SOFTWARE DEVELOPMENT
AN OPEN SOURCE APPROACH

Chapman & Hall/CRC Innovations in Software Engineering and Software Development

Series Editor
Richard LeBlanc
Chair, Department of Computer Science and Software Engineering, Seattle University

AIMS AND SCOPE

This series covers all aspects of software engineering and software development. Books in the series will be innovative reference books, research monographs, and textbooks at the undergraduate and graduate level. Coverage will include traditional subject matter, cutting-edge research, and current industry practice, such as agile software development methods and service-oriented architectures. We also welcome proposals for books that capture the latest results on the domains and conditions in which practices are most effective.

PUBLISHED TITLES

Software Development: An Open Source Approach
Allen Tucker, Ralph Morelli, and Chamindra de Silva

FORTHCOMING TITLES

Fundamentals of Dependable Computing for Software Engineers
John Knight

Software Metrics, Second Edition
Norman Fenton and James Bieman

Designing Software
André van der Hoek, Alex Baker, and Emily Navarro

Systems Engineering Principles for Software Engineers
Ray J. Madachy

Model Based Software Design
Adair Dingle

Software Engineering: The Current Practice
Vaclav Rajlich

CHAPMAN & HALL/CRC INNOVATIONS IN
SOFTWARE ENGINEERING AND SOFTWARE DEVELOPMENT

SOFTWARE DEVELOPMENT

AN OPEN SOURCE APPROACH

ALLEN TUCKER

RALPH MORELLI

CHAMINDRA DE SILVA

CRC Press
Taylor & Francis Group
Boca Raton   London   New York

CRC Press is an imprint of the
Taylor & Francis Group, an **informa** business

The photo on the cover symbolizes the central themes of free and open source software development: the management of chaos (Raymond's "bazaar" metaphor), communities, collaboration, openness, teamwork, and agility.

CRC Press
Taylor & Francis Group
6000 Broken Sound Parkway NW, Suite 300
Boca Raton, FL 33487-2742

© 2011 by Taylor and Francis Group, LLC
CRC Press is an imprint of Taylor & Francis Group, an Informa business

No claim to original U.S. Government works

Printed in the United States of America on acid-free paper
10 9 8 7 6 5 4 3 2 1

International Standard Book Number: 978-1-4398-1290-7 (Hardback)

Visit the Taylor & Francis Web site at
http://www.taylorandfrancis.com

and the CRC Press Web site at
http://www.crcpress.com

Contents

List of Figures xi
List of Tables xv
Preface xvii
Acknowledgments xxv
Authors xxvii

1 Overview and Motivation   **1**
  1.1 Software   1
       1.1.1 Types of Software   2
       1.1.2 The Changing Landscape   5
       1.1.3 Who Are the Developers?   7
       1.1.4 Strategic Choices   8
  1.2 Free and Open Source Software (FOSS)   11
       1.2.1 Origins and Growth   12
       1.2.2 Licensing   16
       1.2.3 Worldwide Impact   18
       1.2.4 Humanitarian FOSS   19
  1.3 Two Case Studies   20
       1.3.1 RMH Homebase   20
       1.3.2 Sahana   20
  1.4 Summary   22
  Exercises   23

2 Working with a Project Team   **27**
  2.1 Key FOSS Activities   27
       2.1.1 Agile Development   27
       2.1.2 Using Patterns   29
       2.1.3 Reading and Writing Code   31
       2.1.4 Documentation   34
       2.1.5 On-Line Help   37
  2.2 Client-Oriented vs Community-Oriented Projects   37
       2.2.1 Project Evolution   40
       2.2.2 Similarities and Differences   42
  2.3 Working on a Client-Oriented Project   44
       2.3.1 Members, Roles, and Tasks   44
       2.3.2 Team Dynamics   47
       2.3.3 Scheduling, Milestones, and To-Do Lists   48
  2.4 Joining a Community-Oriented Project   50

2.4.1 Project Selection 52
2.4.2 First Contact with the Project 53
2.4.3 Norms for Good Citizenship 56
2.4.4 Becoming a User First 58
2.5 Summary 60
Exercises 60

3 Using Project Tools 63
3.1 Collaboration Tools 63
    3.1.1 Asynchronous Communication 64
    3.1.2 Synchronous Communication 65
    3.1.3 Shared Documents 66
3.2 Code Management Tools 67
    3.2.1 The IDE 68
    3.2.2 The Software Stack 70
    3.2.3 The Version Control System 72
    3.2.4 The Bug Tracker 77
3.3 Run-Time System Constraints 82
    3.3.1 Performance 82
    3.3.2 Web Hosting 83
    3.3.3 Licensing 83
    3.3.4 Platform 84
3.4 Summary 84
Exercises 85

4 Software Architecture 87
4.1 Architectural Patterns 87
4.2 Layers, Cohesion, and Coupling 89
    4.2.1 Using Metrics to Evaluate Cohesion and Coupling . . 93
4.3 Security 95
    4.3.1 Architectural Vulnerabilities 96
    4.3.2 User-Level Security 97
4.4 Concurrency, Race Conditions, and Deadlocks 100
4.5 Summary 105
Exercises 105

5 Working with Code 107
5.1 Bad Smells and Metrics 108
    5.1.1 Identifying Bad Smells 108
    5.1.2 Software Metrics 110
5.2 Refactoring 111
    5.2.1 Example 1: Removing Useless Functions 114
    5.2.2 Example 2: Removing a Layering Violation 114
5.3 Testing 117
    5.3.1 Unit Testing Tools 119

	5.3.2	Test Case Design	120
	5.3.3	A Strategy for Sequencing Unit Tests	128
5.4	Debugging		129
	5.4.1	Tool Use vs Developer Skill	130
	5.4.2	Example 1: A User Interface Bug	131
	5.4.3	Example 2: A Multi-Level Bug	133
5.5	Extending the Software for a New Project		134
	5.5.1	A New Use Case	135
	5.5.2	Impact on the Code Base	136
	5.5.3	Team Discussions	139
5.6	Summary		140
	Exercises		140

6 Developing the Domain Classes — **143**

6.1	Understanding the Current System		143
	6.1.1	Reading a Design Document	144
	6.1.2	Reading Code	147
	6.1.3	Examining the Domain Classes	150
6.2	Adding New Features		151
	6.2.1	Top-Down Analysis/Bottom-Up Development	154
	6.2.2	Modifying the Domain Classes	155
	6.2.3	Documentation and Bulletproofing	158
6.3	Class Design Principles and Practice		162
	6.3.1	Using What's Already There	163
	6.3.2	Adding a New Domain Class	164
6.4	Managing the Ripple Effect		166
	6.4.1	Unit Testing the New Code	166
	6.4.2	Refactoring the New Code Base	169
6.5	Summary		171
	Exercises		171

7 Developing the Database Modules — **173**

7.1	Design Principles and Practice		174
	7.1.1	Database Creation	175
	7.1.2	Connecting the Program to the Database	176
	7.1.3	Tables	178
	7.1.4	Normalization and Keys	180
	7.1.5	Backup and Recovery	181
7.2	Working with a Database		182
	7.2.1	Table Creation	184
	7.2.2	Table Searching	185
	7.2.3	Table Insertion, Deletion, and Updating	187
7.3	Database Security and Integrity		188
	7.3.1	Database-Level Permissions	189
	7.3.2	User-Level Permissions	189

        7.3.3   Controlling Concurrency   192
    7.4 Adding New Software Features: Database Impact   193
        7.4.1   Items 1 and 9d: Volunteer Status and Application . .   195
        7.4.2   Item 3: Calendar View   198
    7.5 Summary   201
    Exercises   202

8 Developing the User Interface   **205**
    8.1 Design Principles and Practice   205
        8.1.1   The Model-View-Controller Pattern   207
        8.1.2   Sessions, Query Strings, and Global Variables   210
        8.1.3   Ensuring Security at the User Interface   213
    8.2 Working with Code   218
        8.2.1   Reading Deeply   219
        8.2.2   Debugging as a Community Activity   224
    8.3 Adding New Features: User Interface Impact   230
        8.3.1   Item 1: Volunteer Status   230
        8.3.2   Item 2: Make Active/Inactive   235
        8.3.3   Item 3: Calendar View   237
    8.4 Summary   239
    Exercises   240

9 User Support   **243**
    9.1 Technical Writing   243
        9.1.1   Knowing Your Audience   244
        9.1.2   Principles of Good Writing   246
    9.2 Types of User Support   249
        9.2.1   On-Line Help   249
        9.2.2   Reference Manuals   251
        9.2.3   Open Discussion Forums   253
        9.2.4   User Training and Feedback   257
    9.3 Example: RMH Homebase On-Line Help   258
        9.3.1   Help and the Code Base   258
    9.4 Summary   263
    Exercises   263

10 Project Governance   **265**
    10.1 Origins and Evolution   265
        10.1.1 Starting a Client-Oriented Project   267
        10.1.2 Quality Assessment   271
    10.2 Evolving into a Democratic Meritocracy   273
        10.2.1 Incubation   274
        10.2.2 Organization   277
        10.2.3 Decision Making and Conflict Resolution   281
        10.2.4 Domain Constraints   282

10.3 Releasing Code 284
    10.3.1 Licensing 284
    10.3.2 Finding a Project Host 285
    10.3.3 Release Strategies 287
10.4 Summary 289
Exercises 290

11 New Project Conception   **291**
11.1 Requirements Gathering 292
    11.1.1 Domain Analysis 292
    11.1.2 User Stories 295
    11.1.3 Use Cases 297
11.2 Initial Design 303
    11.2.1 Domain Classes 303
    11.2.2 User Interface 304
    11.2.3 Performance and Platform 305
    11.2.4 System Architecture 307
    11.2.5 Design Alternatives 308
    11.2.6 Design Document 308
11.3 Summary 309
Exercises 309

Appendices   **311**

A Details of the Case Study   **311**
A.1 Requirements 311
    A.1.1 Domain Analysis 312
    A.1.2 Use Cases 317
    A.1.3 System Requirements 327
A.2 Design 328
    A.2.1 Goals 329
    A.2.2 Software Architecture 329
    A.2.3 Domain Classes 330
    A.2.4 Database Design 330
    A.2.5 GUI Design 333
    A.2.6 Implementation Schedule 336
    A.2.7 User-System Interaction 336

B New Features for an Existing Code Base   **341**
B.1 Starting with a Request from the Client 341
B.2 Impact on the Design and the Code Base 343
B.3 Defining a Project that Implements these Features 350

References   **351**

Index   **355**

List of Figures

1.1   Market shares during the "Browser Wars"   3
1.2   Relationships among common FOSS licenses   17

2.1   The traditional software development process.   28
2.2   The agile software development process.   29
2.3   Using the Eclipse environment with Subversion.   31
2.4   Example code from *RMH Homebase*.   32
2.5   Output of the example code in Figure 2.4.   33
2.6   Documentation with indented blocks and control structures. .   34
2.7   Inserting comments in the code.   35
2.8   PHP documentation generated for the Shift class.   36
2.9   Form for filling a vacancy on a shift.   38
2.10   Help screen for filling a vacancy.   39

3.1   Developing within the Eclipse environment.   69
3.2   Software stack for Web-based applications.   70
3.3   A LAMP stack for Web-based applications.   71
3.4   The code synchronization problem.   75
3.5   Resolving the problem: Copy-modify-merge.   76
3.6   Life cycle of a bug, as defined in Bugzilla   78
3.7   Showing the open source license notice in the user interface. .   83
3.8   Displaying the open source license notice in the source code. .   84

4.1   The client-server pattern.   89
4.2   Layers in a multi-tier architecture.   90
4.3   Multi-tier architecture of *RMH Homebase*.   91
4.4   User interface code that violates the layering principle.   92
4.5   A secure login form.   98
4.6   Excerpt from the underlying login code.   99
4.7   *RMH Homebase* Applicant, Volunteer, and Manager menus. .   100
4.8   Code for generating menus.   101
4.9   Deadlock at a traffic intersection.   103

5.1   Refactoring, testing, and debugging are interrelated.   108
5.2   Example bad smell—duplicate code.   109
5.3   Example bad smell removal.   112
5.4   A new search function for the dbPersons module.   116

5.5 A second new search function for the dbPersons module. . . . 116

5.6 A typical PHP unit for testing. 118

5.7 Elements of a unit test for a PHP class or module. 118

5.8 A series of unit tests. 119

5.9 Results of running a series of unit tests. 119

5.10 A partial unit test for the Shift class. 122

5.11 A unit test for the dbShifts module. 124

5.12 The Shift form in the user interface. 124

5.13 A unit test for the editShift module. 126

5.14 A calendar form for the ChangeACalendar use case. 127

5.15 Locating a bug in the calendar.php module. 131

5.16 Locating a bug in the dbDates module. 134

5.17 Use case **Housecleaning**. 137

5.18 A new calendar housecleaning form. 138

6.1 New instance variables for the Person class. 156

6.2 New functions for the Person class. 156

6.3 Revising the instance variables for the Shift class. 158

6.4 Revising the constructor for the Shift class. 159

6.5 Adding a new function to the Shift class. 160

6.6 Original function to return a Shift name. 161

6.7 Instance variables for the Week class. 164

6.8 Instance variables for a new Month class. 165

6.9 Constructor for the new Month class. 166

6.10 Augmenting the unit test for the Shift class. 168

6.11 New unit test for the Month class. 169

6.12 Generating the dates for a new Month. 169

7.1 MySQL commands to create a new user and database. 175

7.2 Creating a new database using LAMP. 176

7.3 Connecting to the *RMH Homebase* database. 177

7.4 A view of the dbDates table. 178

7.5 Shifts in the database for September 2, 2009. 180

7.6 Backing up a database using LAMP. 182

7.7 Template for MySQL table creation. 184

7.8 Creating the dbDates table in the rmhDB database. 185

7.9 Deleting a date from the dbDates table. 191

7.10 New attributes defined in dbPersons table creation. 196

7.11 Inserting a new person into the dbPersons table. 197

7.12 Testing modifications in the dbPersons.php module. 198

7.13 New `setup_dbDates` function in dbDates.php refactoring. . . 200

7.14 New `get_shift_name_from_id` function for dbShifts.php. . . 201

7.15 Upgraded unit test for the dbShifts module 202

8.1 The Model-View-Controller pattern. 207

8.2   The Shift view in *RMH Homebase*. 208
8.3   Overview of the editShift.php module. 211
8.4   Controlling navigation via $_POST variables. 213
8.5   Ensuring security via $_POST and $_SESSION variables. 215
8.6   Password checking during *RMH Homebase* login. 215
8.7   Part of the code base for handling a SubCallList. 219
8.8   Using the SubCallList form. 220
8.9   Using the Shift form to generate an SCL. 220
8.10 Code snippet for removing a person from a Shift. 222
8.11 Reproducing the bug. 225
8.12 Locating the defect. 226
8.13 Designing the fix. 227
8.14 Testing the fix: viewing a person and editing a person. 227
8.15 Showing a person's status. 231
8.16 Changing personForm.php to show a person's status. 231
8.17 Updating a person's database entry. 232
8.18 Showing a person's status in the view. 232
8.19 Changing viewPerson.php to show a person's status. 233
8.20 Searching for "inactive" volunteers and results. 233
8.21 searchPeople.php code that finds "inactive" volunteers. 234
8.22 Changing editMasterSchedule.php to list only "active" volunteers. 234
8.23 Listing only "active" volunteers when filling a vacancy. 234
8.24 Listing volunteers who have not worked recently. 235
8.25 Code for listing volunteers who have not worked recently. . . 236
8.26 New function to search for active or inactive persons. 237
8.27 A view of the new Move Shift feature. 238
8.28 Selecting new start and end times for a Shift. 239

9.1   First page of the *Firefox manual*, including Help and FAQs. . 252
9.2   Accessing the *Sahana* FAQ list. 253
9.3   Point of access to the *Sahana* forums. 254
9.4   Accessing the *Sahana* bug tracking list. 255
9.5   Point of access to the Drupal forums. 256
9.6   Accessing the Firefox user forum. 256
9.7   The main help menu in *RMH Homebase*. 259
9.8   Stepping through the task of filling a vacancy. 260
9.9   Showing a screen shot by selecting its thumbnail. 261
9.10 Integrating help pages within the code base. 262
9.11 HTML code for Step 1 of the help page for filling a vacancy. . 262

10.1 The staging server: Client-Developer interaction. 268
10.2 Organizational levels in the *Sahana* project. 281

11.1 RMH guest referral form. 294

11.2 RMH guest registration card.   295
11.3 RMH guest room schedule.   296
11.4 *RMH Homeroom* use cases.   301
11.5 Some of the initial domain classes for *RMH Homeroom*. . . .   304
11.6 Room view screen draft for *RMH Homeroom*.   305

A.1 RMH Volunteer application form: 12/2007.   314
A.2 RMH master schedule—Group One.   315
A.3 Typical handwritten monthly Volunteer calendar.   316
A.4 Typical scheduled day on the handwritten calendar.   316
A.5 RMH use case diagram.   317
A.6 Use case **UpdateApplicantList**.   318
A.7 Use case **UpdateSubList**.   319
A.8 Use case **UpdateVolunteerList**.   320
A.9 Use case **GenerateACalendar**.   321
A.10 Use case **ChangeASchedule**.   322
A.11 Use case **ChangeACalendar**.   323
A.12 Use case **FindASub**.   324
A.13 Use case **GenerateReminders**.   325
A.14 Use case **ViewAList**.   326
A.15 Key instance variables for the Person class.   330
A.16 Key instance variables for the Shift class.   331
A.17 Key instance variables for the SCL class.   331
A.18 Key instance variables for the RMHdate class.   332
A.19 Key instance variables for the Week class.   332
A.20 Group One master schedule.   333
A.21 First weekend's master schedule.   334
A.22 Example calendar view.   334
A.23 Shift view for 12–3 pm on May 1.   335
A.24 SubCallList view for 12–3 pm on May 1.   335
A.25 Filling the 12–3 pm vacancy on May 1.   336
A.26 Display of a Volunteer in the database.   337
A.27 Manager home page.   338
A.28 Volunteer home page.   339
A.29 On-line Volunteer application form.   339

B.1 Use case **Housecleaning**.   349

List of Tables

2.1 Some Important PHPDoc Tags and Their Meanings 36
2.2 Client-Oriented vs. Community-Oriented Projects 40

4.1 Possible Race Condition Outcomes for Updating a Shift . . . 102

6.1 Two Entries in the dbPersons Table 151
6.2 Formatting Codes Used by the PHP date Function 164

7.1 MySQL Language Connections 176
7.2 Common Relations Used in a MySQL Query 184
7.3 Common Attribute Types in MySQL Tables 185

8.1 Functions in the dbShifts.php Module 223

9.1 *RMH Homebase* User Questionnaire and Results 258

A.1 Overall Structure of the *RMH Homebase* Code Base 329

Preface

To understand the principles and practice of software development, there's no better motivator than participating in a software project that has real world value and a life beyond a single academic semester. The *free and open source software* (FOSS) movement provides a fertile ground for identifying such projects and an exciting new environment for teaching the principles of modern software development.

This book uses a model for teaching software development that combines FOSS principles, agile techniques, modern collaboration tools, community involvement, and teamwork as central themes. Together with its accompanying Web site myopensoftware.org/textbook, this book is designed for use as the main text in a one-semester course on software development.

By completing this course, students should gain a rich appreciation for the principles and practice of FOSS development. As a by-product, they should also become better writers, programmers, and software community members. Our primary goal is that students appreciate the value of collaboration as a fundamental paradigm for software development. They should learn that an effective development team can create a level of software quality that an individual working in isolation cannot typically match.

Why FOSS?

The software development world has evolved rapidly in recent years. The traditional life cycle model is now viewed to have serious weaknesses as a basis for developing, maintaining, and upgrading today's software products. So software developers are using new paradigms to meet these new challenges and they are enjoying significant success. A key component of this evolution is the development of FOSS.

There are many advantages to using FOSS as the medium for a software development course. The main advantage is that FOSS allows source code to be freely read, evaluated, modified, and shared without the licensing constraints that accompany the development of proprietary software. Second, FOSS allows the life of a software project to extend beyond the boundaries of one semester or one institution. Third, FOSS development techniques require a level of openness and collaboration among software developers that proprietary software techniques do not typically match. We discuss these ideas more fully in Chapter 1.

Many FOSS projects are designed to respond to real public and humanitarian needs. Thus, a FOSS focus can add a valuable service learning component to a software development course.[1]

All the FOSS projects discussed in this book respond to real public and humanitarian needs. In this setting, we distinguish between two types of projects, which we call *client-oriented* and *community-oriented*.

- A client-oriented project is one that is in an incubation stage and is usually tailored to fit the needs of a single client. As such, it usually has a small development group and a modest set of design goals, a relatively small initial code base, and a relatively brief but complete requirements statement.

- A community-oriented project is one that has matured to a point that it fulfills the needs of a large group of clients. Such a project usually has a large (often international) development and user group, a large existing code base, and a continuing need for updating and adding new features.

From a software development point of view, both types of projects share a common body of principles and practices. For example, both require developers to be skilled communicators (among themselves and with users) and adept at using modern collaboration tools (such as working with a shared code base). Developers should also be comfortable participating in Web-based discussion threads and finding solutions to technical problems via those threads. Moreover, they should be familiar with modern programming tools and languages, interactive development environments, and database principles.

Both client-oriented and community-oriented projects actively engage the ultimate users of the software as participants in all phases of the development process—not just during requirements analysis and acceptance testing, as in the traditional life cycle model. This process is a derivative of *agile programming*, since it treats the user as a full-fledged member of the development team and it iterates through the development cycle frequently and continuously until the project is complete.

---

[1]Some have argued further that adding service learning activities to the computer science curriculum will improve the attractiveness of computer science as a major field of study, thus increasing enrollment by women and other underrepresented groups. This, for example, is a major theme of the HFOSS project (see hfoss.org and [MTD+09] for more information).

Course Organization

The aim of this book is to immerse students directly into an agile FOSS software development process in the setting of a one-semester course. The projects discussed in this book (and the Web site myopensoftware.org/textbook) are tailored so that they can be completed in a 13-week semester.[2]

Some of the projects are accompanied by a description of new features to be added to an existing code base (see Appendix B for an example). Other projects are accompanied by a design statement, which includes use cases and an initial code base (see Chapter 11 and Appendix A for examples). Either type of project provides an effective starting point for students to implement, adapt, or extend a software artifact during the course of a semester. Other community-oriented project activities can be crafted by connecting students to an ongoing community-oriented project, such as *Sahana*.

Here are two alternative approaches for using this book in a software development course.

One approach is for the instructor to engage students in a client-oriented project. For example, the client can be a local organization on or off campus and the team should include someone familiar with the application that the software will eventually serve (ideally a member of the organization itself). Alternatively, the project can be the *RMH Homebase* project itself, which is the main example used throughout this text. Other examples of this type of project can be found at the book's Web site myopensoftware.org/textbook.

A second approach is for students to contribute to an ongoing community-oriented project, such as *Sahana* (see sahanafoundation.org). In this case, the domain experts are the community of developers and clients who are contributing to the project from many different locations around the world. Thus, student developers who wish to join this community can begin by participating in Web-based discussion threads at the project's Web site. Other examples of community-oriented projects can be found at hfoss.org.

For either approach, this book can be used in a mid-level undergraduate software development course, an advanced projects course, or a service learning course for non-majors who have prior programming experience. The important prerequisite is that students have some programming maturity (for instance, by completing the introductory programming and data structures

---

[2]Since these projects utilize open source (non-proprietary) code, their code base can be freely downloaded and reused.

courses) in advance. A course using this book can either precede or follow a software engineering course.

In this course, we recommend that students begin by covering the material in Chapters 1–5. There, they learn the principles of open source software development that can be applied in either a client-oriented setting or a community-oriented setting. For a client-oriented approach Sections 2.3 and 3.4.1 can be skipped, while for a community-oriented approach Sections 2.2 and 3.4.3 can be skipped.

For a client-oriented approach, we recommend that students continue by covering Chapters 6–9, which provide detailed treatments of coding challenges for three different levels of architecture. If the project chosen for the course uses a language other than PHP (e.g., Java, C++, or Ruby), students will need to adapt those PHP-dependent discussions to the language they are using. Eventually, we expect to expand the book's Web site so that other language options are more directly covered.

For a community-oriented approach, we recommend that students continue by covering Chapters 9–11, which provide additional discussions about forum participation, bug tracking, community building, and project governance. Chapters 10 and 11 provide a kind of "sneak preview" to a software engineering course, since they introduce some principles of project management and requirements analysis that are normally covered in that course.

For either approach, this text provides a team-based, hands-on, agile FOSS development experience, which is its overriding theme.

Sample Syllabi

Below are two sample syllabi that show how a software development course can be structured using the materials in this book. Each one assumes a 13-week semester in which the class meets for 3 hours per week. Both these models are based on syllabi used by the authors while teaching recent software development courses. These syllabi are illustrated in greater detail at the book's Web site myopensoftware.org/textbook.

The first sample syllabus shows the organization of a course where students focus on a *client-oriented project* and work in teams throughout the semester.

Week	Milestone	Topics	Readings (chapters)
1		intro to project, design, collaboration tools	1-2
2		platform/design review, team formation	3
3	Domain classes	refactor, design, team meeting	4
4		code, team meeting	5
5		unit test, client review	6
6	Database modules	refactor, design, team meeting	7
7		code, team meeting	
8		unit test, client review	
9	GUI modules	refactor, design, team meeting	8
10		code, team meeting	
11		unit test, client review	
12	Client documentation	system test, team meeting	9
13		system refactoring	
Exam week	Project presentation		

As shown in this syllabus, a team meeting occurs almost every week. This meeting can be a videoconference (e.g., using Skype), an AIM chat, or a face-to-face meeting in which all team members are present. Each meeting should have representation from users as well as developers.

The second sample syllabus (next page) shows the organization of a course where students engage in a *community-oriented project* and work in teams during much of the semester.

During the first few weeks of this course, students complete a few assignments to familiarize themselves with software development tools, database principles, and the details of an ongoing community-oriented project. Thereafter, the team project dominates weekly assignments and culminates in a project presentation at the end of the course.

With either syllabus, the most important outcome is that students gain new skills as team players and developers for a FOSS project. Thus, students should be graded at least in part on the quality of their contributions to the team project.

Week	Milestone (assignment)	Topics	Readings (chapters)
1	Browse projects, Blog post	Free software vs Open Source	1-2
2	A simple interactive program	3-tier architecture, Software Stack and IDE	3
3	A login script	FOSS methodology, database essentials	4
4	Multideveloper application	Project collaboration, version control systems	5
5	HFOSS project reviews	Project management, documentation	9
6	Project launch	Software architecture	
7	Code review, testing, bug reports	Project code reading	10
8	Project testing, bug reports	FOSS licenses	
9	Project testing, bug reports	Open Source 2.0	11
10	Project patching, bug fixing	Mozilla	
11	Project testing, bug fixing	OS 2.0 beyond open source	
12		Term paper assignment	
13	Project release		
Exam week	Project presentation		

Other Support and Guidance

Students using this text should have completed an introductory programming course and a data structures course, or their equivalent. From that experience, they should be comfortable working with classes and objects, basic data structures (including hash tables or associative arrays), and files.

Students should therefore be familiar with a modern programming language such as Java or C++, and they should be prepared to learn other languages (e.g., PHP and MySQL) depending on the code base for the software project that they select. Familiarity with a modern integrated development environment (IDE) such as Eclipse is also helpful. Students should also be prepared to learn how to use on-line tutorial materials and troubleshooting/debugging support for the languages and tools with which they are less familiar.

A variety of supporting materials are available at the book's Web site my-opensoftware.org/textbook:

- Downloadable FOSS development projects, including their design documents, use cases, and code bases

- A discussion forum for instructors and students to share their experiences and exchange ideas about particular issues raised by these projects

- Supporting materials for common FOSS development tasks, such as setting up a version control system (VCS), an IDE, a project code base, a unit test suite, and so on

- Additional exercises beyond the ones appearing in this book, reflecting a wide variety of software projects and other activities conducted by people using this book

The supporting materials will be tied to individual chapters where they are required by specific exercises. Solutions to end-of-chapter exercises will also be available to instructors via secure password to the book's Web site my-opensoftware.org/textbook.

The software tools used by students in this course should also be open source to the greatest extent possible. This preference is not only a cost-effective way to equip a software lab, it also encourages students to become familiar with downloading and installing useful software tools on their own computers. The resources that are referenced directly in this book are:

Activity	Language/tool	Web source
Programming	PHP	php.org
	MySQL	mysql.org
Documentation	PHPDocumentor	phpdoc.org
Testing	PHPunit	phpunit.de
IDE	Eclipse	eclipse.org, easyeclipse.org
Code synchronization	Subversion (SVN)	apache.org
Discussion threads	Google groups	groups.google.com
Team meetings	Skype	skype.org

While this list is PHP-oriented, we expect that students with strong Java or C++ programming experience will be able to assimilate the PHP syntax and easily follow the examples presented in this book.

The choice of development platform that students make will depend on the programming language required by the project that they choose. For example, many open source projects require Java, so that the tools listed above will need to be replaced by a Java-specific development platform. More extensive and detailed descriptions of these alternatives are provided at the book's Web site myopensoftware.org/textbook.

This book's content is consistent with the Software Engineering recommendations of *Computing Curricula 2008* [ACM08]. It also covers all the topics in the Software Development course described in the *Liberal Arts Model Curriculum* [Con07].

With regard to *Computing Curricula 2008* [ACM08], this book covers all the topics in the Software Engineering section of the core body of knowledge—software design, using APIs and other tools, software processes, requirements, specifications, validation, evolution, and project management. It also covers topics beyond that core body of knowledge—team programming, open source, agile methods, component-based computing, software reliability, and software security.

Finally, students using this text and contributing to an active FOSS project might consider applying for FOSS certification. More information about the FOSS Certificate can be found at the Web site http://hfoss.org.

Acknowledgments

The authors would like to thank the following reviewers, who gave many thoughtful and insightful suggestions on the selection, ordering, and presentation of material in this text: Bob Cupper (Allegheny College), Ed Gehringer (North Carolina State University), Greg Hislop (Drexel University), Charles Kelemen (Swarthmore College), Richard LeBlanc (Seattle University), Bob Noonan (College of William and Mary), Oliver Radwan, Linda Seiter (John Carroll University), and Laurie Williams (North Carolina State University).

This text benefits from work conducted under the *Humanitarian FOSS Project* at Trinity College (http://hfoss.org), with support from the National Science Foundation under Grant No. 0939034. We also thank Bowdoin College for its support, including especially the four Bowdoin students—Oliver Radwan, Maxwell Palmer, Nolan McNair, and Taylor Talmadge—who developed the original release of the *RMH Homebase* software. The staff of the Ronald McDonald House in Portland, Maine, especially Gabrielle Little, provided valuable insight and feedback throughout this project.

Finally, the authors would like to acknowledge and thank our editor Alan Apt for his patient guidance and encouragement throughout the development of this book.

Authors

Allen Tucker is the Anne T. and Robert M. Bass Professor Emeritus at Bowdoin College. He has a BA in mathematics from Wesleyan University and an MS and PhD in computer science from Northwestern University. He is an ACM Fellow and Distinguished Lecturer. Professor Tucker has authored publications in the areas of programming languages, software development, natural language processing, and curriculum development. He has been a Fulbright lecturer in Ukraine and a visiting lecturer in New Zealand, France, and Germany. He is a member of the Humanitarian FOSS Project's executive committee.

Ralph Morelli is professor of computer science at Trinity College in Hartford, Connecticut, where he has been teaching since 1985. He has a BA in mathematics from the University of Connecticut and an MA and PhD in philosophy and an MS in computer science from the University of Hawaii. In addition to a textbook on Java, Professor Morelli has authored publications in the areas of artificial intelligence, FOSS, and computer science education. He is currently one of the principal investigators of the Humanitarian FOSS Project.

Chamindra de Silva has been a project lead and architect on the *Sahana* Free and Open Source Disaster Management Project following the 2004 Asian tsunami. He is the CTO and Director of the Sahana Foundation and has participated in project deployment for governments and NGOs in Pakistan, Philippines, Peru, the U.S., China and Haiti. He co-founded the Humanitarian FOSS community and is on the advisory board of the Humanitarian FOSS Project. He is also an Apache Committer, an OSI Member and a contributor to OLPC. He has represented Sri Lanka in Asian Open Souce forums such as UNDP-IOSN and AsiaOSSS. He has an MEng in engineering and computer science from Oxford University.

Chapter 1

Overview and Motivation

> "Change your opinions, keep your principles;
> Change your leaves, keep intact your roots."
> — *Victor Hugo*

This chapter discusses the short history and current scope of computer software and its development. We focus on the origins and evolution of "free and open source software" (often called *FOSS*), identifying its distinctions from "proprietary software," which is generally neither free nor open source.

You will learn that these two genres of software have different sources of support, goals, development methodologies, and outcomes. Studying the methodologies and goals that drive the development of free and open source software is the main focus of this book.

1.1   Software

Software is a fundamental element of computing. It provides the functionality that allows computers and networks to serve the needs of organizations and individuals. Software and computers are intertwined in a kind of deadly embrace; neither one can survive unless the other one thrives.

In today's developed world, software is *everywhere*. It enables individuals to use an Android phone, Google the Web, communicate with friends, type essays, manage bank accounts, pay taxes, navigate an automobile to an unfamiliar destination, make flight reservations, listen to music, and view photos and videos on their computers. And that's just how individuals use software.

Organizations also rely on software. Small and large businesses, non-profit organizations, banks, government agencies and contractors, universities, research laboratories, and countless other institutions use software to help manage their day-to-day activities.

Without a Web presence for marketing their products and services, most enterprises would not survive in today's world. Organizations also use software to manage their various internal activities—financial accounting, production lines, employee and volunteer recruitment, fundraising, inventory control, payroll, and so on.

Software is also *dynamic*. Every viable software product changes with each new generation of computers, operating systems, and modes of access to worldwide information. If we were to read a definition published in, say, 1965 about the nature of software, we would probably not recognize that definition.[1]

1.1.1 Types of Software

In the last four decades, we have witnessed such a revolution of computing and networking that it now influences nearly all areas of business, scientific, and personal life. This revolution has dramatically changed how individuals and organizations function, and it has also dramatically enlarged the scope and definition of "software" as it is understood today.

Software development methodologies and distribution strategies have also undergone a significant transformation. This transformation has produced the following distinctions:

Bundled vs Unbundled Software Some software items are bundled together in an inseparable way, requiring the client to purchase all of the items at once, even when only one is desired. Further, some software is bundled together with a "native" hardware platform and operating system, making it very difficult for a client to choose among alternatives once the platform has been determined. For example, Microsoft bundles its word processing, spreadsheet, and presentation software into a single package called "Office." To use Microsoft's word processor, called "Word," one must purchase the complete "Office" bundle, whether the other two products are needed or not.

Client "lock-in" is said to occur when such bundling forces the client to stay with a particular software suite or manufacturer even though better alternatives may be available on the market. Monopolistic behavior has been a frequent activity of some software developers, in their ap-

---

[1]In 1965, computers were stand-alone "main-frames" housed in large organizations. Software consisted of an operating system, language compilers, and application programs that enabled computers to maintain the financial and operational activities of businesses, and performed the mathematical and scientific calculations needed by research and engineering organizations.

Software in 1965 was designed by these organizations' in-house programmers. In 1965, there were just two major programming languages—Cobol and Fortran—one for business programming and the other for scientific programming. All computing activities were scheduled to be run on the organization's main-frame computer, usually no more often than once a day.

So in 1965, there were no satellites, networks, laptops, or even desktop computers. There was no Internet, e-mail, or worldwide Web; imagine a world without cell phones! 1965 was surely a different time.

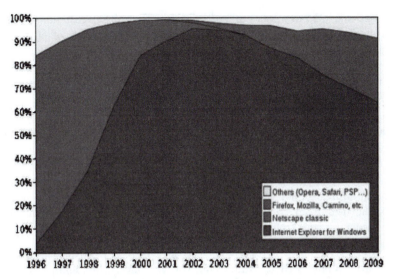

FIGURE 1.1: Market shares during the "Browser Wars" (source: http://en.wikipedia.org/wiki/Browser_wars).

petite for gaining control of entire software markets by eliminating the competition.

For example, Microsoft, which controlled over 90% of the desktop computer market in 1998, began to bundle its Internet Explorer browser with its Windows operating system. Netscape and other browser developers complained that this practice was monopolistic. The U.S. government opened an antitrust investigation, which led to an indictment and a ruling against Microsoft [wp-h]. The ruling was eventually overturned on appeal, but the case's findings of fact—that Microsoft had engaged in monopolistic practices—were allowed to stand and led to an eventual settlement. Nevertheless, the net effect of this action was that Microsoft had effectively taken over the browser market from Netscape, and went on to capture over 90% of that market at its peak in 2001 (see Figure 1.1) [wp-a].

Mass-Marketed vs Custom Software Most commercial software is developed for the mass market, using a "one size fits all" strategy. With this strategy, the price of an individual copy can be kept small, while the degree to which the software matches with the client's actual needs varies. Often, mass-marketed software contains many more features than any one individual needs or wants, and the quality of such software is minimally satisfactory in relation to its price.

Custom software is tailored to fit the needs of a particular client, usually a large client with very specialized needs. Such software is typically more expensive to develop, and so the client must either cost-justify its development or seek less expensive alternatives. Examples of custom software include that which underlies the Federal Air Traffic Control System or the operation of a particular bank's ATM system. The history of these two software development efforts is quite different – the former was a colossal failure and the latter is a resounding success.

Proprietary vs Open Source Software *Proprietary software* is that which is licensed and distributed as a binary executable program to individual and corporate clients. The source code is the private property of the developer. A proprietary software license typically prevents the user from installing the software on more than one computer. It also prevents the user from copying the software, modifying it, or sharing it with associates and friends.

Free and open source software (FOSS) is that which is licensed and distributed along with its underlying source code. Most significantly, "free" means that clients are free to use the software on any computer, to modify the software, and to share the software with associates and friends. Because of this freedom, FOSS is accessible in markets where proprietary software has no interest and little leverage—non-profit organizations, developing countries, and individuals who are either unwilling or unable to pay the (sometimes steep) cost of proprietary software.

From the 1970s to the mid-1980s, nearly all application software development was proprietary.[2] Proprietary sofware is typically developed and maintained by an in-house programming staff of a large organization or by a software vendor targeting a specific mass market.

For example, Microsoft Word was developed to meet the needs of the word processing market, and the "Office" bundle (Word, Excel, and PowerPoint) currently sells for about $400 per copy (students may purchase Office for $150). Office is licensed under the "Microsoft Software License Terms: 2007 Microsoft Office System Desktop Application Software." This license spells out, in 165,181 bytes, all the do's and (mostly) don'ts for clients who purchase the right to install and use a single copy of the Office software on a single computer.

The open source analog for Word is called "Writer" and is available inside the "OpenOffice" bundle, developed by OpenOffice.org. OpenOffice is available for free download, use, and adaptation by any individual or organization (see openoffice.org). It can be run on Windows, Linux, and Macintosh platforms. OpenOffice is distributed under an open source license called the "GNU

---

[2]Since the mid-1980s, FOSS development has had an increasing impact on the overall software market, although most software in use today is still proprietary.

LGPL,"[3] which describes in 8,518 bytes the rights of clients who download and freely use, copy, modify, and redistribute this software.

During the last two decades, open source software development has emerged to become a major player in the software industry. This momentum is spurred by many forces, including the world's need for affordable computing, new developments in software methodology, and the increasing sense of public ownership of the internet and its resources. It is now estimated that open source software is in use on over 20% of all computers worldwide (see [Sal08] p. 161), and this share is steadily growing.

1.1.2 The Changing Landscape

The worldwide growth of the Internet, especially the opportunity it provides for free collaboration, is a primary enabler for the recent emergence of the open source software movement.

Three other major factors have also helped drive this emergence: a persistently high failure rate among proprietary software projects, a high level of frustration among proprietary software customers, and the business model that drives the proprietary software development process itself. These factors are discussed below.

1.1.2.1 Project Failure Rate

Given our personal experience with today's successful proprietary software products, we might be lulled into the belief that a proprietary software development project usually results in a successful product. Nothing could be further from the truth.

A major reason for the emergence of the open source movement is the high rate of failure in proprietary software development over the last four decades. This period is littered with major project failures, such as the 1994 failure of IBM to deliver a working air traffic control system to the FAA after collecting billions of taxpayer dollars over a six-year development period (see www.baselinemag.com/c/a/Projects-Processes/The-Ugly-History-of-Tool-Development-at-the-FAA/).

A more recent failure is Microsoft's "Windows Vista" operating system, which at this writing had captured only 21% of the operating system market, compared with a 67% share by "Windows XP," its aging predecessor (see en.wikipedia.org/wiki/Usage_share_of_desktop_operating_systems).

Mountains of articles have been published about the high frequency of software project failures throughout the last several decades. The 2009 CHAOS Report [Groa] cites software failure rates at the highest level in a decade: 44% of all software projects failed to be delivered on time, on budget, or with full functionality. An additional 24% were cancelled prior to completion.

---

[3]More discussion of open source licensing appears in Section 1.2.2.

This leaves only 32% of all software projects that were completed on time, on budget, and with full functionality—a dismal record indeed.

There are many reasons for software project failure, including:

- inadequate definition of the problem to be solved,

- gross underestimation of the task to be performed,

- inadequate management support or funding,

- overly ambitious development schedule,

- poor design,

- inadequate programmer deployment, and/or

- poor market analysis.

However, improper choice and deployment of an effective development methodology is almost always at the center of a failed software project.

1.1.2.2 Customer Frustration

Added to this history of failure is the current climate of users' frustration with the proprietary software that they have purchased (or that their employer requires them to use). Often an organization's needs are not well met by these proprietary products, but the cost of conversion to a better alternative (along with vendor lock-in) prevents them from making changes.

Since proprietary software licensing is so restrictive, it is virtually impossible for organizations to modify or share the software with other organizations or individuals. In addition, an organization cannot hire a programmer to fix a bug or add useful features to proprietary software. The organization is completely dependent on the vendor for this service, and the vendor may or may not be responsive.

This type of vendor lock-in often even hinders the customer's ability to change its underlying hardware or operating system platform. Lock-in also forces the use of proprietary data formats, which makes it more difficult for an organization to export and use its own data in a different software application. An organization that has invested heavily in a proprietary product is often unable to justify changing to a new product because of the substantial data conversion and training costs involved in moving to a new platform.

1.1.2.3 Business Model

Over the years, we have been taught that selling proprietary software as intellectual property is essential to the economic viability of the software company itself. That is, without the profit motive inherent in the marketing of proprietary software, a company could not pay its highly skilled software developers and thus could not survive in the long run.

However, the belief that the proprietary model is the only viable business model for developing software is now being challenged by the open source movement. A few of the many open source success stories are documented in Section 1.2.

1.1.3 Who Are the Developers?

Programmers and others who develop proprietary software are either individual consultants, members of the IT staffs of medium and large organizations, or employees of software development firms. A major driver for proprietary software development firms is the lure of large profits. In turn, a major motivator for developers working for these firms is the lure of high salaries. Median annual salaries in the proprietary software industry are in the $60,000–$100,000 range (see http://www.payscale.com), depending on years of experience. Major software companies like Microsoft offer significantly higher salaries and benefits to highly qualified individuals.

The open source software industry offers more modest salaries. For example, the median salary at OpenOffice.com is reported to be $55,000 (see http://simplyhired.com). A major motivator for these professionals is the opportunity to contribute to a software project that benefits the global society, especially people and institutions that do not have significant financial resources. Developers in open source projects often have a strong humanitarian motive for making this professional choice. They regularly participate in open forums and other social media to help inform and focus their work.

Beyond the need for programmers, a software project requires contributions from other types of professionals, including testers, writers, graphic artists, user support personnel, marketers, and donors. A proprietary software developer must, of course, hire in-house staff to perform these activities, due to the proprietary nature of the software itself. This overhead contributes to the development cost of the software, which is ultimately passed on to the customer.

In an open source project, the situation is quite different. Much of the coding, testing, debugging, and documentation tasks are done by large numbers of volunteers. Anyone with skills in any of these areas can contribute to a software development project by registering on-line. These volunteers make their open source contributions at times when they are not working their "day jobs" or studying for exams. Open source contributors come from many walks of life – they may be students, retirees, or employees of organizations whose day jobs may or may not include software development.[4]

---

[4]Actually, for some large projects (e.g., Linux, Apache, Mozilla), many programmers are paid by their primary employers to contribute code to a FOSS project. For example, programmers employed by Google regularly contribute to Linux.

1.1.4   Strategic Choices

When working on a software project for the first time, the developers must make some fundamental strategic choices that follow directly from the nature and history of the software project itself. These choices are:

- Top-Down vs Bottom-Up Development

- Individual vs Team Programming

- Coding vs Components

- Legacy vs Greenfield Systems

The following paragraphs explain these choices and their accompanying constraints.

1.1.4.1   Top-Down vs Bottom-Up Development

Should we develop the software serially, starting from a fixed set of requirements, proceeding to a rigorous design specification, followed by writing the code and finally testing the code? Or should we instead develop the code from the "bottom up," starting with a small prototype and incrementally adding new functionality with each iteration?

The traditional model for developing software is called the "waterfall model." It is based on the assumption that a software product's functionality can be fully specified at the outset, so that subsequent steps in the development process can be carried out more-or-less in sequence. These steps are called "requirements analysis," "design," "coding," "testing," and "delivery."

If the requirements can be fully specified at the outset, the waterfall model can work. For example, an embedded software module that measures and reports the altitude of an airplane in real time can be designed and implemented using the waterfall model.

In many applications, however, the waterfall model has inherent problems. First, the assumption that we fully understand the requirements of a software product at the outset, and that those requirements never vary throughout the life of the development process, is often faulty. Various outside factors (such as the emergence of a new line of hardware or operating system) can dramatically alter the requirements. Moreover, users' needs change, and typically they are not fully understood at the outset of a project. Not including end users' needs and feedback throughout the life cycle is a frequent cause for software project failure.

Several alternatives to the waterfall model have emerged to help solve these problems. For example, "spiral development" is an incremental approach that starts with a simple subset of the requirements, implements them, tests the implementation, and then reviews the implementation with end users. The next iteration adds a new feature to the software, tests it, and reviews that with end users. This process is repeated until the resulting software satisfies all the end users' needs.

If this spiraling process occurs frequently enough, say biweekly, the resulting process is called *agile*. If the time interval between successive versions of the software is even shorter, say daily, the process is called *extreme programming*. If, in any of these cases, test cases are developed in advance of the code that implements them, the process is called *test-driven development*, or TDD.

All of these non-traditional development models have been used successfully in recent years. As a group, they tend to be more user oriented, open, and collaborative than the traditional waterfall model. We will return to a more careful treatment of agile development in Chapter 2, and then we will rely on it throughout the remainder of this book.

1.1.4.2 Individual vs Team Programming

Should the members of the development team work more-or-less in isolation on separate components, or should all components be developed jointly by groups of developers sharing all the source code?

There are a few rare cases in which a successful software product has been developed by an individual working more-or-less in isolation. However, the vast majority of software products have been developed by groups of people working together at a very detailed level. Surely, all the FOSS products cited in earlier sections utilize collaboration of this sort, and each one typically has dozens, if not hundreds, of developers.

Software reliability is probably the strongest reason for preferring team programming over individuals working alone. That is, the more pairs of eyes that are reading the code, the more bugs will be caught. In stating this preference, we are tacitly assuming that the software product itself is architecturally large and complex, rather than small or simple.[5]

1.1.4.3 Coding vs Components

Do we develop the software using one or more programming languages, or do we build the software from pre-existing components that can be readily extracted from other systems?

A key principle of computer science is the principle of *abstraction*. Basically, abstraction means to generalize an idea to a level at which it can be reused in other (similar) problem solving settings without reinventing it from scratch each time it is needed.

For example, programmers seldom write a sorting algorithm from scratch anymore – instead, they reuse an existing piece of code, or software compo-

---

[5]Most classroom assignments in computer science courses, since each one is tailored so that an individual student can complete it by working alone, are architecturally small and simple.

nent, that has sorting built in. The advantages of using prewritten components are several.

1. It saves development time.

2. It ensures more reliable software.

3. It allows developers to concentrate more clearly on the application in which the component is being used rather than the minutiae of the component itself.

How do we learn to use components when developing software? Our first encounter with components probably took place when we began to learn about function and class libraries, like the C++ standard template library or the Java class library. We must have been greatly relieved when, for instance, we discovered that "sort" is a pre-implemented function in these libraries, and when we call it with an appropriate collection of items to sort, this function does the whole job of sorting – efficiently and correctly – shazam!

Are all the useful components found in the function and class libraries of our popular programming languages? Luckily, no. Thanks to the recent idea of a *framework*, the use of components has been raised to a far higher level of abstraction, and has thus taken over a much larger portion of a software developer's attention than ever before. Now, more of a developer's time is likely to be spent selecting prewritten components than writing Java or PHP code to implement that functionality.

A fascinating example of this trend is called *Drupal* (see http://drupal.org), which is a software framework for building *content management systems*, or content-rich Web sites. Significantly, Drupal itself is open source, so that the development of its own components is accelerated by contributions from hundreds of developers worldwide.

So what is the role of programming in such a mature world of abstraction? Surely, programming is still at the heart of software, but it can frequently be moved from the foreground of a software project to the background. Rather than developing a component using, say, PHP as a starting point, a programmer can often find a component in an open source library and then "tweak" that component so that it fits the needs of the current application. This tweaking is done by inserting "code snippets" within the prewritten code already present in the component.

1.1.4.4   Legacy vs Greenfield Systems

Does the new software to be developed have a predecessor that already implements many of the desired features, or must we develop the new software more-or-less from scratch?

A *legacy system* is software that has been used for some time and now needs to be modified for use in a new application. For instance, consider an on-line registration system that supports students registering for courses each semester. Suppose we want to enhance that system so that it takes on some of the functions of student advising. For example, we may want it to assist a student to select one from among different courses offered at the same time. To implement these new features, we most likely would start with the existing code that is the current registration system and modify the code so that it supports these new features.

A *greenfield system*, on the other hand, is software that has no reasonable predecessor, and thus must be developed from scratch. This can occur for any of several reasons. For instance, the current software may be so outdated or poorly developed that it cannot be feasibly upgraded to incorporate the needed new functionality. Alternatively, there may simply be no software in existence that has any of the functionality needed by the new system. An example of a greenfield system is the *RMH Homebase* software (see http://rmhportland.org/volunteers/homebase), which was written to replace a completely manual system that used a desk calendar and Rolodex™ file to store volunteer data.

Most software projects tend to start with some amount of prewritten functioning program code, called a *code base*. A particular code base may be chosen as a starting point for a new system because:

- it most closely matches the new requirements,

- it is written in a contemporary programming language that will support the new functionality gracefully, and/or

- the software team is familiar enough with the code and the language that they can effectively implement the new functionality.

The use of legacy code to solve new software problems has been greatly aided by the recent emergence of open source software repositories. A widely known repository for downloading and installing FOSS products is Sourceforge (see **sourceforge.net**), which supports over 230,000 projects and has more than two million developers.[6]

1.2   Free and Open Source Software (FOSS)

As noted above, FOSS allows users to study, modify, and redistribute its source code. Because of its accessibility, affordability, transparency, and association with freedom for the user, FOSS is growing in importance throughout

---

[6]For more discussion of open source repositories and their use in software project management, see Chapter 10.

the world. Businesses, governments, academic institutions, and non-profit organizations are increasingly turning to FOSS for their software needs.

This section summarizes the origins, growth, and licensing distinctions that accompany FOSS. (For more detailed discussions, see [CD07] and [Sal08].)

1.2.1   Origins and Growth

Although they are part of the same movement, the separate terms *free software* and *open source software* actually evolved out of two distinct philosophies. When used alone, the term *free software* emphasizes the freedoms associated with distribution of the software and has a strong ethical and moral dimension, while *open source software* emphasizes the grass roots development model and promotes the practical benefits. The FOSS community emphasizes both of these aspects simultaneously.

The free software movement was started in the early 1980s by Richard Stallman [Sta99, wp-c]. Stallman was a programmer at MIT's Artificial Intelligence lab and learned to program as part of the open and sharing hacker culture that thrived in much of the programming community during the 1960s and 1970s.

Having grown frustrated with the directions that the computing industry was taking, Stallman started the GNU (read "GNU is Not Unix") project in 1983. This project was an effort to build an entirely free and open operating system [Staa]. It is clear from Stallman's original announcement about GNU that his motivations were ethical and humanitarian [GNU]:

> I consider that the golden rule requires that if I like a program I must share it with other people who like it. I cannot in good conscience sign a nondisclosure agreement or a software license agreement. ... I'm looking for people for whom knowing they are helping humanity is as important as money.

Stallman founded the Free Software Foundation (see http://fsf.org) in 1985 to help support this new movement. He developed the definition of free software along with the concept of *copyleft*, which uses software licensing to protect the freedom of software users and developers to share their work [Foud].

Under a copyleft license, *free software* guarantees users the freedom to:

1. run the software for any purpose,

2. study and modify the software (which requires access to the source code),

3. distribute copies of the software to help their neighbors, and

4. improve the software and release those improvements to the public so that the whole community benefits [Foud].

Notice that this definition implies "open source" as well, especially considering items 2 and 4. So using the term *free software* as defined here is equivalent to using the term *free and open source software*, or FOSS.

Despite the ambiguity of the English word "free," this definition of *free software* has nothing to do with the *price* of the software; to borrow Stallman's formulation, it is "free as in 'free speech' not as in 'free beer.'" Practically speaking, however, most software that is licensed under the free software definition is also distributed free of charge.

In 1989, to help protect programs developed as part of the GNU project, Stallman created the GNU General Public License [Fouc]. The GPL is widely regarded as the strongest copyleft license, since it requires that all derivative works be made available under the same protections. (See Section 1.2.2.)

By 1991, Stallman and his collaborators had written an entire operating system, minus the kernel program. It was in this context that Linus Torvalds, working with a broad international community of programmers, developed the Linux kernel program [wp-f]. Linux was licensed under the GPL and became the core of the GNU/Linux operating system [Tor99]. GNU/Linux, or Linux as it is popularly called, is one of the best and most widely known examples of FOSS.

Following the dramatic success of Linux, the Open Source Initiative (OSI) was founded with the purpose of making the FOSS development process acceptable to the software industry itself [Per99]. In his formulation of the *open source definition* Bruce Perens and other founders of OSI hewed closely to Stallman's principles, preserving the basic freedoms that Stallman articulated. Despite this effort, for many the OSI provided a means to distance the movement from what they saw as Stallman's anti-business stance. As a result the OSI has focused more on the practical benefits of the FOSS development model.

As open source gained popularity within the software industry, a schism broke out between free software and open source proponents. Perens eventually resigned from OSI [Per], saying:

> Most hackers know that Free Software and Open Source are just two words for the same thing. Unfortunately, though, Open Source has de-emphasized the importance of the [four] freedoms involved in Free Software. It's time for us to fix that. We must make it clear to the world that those freedoms are still important, and that software such as Linux would not be around without them.

However, despite the efforts of Perens and others to emphasize the moral dimension, the gap between the two branches of FOSS has continued to grow. Stallman himself has continued to emphasize the moral motivation behind the free software movement and has repeatedly emphasized the fact that it is the commitment to software freedom, not the temporary practical advantages, that make the FOSS movement viable [Stab]. Indeed, as recently as July 2009

Stallman was urging the FOSS community to place its emphasis on software freedom [Sta09]:

> As the advocates of open source draw new users into our community, we free software activists must work even more to bring the issue of freedom to those new users' attention. We have to say, "It's free software and it gives you freedom!" more and louder than ever. Every time you say *free software*, rather than *open source*, you help our campaign.

In recent years, the FOSS movement has been highly successful and has grown to encompass a significant share of the software market. Two important events came together to contribute to this success, the emergence of the Red Hat business model and the transformation of the Netscape browser into Mozilla Firefox.

The Red Hat Business Model Red Hat Corporation was the first to show that FOSS development can be sustained by an effective business and economic model [You99]. In 1993, prior to Linux's surge in popularity, Red Hat's founder, Robert Young, was running a software distribution company specializing in Unix applications. As sales of Linux distributions began to pick up, he and Marc Ewing founded Red Hat Software, Inc. in January 1995.

Red Hat's business model is to work with Linux development teams from around the world to put together the hundreds of modules that make up a Linux (or, more accurately, a GNU/Linux) distribution. Rather than selling a license for the software, as a proprietary software vendor would do, Red Hat sells service. In the 1990s, selling service, rather than branding the software as *intellectual property* and selling it, was a revolutionary concept. The Red Hat model thus provides convenience, quality, security, and service to its customers.

Following in Red Hat's footsteps, many other companies have discovered that rather than owning a proprietary software product, a successful business can be built around the concept of supporting and servicing a FOSS product. Thus, contrary to the programmers-need-to-eat skepticism that greeted the GNU Manifesto[7] in the early 1980s [Staa], Stallman defends software freedom as an idea that is compatible with that of financial viability in the software industry.

From Netscape to Firefox The creation of the Mozilla community was another watershed event in the history of the open source movement. Unlike its successful FOSS predecessors (e.g., Linux, Apache, and Perl),

---

[7]Stallman wrote the GNU Manifesto in 1983 to ask for public support for the development of the GNU operating system. It is a philosophical defense of the viability of FOSS as a business model. For a more detailed discussion, see http://gnu.org/gnu/manifesto.html.

which mainly benefit professional programmers, the Firefox browser became the first FOSS product to be successfully distributed to all computer users. Here's how Firefox came into being.

In 1994, Netscape began providing unrestricted distributions of its Navigator browser. In January 1998 Netscape announced that, in addition to freely distributing its browser, it would also freely distribute the source code for its browser software, known as *Mozilla* [HPW99]:

> Netscape was willing to be the first large corporation to open up its proprietary source, because it wanted to foster wider corporate interest in development in open source environments.

These two events forever changed the way software is distributed on the Internet.

As Figure 1.1 illustrates, Mozilla's current open source bowser, called *Firefox*, has now become a highly successful combatant in the browser wars. Firefox is used by over 300 million people, making it the most successful open-source consumer product in the world. It now has over 25% of the browser market share, whereas Internet Explorer's share has declined to around 65%.

Today, the Mozilla Foundation (mozilla.org), originally formed to manage the Mozilla development effort, has evolved to become a model open source community. Mozilla has only about 250 paid employees. Another 1,000 or so volunteer programmers from a broad international community have contributed code to its most recent releases. In addition to programmers and developers, the Mozilla community includes tens of thousands of testers, users, and evangelists, who work to promote the browser and have helped to translate it into more than 70 languages worldwide (see [Foue] for more details).

As the Red Hat, Mozilla, and many other open source projects have demonstrated, the FOSS development model is compatible with the idea of commercial success in the software business. Today, many major software companies, including IBM, Google, Hewlett-Packard, and others, support open-source development in various and substantial ways. Companies that rely on the success of systems such as Linux and Apache assign members of their own software development staffs to work, more or less full time, as contributors to these projects.

At this writing, the FOSS movement has spread far beyond its origins in GNU, Linux, and Mozilla. Many new FOSS communities have emerged to develop important consumer-related software products. Here are two more notable examples:

GIMP The GNU Image Manipulation Program (GIMP) provides a software suite for photographic and other image manipulation. It is a free alternative to the proprietary Adobe Photoshop software. For more information about GIMP, see http://www.gimp.org.

OpenOffice OpenOffice is an office productivity suite that includes word processing, spreadsheets, and presentation modules. As such, it is a free alternative to the proprietary Microsoft Office software, which includes Word, Excel, and PowerPoint. For more information about OpenOffice, see http://www.openoffice.org.

1.2.2 Licensing

Richard Stallman created the GNU General Public License (GPL) to protect the rights of free software users and developers [wp-c]. However, other free software licenses have evolved alongside the GPL to satisfy different needs within the open source community.

Version 2 of the GPL was released in 1991. The GPL is the license preferred by a majority of FOSS projects, and it has been repeatedly upheld in courts around the world as an enforceable license [wp-d]. After 18 months of public discussion and several previous drafts, GPL version 3 (GPLv3) was released on May 31, 2007. It addresses a wide range of issues, including its compatibility with other free software licenses.

At present, there are almost 70 different free and open source licenses.[8] One of the most difficult questions for FOSS developers is how the various licenses relate to each other. Figure 1.2 [Whe] provides an overview of the more widely used licenses and their inter-relationships. Each box represents a particular kind of license.

A license is more or less *protective* depending on how strongly it protects the four freedoms listed in the foregoing definition, particularly the freedom to redistribute derivatives of the software. The left-to-right arrangement of the licenses in Figure 1.2 shows how they progress from least to most protective in this sense.

Here are the main distinctions among the columns in Figure 1.2:

Permissive Software in the *public domain* is, strictly speaking, unlicensed and therefore completely unprotected. Thus, someone can take a piece of public domain software and distribute it under a proprietary license.

Other licenses in the *permissive* column allow derivative products to become *proprietary*. For example, because it allows developers to add

---

[8]The Free Software Foundation's own list of these other licenses provides rulings on which ones are compatible with the GPL as well as guidance on how to define customized FOSS licenses [Foub]. The Open Source Institute maintains a similar list as part of its effort to define *open source software* [OSI].

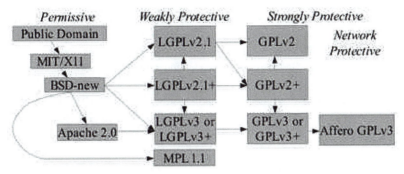

FIGURE 1.2: Relationships among common FOSS licenses (source: http://www.dwheeler.com/essays/floss-license-slide.html).

their own copyright statements to any modifications they make to the software, any software licensed under Apache 2.0 can be turned into a proprietary product.

Weakly protective *Weakly protective licenses* are often used for source code libraries or modules. They protect the software from becoming proprietary but allow it to be used as part of a larger proprietary package. The Lesser General Public License (LGPL) is the most widely used license of this type.

Strongly protective Licenses in the *strongly protective* column in Figure 1.2 require that derivative works must also be licensed, as a whole, under the GPL. This effectively prevents derivatives from becoming proprietary software.

Network protective The GNU Affero GPLv3 expands the reach of the GPL so that users of a Web application can receive its source code. This also applies to network-interactive software, including programs like game servers.

The arrows in this figure represent *compatibility*, indicating where two different FOSS-licensed products can be merged into one. So to determine *compatibility* among licenses, we can trace the arrows in Figure 1.2 to a common license. For example, a software product distributed under an Apache 2.0 license and another product distributed under a GPLv2 license can be combined into a new product and distributed under a GPLv3 or GPLv3+ license. However, a product distributed under the Mozilla public license (MPL) is not compatible with GPL and thus its reuse is somewhat restricted.

Licensing a complex FOSS product is sometimes a complex matter. For example, one of the most challenging issues Mozilla faced was to respect the prior licensing of Firefox's many embedded third-party modules. Agreements with the owners of these modules had to be worked out so that their code could be shipped either as open source or as binary code. The alternative would be to remove them from the code base altogether.

At the same time, Mozilla needed to develop a new license for the Firefox browser that would be compatible with this new code base. This effort produced two separate licenses: the Netscape Public License and the Mozilla Public License. These two licenses are identical, except that the NPL grants extra rights to Netscape to cover the commitments it had previously made to other software companies [HPW99].

1.2.3   Worldwide Impact

By most accounts, free and open source software is growing in usage and significance throughout the world. According to a 2008 report by the Standish Group, FOSS costs proprietary software vendors $60 billion per year in lost revenue [Grob].

A comprehensive 2006 European Union study focusing on the economic potential of FOSS estimated that ICT (information and communication technology) represents almost 10% of the GDP in developed countries. This study concluded that the ICT sector has the potential to be strongly affected by the FOSS movement [Com06].

In terms of FOSS potential impact on European economies, the study recommended that current policies and practices, which favor proprietary software, should be revised as a way to level the playing field and avoid the problem of *vendor lock-in*, particularly in public education.

A recent study by the Red Hat/Georgia Tech Open Source Software Potential Index project (OSSPI) [NBM08] provides a snapshot of worldwide FOSS adoption. The study identified over 750 variables affecting FOSS adoption in public and private sectors. Its main result is an index that rates 75 countries along a number of FOSS-related dimensions.

The two main indices in this study are *activity*, which utilizes concrete data sources (such as the number of Firefox users), and *environment*, which is a more speculative estimate of how strongly the country's environment favors FOSS development. The study concludes that several European countries lead the United States in their FOSS activity index, even though the United States ranks near the top in its FOSS environment index.

This study also acknowledges that some of the best FOSS progress has occurred in developing nations, where governments have seen FOSS as a way to save money and avoid the vendor lock-in problem. For example, the Brazilian government, which received a relatively high activity rank, was one of the first to experiment with FOSS, beginning shortly after the election of Luiz Inacio Lula da Silva in 2002.

As a result of Brazil's leadership, many other South American countries have started initiatives to promote FOSS usage and development, including many grass roots efforts. For example, in April 2009, free software festivals were held in 200 cities within 18 Latin American countries [dIdSL].

- **Installation guides** that provide instructions for how to download, install, and configure the *Sahana* software on various platforms, including Linux, Windows, MacOS, and others

- **Client guides** that describe the functional modules that make up the *Sahana* system and how to use them

- **Administrative guides** that describe how to configure *Sahana* to meet various security and internationalization (multilingual) requirements

- **Source code documentation** that includes comments in the code itself, written to help programmers understand how the program works

- **Wikis**, or collaborative documents, that include a wide range of useful information about a project, from best practices to community standards to project management information and policies

Unfortunately, the tremendous need for disaster management software is not a market that has been targeted by the proprietary software industry. For this reason, the FOSS approach is well positioned to address this kind of humanitarian need.

1.4   Summary

This chapter introduces the notion of software and the process that underlies its development. It focuses on the emergence of free and open source software (FOSS), which is a new force in the software field.

As the examples in this chapter suggest, FOSS has a number of advantages over proprietary software, especially when it is deployed for humanitarian applications [dSdSC+06]:

- **Low cost** FOSS provides a low-cost approach to software development, with high utilization of a volunteer effort. Governmental and non-profit agencies typically do not have the resources to develop such software in-house, and proprietary software developers have limited appetites for developing open source applications.

- **Freely available** A FOSS system is relatively unencumbered by licensing restrictions that would complicate or limit its reuse or redeployment.

- **Global public good** FOSS serves a global public good that can be shared internationally.

- **IT public service** Just as rescue workers, medical personnel, and others volunteer their services and expertise during a crisis, FOSS provides a way for software and IT professionals to contribute.

In addition to FOSS successes in South America, many other adoptions of FOSS have occurred throughout the world. Here are a few examples:

- The French Gendarmerie is reported to have saved an estimated 50 million Euros since 2004 in moving from Microsoft to the Ubuntu/GNU Linux desktop [Hil09b].

- The Amersterdam city government has made OpenOffice and Firefox the default systems on all its desktops [Hil09a].

- In the United Kingdom, the government recently announced an effort to avoid vendor lock-in by considering FOSS alternatives equally when deciding IT procurements [BBC09].

- Many U.S. organizations are making major commitments to FOSS, including the Library of Congress, the U.S. Postal Service, the U.S. Census Bureau, the U.S. Navy, the FBI, and the state governments of Nebraska and Mississippi (see [Sal08] p. 182).

Considering its current momentum, the trend toward FOSS openness, collaboration, and self-forming communities seems sure to grow and expand as the Internet spreads throughout the developing world. But it is also apparent that this growth will be met at each step by opposition from the forces of proprietary software.

Stallman often draws an analogy between the way proprietary software is marketed in the developing world and the ways that colonial powers have maintained their dominance over their colonies [Sta09]. This view is consistent with the conclusion of a comprehensive EU study [Com06] that acknowledges one of biggest threats to FOSS in Europe to be "the increasing moves in some policy circles to support regulation entrenching previous business models for creative industries at the cost of allowing for new businesses and new business models." This appears to be a more diplomatic way of expressing Stallman's view.

1.2.4   Humanitarian FOSS

A significant sub-concept within the FOSS umbrella is called "humanitarian FOSS" (HFOSS for short), which is software designed for use by global relief organizations, non-profit organizations, and society at large. Organizations that serve the public good, whether governmental or non-governmental, need affordable, reliable, and secure software to help them carry out their missions. The particular needs of these organizations have been largely ignored by proprietary software developers.

The goals of HFOSS generally conform to Stallman's original goal in starting the free software movement—namely, to help one's friends and neighbors. Of course, it might be argued that all FOSS serves the public good. While the Linux and Apache systems serve the public good in a generic sense, the following section introduces two examples of HFOSS projects that directly and uniquely impact humanitarian work.

1.3 Two Case Studies

This section illustrates the special nature of HFOSS by introducing two different projects, one small project that was developed for a single client and one large project that is having worldwide impact.[9]

1.3.1 RMH Homebase

RMH Homebase is a Web-based volunteer scheduling and database software system developed for the Ronald McDonald House in Portland, Maine. This software was developed at Bowdoin College by four students and an instructor in Spring 2008. The "live" version of this software can be viewed at http://rmhportland.org/volunteers/homebase.

Since *RMH Homebase* is FOSS, it is available for free download from Sourceforge (sourceforge.net/projects/rmhhomebase). From its completion in May 2008 through September 2009, *RMH Homebase* has been downloaded 480 times by other developers. It has since been adapted for reuse in at least two other organizations.

Because *RMH Homebase* is a smaller custom FOSS product, it provides an accessible example of the FOSS development process, and we will use it frequently for illustration throughout this book. A more detailed summary of the *RMH Homebase* design appears in Appendix A, and a "sandbox" version of the software can be exercised at this book's Web site myopensoftware.org/textbook.

1.3.2 Sahana

Sahana (http://sahanafoundation.org) is a Web-based FOSS disaster management tool that addresses the coordination problems that commonly arise among government groups, non-governmental organizations (NGOs), and victims in a disaster recovery effort. *Sahana* was developed in the immediate aftermath of the December 2004 tsunami that killed nearly 230,000 people in 11 countries [wp-b].

Following the tsunami recovery effort, *Sahana* has been deployed in response to numerous disasters around the world, mostly in poor and developing coun-

---

[9]A more comprehensive view of the breadth and depth of the HFOSS movement can be found at the Web site http://hfoss.org.

tries. These include the 2005 Pakistan earthquake, the 2006 Philippine mudslide, the 2007 Peru earthquake, the 2007 Mayanmar disaster, and the 200 China earthquake [wp-g]. More recently, *Sahana* has been adapted as th basis for a *disaster preparedness system* by the New York City Office of Emergency Preparedness, and has been deployed in response to the 2010 Haitiar earthquake.

Sahana supports a wide range of relief efforts, from finding missing person to managing volunteer workers, keeping track of logistics, and coordinating refugee centers. As a collaboration tool, it helps the various governmental and non-governmental organizations to work together and share information about the recovery effort.

The *Sahana* project has been recognized for its work with numerous awards including the Sourceforge Project of the Month award for June 2006 and the 2006 Award for Social Benefit from the Free Software Foundation [wp-g].

Sahana was first registered on Sourceforge in January 2005, and since then it has grown into an international developer and user community that spans the globe.

Sahana's Sourceforge site http://sourceforge.net/projects/sahana hosts the repository for its code base and various related software development tools. Its Sourceforge community currently has about 75 registered developers whose names and e-mail addresses are available at the site. Many, but not all, of these developers are programmers. Others are domain experts and users from governmental and non-governmental organizations.

The broader *Sahana* community is organized at five different levels:

1. A board of directors manages its growth and adoption.

2. A project management committee manages the project's legal and operational behavior.

3. Its developers (called *committers*) have the authority to commit code directly to the *Sahana* code base.

4. Its sponsors provide financial and in-kind support of the project.

5. Its broader client community of over 200 adopters help promote and apply *Sahana*. Like its developers, *Sahana*'s clients communicate via mailing lists, Internet Relay Chats (IRCs), and other media.

The *Sahana* Web site provides many forms of documentation aimed at informing community members about the project and easing the introduction of newcomers. These include:

- **General descriptions** of the project, its history, management structure, its community, and how others can get involved

- **Licensing information** that describes how the software may be used and distributed

- **Political neutrality** Because of the openness and transparency that defines FOSS, such software is more likely to be trusted across political boundaries than proprietary software.

- **Easily customizable** Unlike proprietary software, FOSS is meant to be customized and redistributed, which is crucial for its ongoing success and utility for solving new problems.

- **No vendor lock-in** Unlike the business strategies of proprietary developers, FOSS products help users avoid vendor lock-in. This can help developing countries and non-profits become more independent and self-sufficient.

The four freedoms of FOSS are its primary asset: freedom to use, freedom to modify, freedom to distribute, and freedom to improve. These freedoms have no parallel in the proprietary software world.

FOSS has great future potential, not only as a force for the betterment of the information and knowledge society, but also as an economic model that supports intellectual openness and provides communities with a broader collection of software choices.

Exercises

1.1 The LaTeX system is a suite of document preparation and typesetting software designed to support writing scientific and technical articles and books. This book, for example, was typeset using LaTeX.

LaTeX is free software and is distributed under the LaTeX Project Public License, or LPPL (see http://www.latex-project.org/lppl/). Review the LPPL and comment on how it differs from the GNU General Public License (GPL) discussed in this chapter.

1.2 Take a look at the OpenOffice software suite at http://openoffice.org. What can you learn about the number of developers contributing to OpenOffice, the number of lines of code in the software, and the number of downloads of this software that have taken place in the last 3 years?

Now take a look at Microsoft's Office suite, which is functionally comparable to OpenOffice. What can you learn about the number of developers contributing to Office, the number of lines of code in the software, and the number of sales (downloads) of this software that have taken place during the last 3 years?

1.3 Adobe provides two proprietary software products, known as "Acrobat Reader" and "Acrobat Writer." The former is avaliable for free download and can be used to read and display a PDF file. The latter allows the user to edit that PDF.

a. Is Adobe Acrobat Reader an example of free and open source software (FOSS)? Explain.

b. Is Adobe Acrobat Writer available for free download? Explain.

1.4 Consider the Drupal (see http://drupal.org) software suite discussed in this chapter. Compare Drupal with the proprietary software products Adobe Dreamweaver and Microsoft FrontPage.

a. Since Drupal is a content management system, does this make its capabilities different from those of Dreamweaver and FrontPage? Explain.

b. How large is Drupal's community of users and developers? Are these size characteristics an essential element of FOSS project vitality? What else do you think matters to the long-term sustainability of a FOSS project? Explain.

1.5 Sourceforge (http://sourceforge.net) invites developers to join project teams, supports downloads of FOSS products, and provides feedback on product usage. Locate an interesting community-oriented project on Sourceforge and summarize the vitality of its developer and user communities—how many developers and users does it have, and what is the volume of activity on its developer and user discussion threads?

1.6 The following examples provide further evidence that the application of FOSS principles have now spread to virtually every corner of modern culture.

Scientific Publication The Public Library of Science (http://plos.org) and similar publishing enterprises have developed FOSS-like models in which peer-reviewed scientific publications are distributed for free by the author's institutions, rather than through a proprietary publisher who pays the production costs).

Open Source Genetics The BioBricks Foundation hosts a repository (http://bbf.openwetware.org) of genetically engineered DNA building blocks, which are distributed freely under open source licenses.

Open Source Agriculture The CAMBIA project (http://cambia.org) hosts a number of open source projects aimed at sharing scientific knowledge and technologies in developing countries, with particular emphasis on open source agricultural products, such as seeds.

Citizen News and Open Source Media Over the past several years a number of independent grass roots media channels have become increasingly important voices in news gathering and reporting. Two influential U.S. sites are the Huffington Post and the DailyKOS (http://huffingtonpost.com and http://dailykos.com).

Find three more examples of the application of FOSS principles in the wider world culture.

1.7 What is FOSSology? How is it useful to an IT organization?

1.8 What is FOSSbazaar? How does it assist persons interested in becoming involved with the FOSS movement?

Chapter 2

Working with a Project Team

> "It takes a whole village to raise a child."
> —*African proverb*

A free and open source software (FOSS) project is distinguished by a development methodology that combines agile techniques with high levels of interaction among developers and users.

This chapter introduces the key ideas behind FOSS development, including agile techniques, the use of frameworks, code reading, documentation, and teamwork.

Two types of FOSS projects, which we call "client-oriented" and "community-oriented" projects, are characterized in this chapter. Participating in a client-oriented project requires a personal level of communication with team members and users. Participating in a community-oriented project requires the use of a different set of communication channels and conventions.

By completing this chapter, readers should be prepared to begin working on a client-oriented FOSS project team or contributing to an ongoing community-oriented FOSS project. The remainder of this book provides guidance for continuing that effort and making a real contribution to an ongoing FOSS project.

2.1 Key FOSS Activities

A number of key activities play important roles in any effective FOSS development effort, whether it be client-oriented or community-oriented. These strategies are summarized in this section and they are illustrated often in later chapters.

2.1.1 Agile Development

The software development world has recently embraced a powerful paradigm called *agile development.* Agile development emerged in response to the many failures of the traditional software process that were noted in Chapter 1.

In a traditional development process, each stage – requirements gathering, design, coding, testing, and delivery – is viewed as a single discrete event. One stage typically does not begin until the previous stage is completed. Typically, the client is involved in the beginning and ending stages of the process, but not in the crucial middle stages. This is illustrated in Figure 2.1.

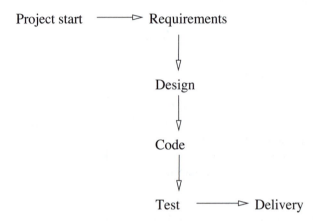

FIGURE 2.1:   The traditional software development process.

The agile process is more fluid, in the sense that each stage has a smaller time scale and all stages repeat in a continuing cycle until the project is complete. The agile development cycle requires that the user be engaged continuously, thus allowing new features to be added from user-provided sce-narios and test cases throughout the development period. Thus, the software product evolves from the bottom up, rather than from the top down. This process is pictured in Figure 2.2.

Since users are involved throughout the agile development process, they play a critical role at each repetition of the design, coding, testing, and review stages. Because these stages are repeated again and again, each iteration provides a new opportunity for *debugging* and *refactoring* the code base in preparation for adding new functionality in the next iteration.

Debugging means finding and correcting errors in the program. Bugs, or instances of incorrect behavior, result from programming errors. Such errors can often be notoriously difficult to find and correct, even when working with a small code base.

Users play a key part in debugging, since they are the ones who most often identify bugs, both during and after the development process has been com-pleted. Continuous communication between users and developers is essential for debugging to be effective. FOSS development, which is an agile process,

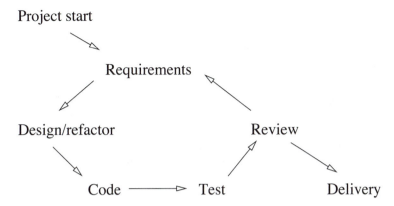

FIGURE 2.2: The agile software development process.

is especially effective in this regard, since it relies on continuous interaction between users and developers.

Refactoring a program means to read the code, find instances of poor programming practice (from either a readability or an efficiency standpoint), and reorganize (usually simplify) the code so that it performs the same functions in a more readable and/or efficient way. No new functionality is added during refactoring, only an improvement in the quality of the code.

The ability to read code with a critical eye, especially code not written by oneself, is a fundamental skill in software development. Software is seldom written by a single person from scratch, contrary to what might have been inferred in introductory programming courses. Instead, software is usually developed incrementally by many developers, each one adding new code to an existing "code base," thus adding a new feature to its overall functionality.

2.1.2 Using Patterns

The overall architecture of a software system refers to the organization of its code base in a way that best reflects the system's functionality, supports its systematic development and deployment, and allows effective distribution of programming tasks among the team's developers.

A *design pattern* is an abstraction from a concrete programming form that keeps reappearing in different coding contexts. Once such an abstraction is identified, it is described and given a name by which programmers can refer to and reuse it.

Examples of design patterns include: Strategy, Visitor, Observer, Mediator, Factory and Prototype (for object creation), and Iterator (for traversals). For more discussions about these and other software design patterns, see **en.wikipedia.org/wiki/Design_pattern**.

An *architectural pattern* moves the idea of a design pattern to the architectural level of a software artifact. At this level, we have patterns for implementing computer-user interaction, such as Client-Server and Model-View-Controller (MVC), as well as others like Multi-Tier, Pipe-and-Filter, and Peer-to-Peer. See http://en.wikipedia.org/wiki/Architectural_pattern) for more discussion of archtectural patterns. The Client-Server, Multi-Tier, and MVC architectural patterns are more fully discussed and illustrated in Chapters 4 and 8.[1]

Once a system's architecture is determined, the code base can be organized appropriately. For example, software organized using a client-server or multi-tier pattern often has the following natural directory structure for its code base.

Domain modules/classes These define the key elements of the application. The domain modules define the name space upon which all other modules are derived. They reflect terminology familiar to users as they exercise the software. Names must be chosen carefully, so as to promote clarity of communication among developers and users. Development of the domain modules in a software system is the subject of Chapter 6.

Database modules/classes These define the tables and variables that comprise the persistent data in the system. The database resides on the server in a client-server software system. Each table is related to one or more core classes/modules. Development of the database modules is the subject of Chapter 7.

User interface modules These implement the system-user interactions that take place on the client side of the software system. The user interface implements the functionality given by the use cases in the requirements document. Development of the user interface is the subject of Chapter 8.

Unit test modules Each of these modules is developed in conjunction with a core, database, or user interface module. Together, the unit test modules comprise a "test suite" for the software system. Whenever any module in the system is changed (refactored, added, or expanded), the test suite must be run to be sure that the system's functionality is not compromised by that change. Unit testing strategies are revisited in each of Chapters 6, 7, and 8.

---

[1]By contrast, a *software framework* is an organizational generalization for a specific type of software application. It is language- and system-specific, and its code inevitably contains instances of various design and architectural patterns. For example, Web application frameworks are implemented in PHP, Java, Ruby, and C++. Well-known PHP frameworks are called CakePHP and the Zend Framework. Well-known Java frameworks are called Apache Struts and Spring. For more discussion of software frameworks, see http://en.wikipedia.org/wiki/Comparison_of_web_application_frameworks.

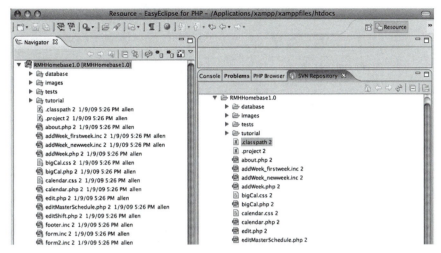

FIGURE 2.3: Using the Eclipse environment with Subversion.

On-line help tutorials These modules are typically developed last, and in conjunction with user training that accompanies delivery of the software. Their structure tends to mirror that of the user interface modules, so that there will be one help screen for each distinct use case that users will be exercising with the system. Writing on-line help modules is covered carefully in Chapter 9.

Organization of individual modules within the code base is initially done by the lead developers. Refinements to this code base are made by individual developers on the project team. To facilitate collaboration, and to ensure the integrity of the code base when several developers are making changes to it simultaneously, a "version control system" is used to synchronize their work.

As shown in Figure 2.3, the code base for *RMH Homebase* follows this general organizational scheme. Figure 2.3 also shows how several developers can synchronize their work using a version control system (SVN in this case). More discussion of version control systems appears in Chapter 3.

2.1.3 Reading and Writing Code

Program reading and writing is, of course, the central activity within software development, since the program is the software. The ability to read and write program code in the language(s) of the application is a key requirement for all the developers in a software project. A corollary requirement is that developers must be able to learn new language features and skills as needed to support the timely implementation of new software elements.

Many fine programming languages are in use for developing contemporary software. This book's examples are shown in PHP and MySQL, although

```
<div id="container">
    <?PHP include('header.php');?>
        <div id="content">
<p>
    <strong>Personnel Input Form</strong><br />
    Here you can enter new personnel into the database.</p>
        <?PHP include('validate.php');?>
        <?PHP
            //Check if they have submitted the form
            if(!array_key_exists('_submit_check', $_POST)) {
                include('form.inc');
            }
            else{
                //in this case, the form has been submitted
                $errors = validate_form(); //step one is validation.
                // errors is an array of problems with their submission
                if($errors){
                    //if any errors exist, display them and give them the form to fill out again
                    show_errors($errors);
                    include('form.inc');
                }
                //otherwise this was a successful form submission
                else {
                    process_form();
                }
            }
        ?>
        <?PHP include('footer.inc');?>
    </div>
</div>
```

FIGURE 2.4:   Example code from *RMH Homebase.*

readers who are familiar with Java or C++ should have no trouble understanding their meaning. Other projects and tutorials appearing at the book's
Web site myopensoftware.org/textbook use different languages, such as Java,
so that readers working with different languages in their projects should look
there for additional support.

Reading code is an especially important skill. The code you read in published programming textbooks is, unfortunately, not typical of the code you
find in most software applications.

In general, code published in textbooks tends to be more uniform and readable than code found in real applications. By contrast, code that appears
in software applications often reflects more than one programming style and
may contain elements that are inefficient, unnecessarily verbose, or just plain
difficult to read.

For example, Figure 2.4 shows some example PHP code from the *RMH
Homebase* project, and Figure 2.5 shows what it produces in a Web browser.
PHP code can be embedded inside the HTML of a Web page by using the
HTML tags <?PHP and ?>. Whenever such a page is rendered, the PHP
code is executed. In this example, the embedded PHP code calls functions that
display the header (which includes the menu bar), the applicant's information
form, and a footer (not shown in Figure 2.5).

Writing good code requires using conventionally accepted coding and documentation practices. This is especially important when the software is being
developed by a team. Unfortunately, much of the code that underlies actual
software products does not reflect the use of good practices. Thus, some of

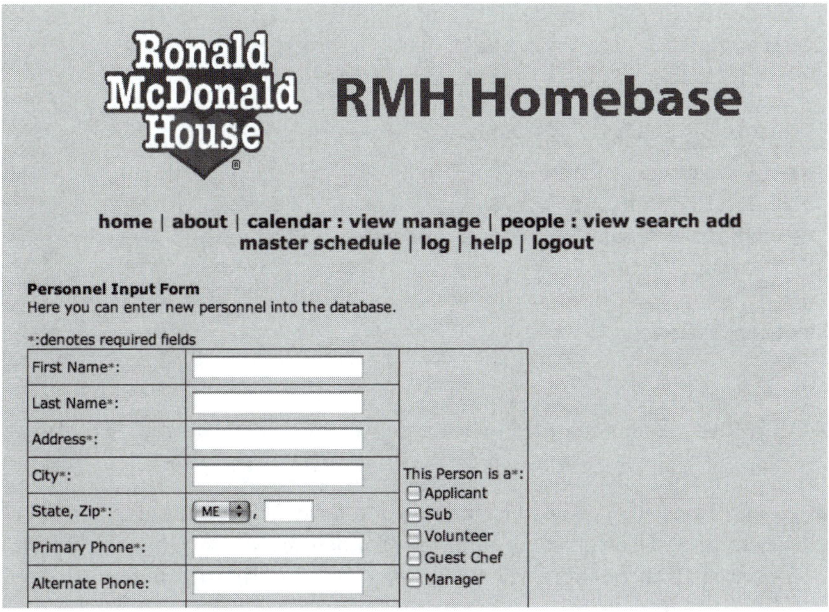

FIGURE 2.5: Output of the example code in Figure 2.4.

a programmer's work includes rewriting poorly written code to make it more readable and receptive to the addition of new features.

Below is a list of widely used coding standards for common program elements. These standards are illustrated here in PHP, though similar standards exist for Java, C++, or any other contemporary programming language.

- Naming and spelling—Class, function, variable and constant names should be descriptive English words. Class names should be capitalized; if they consist of more than one word, each word should be capitalized— e.g., Person, SubCallList.

  - Multiple-word function and variable names should separate their adjacent words by an underscore—e.g., `$primary_phone`. Alternatively, these names can be written with each non-first word capitalized—e.g., `$primaryPhone`.

  - Global variable names should be written in all-caps and begin with an underscore—e.g., `_MY_GLOBAL`.

  - Constant names should be written in all-caps—e.g., `MY_CONSTANT`.

- Line length—A line generally contains no more than one statement or expression. A statement that cannot fit on a single line is broken into two or more lines that are indented from the original.

```
/**
 * fill a vacancy in this shift with a new person
 * @return false if this shift has no vacancy
 */
function fill_vacancy($who) {
    if ($this->vacancies > 0) {
        $this->persons[] = $who;
        $this->vacancies=$this->vacancies-1;
        return true;
    }
    return false;
}
```

FIGURE 2.6:   Documentation with indented blocks and control structures.

- Indentation—Use consistent indentation for control structures and function bodies. Use the same number of indentation spaces (usually four)
  consistently throughout the program—e.g., see Figure 2.6.

The use of coding standards such as these is sometimes met with resistance
by programmers. They argue that pressures to complete projects on time and
on budget prevent them from the luxury of writing clear and well-documented
code all the time.

This argument breaks down when the software being developed is subject to
later revisions and extensions, especially by other programmers who need to
read the code as they revise and extend it. This is especially true in the open
source development world, where the source code typically passes through
several sets of programmers' eyes as it evolves.

2.1.4   Documentation

As a general rule, effective software development requires that the code not
only be well written but also be well documented.

Software is well documented if a programmer unfamiliar with the code can
read it alongside its requirements statement and gain a reasonable understanding of how it works. Minimally, this means that the code should contain a
documentary comment at the beginning of each class and non-trivial method,
as well as a comment describing the purpose of each instance variable in a
class. Additionally, each complex function may contain additional documentation to help clarify its tricky parts.

When reading a code base for the first time, a new developer may find a
shortage (sometimes a complete absence) of commentary documentation. If
the code is well written, the reader may still be able to deduce much of its
functionality from the code itself. In fact, it is a good exercise for a developer
new to a code base to add commentary documentation in places where it is

```
/**
 * class Shift characterizes a time interval for scheduling
 * @version May 1, 2008
 * @author Alex and Malcom
 */
class Shift {
    private $mm_dd_yy;  // String: "mm-dd-yy".
    private $name;      // String: '9-12', '12-3', '3-6',
                        // '6-9', '10-1', '1-4', '12-2', '2-5'
    private $vacancies; // no. of vacancies in this shift
    private $persons;   // array of person ids filling slots,
                        // followed by their name,
                        // e.g. "Malcom1234567890+Malcom+Palmer"
    private $sub_call_list; // "yes" or "no" if SCL exists
    private $day;       // string name of month "Monday"...
    private $id;        // "mm-dd-yy-ss-ss" is a unique key
    private $notes;     // notes written by the manager
    ...
```

FIGURE 2.7: Inserting comments in the code.

lacking. That is, it improves one's own understanding and it contributes to the project by improving future readers' understanding of the code.

A good way to begin refactoring an under-documented code base is to add documentation in places where it is lacking. This helps not only to improve the quality of the code for future readers, but also to reveal bad smells and improve the code's receptiveness to the addition of new features.

Documentation standards exist for most current programming languages, including PHP and Java. These latter are supported by the JavaDoc and PHPDoc tools, respectively. They implement a standard layout for the code and its comments, and they automatically generate a separate set of documentation for the code once it is fully commented.

For example, consider the Shift class in the *RMH Homebase* application discussed above. Its documentation contains a stylized comment of the form:

```
/**
 *
 */
```

at the head of each class and each non-trivial method, as well as an in-line comment alongside each of its instance variables. This is shown in Figure 2.7.

Notice that this documentation contains so-called *tags*, such as @author and @version. When used, each of these tags specifies a particular aspect of the code, such as its author, the date it was created or last updated, and the value returned by a method.

TABLE 2.1:   Some Important PHPDoc Tags and Their Meanings

Tag	Meaning
@author	name of the author of the class or module
@version	date the class or module was created or last updated
@package	name of the package to which the class or module belongs
@return	type and value returned by the function or method
@param	name and purpose of a parameter to a function or method

A short list of the important PHPDoc tags with a brief description of their meanings is shown in Table 2.1.[2] Other languages, such as Java, have similar tagging conventions. It is important for developers using those languages to learn those tagging conventions before writing any documentation.

Once a code base is completely documented, a run of PHPDoc (or JavaDoc, as the case may be) will generate a complete set of documentation for all its classes and modules. For example, Figure 2.8 shows the documentation that is generated for the `Shift` class shown in Figure 2.7.

Class: Shift

Source Location: /database/Shift.php

Class Overview [line 46]

class Shift characterizes a time interval in a day for scheduling volunteers.

Author(s):
Alex and Malcom
Version:
May 1, 2008
Copyright:
Copyright (c) 2008, Orville, Malcom, Nat, Ted, and Alex. This program is part of RMH Homebase, which is free software. It comes with absolutely no warranty. You can redistribute it and/or modify it under the terms of the GNU General Public License as published by the Free Software Foundation (see http://www.gnu.org/licenses/ for more information).

Variables	Methods
$day	__construct
$id	add_vacancy
$mm_dd_yy	assign_persons
$name	close_sub_call_list
$notes	db_shift
$persons	fill_vacancy
$sub_call_list	get_day
$vacancies	get_id
Constants	get_mmddyy
	get_name
	get_notes
	get_persons
	get_sub_call_list
	has_sub_call_list
	ignore_vacancy
	new_shift
	num_slots
	num_vacancies
	open_sub_call_list
	set_notes

FIGURE 2.8:   PHP documentation generated for the Shift class.

---

[2]A more complete list can be found at http://phpdoc.org.

2.1.5 On-Line Help

Documentation serves the needs of developers who are interested in understanding the functionality of a software system. However, it does not serve the needs of users who want to learn the system. For this purpose, separate elements are needed, which often take the form of on-line help tutorials, or equivalently a printable manual that teaches the user how to perform each use case supported by the software.

So, as a separate step from documentation, open source software development requires that on-line help tutorials be developed and integrated within the software itself. These tutorials are written in a language and style familiar to the user, and they should use terminology that is common to the user's domain of activity.

Each help tutorial should correspond to a single user activity, called a "use case,"[3] which typically appears as a group of interactive forms. Thus, the word "Help" in the navigation bar should take the user to that particular tutorial corresponding to the form with which the user is currently working. The tutorial itself should describe a short sequence of steps, with illustrative examples, that shows how to accomplish an instance of the use case that the form implements.

For example, the *RMH Homebase* software has nine distinct use cases (see Appendix A). One of these is called "Change a Calendar" which allows the user to find and fill a vacancy for a shift on a particular day of the week. The corresponding form for that use case is shown in Figure 2.9.

If the user needs assistance, the help tutorial for filling a vacancy can be selected on the menu bar, and the user receives the step-by-step instructions shown in Figure 2.10.

The help tutorial opens in a separate window from the user's current form, so that he/she can work with the form while simultaneously reading the screen.

2.2 Client-Oriented vs Community-Oriented Projects

Prior to the emergence of FOSS development, large-scale proprietary software projects were characterized by a tightly controlled, top-down, hierarchical development process. The newer FOSS development process is characterized by a loosely controlled, bottom-up, distributed community that is highly cooperative and democratic.

This atmosphere of openness and collaboration cannot be emulated in the proprietary development world, since that world demands complete secrecy

---

[3]See Chapter 5 and Appendix A for more discussion and examples of use cases.

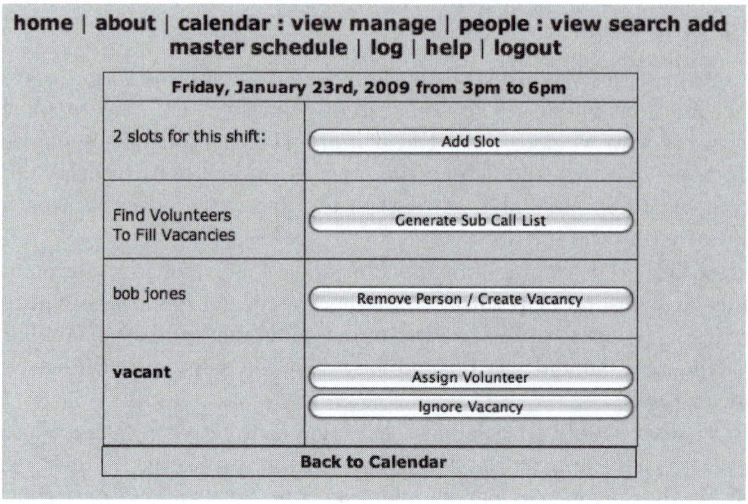

FIGURE 2.9:   Form for filling a vacancy on a shift.

and control over its development processes and products. For example, proprietary software developers are required by their employers to sign a "nondisclosure agreement," or NDA, which restricts them from talking about or sharing any of the source code they read or write with anyone outside the company that owns the software.

NDAs thus legally prevent proprietary software developers from discussing any programming issues in public forums or over e-mail, even if such discussions would benefit their work. For this reason, many feel that NDAs lead to reduced programmer productivity and lower quality in proprietary software projects. NDAs, of course, are not applicable to FOSS developers.

As for FOSS, projects tend to have one of two different but complementary development models, which can be called "community-oriented" and "client-oriented."[4]

Client-Oriented Projects   The client-oriented development model applies to a new FOSS project that has only a few developers and a single client. The client expresses a need for software that could replace an existing system (often a manual system), and the developers set about designing and implementing software which fulfills that need. Typically, the development period is a few months and the software has only a few thousand lines of code. A good example of a client-oriented FOSS project is *RMH Homebase*, which was introduced in an earlier section.

---

[4]The "community-oriented" model actually has several sub-classes, which distinguish single-from multiple-vendor support, single from multiple licensing, etc. These finer variations are discussed in more detail in Chapter 10.

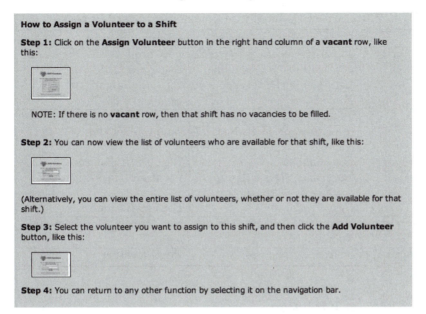

How to Assign a Volunteer to a Shift

Step 1: Click on the **Assign Volunteer** button in the right hand column of a **vacant** row, like this:

NOTE: If there is no **vacant** row, then that shift has no vacancies to be filled.

Step 2: You can now view the list of volunteers who are available for that shift, like this:

(Alternatively, you can view the entire list of volunteers, whether or not they are available for that shift.)

Step 3: Select the volunteer you want to assign to this shift, and then click the **Add Volunteer** button, like this:

Step 4: You can return to any other function by selecting it on the navigation bar.

FIGURE 2.10: Help screen for filling a vacancy.

Community-Oriented Projects The community-oriented model applies to a more mature FOSS project, having a large group of developers, covering a wide geographic spectrum, and serving a diverse group of users who share a common software need. The code base for such a project is large, on the order of tens or hundreds of thousands of lines of code. A good example of a community-oriented project is *Sahana*, which was also introduced in an earlier section.

These two genres have a lot in common. Both aim to develop free and open source software using an agile collaborative process, yielding an artifact that can be widely reused, adapted, and shared. Variants of the GNU General Public License provide assurance that such software cannot be privatized. The notion of team-based agile development with a lot of user interaction is central to both genres.

While they share a common philosophy, community-oriented and client-oriented FOSS projects have some important structural and methodological distinctions. These distinctions arise because of differences in their maturity, code base size, user community size, team size, and geographical distribution. These differences are summarized in Table 2.2.

In the course of this study, readers will be encouraged to participate in either a client-oriented or a community-oriented FOSS development project. Because these alternatives have somewhat different collaboration strategies and goals, they are discussed in more detail in the next two sections.

TABLE 2.2:   Client-Oriented vs. Community-Oriented Projects

	Community-oriented	**Client-oriented**
Maturity	an existing product to which new features can be added E.g., the current version of *Sahana*	new product, no useful existing product E.g., the original version of *Sahana* (2005)
Size	large code base (tens of thousands or more lines of code) E.g., *Sahana*	small code base (a few thousand lines of code) E.g., *RMH Homebase*
Users	large and diverse group of users with similar needs E.g., *Firefox*	few users, single client E.g., *RMH Homebase*
Team size	large team (hundreds of developers)	small team (5–10 developers)
Geography	many locations worldwide	single location

2.2.1   Project Evolution

Many community-oriented FOSS projects begin as client-oriented projects. Others begin as proprietary software and are later converted to open source. Still others start when a lone developer "scratches an itch" and turns a good idea into a viable code base.[5]

If the original product is well-conceived, well-programmed and available for download from a public repository like Sourceforge, it has the potential to be adapted, refined, or expanded for wider use as a community-oriented FOSS project.

Whatever the starting point, the transition of a software product into a community-oriented FOSS project usually occurs in response to requests from new users to expand and generalize that project's functionality, alongside commitments from new developers to help implement this new functionality. Communication and new energy for that project occurs by word of mouth through the project's public discussion forums. The community thus grows organically, based on the perceived quality and usefulness of the product for a larger group of users.[6]

The Linux project provides an excellent example of the transition of a FOSS

---

[5]As an interesting "reverse transition," we note that sometimes a new client-oriented project can emerge out of a larger community-oriented project. For example, a customization of the *Sahana* code base is currently being developed to support the special needs of the New York City Office of Emergency Management.

[6]It is important to note that many (most) small FOSS projects never evolve beyond their original stage of development. Projects fail to mature for various reasons, including the absence of a broader audience beyond the single user, a lack of interest by new developers, or some other reason related to broader technology market dynamics.

product from a lone-developer project into a community-oriented project. The Linux project started almost by accident in August 1991 with the following Usenet post by Linus Torvalds, a graduate student at the time [Tor91]:

> Hello everybody out there using minix - I'm doing a (free) operating system (just a hobby, won't be big and professional like gnu) ... I'd like to know what features most people would want. Any suggestions are welcome, but I won't promise I'll implement them :-)

Torvalds' request was answered by a widespread response [wp-e]. In 1992 Torvalds released the Linux kernel under the GNU General Public License (GPL). By 1993 more than 100 programmers were contributing to kernel development. Today, thousands of programmers around the world contribute to the Linux project. Many contributors are individual volunteers, but today many large corporations also support Linux development, including IBM and Red Hat.

The FOSS development model is also characterized by transparency, openness, and collaborative decision making. These characteristics can be seen in how some of the most successful projects describe themselves. For example, the Mozilla project, which created *Firefox*, describes itself as follows [Foue]:

> The common thread that runs throughout Mozilla is our belief that, as the most significant social and technological development of our time, the Internet is a public resource that must remain open and accessible to all. With this in mind, our efforts are ultimately driven by our mission of encouraging choice, innovation and opportunity online.

> To achieve these goals, we use a highly transparent, collaborative process that brings together thousands of dedicated volunteers and corporate contributors from around the world with a small staff of employees to coordinate the creation of products like the Firefox Web browser.

Similarly, the Apache Software Foundation, the organizational home of numerous FOSS projects, describes itself as "not simply a group of projects, but rather a community of developers and users [Foua]."

Thus, the FOSS development model, as described by Eric Raymond in his popular book *The Cathedral and the Bazaar* [Ray00], has the following central characteristics:

- The source code, both development versions and stable versions, is always publicly available.

- Stable versions of the software, containing the latest bug fixes, are released frequently.

- Software development requires close relationships and interactions with user groups.

- Technical aspects of the project—features, bugs, algorithms—are discussed publicly by the community.

- Although there is some centralized control, individual users and developers have significant ability to influence the project.

- The community is merit based. Prestige and reputation within the community are based on the frequency and quality of one's contributions.

Of course, the highly distributed FOSS model would not be possible without the interconnectivity and modern communication tools provided by the Internet.

2.2.2 Similarities and Differences

While many elements of a community-oriented project are quite different from those of a client-oriented project, the two genres share many methodological similarities. Here are the similarities.

Agile Methods Despite the differences in scale and scope between a large FOSS project and a small one, both types of projects generally use an *agile* development methodology, as described above.

User Role Both client-oriented and community-oriented projects actively engage users in the development process. However, users in community-oriented projects often play the role of beta tester or bug finder as well. For example, the Mozilla project has more than 10,000 users, many of whom serve as beta testers and provide feedback to developers.

Project Leadership Different leadership models have emerged in different FOSS communities. Some, like Linux in its early days, used the "benevolent dictator" model, with Linus Torvalds as the dictator. Others have a "core team" that shares decision making over what makes it into the code base. Still others are more democratic, in the sense that all developers are empowered to suggest new design directions and goals.

Team Roles Developers play different roles—designer, tester, coder, refactorer, documenter—at different times during the project's evolution. Different contributors tend to self-select into specific tasks based on their interests and abilities. Typically, a community-oriented project has a lot of work going on in parallel.

Code Synchronization Repository The *code synchronization repository* (see Chapter 3 for more discussion) is a common tool used by both community-oriented and client-oriented project developers. Many large projects use their Sourceforge site for this purpose, while others, such as *Sahana*, use their own site.

Staging and Live Server The use of a *staging server* (see Chapter 3 for more discussion) in a large project is the same as in a small project. Establishing the software on a live server is the responsibility of the user, since different users have different preferences for integrating the software into their operations.

Team Communication All kinds of communication methods and tools are used in a community-oriented project, including email, list servers, Internet relay channels (IRCs), blogs, and video-conferencing. Most of the same procedures apply here as in client-oriented projects; an agreed-upon agenda for each conference, a central location where to-do lists, discussion threads, and other documents are maintained, and so forth (see Chapter 3 for more details).

Programming Activities Programming languages and tools used are similar between small and large projects. However, since large projects tend to have a longer life, they are more likely to have more than one language in their code base. The choice of an integrated development environment, or IDE, is also independent of the size of a project. While Eclipse is popular among all sizes of projects, different developers in large projects are more likely to use different IDEs (see Chapter 3 for more discussion).

Understanding a community-oriented project with an existing code base and large developer community presents its own set of challenges not found in a client-oriented project. The following differences should be kept in mind.

- Some developers in a community-oriented project may have been engaged in the project from the beginning, while others may be just joining the project. In a large project, team members come and go, and they may play different roles over the life of the project.

- A community-oriented project usually has a large number of users, none of whom has the individual capability or authority to shape the project or its software. This user community exerts collective influence over the software's features and development priorities.

- A community-oriented project might have had an identifiable beginning, but it probably does not have a clear end. It is ongoing in the sense that new code is constantly being contributed as features are added or changed to suit the changing needs of its user community. The project evolves over time as if it were a living organism.

- A community-oriented project's development effort is driven by requirements generated in a distributed and bottom-up fashion by individual users. They are typically adopted using some kind of consensus mechanism among the project's leaders.

- The project's leaders include a group of developers who have "commit privileges," meaning that they can commit actual changes and enhancements to the code base. Others who contribute changes (bug fixes, etc.) must submit their contributions to these developers before they are accepted and committed to the code base.

Community-oriented FOSS projects are usually open and welcoming toward newcomers. The best advice for a newcomer is to take some time to understand how the community accomplishes effective work before attempting to make contributions upon first contact.

2.3 Working on a Client-Oriented Project

A software development team is a group of persons who work together on a project to create a specific software artifact. Throughout the life of the project, individual team members play roles for which they are particularly well suited. Within a particular role, different tasks emerge as the project evolves. Each task is assumed by one or more team members, and remains active until it is completed.

This section describes the general organization of a software team for a client-oriented FOSS project, paying special attention to the roles people play, the tasks they assume, and the tools they use for collaboration, interaction, and code sharing.

2.3.1 Members, Roles, and Tasks

The members of a software team can play any of the following key roles during the life of the project.

- analyst

- developer

- user

- IT technician

- team leader

- observer

The *analyst* role is filled by a person who understands the user's domain, elicits requirements, defines use cases, evaluates risks and alternatives, and sketches the initial design of the software to be developed. The analyst's tasks may also include cost estimation and project scheduling.

The *developer* role is filled by a person who writes test cases from requirements, and reads, writes, tests, debugs, and refactors program code. Developers also refine requirements and use cases, write documentation and on-line help pages, and solicit feedback from users at each stage in the project. In short, a developer is a programmer who can also read, write, and communicate effectively with users.

The *user* role is filled by persons knowledgeable about the application's domain. A user's tasks are to review use cases, provide data for test cases, review the output of code written by developers, provide feedback on the quality of that output, and find bugs in the software after each iteration has been deployed.

The *IT technician* role is filled by persons who configure and maintain the technical environment used by the team. Their tasks are to set up and maintain the code repository, the staging server, the videoconferencing system, the team discussion site, and other software tools needed by the team to develop the software effectively.

The *team leader* role is filled by a person who oversees the development process. The team leader's tasks include setting weekly agendas and milestones, assigning tasks to team members, coordinating overall system architecture, teaching other team members about new techniques, leading regular team discussions, and helping resolve design issues.

The *observer* role is filled by a person interested in watching the project develop and/or whose project management expertise may provide occasional high-level advice on particular design decisions. Overall, the observer role is a fairly passive one.

It is important to note that the same person may play different roles and assume different tasks as different needs arise during the life of a software project. For example, the team leader may also play a developer role when introducing a new concept or technique to other developers.

Moreover, the same person may play two or more roles simultaneously. For example, a developer may also temporarily serve as an IT support person when setting up a master copy of the code base, called a *code repository*, for all the developers to use. Thus, fluidity in role-playing and task assumption is a key element of an agile open source software project.

To illustrate these ideas, the following team was formed to develop the *RMH Homebase* volunteer scheduling system introduced in Chapter 1. This list also identifies the initial role(s) that each person assumed at the beginning of the project.[7]

---

[7]The names used here are pseudonyms, to protect the privacy of the actual team members.

- analyst—Alex

- developers—Orville, Malcom, Ted, Nat

- users—Gina, Karl, Susan

- IT technicians—Ellis, John, Michelle

- team leader—Alex

- observers—Riccardo, Truman

Throughout the three-month life of this project, roles changed. At the beginning, Alex was an analyst while he gathered requirements, wrote use cases, and sketched the initial design. Early in the project, Orville temporarily became an IT support person when he set up the project's code repository.

To illustrate the team dynamics of task assumption, here are some of the discussions following the first videoconference for the *RMH Homebase* project:

Subject: Videochat, 1/30
From: Alex
Date: Tue, 29 Jan 2008 at 7:03pm
Category: Agendas & Meeting Notes

Here's a sketch of an agenda for tomorrow's videoconference:

1. *Discuss each of our new PHP classes.*

2. *Discuss PHP tutorials that will be most useful to us.*

3. *Determine standards for coding, testing, and documenting classes as they develop.*

4. *Determine what each of us can reasonably accomplish for next week.*

5. *Prepare press releases for the project.*

6. *Identify any relationship of the project with other volunteer scheduling systems (e.g., VMOSS).*

Feel free to add anything to this list that I've overlooked.

"See" you at 1:00 tomorrow. I'll try to connect with Orville using my iChat and AIM id = alex. If we get stuck, my phone here is 207-729-1234.

Orville Wed, 30 Jan 2008 at 2:07pm
We had a videochat today. Present were: Alex, Malcom, Nat, Orville, Ted.

We covered our agenda and worked out videochatting bugs. Worked well overall for a first time. Please reply in the comments with the class you will personally work on for next week.

Malcom Wed, 30 Jan 2008 at 2:08pm
I'm working on Calendar, and researching existing PHP Calendar classes.

Orville Wed, 30 Jan 2008 at 2:08pm
I'll break people.php into separate class files, then work on Person (which needs to be done first since the others extend it). Then I'll work on Applicant and Manager. Also, once Alex decides on a structure for our packaging, I'll implement it in the repository.

Nat Wed, 30 Jan 2008 at 2:55pm
I am currently working on SubCallList. I'll post again and take up one (or more) of Orville's classes that extend Person.

As you can see, Alex initiated the discussion by posting the agenda for the videoconference. The developers Orville, Malcom, and Nat had a short follow-up exchange, in which they summarized the videoconference and assigned themselves to the tasks of developing the core classes Calendar, Person, and SubCallList during the upcoming week.[8]

While roles and tasks are often pre-assigned by the team leader, team members may self-select into and out of tasks as the project evolves, depending on personal preferences, skills, and other commitments.

This fluidity is particularly important in the open source development world, where team members are not always working full time on any one project. They usually have commitments to other work, for instance other course work (if they are full-time students) or other professional activities (if they are users or developers in the corporate world).

2.3.2   Team Dynamics

With the tools in place and the programming activities identified, having a coherent and collaborative team dynamic through the life of the project is a key driver for the success of the project. How and when do collaborations occur, and what is the substance of such a collaboration?

The catalyst in team dynamics is usually the project leader. The project leader sets the tone for effective project collaboration. This tone is characterized by trust, inclusiveness, and confidence that the project will succeed and every team member's participation will be crucial to that success.

The project leader also defines a regular schedule for team videoconferences, usually on a weekly basis. An agenda is set for each videoconference, initially by the project leader and refined by suggestions from the team members.

Out of each videoconference comes a review of the prior week's accomplishments and a new set of goals for the upcoming week, accompanied by

---

[8]Detailed descriptions of these elements of *RMH Homebase* can be found in Appendix A.

assignments of tasks to team members. These goals and assignments are determined by consent of the team members.

2.3.3   Scheduling, Milestones, and To-Do Lists

The schedule for a software project must respect the constraints of individual team members. It must also be set so that the goals of the project are substantially met at the end of the development period. While flexibility in the accomplishment of particular tasks is important, some overall view of the main goals of the project must be apparent at the outset. That is, all team members must become confident that the project can be completed within the time frame allotted and that each one can play an important role in reaching that outcome.

To that end, a project *milestone* is an intermediate goal that must be met by a particular calendar date. Examples of goals that can be met as milestones include completion of the project's database modules, completion of the on-line help screens, completion of user training, and so forth. Below are the milestones that had to be completed at the end of the *RMH Homebase* project:

> Wednesday, 23 April, 2008—Complete draft of help tutorials
> Thursday, 24 April, 2008—User training session I at RMH
> Thursday, 1 May, 2008—User training session II at RMH
> Friday, 9 May, 2008—Deliver final system to RMH

A *to-do list* is a collection of smaller units of work that occur in pursuit of a milestone. Unlike a milestone, a to-do list is an assignment of particular tasks to particular individuals on the development team. Below is an example of developing a to-do list that was aimed at the accomplishment of the milestones listed above for the *RMH Homebase* project.

Agenda for 4/16 Videochat
From: Alex
Date: Mon, 14 Apr 2008 at 9:44am
Category: Agendas & Meeting Notes

Here is what I see needs to be done to finish the project, along with debugging. Feel free to add items that I have overlooked.

A. (Nat and Alex) Write and edit the remaining tutorials. Three are now completed, edited, and submitted. Here's a summary of where they stand:

> 1. *Logging on to the Web site—I don't think this one will be needed (the login page is pretty self-explanatory)*
>
> 2. *People: Searching—done*
>
> 3. *People: Editing—done*

4. *People: Adding—done, except .gif images need to be fixed*

5. *Calendar: Viewing*

6. *Calendar: Editing (includes removing persons, SubCallList editing, and adding persons to a shift)*

7. *Calendar: Managing (includes creating slots, generating weeks, and publishing)*

8. *Schedule: Viewing and editing*

B. (Ted and Nat) Organize and conduct workshop sessions at RMH for 4/24 and 5/1.

C. (Alex) Draft evaluation form for workshop participants.

D. (Orville) Write help.php.

E. (Malcom and Alex) Go through the code and add comments for phpdoc and future developers. Add the copyright notice at the top of each source file.

F. (Karl) Ensure that the RMH technical person prepares the RMH server with PHP and MySQL so that the system can be installed there. Add a button to the Web site to link to RMH Homebase.

Orville Mon, 14 Apr 2008 at 2:35pm

help.php is written and committed. Nat, take a look at editPerson-Help.inc.php in the tutorial folder. That's the format your final tutorials should follow. Then look at help.php—it just pulls the relevant tutorial (defaulting to what I call index.inc.php which is the list of all tutorials).

Note the difference in the image paths now, in the editPerson-Help.inc.php file.

To see what it will look like, log in, start editing a person, and click "help."

Also, might I suggest we always include a help footer? With links back to "help index," the URL of which would simply be help.php with no argument passed to it.

Alex Tue, 15 Apr 2008 at 7:29am

Question for Orville and Malcom: When Ted and Nat do the workshops at RMH on the 24th and 1st, they will be using the tutorials which are full of examples from our little "jones" family database. However, the live system at hfoss.bowdoin.edu has an empty database (except for admin/admin) which makes the tutorials pretty useless. Can we set up a temporary "training version" of the database with the "jones" family live, so that the tutorials and the workshop will work together?

It seems that this "training version" of the database might be useful to RMH staff in the future. Ted, I think you need to ask Gina and others at the training sessions about this question.

Orville Tue, 15 Apr 2008 at 7:41am

I just ran testDBSchedules to populate the database for the traning sessions—note that the actual shifts aren't filled yet—you need to actually start publishing some weeks.

I can show Nat or Ted how to reset the tables on-site if you guys are comfortable with unix and terminal-style OSes. If not, it's safer to not do it, because we're working on the actual server, and a mistyped command can cause a lot of damage.

Nat Fri, 18 Apr 2008 at 12:56pm

Alex, I've committed most of the calendar management help tutorials. I went with a main manage calendar tutorial which then lets you pick which specific task you are doing. This avoids redundancy since you need to get to the list of weeks page in order to edit anything.

I've completed all but the editShiftsHelp, which I've been trying to make as simple/easy to follow as possible. So feel free to critique the ones that are done; I should be committing editShiftHelp—I'm aiming for 3pm.

Notice here that Orville has taken the lead on setting up a training version of the database in preparation for the two training sessions. Meanwhile, Nat and Alex are communicating about the completion of the final help tutorials in preparation for those sessions. All of the tasks discussed in this dialogue are "to-do" items, which together lead toward achieving the help tutorial, training, and final delivery milestones.

2.4   Joining a Community-Oriented Project

Before joining a community-oriented FOSS project, it is good to begin with a clear understanding of one's personal motivation. Different individuals have different motives for joining, such as:

Academic The project fulfills a particular learning or research goal. FOSS finds a natural home in academic institutions, since all the code and design documents are transparently available for further analysis and modification. It also presents an excellent way to share an implementation of a hypothesis or the results of data gathering with other researchers who have similar goals.

Philanthropic The project fulfills one's desire to contribute to the benefit of one's neighbors. This is like the motive for an engineer joining Engineers without Borders (http://ewb-international.org/) or a doctor joining Doctors without Borders (http://doctorswithoutborders.org/).

Recognition The project fulfills one's desire to be judged by the quality of their work. FOSS development presents an excellent channel to widely disseminate one's portfolio of contributions to peers and mentors. This can contribute to one's resume, which can in turn secure access to other interesting projects in the future. Unsolicited praise from a distant mentor or colleague is often very satisfying.

Commercial The project provides an avenue through which commercial success can be obtained. Even though the product is FOSS, a developer can often use it while providing service and support for using the product. In addition, successful contributions to a project may yield job offers or consulting opportunities in similar areas that are well aligned with the skills developed while contributing to the project.

Hacker The project provides an opportunity to become energized by writing new code and developing new features and products. Many developers simply enjoy creating new artifacts, or "scratching their own itch" (so to speak) by writing code that does something novel and interesting.

User The product allows a user to contribute to software that can be used internally in their own organization. Often such a contribution ensures that your organization has a say in the product's future functionality. Sometimes this contribution involves quality assurance (testing) and/or writing user documentation that will help colleagues in the organization to effectively use the system.

The exact mixture of participants in any particular FOSS project can vary greatly. The variety and roles of individual developers, sponsors, academics, users, and domain experts are unique to each project's nature and goals. Moreover, project participants often have distinct motivations for joining the project, as explained above.

What brings everyone together in a community-oriented project is that each person contributes to the end result. The determination of future directions for the product is governed typically by a meritocracy. That is, a person's rank or title matters less in their influence on a project than does the quality of their contributions to the end result of the project.

The karma earned by contributing valuable code to a project can thus help a developer to become accepted and recognized in future FOSS projects. Contributions are measured not only by code submissions, but also by feedback provided on helping to improve the project's overall quality and usefulness.

2.4.1   Project Selection

Once the motivations for joining a FOSS project become clear, the next step is to find a project that can fulfill those motivations. And there is a wide spectrum of choices available, ranging from single-developer projects to those maintained by multi-organizational consortia.

Firefox, OpenOffice and Linux are the most visible projects in the spectrum. Persons who manage to contribute something of value to any of these projects will certainly gain recognition, based on the sheer visibility that these projects enjoy in the software world.

However, there are also many small- to medium-sized projects that have potential and are growing rapidly. By participating in one of these, you will probably find more opportunities to contribute something significant. By analogy, it is like being a little fish in a small, growing pond rather than a little fish in a large, established pond.

Places to search first are the large repositories such as http://sourceforge.net and http://launchpad.net, which are two of the most popular. Also, directories like http://freshmeat.net serve as a kind of "yellow pages" for FOSS projects that reside elsewhere on the Internet.

The http://sourceforge.net and http://launchpad.net repositories are designed to be accessible to new developers, providing certain assurances on access, downloading, and reviewing any project's code base. These repositories also have integrated mechanisms for collaboration, bug tracking, planning and release management. After gaining access to one of these projects, a developer has a personal login to access the project's tools and forums, which in turn provide strong support for making real contributions.

Although Sourceforge has over 200,000 projects registered, many of these are either dead or inactive. So selecting a project that will be both challenging and rewarding involves the following additional suggestions:

Seek a popular project. A good indicator of a project's popularity is how many downloads its software has each month and how active its user and developer forums are. The user forum enables users to get help and give feedback on the project. Since the users represent the project's target group, it is important to know the size of this group to help understand the project's current and future vitality.

Seek a project with a lot of vitality. A project's statistics often include the number of new code contributions that have been made, the number of feature requests/bugs that have been submitted, and/or the number of new releases that are created each year. All these are measures of a project's vitality and hence its receptiveness to the addition of newcomers.

Seek a project with growth potential. Some projects have a large user base and deliver a lot of value but are now mature and have reached a plateau in terms of future growth. Thus, these projects will provide very little opportunity for a newcomer to make an impact.

Seek a project that welcomes diversity and promotes contributions. Not all open source projects operate as diverse open communities; some are run by a closely knit group of people with a lot in common. A project that instead has a lot of diversity (e.g., representing various nationalities, types of contributions and motivations) is likely to be more welcoming to newcomers.

Seek a project that will be enjoyable. Newcomers interested in content management systems, business intelligence applications, disaster management systems, or medical information systems should seek projects that are targeted to those applications. Whatever project is selected, it should energize the newcomer every time a contribution is made and the results are posted.

2.4.2 First Contact with the Project

Once a project is selected, the newcomer may take each of the following three steps, in turn, to initiate their involvement with a community-oriented FOSS project:

1. Reading and improving the documentation

2. Using communication channels

3. Working with the code

Each of these steps is enabled by interacting with the project's Web site. Here's some more information about what these steps involve.

2.4.2.1 Reading and Improving the Documentation

The first step to getting involved with a community-oriented FOSS project is to visit its Web site and learn as much as possible about the nature of the project. This step naturally evokes questions, which may be answered by digging into the project's documentation. If answers are elusive, a newcomer may post a question to the community through one of its communication channels.

Of course, the *quality* of different FOSS projects' documentation is highly variable. Some projects provide ample, well-written documents; others provide little or none; and still others provide unhelpful or poorly written documentation.[9]

---

[9]Programmers are notorious for focusing all their attention on the code and undervaluing the documentation that should accompany it.

Thus, one of the best ways for a newcomer to begin contributing to a FOSS project is to contribute to its documentation. For example, if a project is lacking a good user guide for a module or function, a newcomer could take notes while exercising the system, and then use the notes to write a guide that will help other users.

Similarly, if a newcomer is interested in working on a particular segment of the source code, for example fixing a bug, a good way to start is to read the code itself, along with its documentation. In places where the documentation is missing or unclear, a newcomer may rewrite it. The project's developer community is usually grateful for all contributions like this.

2.4.2.2   Using Communication Channels

Three popular mechanisms are available for users to engage with a project's development community: mailing lists, forums, and IRC channels. The first two are not time zone dependent, so the entire community has an opportunity to access and reply to one's posts. The latter, however, is a long-standing medium (IRC) and is very popular as a hangout area for open source projects.

Each project typically creates its own chat rooms and those interested can join without being invited. The IRC chat room might therefore be useful as an informal place for finding out more about community, before a newcomer starts using the mailing lists more frequently.

For example, the *Sahana* project provides separate mailing lists for developers and users (and there are others for directors and members of the project management team). These are linked to the *Sahana* Web site and include a complete archive of all the project's communications. For example, once a newcomer joins the *Sahana* user list, he/she can read through its entire history. Skimming this history is a good way to get a feel for the community and its current focus areas.

The *Sahana* project is open and welcoming to newcomers, since it explicitly invites them to "Join us and contribute." Its Web site **sahanafoundation.org** greets visitors with a concise overview of the various ways to join its community, as either a developer, a user, or a donor. As noted above, *Sahana* provides a wealth of documentation to help newcomers become familiar with the project.

To join in a project's discussion, newcomers may first need to "register" as a new community member. At that point, it is useful to join the project's mailing lists and chat rooms and try to identify some of its ongoing issues and current goals.

In this activity, it is pragmatic for newcomers to choose tasks and contributions that are within their capabilities and can help improve their overall understanding of the project. It is also good to "scratch one's itch" and focus on those aspects of the project about which one is most passionate.

2.4.2.3 Working with the Code

Finally, a newcomer will eventually want to get involved with the code base itself; adding features, improving documentation, or fixing bugs and refactoring. This activity is best initiated by reading and analyzing the code, especially parts that relate to features that allow "scratching one's itch!"

Newcomers may start this activity by becoming a user and tester for the project's code base. That is, they will download and "play" with the software until they become familiar with its overall organization and functionalities.

During this activity, they will also note any apparent bugs or missing features, as well as features that they think need to be revised. These concerns should be communicated to the project's developer community.

While contributing code is a central component of any software project, that activity is not the only one needed by a successful software project. In the case of FOSS, it is often the non-coding contributions where most of the demand lies. Here is a summary of the different types of contributions that can be made to a FOSS project:

Bug Fixing and Core Development Development fuels the growth of the project and thus is a core contribution. Bug fixing is a valuable entry point for new developers. It is a good way to demonstrate one's capability to contribute something significant to the project, since bug fixes and patches are reviewed by senior developers and are ultimately credited to the contributor if they are accepted.

Testing and Quality Assurance Every time a new release or build is made, new bugs can creep in due to newly coded features or unexpected changes in the system's dependencies. Testing is thus a critical role to ensure the quality of the product for the user base. Testers are the last line of defense on ensuring product quality. However, to play this role, a newcomer does not need to have specific technical expertise. The requirement here is for someone who has a good affinity for quality and can put themselves in the shoes of a typical user.

Documentation Some developers believe that the code is the documentation and should be more than sufficient for anyone to understand the functionality of the software. This belief is often seconded by the fact that documentation itself is an afterthought and is often not kept up-to-date with the code. Of course, every software system is designed expecting that code readers have a certain level of IT literacy. However, not all users are as familiar and literate with common coding conventions and practices. Thus, user documentation, installation guides, on-line help, and quick references are critical elements of a well-documented software artifact.

Release Management Once the core product is built, it needs to be packaged into the various computer environments that the product should support, which typically includes Windows, Max OS, and Linux. This requires additional work to package the software in a form that is natural to the installation process of the target computer environments.

Creative Design Work Finding a talented developer who is a good creative designer is sometimes a challenge. The skill and discipline needed to develop robust code do not propagate well to the arts. A good creative designer can greatly enhance the user experience and affinity to the product, and thus can have a strong impact on the system's usability. Persons with artistic backgrounds typically excel in this form of contribution.

Infrastructure Support Sustaining the supporting IT infrastructure for a FOSS project can be demanding. It typically involves maintaining Web sites, wikis, mailing lists, IRC channels, forums, a version control system, and a bug tracker. Ensuring that these supporting tools are kept up-to-date is a lot of work, as is the key task of developing a backup and recovery mechanism should the development site fail catastrophically.

Translation As much as English is an established *lingua franca* of the international community, not all users may be able to speak it or understand it. Thus translators are needed to build language packs that translate the user interfaces and supporting documentation into appropriate non-English languages. Here lies the opportunity for diversifying the user community, since anyone who finds that their native language is not supported can contribute translations to the community. The only skills needed are the ability to read English sentences and translate them into one's native language.

2.4.3 Norms for Good Citizenship

When joining a community-oriented FOSS project, newcomers need to understand how the community ticks. Every community has a distinctive culture and norms and it is important to understand them. The most important step is to begin actively participating in discussions, so that the newcomer's name and interests become recognized by other active community members.

Despite their different cultures, most FOSS developers and users follow widely accepted commonsense norms when communicating in a mailing list, forum, or IRC session. Here is a summary of these norms:

Post appropriate material There are often multiple mailing lists for development, users, and other specialist areas per project. One should post questions and comments to the appropriate mailing list, since those supervising that list will be more likely to respond.

Be brief and to the point Shorter is always better. Most people on the list are busy people. It's much easier to hold people's attention with three paragraphs than with three pages. Sending anything that's larger than it needs to be is an imposition on other readers on the list. If what you're saying requires a comprehensive treatment, it's probably worthwhile to write a brief summary at the start, so that subscribers don't have to spend a lot of time deciding whether what you've written really interests them.

Remove unnecessary "quoted text" Often email users allow you to quote the text of the message to which you are replying—and over the course of an animated email conversation, the back-and-forth trail of quoted text can become very long. To avoid wasting space, quoted text should be minimized.

Avoid kneejerk e-mails Try to make each e-mail constructive, with well-supported points and links to references whenever appropriate. Avoid simplistic, emotive, kneejerk reactions and other messages that you may regret later on. Kneejerk reactions usually aren't interesting reading for other community members.

Stay on topic Once a thread of discussion is started, try to stay on topic of the original discussion. If you digress the original topic might get lost in the discussion. If you need to digress to a new topic, start a new discussion thread (i.e., use a new subject line).

Avoid large attachments Not everyone on this mailing list will have broadband, so avoid sending large attachments and try your best to send links to large files instead.

Proofread your post E-mail doesn't offer the additional modes of communication of in-person communication. Body language, tone, eye contact, etc. aren't available to help you get your point across. Be sure your message is free of errors. You have no idea who is going to read your message—it's not quite the same as personal e-mail.

Don't write in CAPITALS In the e-mail world, this is equivalent to shouting. Text is a somewhat limited medium when it comes to being demonstrative. Use it conservatively.

Refrain from using obscure abbreviations Using abbreviations like *wrt* and *rtfm* is useful, but only if the person reading your message knows what they mean. In other cases, the message may look pretentious and exclusionary.

Avoid making comments that can be mistaken as sarcasm Some messages don't always come across in text for others as they might be intended. Despite their smarminess, "emoticons" or sideways smileys should be used sparingly.

Respect the diversity of the community Successful FOSS projects have contributors from all around the world and from different native languages and cultures. There are also contributors from different communities from academics, emergency management, civil society, and the software development world. Also, since English is not everyone's primary language, not everyone writes e-mail in the same style, so some tolerance for these differences is appropriate.

Avoid foul language and flaming Posting extremely foul or abusive language aimed at a fellow list member is a deal breaker. This includes obscenities, verbal harassment, or comments that would prove offensive based on race, religion, or sexual orientation.

Avoid encouraging (and using) "Read the f...ing manual" responses It is quite likely when you start on a new open source project that you will ask questions to clarify your understanding that have been asked on the same mailing list or otherwise numerous times before. Some developers become agitated having to repeat themselves, and often they place those questions and answers in a FAQ or a manual. Thus, it is best to read the documentation and try first to find the information for oneself before asking a question that's already been answered before.

2.4.4   Becoming a User First

The primary voice to be heard by a FOSS developer is the user's voice. Ultimately, the success or failure of the project depends on how widely it is adopted by users.

Unlike traditionally developed software products, FOSS projects do not typically provide a clear set of requirements specifications at the outset. Instead, that knowledge is held by the user community at large. The only way to learn about requirements is to employ common collaboration mechanisms, ask questions and learn about what the application should do from its user base.

By "becoming a user first," a newcomer may either find bugs that need fixing or suggest ideas for new features that can improve the software's usefulness. So, submitting bug reports and enhancement suggestions is a real contribution, since users are an integral part of the FOSS community and their feedback is important.

Here are a few steps that can be taken by a newcomer to become a user first:

Understand the project's goals The mission statement of the project, often found in the project's **About Us** page, will provide an initial understanding of why the project exists and what common goals drive everyone in its community.

Understand the itch Understand what is compelling people to contribute to develop something in this problem domain by identifying the key problem the system is trying to help solve.

Understand the alternatives Learn about all the alternative open source, freeware, and/or proprietary products that compete for the same target user base, and see how this system differentiates itself from these alternatives. Often the commercial products are ahead of the open source alternatives, so they are a good source for understanding the gaps.

Install the system and play the role of the user There is no better test to understand the user experience with a system than to download, install, and try it for oneself. This will also provide insight into improvements that can be made to better address the needs of the target user base.

Ask questions Asking questions on the user mailing list can clarify one's understanding of the product and confirm that potential bugs and enhancements are really valid. Even simple questions are welcome; this constitutes participation and answering questions also constitutes a contribution in its own right. For example, Launchpad actually gives credit to people who answer users' questions.

Submit bug reports Once a bug is found and it can be confirmed that the system is not performing as it should, one can submit a bug report to the project's bug tracker. A bug report needs to be written so that a developer can recreate the bug without having to ask for further clarificaition. Below is an example of a good bug report that was recently submitted to the *Sahana* project:

```
--------------

Release Version:
Sahana r603 (2010-01-24 13:02:53) - You can obtain this
from the Help->About menu
(http://haiti.sahanafoundation.org/prod/default/about)

Environment:
Firefox 3.5
Windows XP

Prerequisites:
User should be logged in to the system.

Steps:
1) Click 'Mapping'.
```

```
2) Click 'Map Service Catalogue'.
3) Click 'Features'.
4) Click on an ID in the Location list.
   (The 'Edit location' page will appear.)
5) Remove the value in the 'Latitude' field.
   (This step is optional)
6) Click on 'Conversion Tool' link.

Expected Result:

   The Converter should appear.

Actual Result:

   Clicking the link results in nothing. Converter doesn't
   appear.
```

2.5   Summary

A FOSS project is distinguished by a development methodology that combines agile techniques with high levels of interaction among developers and users. FOSS development includes not only coding and debugging, but also communicating, writing documentation, and submitting bug reports.

Two genres of FOSS projects, called "client-oriented" and "community-oriented" projects, are also distinguished. Both share common methodologies, such as agile development and user involvement.

However, the two have different development paradigms because of their different maturity levels, user base size, and diversity of their developer communities. Working on a client-oriented project requires a personal level of communication with team members and users, while joining a community-oriented project requires initiating a different collection of communication techniques and activities.

Exercises

The exercises below are aimed at facilitating the team-formation and team-joining activities for a FOSS development project that can be carried out throughout the remainder of a one-semester course. The first three exercises are appropriate for beginning work on a client-oriented project, while the second three are suited to joining an ongoing community-oriented project.

2.1 Read the requirements document and initial code base for a client-oriented FOSS project that your team will be conducting in this course.

    a. Identify your teammates and the role that each one will play in the project.

    b. Evaluate the condition of the code base. In your view, is it well written and documented? What needs to be done to improve its readability and extendability to new functionality?

    c. Evaluate the requirements document. Does it clearly state the objectives of your project? Does it relate well to the code base, in the sense that its use cases relate clearly to the organization of the code base?

2.2 Participate in the first team meeting for your client-oriented project. There, an initial task assignment will be given.

    a. Evaluate and discuss your preparation and willingness to perform the tasks that are assigned to you. Feel free to suggest changes appropriately.

    b. If you have questions about the requirements document, ask users to clarify those questions.

    c. If you have questions about the code base, ask the project leader to clarify those questions.

2.3 Complete the initial task(s) assigned to you for your client-oriented project. In this exercise, you should be comfortable collaborating with teammates as needed. Communicate your progress and completion of your task(s) to all teammates on or before the due date for your task(s).

2.4 Visit http://sourceforge.net and find five active, vibrant FOSS projects and five moribund ones. Explain how you came to each of these assessments.

2.5 Revisit http://sourceforge.net and locate two interesting community-oriented projects.

    a. Compare the two with regard to their apparent vitality, receptiveness to newcomers, and compatibility with your particular programming and other development skills.

    b. Visit each one's IRC channel and observe the conversations that are taking place among developers and users. Do the conversations seem to be welcoming? Do the posts seem to be constructive?

    c.   Browse the source code for each project and make a brief assessment of how well organized and documented it is.

2.6 Select a community-oriented project and explore the current issues being discussed on its IRC channels (developer and user forums) and email archives. If necessary, take appropriate steps to join the project by obtaining a user id and password. Read the user documentation and, if possible, exercise an on-line test version of the software.

Chapter 3

Using Project Tools

> "What we have to learn to do, we learn by doing."
> —*Aristotle*

Whether the free and open source software (FOSS) project is client-oriented or community-oriented, the code base is the central object in the development process. Working with the code base as a member of a development team requires special tools and skills, many of which are not needed when working on a single programming task in isolation.

In any collaborative process where a single product is being built by many hands, the collaborators need to find a way to communicate with each other about their individual activities. They also need shared access to the code base they are constructing. Thus, developer tools can be divided into two broad categories: *collaboration tools* and *code management tools*. The former is about strategies for working as a team, while the latter is about strategies for organizing and working with the code base.

This chapter describes and illustrates the key tools that FOSS developers use when collaborating and working with the code base.

3.1 Collaboration Tools

As in all group projects, a collaborative software project depends in large part on successful communication strategies. Fortunately, there are many tools available that support communication among team members, including those who are spread across geographical areas and time zones.

The developers of a typical FOSS project regularly use the following kinds of basic collaborative tools [Fog09]:

- A Web site for public outreach

- Mailing lists for team communication

- Version control to manage the code base

- Bug tracking tools

- Real-time chat (IRC) channels

As you can see, this tool set supports both interpersonal communication (Web site, e-mail lists, chat software) and interaction with the code itself (version control, bug tracking).

3.1.1   Asynchronous Communication

Perhaps the most versatile collaborative tool, one seen in just about every FOSS project, is the *mailing list*. A mailing list is a distribution list. When a member of the list sends a message to the project's list server, it is distributed to all other list members. It thereby supports *asynchronous communication* within the project's development community.

For many projects different lists and sub-lists can be set up to support different aspects of the project—e.g., coding, documentation, and management. For example, the *Sahana* project maintains the following lists:

- The *Sahana-user* list enables users and administrators of *Sahana* to submit queries about using, deploying, and administering the software.

- The *Humanitarian-ICT* list serves non-technical members of the community who specialize in emergency management.

- The *Sahana-maindev* list is for software developers and focuses on technical design, quality assurance, documentation, deployment, and "geeky discussions" about the *Sahana* code base.

An important feature of mailing lists is that they can also serve as an historical *archive* for the project, thereby providing a record of important design and policy decisions that took place throughout the life of the development process.

As discussed in Chapter 2, an important aspect of participating in a mailing list is using appropriate etiquette. Many communities publish documents describing their expectations in this regard.

For example, the *Sahana* project's expectations are linked to an etiquette guideline published by the New Zealand Open Source Society (NZOSS) (see http://nzoss.org.nz/nzoss-openchat-acceptable-use-policy), which provides the following general guideline:

> The NZOSS recognizes that it represents a very diverse community. The overriding tone we promote is 'consideration and respect for others.' If in doubt, use this as your primary guideline.

This and similar guidelines provide commonsense advice on appropriate list behavior—the need for brevity, civility, and appropriate writing style.

However, the use of mailing lists as the sole medium for written communication among software team members is a bad idea. Additional tools are needed that support project-specific discussion threads that can be initiated by any team member, and whose discussions are accessible only to team members.

To this end, other forms of asynchronous communication tools have been used by FOSS projects, and more are being developed all the time. For example, *forums* can be used to manage group discussions for a project. Because a forum is topic based, it fits particularly well with the dynamics of FOSS project development.

The forum provides a unique location where a project's discussion threads can be initiated and maintained by team members, and from which every new message is broadcast (via e-mail) to all members of the team who are participating in that thread.

Unlike mailing lists, forums require members to visit a certain Web site in order to participate. Forums also allow users to subscribe to *really simple syndication* (RSS) feeds that notify every subscriber whenever a new post is made.

Many tools are available that support asynchronous communication in this way. We recommend ones that are either free or inexpensive, multi-platform, and multi-functional, such as Google Groups (http://groups.google.com) and Basecamp (http://www.basecamphq.com).

3.1.2 Synchronous Communication

In the early days of software development, all the members of a software team would work in the same room from the beginning to the end of the project. This model, however, is no longer realistic. In today's world, the members of a software team are geographically dispersed. To accommodate this constraint and ensure continuous communication, the team must maintain a regular schedule of synchronized communication.

Virtual meetings are sometimes needed to set goals, evaluate progress, or discuss some other global issue. Synchronous communication tools are thus also needed to supplement the asynchronous tools presented above.

A classical synchronous communication tool is Internet Relay Chat (IRC), which provides real-time text communication over the Internet to support *synchronous conferencing*. In a typicial IRC environment, a single channel is used by all community members who are engaged in, for example, a distributed plenary conference session. Such a dedicated communication channel can also be used on an *ad hoc* basis to support one-on-one, small group or team discussions. Many different freely licensed IRC clients are available (see http://ircreviews.org/clients).

Videoconferencing is a more sophisticated tool for managing synchronized communication. It has the advantage of allowing participants to share information visually, as well as through the use of audio and text. Good tools for videoconferencing are freely available, for example Skype (http://skype.com) and AIM/iChat (http://aim.com).[1]

In any case, each synchronous communication session should have an agenda that covers the team's accomplishments since its last session, an identification and initial assignment of upcoming tasks to team members, and a discussion of new issues that need to be addressed.

The use of synchronized communication is a critical activity through which software team members can negotiate and set new goals, assess their progress, and discuss design and implementation alternatives at a high level of abstraction. However, synchronized communication is not usually the best place for discussing detailed technical issues or bug fixes; those are better handled off-line on an individual basis, using discussion forums or other asynchronous methods.

3.1.3　Shared Documents

Maintaining shared documents—such as to-do lists, milestones, and files—is vital to a collaborative software project.

To-Do Lists are lists of tasks to be completed in the near term, along with the names of team members who have committed to complete those tasks. Bug-fixing assignment is a particularly popular use of to-do lists.

Milestones are calendar events that identify deadlines for completing major steps in the project.

Files are artifacts like design documents, client-provided scenarios, community outreach documents, or help pages that support the project's development.

Project management and collaboration tools, such as Google Groups, typically support the sharing and maintenance of such documents.

Often, several people may need to share the editing of a single document, in which case the wiki becomes an important tool. That is, a wiki supports collaborative development of a document through group editing. Like version control systems (see Section 3.2.3), wikis come with features such as history and change tracking. A wiki also supports discussion threads associated with each page of a shared document.

For example, the *Sahana* wiki at http://wiki.sahanafoundation.org has the following valuable threads:

---

[1] A more comprehensive survey of current videoconferencing tools can be found at Videoconferencing Reviews (http://thinkofit.com/webconf/videoreview.htm?p=aim#aim), which contains detailed reviews and articles about video conferencing, VOIP, phone, and audio conferencing.

Foundation has discussions about the Sahana Foundation and help for getting involved with the *Sahana* community.

Deployments has discussions about *Sahana* deployments, project standards, and best practices.

Translate has discussions among members of the *Sahana* translators community.

Requirements has discussions about new requirements among domain experts and clients.

3.2 Code Management Tools

Beyond interpersonal collaboration, FOSS developers must master several key concepts that directly relate to the code base itself.[2]

The key components of a typical development environment range from tools (such as editors and compilers) that reside and run on the developer's workstation to the tools that reside on remote servers to ensure effective collaboration. These components fall into the following categories:

The IDE allows a single developer to work with the code base using appropriate coding, compiling, debugging, and testing tools.

The Software Stack provides a run-time environment so that developers can test their changes in a realistic setting.

The Version Control System supports asynchronous reading and writing into a code base among several developers using a shared code repository.

The Bug Tracker keeps track of the status of all current and past bugs in the software, so that users and developers can submit and resolve bug reports.

These components are discussed more fully in the sections below.

---

[2]Sharing a code base is not unique to FOSS development. This kind of sharing takes place in any collaborative software process, whether the artifact is proprietary or open source. What distinguishes collaborative FOSS projects from collaborative proprietary projects is that in FOSS projects, all of the shared code is publicly visible.

3.2.1   The IDE

An *integrated development environment* (IDE) is a software application that
supports the development of software in a particular programming language.
This activity includes coding, compiling, tracing, debugging, and running
individual programs that comprise the code base for a software system.

Examples of IDEs include Eclipse, NetBeans, Microsoft Visual Studio, and
XCode. All of these are multi-language IDEs, so that any one can be configured to support development in a particular programming language.

Each member of the development team must install an IDE on his/her own
computer, which provides integrated access to the following kinds of support
tools:

- *Source code editor*, typically a text editor that has such features as *syntax
  highlighting, syntax checking, autocompletion* of language-specific terms,
  and others that simplify the coding process

- *Source code translators*, including *compilers* and *interpretors* depending
  on the programming language being used

- *Package build tools* that link programmer-developed source code with
  binaries, libraries, and other resources that make up an application

- *Debugging and unit testing tools* that assist the programmer in finding
  and fixing run-time errors

- *Version control tools* that help to synchronize the code base with the
  repository

- *Documentation tools* that support the maintenance of consistent documentation of individual modules and functions in the code base

For example, the Eclipse IDE (http://eclipse.org) is particularly popular.
Historically, Eclipse began as an IBM Canada project, but it is now overseen
by the Eclipse Foundation, supported by many software firms, and licensed
under the Eclipse Public License. Eclipse is now open source, cross-platform,
and supportive of several different programming languages and associated
development tools.

Eclipse has a *plug-in architecture*, which allows it to be extended to new
programming languages and to incorporate new features. It can be configured to support programming in Java, C, C++, Python, Perl, PHP, or any
of various other languages. For example, different configurations of Eclipse
with PHP and MySQL were used for the development of *Sahana* and for the
development of *RMH Homebase*.

Figure 3.1 shows a snapshot of an Eclipse session, in which a developer's
version of *RMH Homebase* is in use and is also synchronized with a version
control code repository. The Eclipse graphical user interface (GUI) is divided
into various frames which provide different *perspectives* or *views* of the project.

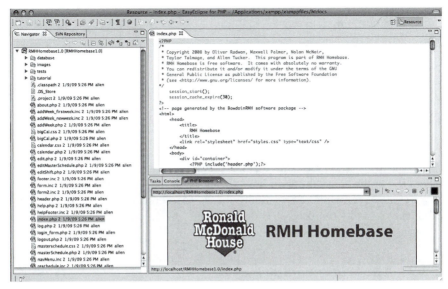

FIGURE 3.1: Developing within the Eclipse environment.

Notice the hierarchy perspective shown on the left-hand side of the Eclipse window. It reveals the overall directory and file structure of the code base. With this perspective, the programmer can easily browse the code base, add or delete files, or open files for editing. Various icons are used to provide the experienced programmer with a snapshot of the file's status—e.g., new, modified, saved, etc.

The middle pane is the editing window. Notice the use of *syntax-aware* highlighting, which distinguishes keywords, comments, and other features of the code. Not shown here are the special icons that Eclipse uses to highlight syntax errors and other problems with the code. By navigating over a syntax error flag, the programmer is given an error message and often one or more suggestions on how to resolve the syntax error.

Also not shown here is Eclipse's ability to *auto complete* code as it is being typed. For example, for an object-oriented language like Java, when the programmer types the name of a reference variable to a particular type of object, Eclipse will display a pop-up window that includes all the various methods that can be called on that object. These and other features help reduce errors and shorten development time.

A debugger is a tool built into an IDE that can help the developer locate and correct errors in the code base. Whenever that code crashes while it is running, the debugger can show the instruction in the source code that was executing at the time of the crash. The debugger also provides tools like running a program step by step, stopping at some pre-specified step (called a *breakpoint*), and tracking the values of pre-selected variables as such breakpoints are reached.

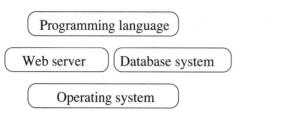

FIGURE 3.2:   Software stack for Web-based applications.

The bottom pane provides various other views, including a console view where the program's command-line output would be displayed and the output of a debugging session. Thus, Eclipse pulls together, within one application, all of the elements required to code, test, run, debug, and document a unit of code within a large software system.

3.2.2   The Software Stack

To contribute effectively to a software project, a developer must set up a run-time environment for the code base so that new code can be immediately tested as it is written. This environment is called a *software stack*,[3] since it is a hierarchy containing (at least) a particular operating system, database system, and programming language that will be used to develop and support the application. The software stack is connected with the IDE, so that the developer can run a program in a particular operating system environment as new code is developed.

The elements of a software stack for Web-based applications are visualized in Figure 3.2. This shows an additional Web server element above the operating system and alongside the database system.

Many different software stacks are in use, depending on the particular platform for which the software is being developed. For example, developing Web-based software in PHP for a Linux platform might use a LAMP (Linux, Apache, MySQL, and PHP) stack. On the other hand, developing Web-based software in C# for a Windows platform might use a WINS (Windows, Internet Information Service, .NET, and SQL) stack. For more information on different software stacks, see **en.wikipedia.org/wiki/Solution_stack**.

The LAMP software stack is a particularly popular software environment for open source Web applications, since it is open source and easy to install and manage. LAMP also comes in other OS-dependent variations, such as WAMP (Windows) and MAMP (Mac OS), making it possible to turn just about any personal computer into a convenient platform for developing Web applications. Because LAMP is in widespread use on the Web, locally developed applications can be easily ported and deployed to commercial servers.

---

[3]It is also known as a "software bundle" or "solution stack."

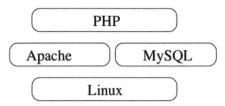

FIGURE 3.3: A LAMP stack for Web-based applications.

As depicted in Figure 3.3, the so-called *LAMP stack* can be used to support *three-tiered* Web applications. Generally, these are client-server applications that include a database.

What are the components that make up the LAMP stack? Linux (or MacOS or Windows), of course, is the operating system, which manages all of the computer's basic functions, from file storage to process scheduling and the user interface.

At the next level is the Apache Web server,[4] which is an application that supports the *HyperText Transfer Protocol*, a collection of rules that governs how Web pages are transported across the Internet. Web servers are part of the *client-server* architecture that characterizes the World Wide Web. The client side of such an architecture is represented by various Web browsers, such as Firefox, Internet Explorer, and Chrome.

For most Web applications, the Web server works in conjunction with a database. MySQL is a free and open source relational database management system. It is the most widely used database server for Web applications. A *relational database* is a collection of interrelated *tables* that store data for a particular application. Chapter 7 discusses the principles and practices behind database organization and programming in more detail.

For example, Amazon's database contains thousands of tables, including a table that stores information about its customers and another table that stores information about purchases. The data from both tables are linked (or related) because the purchases table contains a field that gives the customer id for each purchase.

Finally, PHP is a scripting (or programming) language used for creating dynamic Web pages. PHP scripts can be embedded in HTML code and run on nearly all Web servers. PHP is considered a *server-side* scripting language because PHP scripts are interpreted by the Apache Web server.

For example, when a browser loads the URL http://myserver.org/index.php, this initiates a request for the index.php page from the Apache server located at myserver.org. If that page contains a PHP script, the server will interpret

---

[4]The Apache Web server is a free and open source server developed by the Apache Software Foundation. It is a fast, scalable Web server that is used by approximately 65% of the sites on the Web, including some of the largest and busiest sites.

the script directly, possibly retrieving information from a MySQL database and returning that result to the browser.

Installing the LAMP stack on a personal machine is a straightforward and well-documented process. For instance, the MAMP version for Macintosh is available with a one-click installer (http://www.mamp.info/en/index.html). It will install a local server environment on any Mac running Mac OS X version 10.4 or higher. MAMP is licensed under the GNU GPL.

Several different open source WAMP servers are available for Windows machines, such as WAMPServer (http://www.wampserver.com/en) and easyPHP (http://www.easyphp.org). Both of these are distributed under free software licenses and are easy to install on a personal computer.

3.2.3 The Version Control System

Software systems are made up of a large number of files that change over time as additions, deletions, and modifications are made to the code base. For all but the very smallest projects, it is essential to use a *version control system* (VCS) to help manage this process.

A VCS (also known as *revision control* or *source control*) is software that helps manage changes to a collection of source code files. Such software is useful even if there is only a single developer, but it is essential when there is a team or a community of developers all sharing the same code base.

A VCS tracks all changes to the code base. That means that whenever a programmer adds a new piece of code to the code base, it doesn't simply overwrite the previous version. Rather, the VCS keeps both copies of the system, making it possible to revert to a previous version if a current line of development proves to be incorrect.

In addition, the VCS keeps track of who contributed the code, when it was contributed, and so forth. It provides tools to compare one version of the software with another, making it easy to see what has changed, incrementally, from one version to the next as the code base grows or shrinks.

A good (non-software) example of a VCS is Wikipedia. For any page in Wikipedia, it is possible to examine the history of the page, which will show exactly what changes were made, by whom they were made, and when they were made. If a user believes that a set of changes is incorrect, he or she can revert to a previous version. A major difference between Wikipedia and a FOSS code repository is that not every programmer has direct write access to the code base, a point we take up more fully below.

In general, a VCS supports the following code management functions:

- Multiple revisions of the same code base

- Multiple concurrent developers

- Locking, synchronization, and concurrency of the code base

- Support for versioning history and project forking, meaning that certain parts of a project or the entire project itself can be split off (forked) into a separate project

Some of the common VCS concepts and operations that support these functions include:

- *Repository:* The repository is the place where the shared code base is stored. While anyone can download and read code from a FOSS respository, typically only certain programmers—*the core team* or *committers*—have authority to write code into the repository.

- *Working copy:* This refers to the individual programmer's copy of the code base.

- *Check out:* Individual programmers can check out a working copy of the code base, downloading it to his or her computer, often linking to the code to an IDE such as Eclipse.

- *Update:* The programmer can download the most recent version of a code base that was previously checked out. The updated version will include changes made by other programmers.

- *Commit:* Programmers who have sufficient write privileges with the repository can contribute new code directly. These programmers' working copies of the code are immediately merged with the existing code base. The VCS figures out which pieces of code have changed in the working copy and need to be merged.

- *Merge:* Two pieces of code are merged whenever they both apply to the same file or code segment.

- *Patch:* A patch is piece of code that is added to the code base. It usually describes what code is to be added or removed from the code base.

- *Trunk:* Repositories are organized into hierarchies, which are tree structures. The trunk is usually the main development line for a project.

- *Branch:* A branch is a copy of the software that can undergo separate and independent development. Branches are often used to package *releases* of the software or to allow experimentation. In some cases a branch can break off (or *fork*) into a separate or competing project. In many cases, branches are later merged back into the trunk.

Many different VCSs are currently in use. Two popular ones are the Concurrent Versions System (CVS) at http://nongnu.org/cvs and Subversion (SVN) at http://subversion.apache.org. They are both open source. CVS is the older of the two, but it has some serious restrictions. For instance the module structure in a CVS repository cannot easily be reorganized. SVN is a newer code synchronization tool that addresses the restrictions posed by CVS.

For example, recall Figure 2.3 in Chapter 2, which shows how several developers can synchronize their work using SVN. The left-hand window in that figure shows the developer's own copy of the code repository, while the right-hand window shows the modules in the repository itself. Alongside each module is an integer *version number*, which reveals the developer's version compared with the version that is current in the repository.

Additionally, the developer may wish to view the differences between his/her version of a module and the version that is in the repository. To do this in Eclipse/SVN, the developer highlights that module in the left-hand window and then selects "Compare with Latest Version in Repository." Detailed instructions for setting up and working with an SVN repository can be found at the Web site myopensoftware.org/textbook.

Different VCSs take different approaches to managing a repository. Some, such as CVS and SVN, use a centralized *client-server* approach. Working copies are related to the repository as clients to the server, in the same way that spokes of a wheel are related to the hub. Others, such as Git (http://git-scm.com), Mercurial (http://mercurial.selenic.com), and Bazaar (http://bazaar.canonical.com), use a distributed approach, where there is no single centralized repository. Instead, changes are distributed in a *peer-to-peer* fashion.

Regardless of how the VCS is designed, they all provide more or less the same functionality. They are all well integrated with modern development environments, such as Eclipse. Typically, each developer has a complete working copy of the code repository inside his/her own IDE. All code synchronization activities are supported by that IDE, so that any developer can autonomously synchronize, write code, test code, and commit changes to the code repository directly from within a unified setting.

3.2.3.1 VCS Conflict Management

While a VCS helps manage the code base, it does not automatically resolve all possible *conflicts* that can arise during a collaborative project. To illustrate, suppose two developers decide simultaneously and independently to work on module A in a software project, whose code base has, say, five modules A, B, C, D, and E. The code base sits on a separate server, called a *code repository*, from which each developer has downloaded a working copy to their own local machine (see Figure 3.4).

Since both developers initially have a copy of module A, they begin working on it. After completing their work, these two developers typically produce two different variations, say A' and A", of the original module A. Neither variation incorporates the changes contained in the other, so no matter which variation finally replaces A in the code repository the other will be lost. This problem is illustrated in Figure 3.4.

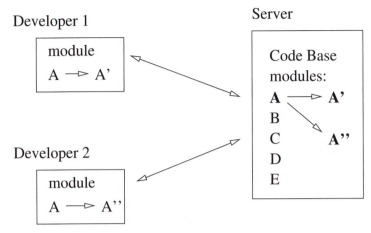

FIGURE 3.4: The code synchronization problem.

The use of a VCS can avoid this problem. Here's how it works. Suppose Developers 1 and 2 both want to modify module A in the repository. Each of them starts working with a local copy of A that is identical with module A in the repository. Suppose further that Developer 1 completes his/her modifications first and *commits* the changed module A' to replace A in the repository.

Now when Developer 2 completes his/her modifications to A" and attempts to save them in the repository, the repository will reply that his/her modifications are based on an *out of date* version of module A. That is, a new version A' has replaced A in the repository since Developer 2 began working on A to obtain A".

However, there is good news: Developer 2 may ask the repository to *merge* and display all the differences between A' and A", as shown in Figure 3.5. Such a merge will reveal either (or both) of two situations:

1. The changes in A' are separate and distinct from those that Developer 2 has made to module A.

2. The changes in A' *conflict* or overlap with those that Developer 2 has made to module A.

Resolving situation 1 is simple. Developer 2 simply asks the synchronization repository to update his/her version A" of A with the changes in A', and then commits the resulting version A'" back into the repository.

Resolving situation 2 is not as simple. In this case, Developer 2 must examine each part of A' that conflicts with a change that he/she has made to module A, and then manually combine these parts together so that the intended functionalities from both developers are properly implemented in

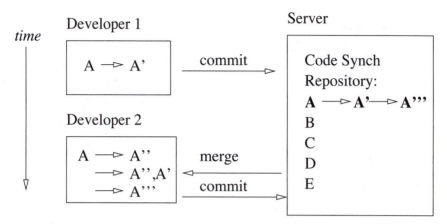

FIGURE 3.5:   Resolving the problem: Copy-modify-merge.

the new version A"'. Sometimes a conversation between the two developers is needed to resolve this kind of conflict.

In some cases, it may be strategic for one developer to obtain a temporary and exclusive *lock* on a module. Until the lock is released, no other developer can make changes to that module. This strategy is useful in cases where situation 2 would create so many conflicts that their resolution would be better handled by a single developer working alone on all the modifications of module A rather than distributing the modifications among several developers working simultaneously.

In any case, it should be clear from this example that the use of a code synchronization repository by project developers is not a panacea. Developers must still collaborate effectively to resolve (or prevent) conflicts in the repository whenever they arise.

3.2.3.2   Managing a Code Repository

Collaborative software development is a little like the collaborative encyclopedia building in the Wikipedia project. A software code repository is like a Wikipedia site. The software development team or community is similar to the community of Wikipedians. However, the Wikipedia "code base"—i.e., a Wikipedia page—is completely open for anyone to read or write. This is not the case for most FOSS development projects.

Not everyone in a community-oriented FOSS project has privileges to write new code directly to the code base. Certain members of the team or the community serve as gatekeepers who need to approve code contributions before they are added to the code base.

In a community-oriented FOSS project everybody has *read access* but only a select few have *write access* and even fewer still have *admin access*. In other words, the repository is not as "democratic" as a Wikipedia site where everyone has both read and write access.

Adding source code to a shared repository is the responsibility of a relatively small group of *core developers*. Because these developers have gained the most experience and trust within the community, they enjoy *commit privileges* on the repository. For smaller client-oriented projects, commit privileges may reside in a single person, such as the *lead developer*, or be shared among all developers.

Other members of the development team contribute code by submitting *patches*, which are pieces of code designed to fix specific problems with or add minor features to the code base. Before they are committed to the code base, patches must be reviewed and tested by other developers for correctness. Particularly well-organized projects may have *quality assurance* teams that specialize in testing patches before they are accepted into the code base. Many IDEs, such as Eclipse, include fucntionality to support the creation and processing of patches.

A community-based FOSS project may provide documentation that describes the development process and practices that apply to that particular community. In *Sahana*, for example, commit status comes by being nominated by a member of the Project Management Committee. Such a nomination is based on the number and quality of contributions in the form of bug fixes and patches to the code base, as well as a candidate's adherence to the coding standards set by *Sahana* itself. Thus, *Sahana* commit status is granted by consensus. For more discussion of project governance, see Chapter 10.

3.2.4   The Bug Tracker

As the code base becomes complex and its community grows, an open source software project should establish a viable process for identifying and tracking the status of bugs that are reported by users and developers. Bug tracking is an important process, especially in a development culture in which Linus' Law, "given enough eyeballs, all bugs are shallow," is held in such high esteem.

What is *bug tracking*? It is a formalized process established by a software project that governs how bugs are identified and how their resolution is managed by the developers who work with the code base. A particularly interesting bug tracking process is the one established by the Mozilla Foundation, based on its open source bug-management tool called *Bugzilla* (see http://www.bugzilla.org/about).

The "life cycle of a bug" refers to a bug's progress through a series of discrete states. Such a life cycle can be described in the form of a state diagram, as shown in Figure 3.6 for Bugzilla (Source: www.bugzilla.org/docs/2.18/html/ lifecycle.html June 30, 2010). In Bugzilla, a bug has several attributes, which are summarized below [asterisk (*) means optional].

Product and Component Bugs are divided up by Product and Component, with a Product having one or more Components in it.

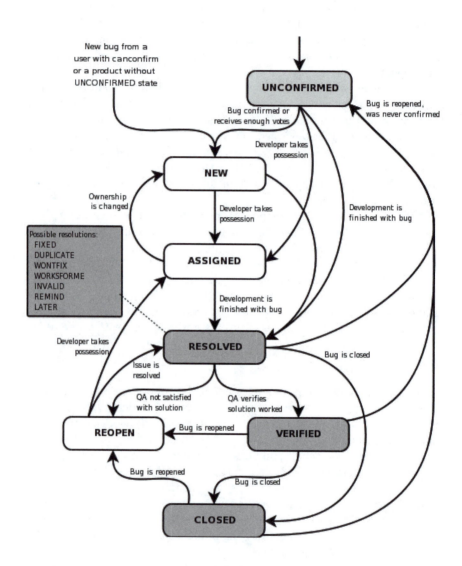

FIGURE 3.6: Life cycle of a bug, as defined in Bugzilla
(source: http://www.bugzilla.org/docs/2.18/html/lifecycle.html).

Status and Resolution These define what state the bug is in—from unconfirmed to fixed.

Assigned To The person responsible for fixing the bug.

*URL A URL associated with the bug.

Summary A one-sentence summary of the problem.

*Whiteboard A free-form text area for adding short notes to a bug.

*Keywords The administrator can define keywords used to tag and categorize a bug.

Platform and OS The computing environment where the bug was found.

Version Version of a product that the particular bug report is about.

Priority The person assigning the bug sets its priority.

Severity Severity of the problem—from blocker ("application unusable") to trivial ("minor cosmetic issue"). Also may be used to indicate whether a bug is an enhancement request.

*Target (a.k.a. Target Milestone) A future version by which the bug is to be fixed.

Reporter The person who filed the bug.

CC list A list of people who get mail when any of these attributes change.

*Time Tracking This form can be used for time tracking.

Attachments You can attach files (e.g., test cases or patches) to bugs. If there are any attachments, they are listed in this section.

*Dependencies If this bug cannot be fixed unless other bugs are fixed (depends on), or this bug stops other bugs being fixed (blocks), their numbers are recorded here.

*Votes Whether this bug has any votes.

Additional Comments You can add your two cents to the bug discussion here, if you have something worthwhile to say.

As Figure 3.6 shows, a bug can be in any of seven states: "unconfirmed," "new," "assigned," "resolved," "reopened," "verified," and "closed." A bug can be introduced by any user. The management of a bug is done by developers with commit privileges, and the whole process can be quite complex.

For example, the Eclipse community uses Bugzilla. Below is a summary of how the process works for a software project/component in that community (paraphrased from http://wiki.eclipse.org, June 30, 2010).

- Users "own" the following attributes: component, version, platform, OS, severity, summary, and description.

- Committers "own" the following attributes: status, resolution, and priority.

- Users may not change the Committer owned fields—this is enforced by social convention.

- Developers are expected to watch the component owner's e-mail address to monitor the incoming bugs for their projects/components.

1. At the start of each day, each project/component team leader does bug triage. He or she assesses each NEW bug by validating and prioritizing it:

   - Validation—ensure that the bug really exists and that it really belongs to the current project/component.

     (a) If the bug needs more information to be validated as a bug, add a request for more information/steps to reproduce, etc. The bug remains in the NEW state until enough information is received to validate it.

     (b) If there is no response within a week, close the bug (RESOLVED, INVALID, or WONTFIX) telling the submitter to re-open once they have more info.

     (c) The bug may get moved to another component/product.

     (d) The bug may be a user problem or an intended behavior—these are annotated with the reason and then are RESOLVED to INVALID, WONTFIX, or WORKSFORME (generally, INVALID means the report is just bogus, WORKSFORME means the report is not a problem, and WONTFIX is used for things that are valid requests, but that the team can't do).

     (e) Once a bug is validated, it goes to prioritization.

   - Prioritization—assign a priority to the bug. If it is a feature request, change its severity to "enhancement."

     (a) If the bug should be fixed in the current release, the status gets changed to ASSIGNED and a target milestone is set appropriately.

     (b) If the fix is critical, the target will be the next release milestone. Otherwise, it will go into the current release milestone, meaning it should be addressed in the current release.

     (c) If the bug/feature will not be fixed in the current release, the status is set to RESOLVED LATER.

     (d) Set the priority with these guidelines:

P1 stop development fix: needs immediate attention before other work continues

P2 must fix before the next release, but can make progress without fix

P3 should fix before the next release

P4 would be nice, but not critical, can issue the next release without fixing

The severity tags aren't used much, except to distinguish enhancements from bugs. Typically, users specify severities as they see fit. The bug will remain ASSIGNED to the "inbox" account until a developer takes the bug, or the team leader assigns it to someone.

The developers then work on the bug.

- When a developer fixes the bug, the status is set to RESOLVED - FIXED, and it is assigned to another committer on the team to verify. It is important that the verifier be a different person from the fixer because the fixer is too close to the code and thus may not be as diligent at testing the corner cases.

- When a developer commits code, she includes the bug#(s) in the commit message.

- It is possible for a bug to be RESOLVED to LATER or WONTFIX or INVALID as well if the developer discovers that the fix is too complex/risky or that it is not really a bug.

2. Verify: When a committer verifies a fix, the status is changed to VERIFIED. All bugs should be verified before the next integration build.

3. When the project does a major release, the VERIFIED bugs are changed to CLOSED.

This example shows that the process of bug management is not trivial. The process works only if the project has both an active user community for detecting and reporting bugs, and an active developer/committer community for fixing, resolving, and verifying the fixes.

For projects with large user and developer communities, this summary provides a lot of insight into how to implement Linus' Law in a practical setting. It also shows that the process of fixing a bug and verifying that fix relies strongly on both the openness of the code base and the atmosphere of trust that exists among users and developers.

3.3   Run-Time System Constraints

The development of an effective software application is always constrained by the limitations of the existing code base, hardware, networks, budgets, and other resources that are available in settings where the software will eventually be used.

These constraints are dictated by the user community and code base and are often inflexible. For instance, if a client-oriented project is developing software for a non-profit organization whose daily operations use a local network of Windows-XP machines, those machines will likely be the platform on which the new software must reside. The following sections briefly discuss the major constraints faced by a software development project.

3.3.1   Performance

When reading the code base for an existing system and planning the development of an enhancement, several general performance requirements need to be kept in mind.

For example, a Web-based application should meet the following general performance goals:

User interface should be consistent and compatible with modern Web-based applications. It should be easy to learn by persons with a variety of backgrounds and minimum technical training. Entry, exit, and navigation among the various forms in the user interface should be straightforward and intuitive.

On-line help pages should be available and well aligned with each of the functional elements of the system.

Availability and reliability The system should be available 24/7 and accessible from any Web browser connected to the Internet. The system should run correctly; all user actions should be reversible and repeatable.

Backup and recovery should be executable by the system administrator. If the system fails or the database is lost, the system administrator should be able to recover all data and functionality from a recent backup.

Error correction The system should be designed and documented so as to facilitate quick correction of minor defects as well as major future enhancements.

In particular, developers of new features for existing systems should be on the lookout for weaknesses in any of these areas.

3.3.2 Web Hosting

It is fair to assume that users of the software will have Internet and e-mail access, and maybe even their own Web sites. These assumptions can help inform the development of a baseline architecture for a new client-oriented application. If the application itself must be Web accessible, the particular hosting configuration currently being used by the client may pose additional system constraints that affect the new software design.

For instance, if the client's current Web host does not provide PHP and MySQL support, then either the host must be changed or the new software must be developed without PHP or MySQL.

The good news is that most Web hosting providers support most of the popular programming tools used in Web based applications. Moreover, moving from one Web host to another is not difficult if the situation requires such a move.

3.3.3 Licensing

The system and its source code should be freely available and adaptable by any other organization that has a similar need. But what particular FOSS license (as discussed in Chapter 1) is appropriate for the software, and why?

To implement and disseminate these goals to future users and developers, the particular license chosen (e.g., the GPL) should be identified on all pages of the user interface (usually as a footnote), as well as in the headers of all major classes and modules in the source code.

Figure 3.7 shows how this notice appears in the footer of every page of the user interface for *RMH Homebase*. Typically, the original authors of the software share its copyright and the users of the software acknowledge that their use will comply with the terms of that particular license.

Copyright © 2008 by: Oliver Radwan, Maxwell Palmer, Nolan McNair, Taylor Talmage, and Allen Tucker. RMH Homebase was designed at Bowdoin College for the Ronald McDonald House of Portland, ME.

RMH Homebase v1.4 is free software. It comes with absolutely no warranty. You can redistribute it and/or modify it under the terms of the GNU General Public License as published by the Free Software Foundation.

FIGURE 3.7: Showing the open source license notice in the user interface.

Figure 3.8 shows how this notice appears at the top of a class or module in the *RMH Homebase* code base. This notice is written for developers who are debugging the code or modifying it for future uses. The GPL basically requires developers to retain this notice in all future versions and distributions of the modified code.

Recall from Chapter 1 that licensing software as FOSS affirms that the software is *free* as in *free to use, modify, and distribute*. This freedom provides a strong incentive for other developers to examine the code base and freely

```
/*
 * Copyright 2008 by Orville, Malcom, Ted, Nat, and Alex.
 * This program is part of {\it RMH Homebase}, which is free
 * software.  It comes with absolutely no warranty.
 * You can redistribute it and/or modify it under the terms
 * of the GNU General Public License as published by
 * the Free Software Foundation (see gnu.org/licenses/).
 */
```

FIGURE 3.8: Displaying the open source license notice in the source code.

adapt and reuse its best elements in other FOSS applications.

3.3.4   Platform

In general, open source software should be developed to run on as wide a variety of platforms as possible. For example, Web based applications should run on all types of computers that access the Web—Windows, Mac, or Linux systems at the least, and increasingly intelligent cell phones and tablet devices as well.

Moreover, interoperability suggests that the software and database be hosted on a Linux system and that users may access it from any Windows, Mac, or hand-held device via its Web browser.

A corollary to this is that the development process itself should strive to use open source tools as much as possible. This includes the IDE, VCS, programming language, database system, and Web server technologies that are both freely available and supportive of the interoperability suggested above.

For example, the Eclipse, SVN, and LAMP tools discussed earlier combine all these capabilities in a unified easily installable environment for a software development team. For Android developers, similar capabilities are provided by the Android Development Tools (ADT) Eclipse plugin. For more information, see http://developer.android.com/guide/developing/eclipse-adt.html.

3.4   Summary

This chapter has introduced the key collaboration and development tools and strategies in use by FOSS project participants. Some of the tools are more heavily used by community-oriented projects, while others are heavily used by both client-oriented and community-oriented projects.

Participants in a dynamic FOSS project know how to manage both collaboration and code sharing. They have learned how to use tools that facilitate both these types of activities. Projects whose participants communicate well and often, and also synchronize their work effectively, are likely to attract the most clients and new developers in the future.

In these early chapters, readers have studied FOSS principles and briefly explored the work of others who are engaged in FOSS projects. The next few chapters will shift gears and encourage readers to directly participate in an ongoing project from the inside. That is where the "rubber meets the road," so to speak, and where readers can learn a lot by making actual contributions to FOSS projects.

Exercises

3.1 Participate in the second team meeting for your client-oriented project.

    a. Discuss your completion of the tasks that were assigned to you in the first team meeting.

    b. Discuss the assignment of new tasks and suggest changes as appropriate.

3.2 Perform a preliminary evaluation of the community-oriented project that you will be working on throughout the remainder of this study. That is, write a brief review by answering the following questions:

    a. Does the project's Web site provide a clear and concise mission statement? Does it describe the main features of the software? Is the project's FOSS license identified?

    b. Does the project have a user guide? A developer guide? How well are they written?

    c. Is there a developer's guide and how informative is it?

    d. Is the source code appropriately documented according to standards such as PhpDoc or JavaDoc?

    e. Does each file in the code base contain an initial comment block with appropriate information, including the software's license?

    f. How easy will it be for you (a newcomer) to contribute to this project?

3.3 Set up an appropriate software stack on your computer for the project that you will be working with throughout this study. This stack may be a LAMP stack if your project runs on a Linux-Apache-MySQL-PHP platform, or another stack depending on your project's platform needs.

3.4 Set up your computer with an IDE (Eclipse or other), including repository access (CVS, SVN, or other) and unit testing support.

    a.   Synchronize your IDE with your project's repository and download a copy of the code base for your use.

    b.   Connect your IDE with the software stack that you set up in the previous exercise, so that you can run the project directly from your IDE.

    c.   Run the project and be sure that its functionality agrees with its documentation. For example, run all the unit tests and ensure that they all succeed.

3.5 Visit http://sourceforge.net and find a project that has an active bug-tracking forum. For that project, briefly describe one bug that falls into each of the following categories, and answer the questions below as well:

New How long has it been active?

Assigned For how long has it been assigned?

Resolved How long did it take to resolve?

Closed Why was the bug closed?

Chapter 4

Software Architecture

> "Good judgment comes from experience, and experience comes from bad judgment."
> —*Fred Brooks*

A software architecture is an organizational model for a moderate or large software system. Such a model divides the software into graphical user interface (GUI) forms, classes, modules, and database tables. A software architecture provides strong guidance on how modules interact with each other, how a test suite can be designed, how refactoring strategies can be exercised, and how program bugs can be detected and removed.

This chapter focuses on four central ideas related to software architecture. First, we introduce the concepts of architectural patterns and how they help developers organize software systems. Second, we introduce the ideas of layers, cohesion, and coupling and how they help designers organize individual classes and modules. Third, we introduce the idea of software security and discuss its relationship with software architecture. Fourth, we discuss the concepts of concurrency and synchronization, and their relationships with software architecture.

4.1 Architectural Patterns

The architecture of a software system provides a template within which all subsequent development activities can be organized. Understanding the general concepts and utility of a software architecture, therefore, is crucial to successful software development.

A small number of common organizational schemes tend to guide the development of many software systems. An organizational scheme that is repeated over and over for different applications can be abstracted in the form of a "pattern." The following patterns are frequently used in software architectures:

The Multi-Tier pattern distinguishes the user interface layer from the core (domain) class layer from the database layer. In this pattern, GUI components are isolated within the user interface layer and database interactions are isolated within the database layer. The domain class layer serves as the "glue" that facilitates interaction between these layers, in addition to providing a basic vocabulary, or "namespace," for referencing concepts that are unique to the application.

The Client-Server pattern separates the functionality of a typical user of the system from that of the server that hosts the database that all users access. Developers often refer to "client-side" code as that which resides on the user's computer, including the GUI components. "Server-side" code is that which resides on the server's computer, including the database components.

The Transaction Processing pattern is useful for systems that accept a stream of transactions and process each transaction fully before moving on to the next. The software that drives an ATM, for instance, is organized around this pattern, since each customer's transaction must be completed before the next one can begin.

The Model-View-Controller (MVC) pattern is useful for systems that have substantially complex user interfaces. The idea of MVC is to separate the functionality (the model) that underlies the user interface from the code that controls how the user sees (the view) and interacts with (the controller) the system. This pattern will be explored in more detail in Chapter 8.

Let's look at the Client-Server pattern in more detail. This pattern is pictured in Figure 4.1. The Client-Server pattern is an especially common and versatile framework for developing Web based applications. Its basic organization allows several different clients to communicate with a shared database over the Web. *RMH Homebase* uses the Client-Server pattern.

Software organized around the Client-Server pattern naturally supports synchronization, which allows two or more clients to access a shared database at the same time without interfering with each other. For example, *RMH Homebase* has three levels of clients—managers, volunteers, and applicants. Its database has two kinds of data—personnel data and calendar schedules. Synchronization is enforced whenever two or more clients try to update the same calendar schedule entry at the same time.

The Client-Server pattern also supports database security by providing a different level of database access to each level of client. For example, *RMH Homebase* security allows a manager complete read/write access to all volunteers' personal data and the calendar schedules. However, a volunteer has read/write access to only his/her own personal data entry but nobody else's, and an applicant has read/write access to neither.

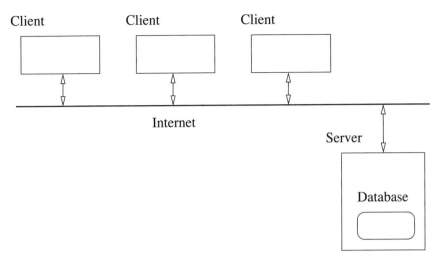

FIGURE 4.1: The client-server pattern.

In general, the use of any particular design pattern in a new software project is constrained by the the architecture of the current system upon which that project is based. If the current system is Web based, its architecture may well utilize a Multi-Tier pattern, the Client-Server pattern, and/or the MVC pattern. The *RMH Homebase* system architecture utilizes a Multi-Tier pattern, the Client-Server pattern, and to a lesser extent the MVC pattern. We shall illustrate the use of these patterns later in this chapter and in Chapter 8.

4.2 Layers, Cohesion, and Coupling

When we first consider the overall architecture of a software system, it is useful to model its functionality as a group of smaller, more manageable components. Such a "divide and conquer" approach allows us to manage the system as a coherent arrangement of individual components rather than one large clump of code. Organizing the components into a conceptually logical and manageable arrangement is thus a basic challenge of software architecture.

Three important principles guide the development of a software architecture: the *layering principle*, the *maximum cohesion principle*, and the *minimum coupling principle*.

An architecture that follows the *layering principle* allows developers to visualize the system as a small number of interconnected vertical layers. Under the layering principle, each component appears in a single layer; the user sits at the top layer and the database is at the bottom layer.

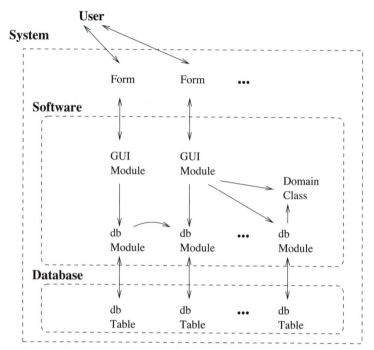

FIGURE 4.2:   Layers in a multi-tier architecture.
($\leftrightarrow$ denotes information flow and $\rightarrow$ denotes control flow.)

> **The Layering Principle**: Every module belongs in a single layer.
> No module should skip over its neighbors in the layer immediately
> above or below it, in order to provide or obtain services from
> another layer.

Figure 4.2 shows a typical Multi-Tier software architecture that has six
distinct layers—the user, the user's GUI forms, the GUI modules, the domain
classes, the database modules, and the database tables. The double-headed
arrows in Figure 4.2 denote two-way information flow, while the single-headed
arrows denote one-way control flow (i.e., $a \rightarrow b$ denotes that a calls functions
in b) for a typical user-system session.

The positioning of the arrows suggests that each layer should call only those
functions in layers that are directly above and below it. The user, for example,
interacts only with the forms, while information flows back and forth between
the forms and their corresponding GUI modules. Generally, a single GUI
module corresponds to a form that appears in the user interface. Thus, the
forms allow information to flow back and forth between the user and their
corresponding GUI modules.

In turn, each GUI module receives services from database modules and/or
domain classes. And each of the database modules has a single associated

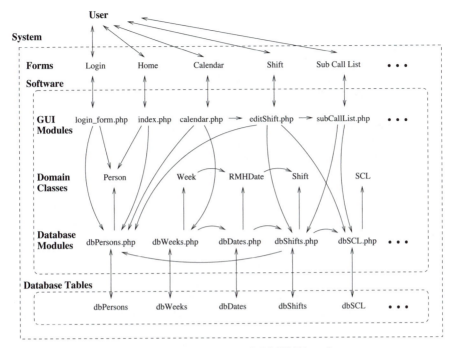

FIGURE 4.3: Multi-tier architecture of *RMH Homebase*.

database table, with which it exchanges information back and forth as called upon from various GUI modules.[1]

Under the layering principle, no GUI module should need to directly access a database table to obtain information. If that need exists, it usually means that the corresponding database module does not provide sufficient functionality to serve the GUI module's need directly. Thus, the proper way to satisfy this need would be to add a function to that database module, so that the GUI module can obtain the required information by calling that function.

RMH Homebase generally exemplifies the layering principle. Its GUI modules support all the interactive forms that the user sees—user interactions are not directly supported by any database module or domain class. Figure 4.3 shows many of the key modules and classes in *RMH Homebase*, and how they fit together to form the user interface, domain class, and database layers.

However, *RMH Homebase* occasionally violates the layering principle. For example, not shown in Figure 4.3 is a connection between the GUI layer and the database when the editShift.php module directly accesses a database table. Figure 4.4 shows some of the offending code that appears in the get_available_volunteer_options function in the editShift.php module.

---

[1]In general, a database module may interact with more than one database table, for example when it needs to implement a familiar "join" operation.

```
connect();
if ($fam=="Fam")
    $query="SELECT * FROM dbPersons WHERE" .
           "(type LIKE '%family_room%') AND " .
           "availability LIKE '%".$day.$time."%' " .
           "ORDER BY last_name,first_name";
else
    $query="SELECT * FROM dbPersons WHERE" .
           "(NOT (type LIKE '%family_room%')) AND " .
           "availability LIKE '%".$day.$time."%' " .
           "ORDER BY last_name,first_name";
$result=mysql_query($query);
mysql_close();
```

FIGURE 4.4:   User interface code that violates the layering principle.

This GUI code is interacting directly with the dbPersons database table since it issues a MySQL query rather than calling a function in the dbPersons.php module. While this code works correctly, a better design would be to refactor it in the following way:

- Add a function to the dbPersons.php module that performs this type of query, and

- Replace the code in the editShift.php module (shown in Figure 4.4) by a call to that new function.

The details of this refactoring activity are presented in Section 5.2.2.

The layering principle leads to two other related principles of software architecture, the *maximum cohesion principle* and the *minimum coupling principle*. The former is a property of each individual module in the code base, while the latter is a property of the interconnectedness among all the modules in the code base.

> **The Maximum Cohesion Principle**: All the functions that relate to a single concept are gathered into a single module or class. A software architecture is maximally cohesive if all its modules and classes are cohesive in this way.

For example, *RMH Homebase* has at least two distinct concepts—persons and calendar shifts. When designing or exploring this system, we should find two distinct classes—one that characterizes all the functions relating to a person and another that characterizes all the functions relating to a calendar shift. A maximally cohesive architecture would not allow any function that manipulates a person's data to creep into the Shift class, or vice versa. Moreover, the Shift class should encapsulate all the functionality required by other modules to manipulate any Shift object.

The Minimum Coupling Principle: Two modules are *coupled* if either one shares information or receives services directly from the other. A software system is *minimally coupled* when the number of interactions between all pairs of modules is kept to a minimum.

Minimal coupling means that no two modules are functionally connected unless they are in adjacent layers or the same layer. Moreover, any such pair of modules should be coupled only to the extent required by the use cases in the design document. Addition of superfluous couplings between pairs of modules in a code base should be avoided.

For example, the only interactions between a person and a calendar shift in *RMH Homebase* should be either to schedule a person for a shift or to remove a person from a shift. No other interactions between these two modules should be needed. If the code supports this, the dbPersons and dbShifts modules are said to be minimally coupled.

The advantages of following the layering, cohesion, and coupling principles in a software design are many. Here are a few:

- Improved system readability—ideas related to a single concept are found together in the same place; loosely-related or unrelated ideas are easily ignored when reading a single module.

- Improved system extendability—adding new features to an existing system is enhanced when the existing concepts and their interrelationships are clearly modeled by the architecture.

- Support for debugging—bugs tend to appear in modules where they ought to appear; the occurrence of undesirable side effects from modifying or enhancing a piece of code can thus be better controlled.

- Support for code reuse—maximally cohesive and minimally-coupled modules tend to be easier to extract and reuse in a different software system that includes similar concepts.

- Support for refactoring—a group of modules that doesn't follow these principles is always a good candidate for refactoring.

4.2.1 Using Metrics to Evaluate Cohesion and Coupling

Two specific software metrics are designed to estimate the level of cohesion and coupling among the modules in a code base. These are called:

- Lack of cohesion of methods (LCOM), and

- Efferent coupling.

These metrics can be especially useful when the code base is especially large, complex, and/or unfamiliar to the reader. Here's what they mean:

Lack of Cohesion of Methods (LCOM) measures the cohesiveness of a class or module, and is computed as follows:

$$LCOM = 1 - \sum_a m(a)/\mid m \parallel a \mid$$

where m is a method (function or constructor), a is an instance variable in the class or module and $m(a)$ is the number of methods referencing a. The calculation of $LCOM$ always gives a value between 0 and 1.

A low value for $LCOM$ indicates a cohesive class. A value close to 1 suggests lack of cohesion, in which case the class might best be split into two or more distinct classes.

For example, look at the module Shift.php in the *RMH Homebase* code base. It has $\mid a \mid= 8$ instance variables and $\mid m \mid= 24$ functions and constructors. For each of these variables, here is a breakdown of the number of methods referencing it:

a	$m(a)$
$mm_dd_yy	1
$name	2
$vacancies	6
$persons	7
$sub_call_list	6
$day	2
$id	2
$notes	4

So $m(a) = 30$, which gives a value of $LCOM = 1 - 30/192 \approx 0.85$. This relatively high value indicates that the Shift.php module isn't particularly cohesive, and thus may be a candidate for refactoring.

Efferent Coupling of a class or module (Ce) is the number of other classes or modules that call on its services.[2]

A class or module with $Ce > 50$ depends on too many other classes or modules, in the sense that it is too complex and has too many responsibilities. Such a class is a good candidate for refactoring.

For example, look at the dbPersons module in the *RMH Homebase* code base. From Figure 4.3, we can see from its incoming arrows that it has five other modules that call on its services; thus, its efferent coupling is 5. All other modules shown in Figure 4.3 have smaller efferent coupling, which suggests that the system is loosely coupled—a good feature.

Both these calculations can be done automatically if the IDE provides metrics services via a plugin. In the case of PHP, no such metrics are

---

[2]**Afferent Coupling** of a class or module (Ca) measures the number of other classes that call directly on its services. So Ca and Ce are somewhat redundant with each other.

available at this writing. In the case of Java, however, metrics plugins are widely available (see, for instance, metrics.sourceforge.net).

These metrics can be especially useful when used in conjunction with code reading, debugging, refactoring, or adding new features to a large software system. However, for a small- or medium-sized code base, they are not a particularly good substitute for careful code reading, using the techniques to be introduced in Chapter 6.

4.3   Security

Software is often easy for attackers to target because it is almost guaranteed to have vulnerabilities. Most successful attacks result from targeting and exploiting known vulnerabilities introduced while the software is developed. In a report titled "Cyber Security: A Crisis of Prioritization" [Com05], the President's Information Technology Advisory Committee summed up the problem of non-secure software as follows:

> Software development is not yet a science or a rigorous discipline, and the development process by and large is not controlled to minimize the vulnerabilities that attackers exploit. Today, as with cancer, vulnerable software can be invaded and modified to cause damage ... and infected software can replicate itself and be carried across networks to cause damage in other systems. As in cancer, both preventive actions and research are critical, the former to minimize damage today and the latter to establish a foundation of knowledge and capabilities that will ... reduce risk and minimize damage for the long term.

The security of a software product can be threatened at different times during its development and usable life. Such threats can be either inadvertent or intentional, and they can originate either from outsiders or from "insiders" who have knowledge of the project—developers, clients, or end-users.

Software security is thus a very important concept for developers to understand and take into account throughout the development process. Some software projects, like designing an Internet game, may have no security requirements, since their use is recreational and does not involve access to sensitive or confidential information.

The first step in ensuring security is to understand the client's requirement that the new software protect confidential and other sensitive information from unauthorized access. A software security policy must be defined for the new system that implements that requirement, and the software must incorporate that policy in a transparent and verifiable way.

Failure to incorporate the client's security requirements into the development process will threaten the project's overall success. In the case of *RMH Homebase*, for example, the software must prevent Applicants from accessing the personal data of any Volunteer or the House Manager. In addition, the software must also prevent a Volunteer from accessing the personal data of any Person other than themselves.

4.3.1   Architectural Vulnerabilities

Recall the quote from the previous section that talked about software's vulnerabilities that attackers tend to exploit. From a software architecture point of view, we need to ask:

> "What are these vulnerabilities, and how can we develop software that minimizes them?"

The following brief discussion is adapted from the Wikipedia article http://en.wikipedia.org/wiki/Vulnerability_ "computer_science".

> Vulnerabilities may result from weak passwords, software bugs, a computer virus or other malware, a script code injection, a SQL injection or misconfiguration. Three examples: an attacker finds and uses an overflow weakness to install malware to export sensitive data; an attacker convinces a user to open an e-mail message with attached malware; an insider copies a hardened, encrypted program onto a thumb drive and cracks it at home.

> Common types of software flaws that lead to vulnerabilities include:

> - Memory safety violations, such as buffer overflows and dangling pointers
> - Input validation errors, such as format string bugs, SQL injection, code injection, e-mail injection, directory traversal, cross-site scripting in Web applications, HTTP header injection, and HTTP response splitting
> - Race conditions, such as time-of-check-to-time-of-use bugs and symlink races
> - Privilege-confusion bugs, such as cross-site request forgery in Web applications, clickjacking, and FTP bounce attack
> - Privilege escalation
> - User interface failures, such as user conditioning, blaming the victim, and race conditions.

While some of these flaws are obvious (e.g., we have seen buffer overflows in other programming situations), others are pretty vague.

What is *SQL injection*? This is a code injection technique that exploits a security vulnerability to corrupt or destroy information stored in the database layer of a software architecture. The vulnerability is present when user input is inadequately filtered for string literal escape characters embedded inside database queries.

What is *cross-site scripting*? This technique injects unwanted external information into Web pages viewed by other users. Any information that is not already in the code or the database must come from an external source. Cross-site scripting also occurs when user input is inadequately filtered.

Thus, both these vulnerabilities are exploited at the user interface layer of a software architecture. We illustrate each of them in Chapter 8, where we also discuss steps that can be taken to help eliminate them. Readers are encouraged to read more of the abundant literature on software security and its relationship with software development. For example, see [McG06].

4.3.2 User-Level Security

When reviewing the security aspects of a software system, we need to ensure that the system enforces the following constraints on users:

1. Each authenticated user has a unique login id and password, and access to all system functions is provided only after the person enters his/her id and password.

2. Each authenticated user has access to only those system functions that are appropriate for their level of access, and no others.

3. Each visitor to the system has access only to those system functions that are appropriate for the general public to access.

Therefore, the starting point for ensuring user-level security in a software system is to implement a secure login strategy and a database of id's and passwords for all authenticated users.

Secure login is often called "authentication," and there a few different ways to implement it. Minimally, each authenticated user has a unique id and password, and provisions are built into the system for adding a new user to the system, assigning a unique id and password, and allowing them to change their password after logging in.

In *RMH Homebase*, authentication begins when the user encounters the form shown in Figure 4.5. As noted above, the user's id is the concatenation of their first name and their 10-digit phone number, and this value is their default password also.

The code that underlies this login form checks that the Username and Password entered match with that of a Person in the database dbPersons. It is

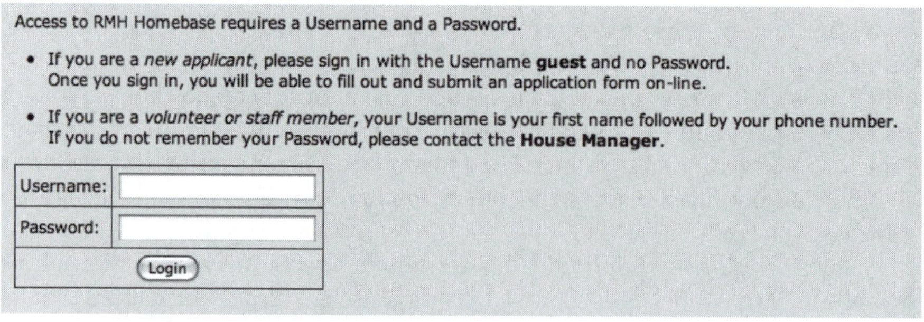

Access to RMH Homebase requires a Username and a Password.

- If you are a *new applicant*, please sign in with the Username **guest** and no Password. Once you sign in, you will be able to fill out and submit an application form on-line.

- If you are a *volunteer or staff member*, your Username is your first name followed by your phone number. If you do not remember your Password, please contact the **House Manager**.

Username: [   ]

Password: [   ]

(Login)

FIGURE 4.5:   A secure login form.

part of the PHP module `login_form.php`, which is summarized in Figure 4.6 (for a full description, see the file `login_form.php` in the code base).

This code establishes a valid login by checking whether the user is a "guest," in which case their password is "", or an authentic volunteer or manager in the `dbPersons` database table. The query `get_person($db_id)` retrieves that person and, if there, checks the person's type to see whether or not they are a manager.

If the password entered matches the password in the database for this person, then the `SESSION` variable `$session_id` is established as the id of the person logging in. If not, the module denies access and tries to provide help for the user to enter a correct Username and Password.

The `SESSION` variable `access_level` is set to 0, 1, or 2, accordingly as the person's type is "guest", "volunteer," or "manager," respectively.[3]

The second consideration related to software security is to ask, "Are there some functions that the software should make available to some types of authenticated users but not to others?" If the answer is "Yes" then the design should provide a longer menu of options to some users than it provides to others.

In the case of *RMH Homebase*, there are three types of authenticated users, an Applicant (called "guest"), a Volunteer, and a (House) Manager. The Manager has access to virtually all functions and data in the system, while a Volunteer has access only to the calendar and his/her own database entry. An Applicant has access only to the application form, which allows an anonymous on-line application to be submitted and sent directly to the House Manager.

To enforce these levels of access, a person logging in as an Applicant, Volunteer, or Manager has `SESSION['access_level']` set to 0, 1, or 2, respectively.

---

[3]The PHP `SESSION` variables stay active throughout the time that a person is logged in, and they remain globally accessible to the code base until the person logs out. Each separate person who logs in to *RMH Homebase* has their own set of `SESSION` variables. More discussion and illustration of sessions appears in Chapter 8.

```
// check if they logged in as a guest:
if ($_POST['user']==''guest" && $_POST['pass']==""){
    $_SESSION['logged_in']=1;
    $_SESSION['access_level']=0;
    $_SESSION['_id']="guest";
    ...
else {
    $db_pass = md5($_POST['pass']);
    $db_id = $_POST['user'];
    $password_query_result = get_person($db_id);
    if($password_query_result)  { // this id is in the database
        $person = mysql_fetch_array(
            $password_query_result, MYSQL_ASSOC);
        if($person['password']==$db_pass){ // passwords match
            $_SESSION['logged_in']=1;
            $type_array = explode(",",$person['type']);
            if (in_array('applicant', $type_array))
                $_SESSION['access_level'] = 0;
            else if (in_array('manager', $type_array))
                $_SESSION['access_level'] = 2;
            else $_SESSION['access_level'] = 1;
            $_SESSION['f_name']=$person['first_name'];
            $_SESSION['l_name']=$person['last_name'];
            $_SESSION['_id']=$_POST['user'];
            ...
        }
        else {
            //  invalid user id or password, provide some help
            ...
        }
        ...
    }
}
```

FIGURE 4.6: Excerpt from the underlying login code.

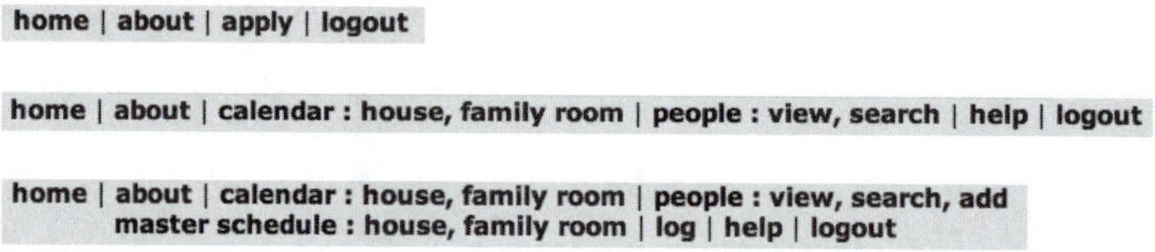

home | about | apply | logout

home | about | calendar : house, family room | people : view, search | help | logout

home | about | calendar : house, family room | people : view, search, add
master schedule : house, family room | log | help | logout

FIGURE 4.7:   *RMH Homebase* Applicant, Volunteer, and Manager menus.

After logging in, this person sees a menu of only those system functions that they are authorized to access. These three menus are shown in Figure 4.7.

The code that generates these three kinds of menus is encapsulated in the `header.php` module, which is summarized in Figure 4.8. Since the `header.php` module is called by every other user interface module, it limits access to system functions depending on the setting of `SESSION['access_level']`. Notice also that each link in the menu is associated with a distinct PHP module in the user interface that implements a particular user function. We shall discuss this organization in more detail in Chapter 8.

The third consideration related to software security is to ask the question, "Are there legitimate functions that the software should make available to the general public?" If the answer to this is "Yes," then the design should make those functions easily accessible, while keeping all other functions inaccessible to persons without a secure login.

For example, *RMH Homebase* considers anyone in the general public as potentially someone who might become interested in applying for a volunteer position. So the "guest" login discussed above is open to the general public because it has a blank password and is clearly described on the login form itself (Figure 4.5.

4.4   Concurrency, Race Conditions, and Deadlocks

In the foregoing discussion of security vulnerabilities, the term "race condition" was introduced. It is very important to understand this particular security flaw, since it can occur easily in a multi-user Web based system. To provide a setting for this discussion, we first introduce the idea of a "session."

When a software system has a client-server architecture, it must allow several users to concurrently and independently use the system. Each user sees all the features of the system that any other user can see, within the limits allowed by system security (recall Section 4.3.2).

Concurrency is enabled in a Web based software architecture by establishing a so-called *session*. As illustrated in Figure 4.6, each separate user who is logged into the system has a unique session, distinguished by a set of "session

```
//they're logged in and session variables are set.
if($_SESSION['access_level']>=0){
  echo('<a href="'.$path.'index.php">home</a> | ');
  echo('<a href="'.$path.'about.php">about</a>');
 }
if ($_SESSION['access_level']==0)
  echo(' | <a href="'.$path.'personEdit.php?id='.'new'.'">
    apply</a>');
if ($_SESSION['access_level']>=1){
  echo(' | calendar : <a href="'.$path.'calendar.php">house,
    </a> <a href="'.$path.
    'calendarFam.php">family room</a> | ');
  echo('people : <a href="'.$path.'view.php">view,</a>
    <a href="'.$path.'searchPeople.php">search</a>');
 }
if ($_SESSION['access_level']>=2){
  echo('<a href="personEdit.php?id='.'new'.'">, add</a><br> '.
    'master schedule : <a href="'.$path.
    'masterSchedule.php">house,</a> ' .
    '<a href="'.$path.'masterScheduleFam.php">family room</a> '.
    '| <a href="'.$path.'log.php">log</a>');
 }
if ($_SESSION['access_level']>=1)
  echo(' | <a href="'.$path.'help.php?helpPage='.$current_page.
    '"target="_BLANK">help</a>');
echo( ' | <a href="'.$path.'logout.php">logout</a> <br>');
```

FIGURE 4.8: Code for generating menus.

variables" that persist until the user logs out. In *RMH Homebase*, these variables are:

$_SESSION['access_level'] 0, 1, or 2 denotes "guest," "volunteer," or "manager"
$_SESSION['logged_in'] 1 means that the user is logged in
$_SESSION['f_name'] the user's first name
$_SESSION['l_name'] the user's last name
$_SESSION['_id'] the session id, which is unique for every logged-in user

In PHP, a session is created in the code base by a call to the function session_start(). This call should be executed when the page index.php is encountered by the user. That page typically contains a login form through which the user can gain secure access to the system.

After the user logs in, various system functions are enabled or disabled, depending on that user's access level. This applies not only to the menu bar at the top of each page, as discussed in Section 4.3.2, but also to other functions like the ability to edit the notes on an individual shift. The way this is accomplished is by examining the $_SESSION['access_level'] variable whenever such a function could be made available. An example of this occurs in the editShift module, where only a person at the access level of "manager" can edit the notes on a shift.

Having several users simultaneously logged in to a system also introduces other complexities. That is, when two or more different user sessions try to simultaneously access (read and/or write) the same element of a shared database, the system must guarantee integrity of the database after those accesses are completed. This sort of guarantee is called *synchronization*.

Effective synchronization must address two potential problems: *race conditions* and *deadlocks*. A race condition occurs when the resulting value of a particular database element would be different depending on the order in which the two users' requests are processed. A deadlock occurs when one user's request becomes stuck waiting for an event that will never happen.

Suppose, for the moment, that the database underlying *RMH Homebase* had no synchronization. And suppose that two users are trying to simultaneously access the September 2, 2009 6-9pm shift, where "jeremy jones" is scheduled to work and there are two vacancies. Finally, suppose that User 1 is trying to add "mary jones" to this shift, while User 2 is trying to add "joe jones" to this shift at the same time.

When a race condition occurs, these two transactions will be completed, but the outcome is unpredictable. Table 4.1 shows how any of four different outcomes can occur, depending on the temporal order in which the two transactions begin and end.

A deadlock can occur when User 1 tries to access the dbShifts table at precisely the same time as User 2, causing neither one to gain access to it. If this happens, both users can wait indefinitely with a locked screen, neither

TABLE 4.1:   Possible Race Condition Outcomes for Updating a Shift

Outcome	time = t1	t2	t3	t4
1. jeremy mary joe	1 gets jeremy	1 adds mary	2 gets jeremy, mary	2 adds joe
2. jeremy mary	1 gets jeremy	2 gets jeremy	2 adds joe	1 adds mary
3. jeremy joe	1 gets jeremy	2 gets jeremy	1 adds mary	2 adds joe
4. jeremy joe mary	2 gets jeremy	2 adds joe	1 gets jeremy, joe	1 adds mary

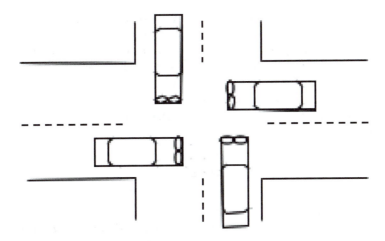

FIGURE 4.9: Deadlock at a traffic intersection.

one knowing what caused this deadlock to occur. This is similar to a traffic deadlock at an intersection, as shown in Figure 4.9.

Both these synchronization problems can be avoided by using a technique called *locking*. This means that any session accessing a resource (table or row) in a database gains exclusive control of (a "lock" on) that resource throughout the time required to complete that access (read, write, or update). If a second session tries to access the same resource while the first session has a lock on it, the second session's request is put into a queue until the lock is released. All requests for access to the same resource are handled in a first-come-first-served order.

Locking thus prevents race conditions like the one described in Table 4.1 from occurring. That is, locking prevents either of outcomes 2 or 3 in that table from occurring, since the two users' requests cannot be interleaved. If User 1's request arrives first, then outcome 1 occurs; while if User 2's request arrives first, then outcome 4 occurs.

Locking is built into most database systems. For example, MySQL supports both table-level locking and row-level locking, depending on the storage engine that the developer selects. Its default storage engine is called MyISAM, which supports table-level locking. This means that every time a session issues a MySQL query to a particular table, the entire table is locked from access by any other active session. The lock is released when the query is completed.

The alternative MySQL storage engine is called InnoDB, and it supports row-level locking. This means that every time a session issues a MySQL query to a particular table, only the rows affected by the query are locked from access by any other active connection.

The good news is that, no matter which storage engine the developer chooses, there is no impact on the way that MySQL queries are written or database tables are designed. The two storage engines yield different performance levels. In general, InnoDB should be considered when the tables are large and/or the volume of queries is high. Otherwise, the default MyISAM engine is sufficient.

Selection of a storage engine for a given table is made at the time the table is created. To select, for instance, InnoDB, for table t, one would issue the query:

```
CREATE TABLE t (...) ENGINE=InnoDB;
```

Omission of the `ENGINE=` clause causes MySQL to use the default MyISAM engine for the table. For a more detailed discussion on these choices, look at http://dev.mysql.com/tech-resources/articles/storage-engine/part_1.html.

Notice that table-level or row-level locking removes responsibility for its prevention from the architecture itself. That is, no two sessions can execute a query to the same database table (or row) at the same time. If two sessions are connected to the database at the same time, still only one will have access to that table (row) because locking is built-in.

However, the software architecture can take steps to limit the number of sessions that are simultaneously connected to a database, and thus improve overall system performance. To accomplish this, all database accesses should be confined to the database layer (again heeding the layering principle), and every such access should use the following protocol for executing a query:

1. Connect to the database

2. Execute the query

3. Disconnect from the database

Following this protocol, each session is only connected to the database at times when it is executing a query (read, write, or update) to the database, and at no other time. This enhances overall database access performance by minimizing the number of simultaneous sessions connected to it at any one time. However, this protocol slightly degrades individual session performance since the session connects and disconnects from the database once for every query.

We shall illustrate this strategy for database access in Chapter 7, after readers have gained some experience working with a database and its query language.

4.5 Summary

Software architecture provides an underpinning for many key software development activities—especially refactoring, testing, and debugging. Understanding the architecture of a code base is therefore critical to effectively carrying out those activities.

A client-server architecture provides a framework within which concurrent access by many users can be rationalized. Support for concurrency requires the architecture to provide session-level globals, so as to distinguish one user from another while both are simultaneously accessing system resources.

Concurrency also admits the possibility that two or more users will want to access the same resource at the same time. Thus an effective software architecture must ensure that simultaneous accesses be effectively synchronized so that the integrity of the underlying database is not compromised.

Finally, the architecture of any software developed for Internet access must include effective security measures. These measures ensure that secure system functions are accessible only to authenticated users and that the system architecture is well protected from various types of external attacks.

Exercises

4.1 Find another violation of the layering principle in *RMH Homebase* besides the one identified in this chapter. Eliminate that violation through refactoring the offending code. Rerun the test suite to gain confidence that your changes didn't introduce other errors into the software.

4.2 Using search tools provided in your IDE, find three examples of useless functions in the *RMH Homebase* code base besides the ones identified in this chapter. Remove those functions and run the project's test suite to gain confidence that your changes didn't introduce errors into the software.

4.3 Compute the LCOM statistic for each of the other classes in *RMH Homebase*. Which ones are the most (least) cohesive, according to your computations?

4.4 There is a software tool called Metrics (http://metrics.sourceforge.net/) that computes a number of metrics for Java programs. Is there a comparable tool that computes metrics like LCOM and Efferent Coupling for the modules in a PHP code base? Explain the challenges for developing such a tool for PHP vs Java.

4.5 There are a number of additional modules in *RMH Homebase* beyond the ones shown in Figure 4.3.

    a. Show how these additional modules are interrelated by extending that figure to include all of them. Be sure to place each module in the layer to which it belongs.

    b. Find at least one layering violation among these additional modules. Suggest a way to refactor the code so as to remove that violation.

    c. Find at least one useless function among these modules and remove all that you find.

4.6 Considering the various security vulnerabilities described in this chapter, examine the code base and user/developer forums for the community-oriented FOSS project that you are working on. Find a security vulnerability in the code base. Is this vulnerability, or any other vulnerability for that matter, being discussed in the forums? Why or why not?

4.7 Consider the four race conditions illustrated in Table 4.1. Now suppose that a third user, User 3, is simultaneously trying to add "sandy jones" to the database, in addition to the additions being made by User 1 and User 2.

    a. Describe all the possible outcomes that can occur in this instance, assuming again that no locking takes place.

    b. Describe all the possible outcomes that can occur if locking does take place.

Chapter 5

Working with Code

> "A designer knows [s]he has achieved perfection
> not when there is nothing left to add, but
> when there is nothing left to take away."
> —*Antoine de Saint-Exupery*

Effective software development requires a mastery of both the architecture and specific strategies for improving, testing, and debugging the code base.

This chapter introduces these strategies, which can be used either for correcting a defect or adding a new feature to the software. Both these activities require the use of refactoring, testing, and debugging tools and techniques.[1]

When we work with code, we use both synthesis (writing new code) and analysis (criticizing and revising existing code). Four central activities are associated with code analysis:

- Identifying "bad smells," or poorly written code fragments

- Refactoring

- Testing

- Debugging

These are strongly interrelated activities in the software development process (see Figure 5.1). One cannot usually occur in isolation.

The following sections present and illustrate some basic techniques associated with each of these activities.

---

[1]To facilitate hands-on engagement with refactoring, testing, and debugging, readers are encouraged to download and install a *sandbox version* of their project's code base. The *RMH Homebase* release 1.5 code base is used in the examples in this chapter, and it can be downloaded from the book's Web site myopensoftware.org/textbook. A *sandbox version* of a code base is an implementation where developers can "play" with the code base and the run-time system in order to understand it better. Since developers are not using the *live version* of the software, errors that they make while playing in the sandbox have no disastrous side effects on users.

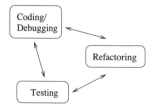

FIGURE 5.1:   Refactoring, testing, and debugging are interrelated.

5.1   Bad Smells and Metrics

Before adding new features to an existing code base, the code itself needs to be examined for quality and receptivity to those new features. Many times, such an examination reveals bugs that need to be fixed, or at least organizational characteristics that need to be improved, before the new features can be added.

This section discusses two strategies for finding code that needs to be improved: identifying bad smells and using software metrics.

5.1.1   Identifying Bad Smells

The code we read while testing or preparing to add a new feature to a software product may have many "bad smells" (a term coined by Kent Beck in [Fow00], p. 75). A bad smell is a segment of code that doesn't read clearly and concisely, and hence probably can be improved.

Such code may have been developed by a novice, a person not familiar with standards for good programming practice, or someone interested only in "making the program work" rather than "making the program readable." In any case, the original author of the smelly code is likely not within shouting distance. So it falls to the current developer to remove bad smells from the code so that future developers will have an easier time understanding it.

To illustrate this idea, consider the PHP program text in Figure 5.2, which contains several duplicate copies of a very technical piece of text. The removal of this bad smell by refactoring renders the code more readable, as illustrated in Figure 5.3.

Several different types of bad smells can occur in programs. Here are a few common types of bad smells that commonly occur in existing software artifacts (see Fowler [Fow00] for a more detailed discussion):

- Poorly Named Variable, Method, or Class—the variable, method, or class name does not clearly represent its purpose in the code. For example, the name `$sch` is a poor name for a variable instead of `$schedule`.

```
/**
* process_form sanitizes data, concatenates needed data, and enters it all into a database
*/
function process_form(){
    //step one: sanitize data by replacing HTML entities and escaping the ' character
    $first_name = trim(str_replace('\'','\\\'',htmlentities($_POST['first_name'])));
    $last_name = trim(str_replace('\'','\\\'',htmlentities($_POST['last_name'])));
    $address = trim(str_replace('\'','\\\'',htmlentities($_POST['address'])));
    $city = trim(str_replace('\'','\\\'',htmlentities($_POST['city'])));
    $state = trim(str_replace('\'','\\\'',htmlentities($_POST['state'])));
    $zip = trim(str_replace('\'','\\\'',htmlentities($_POST['zip'])));
    $phone1 = trim(str_replace(' ','',str_replace('\'','\\\'',htmlentities($_POST['phone1']))));
    $phone2 = trim(str_replace(' ','',str_replace('\'','\\\'',htmlentities($_POST['phone2']))));
    $private_notes = trim(str_replace('\'','\\\'',htmlentities($_POST['private_notes'])));
    $public_notes = trim(str_replace('\'','\\\'',htmlentities($_POST['public_notes'])));
    $my_notes = trim(str_replace('\'','\\\'',htmlentities($_POST['my_notes'])));
```

FIGURE 5.2:   Example bad smell—duplicate code.

- Duplicate Code—the same sequence of expressions or instructions appears in several places. For example, see Figure 5.2.

- Long Method—a method contains a lot of code that accomplishes several sub-tasks. For example, writing a method `AvMaxMin($list)` is a poor way to compute the average, maximum, and minimum value in a list, compared with writing three separate methods.

- Large Class—a class has an unusually large and diverse collection of instance variables or methods. Often this signals a lack of *cohesion* for a class, in the sense that it is trying to represent more than one object at a time. For example, the class `AlarmClock` might have features of an alarm and other features of a clock. A better design would define two classes, `Alarm` and `Clock`, and specify that a `Clock` may have an `Alarm` as a component.

- Too Many/Too Few Comments—too many comments can hide bad code (i.e., they can be "used as a deodorant"), while too few can make code difficult to read. As a rule of thumb, use the guidance discussed in Section 2.1.3 for inserting an appropriate level of commentary in the code base.

- Data Clumps—the same three or four variables appear together in several different places. This may signal an opportunity for defining, or "extracting," a new class that has these variables as instance variables.

- Parallel Inheritance Hierarchies—each time a sub-class is added to one hierarchy, it must be added to other hierarchies. This may signal a need to reorganize the hierarchies so that the sub-class is added only once.

- Feature Envy—a method requires lots of information from a different class. Perhaps that method should be embedded inside that class.

- Primitive Obsession—the code is reluctant to use classes instead of primitive data types. This signals an opportunity to simplify the code and improve its reliability by using classes rather than primitives.

- Lazy Class—a class that no longer "pays its way"; it is seldom used and its methods are seldom called. This usually suggests replacing those calls by calls to methods in other classes, and then removing the class from the code base.

- Speculative Generality—inserting features into the code for functionality that is not part of the current requirements. Generally, these clutter the code and should be removed.

- Temporary Fields—instance variables in a class that are set only in certain circumstances. All instance variables should be set and accessible all the time.

- Inappropriate Intimacy—pairs of classes that know too much about each other's private details. This usually suggests making each class's instance variables private and adding appropriate methods to access or modify them as needed by the other class in the pair.

- Incomplete Class—one that doesn't do everything you need. The fix is to complete the class's functionality by adding methods that do everything that is needed.

- Refused Bequest—a sub-class ignores most of the functionality provided by its superclass. The fix is to remove methods from the sub-class that duplicate that functionality.

5.1.2 Software Metrics

Another way to evaluate the quality of a code base is to calculate its so-called "software metrics." A metric is a quantification of some aspect of the syntactic structure of a program, which aims to expose potential weaknesses (bugs, or risks of run-time failures) in that structure.

Several different metrics can be used to measure the quality of a program. If the metrics of a code base are not all within a normal range, this may indicate poor code quality. Here is a short list of metrics that can help measure the quality of a Java program:

- Count Metrics—the number of packages, classes, instance variables and methods for each class, and parameters and lines of code for each method. Good design tries to minimize these numbers in accordance with the nature of the application and its individual classes.

- Clarity Metric—"McCabe cyclometric complexity" counts the number of distinct paths through each method, considering all its if, for, while, do, case, and catch statements. A good design tries to keep this number under 10 for every method in the code base.

- Cohesion Metric—lack of cohesion of methods (LCOM) in a class with m methods means that the ratio of the average number of methods accessing each instance variable to $m - 1$ is near 1. That is, a class is completely cohesive if all its methods access all its instance variables, which means that $LCOM = 0$. So the more cohesive the class, the closer LCOM is to 0, which is another indicator of good design.

- Coupling Metrics—indicate how strongly the packages in a code base are interdependent. Good design tries to minimize coupling.

Metrics calculators are available as a plugin for any Eclipse/Java IDE.[2] When metrics are enabled, they are recalculated automatically whenever the code base is changed. Unfortunately, no similar plugin for Eclipse/PHP is available at this writing.

Bad smells and metrics tend to be complementary, in the sense that each metric corresponds to a particular bad smell that can be detected by examining the code.

The main advantage of using metrics over looking for bad smells is that they can be quickly applied to a very large code base, highlighting areas that need a closer look. That is, reading all the text of a million-line code base, without the aid of metrics, would be a very tedious exercise.

5.2   Refactoring

Once a bad smell is detected, or a metric reveals a probable instance of poor coding, the offending code segment needs to be improved. Modifying code to improve its readability, efficiency, or modifiability is called *refactoring.*

No new features should be added during refactoring: the goal of refactoring is simply to improve the quality of the code without changing its observable behavior (i.e., its functionality in the eyes of the user). Often refactoring substantially reduces the size of the code base. Refactoring may also transform complex structures into simpler ones that are easier to maintain and understand.

What particular types of refactoring can be done? One kind of refactoring is to eliminate instances of duplicate code, which usually involves defining a new function with one copy of that code and replacing all the duplicate copies

---

[2]The use of Eclipse/Java metrics is illustrated at the book's Web site myopensoftware.org/textbook.

```
/**
* process_form sanitizes data, concatenates needed data, and enters it all into a database
*/
function sanitize_post ($s) {
    return trim(str_replace('\'','\\\'',htmlentities($_POST[$s])));
}
function process_form(){
    //step one: sanitize data by replacing HTML entities and escaping the ' character
    $first_name = sanitize_post('first_name');
    $last_name = sanitize_post('last_name');
    $address = sanitize_post('address');
    $city = sanitize_post('city');
    $state = sanitize_post('state');
    $zip = sanitize_post('zip');
    $phone1 = sanitize_post('phone1');
    $phone2 = sanitize_post('phone2');
    $private_notes = sanitize_post('private_notes');
    $public_notes = sanitize_post('public_notes');
    $my_notes = sanitize_post('my_notes');
```

FIGURE 5.3:   Example bad smell removal.

by a function call. The bigger the size of the duplicated code, the worse it smells! Figure 5.3 shows how creating a new function can eliminate the bad smell of duplicate code that appears in Figure 5.2.

This type of refactoring is called "method extraction." Many other types of refactoring are also possible.[3] To support this activity, the integrated development environment (IDE) can be configured to perform some types of refactoring automatically.

Here is a short list of important refactoring types that can be useful for developers working with a code base as they begin to add new features or track down bugs:

Renaming a variable, method, or class to add clarity for the reader and consistency with the user's domain and design document.

Extracting a method to eliminate duplicate code, and then replace each duplicate appearance by a call to that method.

Extracting methods to reduce the size of a long method. That is, logically divide the long method into smaller segments, extracting each segment as a separate method, and then replace the original segments by a series of calls.

Reorganizing a class to improve its logical cohesion. If two or more kinds of objects are encapsulated by the class, break it into two or more separate classes.

Unifying data clumps If a clump of data declarations characterizes an object, define a new class with them as its instance variables. Each original

---

[3]In fact, entire books have been written on this subject (for example, [Fow00]).

appearance of these variables can be replaced by a call to a new method, which can be defined within the new class.

Removing a parameter Sometimes a parameter is superfluous, for example when it is functionally dependent on one or more other parameters. Such a parameter can be eliminated.

Simplifying conditionals Sometimes a collection of conditionals can become so deeply nested that the underlying logic becomes impossible to understand. Such a nest can be simplified by rethinking and disentangling the logic.

The following additional types of refactoring rely on the principles of software architecture—layers, cohesion, and coupling—that were discussed in Chapter 4.

Removing Useless Code When reviewing the code base alongside the design document, look for code that has no purpose in relation to the existing requirements or the rest of the code base. This may take the form of a function, variable, or an entire class or module that is never referenced. All such code should be removed.[4]

Removing Violations to Layering Principles When layer, cohesion, and coupling principles are violated, refactoring should be done to remove the violations. This often involves other refactorings, such as extracting a new method or function.

Merging Similar Functions/Modules During different stages in development, a developer may not be aware that a function/module already exists that (nearly) fulfills a certain requirement, and thus may reimplement that function/module. When this redundancy is discovered later, it becomes a candidate for refactoring.

Separating Model, View, and Controller Code In a graphical user interface (GUI) module, confusion can occur if the model, view, and controller code are intertwined. Separating the code for these three may help clarify the code and make it more robust. We shall discuss this activity in more detail in Chapter 8.

Note that some refactoring activities may combine two or more of these techniques in a single step. For example, when combining two similar methods into one, we may also eliminate or add a parameter to clarify the new code.

Note finally that many of these refactorings tend to *reduce* the size of the code base rather than enlarge it. In general, a good architecture is often one

---

[4]A modern IDE, such as Eclipse, will automatically flag instances of unused code sections or unreferenced variables, so that they can be easily spotted and removed.

that has less code rather than more. Effective software, like effective writing, has little tolerance for redundancy and superfluity. Remember the words of Saint-Exupery!

The refactoring examples in the following sections are all taken from the *RMH Homebase* release 1.5 code base.

5.2.1   Example 1: Removing Useless Functions

A function is *useless* if it is not called from anywhere else in the code base. Identifying useless functions is relatively easy with a modern IDE. One way to do this is to highlight the function name and then search the code base (project) for all references to that name. If there are none, the function is useless.

For example, consider the Shift class in *RMH Homebase*. It has 24 functions and constructors. Utilizing the search tools provided in our IDE, we find that the following functions are not called from anywhere else in the code base, and therefore can be safely eliminated:

```
fill_vacancy
find_person
remove_person
```

The reason these can be removed is that the responsibilities for adding and removing individual persons in a shift are handled directly by the dbShifts module. The only services the dbShifts.php module requires from the Shift module are adding and removing all the persons from a shift at once, using the get_persons and assign_persons functions.

Why were these three functions included in the Shift class in the first place? Probably because the Shift class was developed before, and independently from, the development of the dbShifts database module and the editShift user interface module. Now is a good time to clean house and remove them; in preparing to add new features to the code base, we want it to be as lean as possible at the outset.

5.2.2   Example 2: Removing a Layering Violation

In Chapter 4, we introduced an example in the editShift module from *RMH Homebase* that violates the layering principle (recall Figure 4.4). We return to that example now and illustrate how we can remove that violation by extracting a new method.

The code shown in Figure 4.4 builds an array of all persons who have/do not have "family_room" in their type and are available on a certain $day and $time. This code, which occurs in a user interface module, is directly executing a database query rather than calling a function in a database module, thus violating the layering principle.

Looking further into the editShift.php module, we see a second layering violation of the same sort:

```
connect();
$query="SELECT * FROM dbPersons WHERE " .
    "(type LIKE '%volunteer%' OR type LIKE '%sub%') " .
    "ORDER BY last_name,first_name";
$result=mysql_query($query);
mysql_close();
```

This code builds an array of all persons who have "volunteer" or "sub" in their type, but for no particular day or time. Both sections return the array ordered by last_name and first_name.

It would be good to try to remove both these violations at once. To do this, we need to find or define one or more functions in the dbPersons module that satisfy both needs and then replace these two sections of code by appropriate function calls.

The dbPersons module already has a few search functions predefined. These are:

getall_persons() : Find all persons.

getall_type($t) : Find all persons of type $t.

getall_available($t, $day, $time) : Find all persons of type $t who are available on $day and $time.

getall_availables($t, $u, $day, $time) : Find all persons of type $t and $u who are available on $day and $time.

getall_scheduled($t, $group, $day, $time) : Find all persons of type $t who are scheduled in in $group, $day, and $time.

A quick look at the utility of these search functions reveals that only the first two are called from anywhere else in the code base. The other three can thus be removed. In their place, we can add two new search functions to the dbPersons module that address our newfound refactoring needs. These new functions are shown in Figures 5.4 and 5.5.

Now returning to the code in editShift.php, we can replace the first violation of the layering principle by the following call:

```
$result = getall_available($fam, $day, $time);
```

and the second violation by the following call:

```
$result = getall_eithertype("volunteer", "sub");
```

Now these layering violations have been eliminated from the editShift module and two new useful search functions have replaced three useless ones in the dbPersons module. Since either call returns `$result === false` if the search returns nothing, the remaining code in the editShift module is unaffected.

```
/*
 *   get all available volunteers for venue $venue on
 *   a particular $day and $time.
 *   $venue == "" means House and "Fam" means Family Room.
 *   return false if none are available
 */
function getall_available($venue, $day, $time) {
    connect();
    if ($venue=="Fam")
        $query="SELECT * FROM dbPersons
            WHERE (type LIKE '%family_room%')" .
            " AND availability LIKE '%" . $day . $time .
            "%' ORDER BY last_name,first_name";
    else
        $query="SELECT * FROM dbPersons
            WHERE (NOT (type LIKE '%family_room%'))" .
            " AND availability LIKE '%" . $day . $time .
            "%' ORDER BY last_name,first_name";
    $result=mysql_query($query);
    mysql_close();
    return $result;
}
```

FIGURE 5.4:   A new search function for the dbPersons module.

```
/*
 *   get all available volunteers with either type $t or type $u
 *   return false if none available
 */
function getall_eithertype ($t, $u) {
    connect();
    $query="SELECT * FROM dbPersons WHERE (type LIKE '%" .
        $t . "%' OR type LIKE '%" . $u .
        "%') ORDER BY last_name,first_name";
    $result=mysql_query($query);
    mysql_close();
    return $result;
}
```

FIGURE 5.5:   A second new search function for the dbPersons module.

5.3 Testing

Developing and using an effective test suite is a key step in software development. Traditional views place this activity sometime after the coding is done. That is the wrong placement.

A more aggressive approach to developing a test suite is to do it hand-in-hand with the coding process. A *most* aggressive approach to developing a test suite is to do it hand-in-hand with requirements gathering, and before any coding is done. This approach is advocated by the agile philosophy, and it is called *test-driven development* or TDD.

TDD is especially valuable because it keeps the client in the game, so to speak. That is, discussions between developers and clients can evoke examples of system and user interface behavior before the system is actually built. These examples thus become tests that drive the writing of the initial code for the new software.

When a test suite is developed either during or before the coding process, the test cases can motivate effective and focused code development. The code is clearly a prototype at this stage, since it is designed to respond specifically to the tests at hand. However, once an iteration or two of this agile process has taken place, the code (and the tests) will begin to mature and become more generally applicable.

A good development environment, such as Eclipse, supports this parallel process of test suite development alongside coding. Unit testing tools, like PHPUnit for PHP or JUnit for Java, can be easily integrated within the Eclipse environment.

The organization of the code base should also support unit testing, in the sense that a separate directory of test cases should live alongside the code directories themselves. Keeping the test modules together with the code base is good practice, even though it adds some storage overhead to the system as a whole. This practice facilitates unit testing of existing code whenever refactoring is done or new functionality is added.

For example, *RMH Homebase* has a collection of unit tests in the directory **tests**. Each test is aligned with a particular class or database module in the system. This directory has no unit tests for the user interface modules. Instead, each of those modules has been tested by exercising all the paths through the forms using a hypothetical database of users and a master schedule.

Each unit test usually applies to a single class or module. For example, Figure 5.6 shows the methods to be tested that are defined inside the **Shift** class in *RMH Homebase*.

The unit test itself contains a series of **assert** statements that must all be true for the code to "pass" the test. Each **assert** statement typically exercises

```
* construct an empty shift with a certain number of vacant vacancies
function __construct ($id, $vacancies) {
 * For creating a new shift
function new_shift() {
 * create a shift from the database
function db_shift($persons, $sub_call_list,$notes) {
 * @return the number of vacancies in this shift.
function num_vacancies() {
 * remove a slot from the shift
function ignore_vacancy() {
 * add a slot to the shift
function add_vacancy() {
function num_slots() {
 * fill a vacancy in this shift with a new person
function fill_vacancy($who) {
 * Build a SubCallList for this shift
function has_sub_call_list () {
function open_sub_call_list() {
function close_sub_call_list() {
function assign_persons($p) {
 * getters and setters
function get_mmddyy() {
function get_name() {
function get_persons() {
function get_sub_call_list()
function get_id() {
function get_day() {
function get_notes() {
function set_notes($notes) {
```

FIGURE 5.6: A typical PHP unit for testing.

a call to a single method within the module or class, using typical and atypical values for its arguments.

A unit test should have at least one method call for each non-trivial method in the module or class. For example, Figure 5.7 shows some elements of the unit test that were written to exercise the methods inside the Shift class shown in Figure 5.6.

```
class testShift extends UnitTestCase {
    function testShiftModule() {
        $noonshift = generate_new_shift("03-28-08-12-3",3);
        $this->assertEqual($noonshift->get_name(), "12-3");
        $this->assertTrue($noonshift->get_id() == "03-28-08-12-3");
        $this->assertTrue($noonshift->num_vacancies() == 3);
        $this->assertTrue($noonshift->get_day() == "Fri");
        $this->assertFalse($noonshift->has_sub_call_list());
        ...
```

FIGURE 5.7:   Elements of a unit test for a PHP class or module.

```
class AllTests extends GroupTest {
  function AllTests() {
...
    $this->addTestFile(dirname(__FILE__).'/testShift.php');
...
    $this->addTestFile(dirname(__FILE__).'/testdbShifts.php');
...
    $this->addTestFile(dirname(__FILE__).'/testeditShift.php');
...
    echo("\nAll tests complete");
  }
}
```

FIGURE 5.8: A series of unit tests.

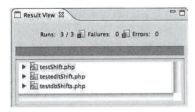

FIGURE 5.9: Results of running a series of unit tests.

5.3.1 Unit Testing Tools

Software tools for unit testing provide a convenient way to package a sequence of unit tests and run them all at once, relieving the developer of the effort that would be required to run each unit test individually.

In PHP, for example, one such tool is called SimpleTest. A series of unit tests for *RMH Homebase* code base is shown in Figure 5.8. Here, the ellipses (...) are placeholders for tests developed for the remaining classes, modules, and use cases indicated in the above list.

The results of running the three tests discussed in the foregoing section are displayed in Figure 5.9. If this figure were in color, the horizontal bar in the middle would be green when all tests had run with no failures or errors. A blue bar would indicate that one of the `assert` statements had failed, while a red bar would indicate that a run-time error had occurred in the code itself. So this feedback provides the developer with quick visual information about the status of the code base after exercising it with a complete test suite.

As a final note on testing, it is important to acknowledge its fallibility. That is, systematic unit testing does not guarantee that the code is free of errors. Only a strategy that uses *formal methods* would guarantee that.[5]

---

[5]The study of formal methods is beyond the scope of the present text. For more in-

5.3.2   Test Case Design

A well-architected software system must be hospitable to a rigorous testing strategy. To facilitate development, we need to design a collection, or *suite*, of test cases that cover all the modules and functions in the system. A Multi-Tier software architecture can provide a clear framework for developing such a test suite.

If the software we are writing is an extension of an existing system, the existing code base should ideally contain a complete suite of good unit tests. If it does not, our first step is to complete the test suite for the existing system—perhaps not a simple task in itself. Thus, when we build the test suite for the new system, it will be anchored in a reliable initial test suite.

It may be a surprise to suggest that a test suite for adding new features to a code base can be developed *before* any new code is written to implement those features. This process is formally known as *test-driven development (TDD)*. The motivation for this horse-before-the-cart approach is twofold:

1. New code is better focused when it responds to specific use-case-driven examples in the form of test cases.

2. Users can suggest the best test cases because they have the clearest idea of the new application's use cases.

The pre-existence of a test suite provides programmers with "live" goals for the code to achieve as they write, along with a suite of realistic examples that can test the validity of the new code itself. How do we begin designing a useful test suite for a code base? Here is the beginning of a discussion of this very complex question[6]:

> A *test suite* is a collection of "unit tests." The suite should have one unit test for every module or class in the code base and one unit test for each use case.

Each unit test should contain a group of calls that exercise all of the module's functions (and constructors, in the case of a class). For each such call, the unit test contains an assertion that delivers "true" exactly when that call is successful, and "false" otherwise.

> A unit test should aim for *100% code coverage and 100% use case coverage.* That is, every line of code in each module being tested

---

formation about formal methods in software development, readers may want to visit http://en.wikipedia.org/wiki/Formal_methods.

[6]For a more thorough treatment of software testing, readers may explore the subject more deeply by starting at **en.wikipedia.org/wiki/Software_testing**. The discussion on these pages identifies only the beginning stages in designing unit tests, and should not be considered a complete treatment of software testing.

should be exercised by at least one call in the unit test. Moreover, every step of each use case being tested should also be covered.[7]

Designing a unit test for a domain class or database module begins by writing at least one call for every function and constructor in that class or module.

Designing a unit test for a user interface module is more difficult, since each user interface module contains a mix of PHP and HTML code that supports a particular user form. Nevertheless, the unit test must begin with a test for every user option that appears on the form. Usually, these options appear as buttons, menus, text boxes, or other widgets common to an interactive Web page.

To unit test a use case, we begin by identifying as a "unit" those user interface elements—forms and associated modules—that combine to implement that use case. The question our unit test addresses is, "Does that unit correctly and fully support a user executing all the steps of that use case?"

In this sense, the complete set of unit tests stands as a basis for "integration testing" or "acceptance testing" the system in the eyes of the user. Implicit in this definition is the assumption that the unit testing of the use cases follows the separate testing of all the underlying domain classes, database modules, and user interface forms individually.

Examining the code base for *RMH Homebase* release 1.5, we see that it has a test suite (the `tests` directory), and the test suite has unit tests for many of the classes, modules, and use cases implemented by the code base. To test the entire system, a complete collection of unit tests would need to be designed and exercised.

Since *RMH Homebase* has at least 15 classes and modules (see Figure 4.3) and 9 use cases, a complete test suite should contain at least 24 unit tests. In the sections below, we use this code base to illustrate the design of unit tests for a domain class, a database module, a user interface module, and a use case.

5.3.2.1   Example 1: Testing a Domain Class

As our first unit testing example, consider the design of a unit test for the Shift class. A complete unit test for this class should exercise every function and constructor in the class. A partial unit test for this class is shown in Figure 5.10.

The Shift class (summarized in Figure 5.6) has 20 different functions (17 after refactoring), each of which should be invoked during the unit test to be sure that it delivers the correct results. That is the purpose of the `assertTrue` statements in Figure 5.10, each of which succeeds if and only if its argument

---

[7]In fact, aiming for 100% code coverage is often a weak testing strategy. For example, there may be boundary conditions occurring in the use case that are not covered by the code or identified in the use case itself.

```
class testShift extends UnitTestCase {
    function testShiftModule() {
        $noonshift = generate_new_shift("03-28-08-12-3",3);
        $this->assertEqual($noonshift->get_name(), "12-3");
        $this->assertTrue($noonshift->get_id()
            == "03-28-08-12-3");
        $this->assertTrue($noonshift->num_vacancies() == 3);
        $this->assertTrue($noonshift->get_day() == "Fri");
        $this->assertFalse($noonshift->has_sub_call_list());

        $persons = array();
        $persons[] = "alex1234567890+alex+jones";
        $noonshift->assign_persons($persons);
        $noonshift->ignore_vacancy();
        $persons[] = "malcom1234567890+malcom+jones";
        $noonshift->assign_persons($persons);
        $noonshift->ignore_vacancy();
        $persons[] = "nat1234567890+nat+jones";
        $noonshift->assign_persons($persons);
        $noonshift->ignore_vacancy();
        $this->assertTrue($noonshift->num_vacancies() == 0);
        $noonshift->add_vacancy();
        $this->assertTrue($noonshift->num_slots() == 4);
        $noonshift->ignore_vacancy();
        $this->assertTrue($noonshift->num_slots() == 3);

        $noonshift->set_notes("Hello 12-3 shift!");
        $this->assertTrue($noonshift->get_notes()
            == "Hello 12-3 shift!");
        echo ("testShift complete");
    }
}
```

FIGURE 5.10: A partial unit test for the Shift class.

delivers a `true` result. Altogether, this partial unit test contains calls to 10 different functions in the Shift class.

Running a unit test can produce one of three outcomes:

Success All the assertions in the unit test are `true`.

Failure One or more of the assertions in the unit test is `false`.

Error An error occurred in the code base being tested.

A unit test succeeds, of course, only when the Success outcome is achieved. In either of the other two cases, work remains to be done to understand why a particular test failed or what is wrong with the underlying code base.

5.3.2.2   Example 2: Testing a Database Module

Once the Shift class is fully tested, we can move on to design a unit test for the dbShifts module. The dbShifts module has five major functions:

setup_dbShifts creates an empty dbShifts table in the database.

insert_dbShifts inserts a new shift (row) into the dbShifts table.

select_dbShifts selects a unique shift (row) from the dbShifts table.

delete_dbShifts removes a shift (row) from the dbShifts table.

update_dbShifts replaces an existing shift in the dbShifts table by another with the same key.

This is a straightforward module, so its unit testing can contain one call for each of these five functions. A unit test for dbShifts is shown in Figure 5.11. It has calls to four of the five distinct functions in the module.

The reason we cannot test the dbShifts module until after the Shift class has been fully tested is because dbShifts uses some of the Shift class's functions (generate_new_shift in particular) to enable the testing of the dbShifts functions. Knowing *a priori* that the former are reliable helps us pin down problems in the testing of the dbShifts functions themselves.

The reason we do not test the `setup_dbShifts` function is that this function clears the dbShifts table completely. A non-empty dbShifts table is needed for the testing of other modules, as we shall see below.

5.3.2.3   Example 3: Testing a User Interface Module

Having tested both the Shift and dbShifts modules, we can now design a unit test for the user interface module editShift, which supports the user options on the Shift form shown in Figure 5.12.

We can see that this form has several buttons: "Add Slot," "Clear Entire Shift," "Generate Sub Call List," "Remove Person," "Assign Volunteer," "Ignore

```
class testdbShifts extends UnitTestCase {
  function testdbShiftModule() {
    $s1=generate_new_shift("02-25-08-night",3);
    $this->assertTrue(insert_dbShifts($s1));
    $s2=generate_new_shift("02-25-08-3-6",3);
    $this->assertTrue(insert_dbShifts($s2));
    $this->assertTrue(select_dbShifts("02-25-08-3-6")!==null);
    print_r(select_dbShifts("02-25-08-3-6"));

    $this->assertTrue(delete_dbShifts($s1));
    $s2=generate_new_shift("02-25-08-3-6",2);
    $this->assertTrue(update_dbShifts($s2));
    $this->assertTrue(delete_dbShifts($s2));
    echo ("testdbShifts complete");
  }
}
```

FIGURE 5.11: A unit test for the dbShifts module.

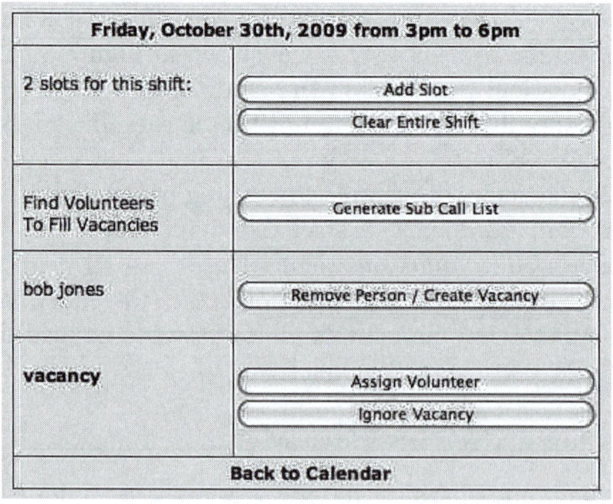

FIGURE 5.12: The Shift form in the user interface.

Vacancy," and "Back to Calendar." Our unit tests must eventually cover each of these possible user actions separately. A unit test for this form is shown in Figure 5.13.

This unit test relies on the existence of a calendar week that includes the date October 30, 2009, from which the 3–6 shift is being retrieved. Without that assumption, we would need to create a new shift equivalent to the one that is retrieved by the line:

```
$myshift = select_dbShifts("10-30-09-3-6");
```

This unit test has five parts, corresponding to five of the seven distinct buttons on the Shift form. It does not include a test for the "Generate Sub Call List" button or the "Back to Calendar" button because these are included in other unit tests.

Notice, after each of the first four parts of this unit test is completed, that the line

```
$myshift = select_dbShifts("10-30-09-3-6");
```

is repeated. This is needed because the variable $myshift must be updated by the new value stored in the database for this shift by the previous assertion. Otherwise, this variable would not be up-to-date with its corresponding database entry.

5.3.2.4 Example 4: Testing a Use Case

As a final unit testing example, consider the testing of the entire use case ChangeACalendar, described in Figure A.11. This is a very different process from the individual unit tests described above. Here, we are examining the integrity of the entire system, not a single module.

To do this, we start by assuming that all the individual forms in the use case have been individually tested. In the case of ChangeACalendar, this includes the calendar form as well as the Shift form and the Sub Call List form.

Then we follow each individual step in the use case by exercising the user interface elements that support that step. In the case of ChangeACalendar, we start by editing a week's calendar such as the one shown in Figure 5.14.

This form can initiate any one of the following user activities:

- Editing a shift

- Adding or changing notes for an individual shift

- Adding or changing manager notes for an individual day

- Adding or changing the guest chef for an individual day

```
class testeditShift extends UnitTestCase {
  function testeditShiftModule() {
    // get a shift from the database
    $myshift = select_dbShifts("10-30-09-3-6");
    print_r($myshift);

    // test generate sub call list/view sub call list button
    // test clear shift button
    $this->assertTrue(process_clear_shift(
        array('_submit_clear_shift'=>true), $myshift, ""));
    // test assign volunteer button
    $myshift = select_dbShifts("10-30-09-3-6");
    $this->assertFalse(process_add_volunteer(
        array('_submit_add_volunteer'=>true, 'all_vol'=>"0",
        'scheduled_vol'=>'rob2077291234+rob+jones'),$myshift,""));
    // test add slot button
    $myshift = select_dbShifts("10-30-09-3-6");
    $this->assertTrue(process_add_slot(
        array('_submit_add_slot'=>true), $myshift, ""));
    // test ignore vacancy button
    $myshift = select_dbShifts("10-30-09-3-6");
    $this->assertTrue(process_ignore_slot(
        array('_submit_ignore_vacancy'=>true), $myshift, ""));
    // test assign volunteer button
    $myshift = select_dbShifts("10-30-09-3-6");
    $this->assertFalse(process_add_volunteer(
        array('_submit_add_volunteer'=>true,'all_vol'=>"0",
        'scheduled_vol'=>'jon2077291234+jon+jones'),$myshift,""));
    // test remove person/create vacancy button
    $myshift = select_dbShifts("10-30-09-3-6");
    $this->assertTrue(process_unfill_shift(
        array('_submit_filled_slot_0'=>true), $myshift, ""));
    $myshift = select_dbShifts("10-30-09-3-6");
    print_r($myshift);
    echo ("testeditShift complete");
  }
}
```

FIGURE 5.13: A unit test for the editShift module.

House Calendar: October 26, 2009 to November 1, 2009							
	26 Monday	**27** Tuesday	**28** Wednesday	**29** Thursday	**30** Friday	**31** Saturday	**1** Sunday
9am / 10am	jane jones / linda jones	lynne jones / arla jones	linda jones / orminia jones	dottie jones / joy jones	becky jones / sally jones	rita jones	nancy jones
11am							
12pm / 1pm	mary jones / gerry jones	judy jones / jenny jones	mary jones / meg jones	ann jones / **Vacancies (1)**	pat jones / evelyn jones	beverly jones	
2pm							**Vacancies (1)**
3pm / 4pm	sharon jones / laura jones	becky jones / betsy jones	esther jones / **Vacancies (1)**	jane jones / nancy jones	phyllis jones / bob jones		
5pm							mary jones
6pm / 7pm / 8pm	ellen jones / kelly jones / meghan jones	cathy jones / joan jones / carol jones	claudia jones / marilee jones / **Vacancies (1)**	ron jones / derek jones / **Vacancies (1)**			
night					**Vacancies (1)**	**Vacancies (1)**	
manager notes							
guest chef							

Save changes to all notes

FIGURE 5.14: A calendar form for the ChangeACalendar use case.

At this point, we assume that each of these activities has already been tested individually. Now we are interested in verifying that all the steps of the use case can be effectively carried out by a sequence of actions that may invoke several other forms in the process. In that sense, we are basically testing the integrity of the links that connect the individual forms together, as summarized below.

- Editing a shift—user selects the shift to be edited. The user should be transferred to the Shift form (see Figure 5.12) for that shift.

- Adding or changing notes for an individual shift—user edits the shift's notes and then selects the "Save changes" button at the bottom of the form. The user should see the calendar refreshed with an acknowledgment that the changes have been made.

- Adding or changing manager notes for an individual day—user edits the manager notes line and then selects "Save changes." The user should see the calendar refreshed with an acknowledgment that the changes have been made.

- Adding or changing the guest chef for an individual day—user edits the guest chef line and then selects "Save changes." The user should see the calendar refreshed with an acknowledgment that the changes have been made.

The guide in this exercise is the use case itself. A "Success" is achieved when all the steps of the use case can be completed and the desired result (making a change on the calendar) can be achieved by the user. Otherwise, either a "Failure" will occur (when a different result from the one expected is observed) or an "Error" will occur (when the code base fails to execute for some particular step).

5.3.3   A Strategy for Sequencing Unit Tests

As the above examples suggest, there is a certain order in which the individual unit tests can be conducted. This order is determined by the functional dependencies that occur among the modules at the different layers in the architecture.

For instance, to find a sub, the user must begin by editing the Sub Call List form, which is managed by the subCallList.php module. Looking back at Figure 4.3, we see that this module requires the services of both the dbShifts.php module and the dbSCL.php module. These in turn require the services of the Shift.php and SCL.php classes, and so on.

So before we can begin to test the Sub Call List form, we must first unit-test all the modules from which it requires services. Then, if that unit test fails, we can assume that the error is most likely confined to the subCallList.php module, rather than a module upon which it is functionally dependent.

An overall strategy for designing and conducting a complete suite of unit tests for a Multi-Tier architecture can be developed in the following way.[8]

1. Begin by testing all the classes/modules that do not receive services from any other classes or modules.

2. Next, test each class/module that only receives services from classes or modules that have already been tested.

3. Repeat step 2 until no more classes/modules remain to be tested.

4. Finally, test each use case.

Using this strategy for testing *RMH Homebase*, we should test the classes and modules in Figure 4.3 in a sequence that respects the dependencies among them:

1. Begin by testing the classes Person, Shift, and SCL.

2. Test the class RMHDate and the modules dbSCL, dbPersons, login_form, and index.

---

[8]Notice that this strategy requires that there be no circular dependencies in the architecture. If there were, repetition of step 2 would not necessarily result in the testing of all classes/modules in the system.

3. Test the class Week and the module dbShifts.

   Test the modules dbDates and subCallList.

   Test the modules dbWeeks and editShift.

   Test the module calendar.

4. Test each of the nine use cases.

By the time we test the use cases, this testing sequence gives us reasonable confidence that all the underlying classes and modules are reliable, since they themselves have already been unit tested.

5.4 Debugging

We can expect that, throughout the development and useful life of a software product, errors in the code will occur. Importantly, the users provide the first line of defense in locating software errors. Perhaps this is because the users exercise the code far more rigorously than any suite of tests. Users thus provide the most reliable and thorough source of feedback to developers, especially for the existence of errors, or *bugs*, in the software itself.

> Technically, the term *bug* refers to a *defect* or *flaw* in the code base that contributes to the occurrence of a *failure*.

> The term *failure* refers to any unacceptable behavior in the software that can be observed by the user.

In this book we use the term *bug* rather informally, in the sense that it will simultaneously refer to both a failure in the software and its related defect in the underlying code base.

A most severe kind of bug is one that causes the software to "crash," or go into a permanent dysfunctional state from which the user cannot recover. One example of such a crash is the occurrence of a so-called "white screen of death" (WSOD, for short), where the user suddenly ends up staring at a blank screen. Little evidence of the source of the bug is apparent when this happens. So one debugging strategy for this case is to gather all the information that was available just before the WSOD happened (by restarting, repeating the steps, and gathering information along the way).

In any case, when finding and correcting a bug, the developer should add a new test to the test suite that addresses that particular error. Severe defects may even cause developers to refactor parts of the code base, perhaps even modifying the architecture itself. Thus, the interplay among software architecture, refactoring, test case design, and debugging is intimate.

5.4.1   Tool Use vs Developer Skill

Recall from Chapter 3 that some important tools are available for reporting, tracking, finding, and correcting software bugs. For example, the IDE contains debugging support for developers. The bug tracker provides support for reporting and updating the status of a bug in a community-oriented software project from its inception to its resolution. Yet the tools alone are often insufficient for effectively locating and removing a bug from a code base.

Earlier chapters illustrate that a healthy open source software project relies on the wide participation of users and developers to help keep the code base up to date and reasonably free of errors.[9] FOSS developers thus rely on the active participation of users to help them test new releases and verify bug corrections in the code base.

Beyond tool use and collaboration with users, developers need two additional skills for effectively diagnosing and removing a bug from the code base: a healthy understanding of the software architecture and an ability to traverse and analyze the code base to find and correct the bug.

In the absence of a coherent software architecture, finding a bug in a large code base can be equivalent to finding a needle in a haystack. How can the architecture help find and correct a software error?

The major challenge in finding a bug in a large system is to use the architecture to narrow the search to a particular module or level where the bug is most likely to occur. For instance, if the bug seems to be "cosmetic" in nature, with no apparent impact on the permanent data maintained by the system, it may be traceable to a single user interface module.

On the other hand, if the bug seems to have a more permanent impact on the system's data, the developer may need to follow the bug all the way down from the user interface level to a related module at the database level. In either case, the developer should understand the code base at different levels, including the interdependencies among different modules.

The examples in the following sections illustrate the effective interplay between tools, users, software architecture, and developer skills in identifying and removing bugs from an active code base.[10]

---

[9]Projects like Linux and Apache, and language projects like Perl, PhP, and MySQL, maintain an especially close connection between developers and users, since the developers *are* the users. Mozilla, which maintains the open source Firefox browser, is a good example where a user community of non-developers participates directly and closely with developers. Moreover, there are many examples of proprietary software projects that have wide participation of their user base through alpha and beta testing processes.

[10]These examples represent actual errors that were discovered by users and corrected by developers during the first year after the *RMH Homebase* project was installed and put into productive use.

```
if ($edit==true &&
    ! ($days[6]->get_year()<$year ||
        ($days[6]->get_year()>=$year &&
            $days[6]->get_day_of_year()<$doy)
    ) &&
    $_SESSION['access_level']>=2)
```

FIGURE 5.15: Locating a bug in the calendar.php module.

5.4.2 Example 1: A User Interface Bug

The simplest kind of bug to detect and correct is one that can be isolated in a single module in the user interface part of the code base.

Here is a bug recently reported by one of the users of *RMH Homebase*:

> Hi Alex,
>
> On the calendar, beginning in January the button to click to save notes is missing. The last week it appears on is December 21–27.
>
> Thank you!
>
> Gina

To recreate this error, Alex tried to edit the calendar page for the same week reported by the user. He used a sandbox version of *RMH Homebase*, so as not to interfere with the "live" version.

At the bottom of each calendar week, the button "Save changes to all notes" should appear, as it does in Figure 5.14. For some reason, this button does not appear on any calendar week after the week of December 21–27.

So the first step in debugging is to locate the module that manages the calendar form, which is called `calendar.php`. We locate this by referring back to the RMH system architecture, which has the structure shown in Figure 4.3.

The next step is to think about what causes this button to appear in the first place. The particular date on which the calendar is being edited must play a role in this determination, since we know it is not possible to edit calendar shifts for weeks that are fully gone by (try it!).

So the appearance of this button must be determined by a comparison of the date when editing took place with the dates of the calendar week being edited. If the week is fully in the past, then this button should not appear.

We can begin examining the calendar.php module for a code snippet that determines whether or not to display this button. Such a snippet occurs near the bottom of the calendar module in the code shown in Figure 5.15.

This is pretty ugly, so let's parse it a bit more. We quickly learn that `$edit==true` is the test that determines whether the calendar is in "edit" mode or "view mode," respectively. We also learn that `$edit==true` is the test to be sure that the user has edit access to the calendar notes ... more about this in Chapter 8.

Now for the gritty middle part of this code. A week is an array of 7 days, indexed from 0 to 6, and so the reference `$days[6]` is talking about the last day of the week. The references `$year` and `$doy` are talking about the year and the day of the year (0 to 365) in which the calendar editing is currently taking place.

So literally this code is displaying the "Save changes to all notes" button when the following three conditions are met:

1. the user is editing a calendar week,

2. that calendar week being edited does not fully precede the current week, and

3. the user is authorized to edit the notes.

Clearly, the fault must lie with item 2, since otherwise the error would not appear only in selected weeks. Looking at the logic of item 2, we can break down the code a little more finely to read:

```
the calendar week being edited is:
  not (last year or
     (this year or later and its day of the year precedes today)
  )
```

Now the error becomes more apparent, since the clause "or later" allows the earlier part of a future year to "precede" today, which is incorrect. This would explain why the "Save changes to all notes" button disappears at the beginning of next year but not for the week of December 21–27.

To correct that error, we need to eliminate that clause so that the text reads:

```
the calendar week being edited is:
  not (last year or
     (this year and its day of the year precedes today)
  )
```

To fix the code, we need only to change the `>=` operator in the third line of Figure 5.15 to `==`, and then retest the calendar editing form to be sure we have corrected the error properly.

We note also that this sort of bug can occur whenever a calendar is being displayed—not only in the calendar.php module but also in the calendar-Fam.php module (which displays a week on the Family Room Calendar). A careful checking of the code in the latter module reveals that the same bug reoccurs there as well.

An important lesson comes out of this discovery. That is, when the same bug occurs identically in two or more places (because the code is identically wrong in both places), we may have an opportunity for refactoring. In our example, we can extract a new function and replace all occurrences of the duplicated code by appropriate calls to that new function. This activity is left as an exercise.

5.4.3 Example 2: A Multi-Level Bug

Many bugs in complex software systems require the developer to navigate through the architecture and utilize information that the IDE provides about coupling between modules.

Here is a bug reported by one of the users of *RMH Homebase*:

> Hello!
>
> I think we may have discovered another bug: a volunteer created a sub call list and began making calls, she saved the information in the sub call list. I went in and added notes under the shifts which then deleted her sub call lists and the information. If it would be helpful, I can try to recreate this with you over the phone.
>
> Thanks and no hurry
>
> Gina

The first response from the developer was to confirm and understand the error more precisely by trying to recreate it on the sandbox version of *RMH Homebase*, so as not to interfere with the "live" version. This exercise invoked services from the following modules (the date reflects the week for which the exercise was being conducted, and is arbitrary):

```
calendar.php?id=10-29-09&edit=true
editShift.php?shift=10-29-09-12-3
subCallList.php
```

Now when we return to the calendar.php module and edit and save the notes for some other shift, the sub call list associated with the shift 10-29-09-12-3 suddenly vanishes.

Let's look at the code that is responsible for saving the shift, day, and guest chef notes. That code is in the function process_edit_notes inside the calendar.inc module. Within that code, there are only two ways in which the shift in question ($shift), and hence its sub call list, can be permanently changed. One would be to execute the update_dbShifts($shift) call midway through that function. The other would be to execute the update_dbDates($days[$i]) call near the end of that function.

Looking at the update_dbShifts function inside the dbShifts module, we see that it is accomplished through a delete_dbShifts call followed by an insert_dbShifts call. No other side-effects seem to be taking place here.

Looking at the update_dbDates function inside the dbDates module, we see a similar pattern—a delete followed by an insert. However, there is something else going on here, as shown in Figure 5.16.

```
function delete_dbDates($d) {
...
    $shifts=$d->get_shifts();
    foreach ($shifts as $key => $value) {
      $s = $d->get_shift($key);
      delete_dbShifts($s);
      delete_dbSCL(new SCL($s->get_id(),null,null,null,null));
    }
}
function update_dbDates($d) {
    if (! $d instanceof RMHdate)
      die ("Invalid argument for dbDates->update_dbDates call");
    delete_dbDates($d);
    insert_dbDates($d);
}
```

FIGURE 5.16:   Locating a bug in the dbDates module.

That is, while an update is accomplished by deleting and adding the same shift to dbShifts, each shift's sub call list is also deleted at the same time. Once gone from the database, that sub call list cannot be re-added, since sub call lists are stored in a separate table.

So the proper correction for this bug is to remove the delete_dbSCL call from the delete_dbDates function, leaving each sub call list unchanged in the database even though its corresponding shift has been deleted.[11] Once the shift is re-inserted into the database to complete the update, it is reunited with its old sub call list (if it had one).

5.5   Extending the Software for a New Project

So far in this chapter, we have focused on techniques for understanding the elements of a software system by analyzing, refactoring, testing, and debugging an existing code base. Our focus on architecture, testing, and debugging shows how classes and modules relate to an existing system's functionality at the user level.

At this point, we are prepared to consider the addition of new features to a code base, which will be guided by a new set of requirements. The ultimate

---

[11]This may seem odd for cases where a shift is simply deleted, rather than updated, but it turns out that these cases can never occur.

goal, of course, is to create an enhanced software system that will provide new functionality for the user.

The first step in reaching that goal is to listen to users, learn the new system requirements, and then adapt and create new classes and modules to implement the enhanced functionality suggested by the users and the new requirements and use cases.

New requirements for an open source software artifact usually originate from the collected views of current system users. Often these requirements appear in a post on a discussion thread. In the case of *RMH Homebase*, the user sent an e-mail to the developer outlining a "wish list" of nine new features that would be useful and bugs that should be removed. The text of that e-mail, along with a complete list of the new features and bugs that it identifies, appears in Appendix B.

The entire e-mail from the user suggests a collection of development activities that will be revisited incrementally throughout the next four chapters. Most of these involve additions to different parts of the code base (Chapters 6, 7, and 8). Many of these new features require additions to the user documentation (Chapter 9).

In this section, we concentrate on taking the first step toward implementing these new features: reading and understanding the new use case that comes directly from four of these nine new requirements.

5.5.1 A New Use Case

Suppose we want to add new functionality to *RMH Homebase* that will improve its searching and reporting capabilities. In particular, the House Manager has asked for modifications so that the following new kinds of information can be retrieved:

1. A summary of the total and average number of vacancies for each day and shift, for any series of weeks in the archive, accessible only to the House Manager

2. A summary of the total and average number of shifts worked by any volunteer, for any series of weeks in the archive, accessible only to the House Manager

3. A list of all volunteers who have not been scheduled for any series of dates in the past

4. A list of all inactive volunteers

5. The ability to export the data for any volunteer so that it can be imported by another application

The House Manager should be able to change the status (active/inactive) of any volunteer(s) in the list, and the entire database entry for any volunteer(s)

in the list should also be exportable as a comma-separated list suitable for import to a spreadsheet or other application.

Figure 5.17 describes a new use case that encapsulates this requirement. The use case is called "Housecleaning," and it is an extension of the original use case "ViewAList" shown in Figure A.14.

This use case suggests several questions for the developers to answer as they consider extending the existing code base to satisfy these new requirements.

1. What user interface modifications, including navigation changes, are needed for these functions to be effectively added to *RMH Homebase*?

2. What new or modified domain classes are required for accomplishing this task?

3. What new or modified database tables are needed?

4. What are the security implications of this new functionality?

5. What new user documentation is needed to support these new capabilities?

5.5.2 Impact on the Code Base

Several modules in the code base will be affected when this use case is implemented. Our task in the following sections is to identify those modules and sketch what will be needed to implement the new requirements. The implementation itself, along with the associated refactoring and testing, will be fully treated in later chapters.

5.5.2.1 User Interface

A review of the current system suggests that the items in this use case can be accommodated by developing a new **Calendar Housecleaning** form, like the one sketched in Figure 5.18.

In making this addition, we can also streamline the user interface by adding a new **calendar: search** tab to the main menu which will lead the user to the new form. This will allow the House Manager to view vacancy summaries and manage inactive volunteer lists directly.

With this change, the new main menu that the House Manager sees could look like this:

> **home | about | calendar: house, family room, search |**
> **people: view, search, add**
> **master schedule: house | family room | log | help | logout**

Housecleaning

Description: Occasionally, the House Manager needs to view the total and average number of vacancies for each shift and each day, over a period of weeks in the recent past. Various other information about volunteer schedules should also be retrievable, such as the total and average number of shifts worked by any particular volunteer for any such period, a list of active volunteers who have not been scheduled during that period, and a list of all the inactive volunteers. The active/inactive status of any person on such a list should be reversible. The database entries for any group of volunteers should be exportable as a comma-separated list so that they can be imported into a spreadsheet or another application.

Actor: the House Manager

Goals: Different selections should be possible, in particular:

"View the total and average number of vacancies for each day and shift, over any period of time in the past."

"View the total and average number of shifts worked by any volunteer, over any period of time in the past."

"View all active volunteers who have not been scheduled for a shift over any period of time (change their status to inactive)."

"View all inactive volunteers (change anyone's status to active)."

"Export the database entries for any group of volunteers in the list."

Preconditions: 1. A beginning and ending date for the period of time has been specified.
2. One of the above selections has been made.

Postconditions: 1. The desired list is displayed, and some volunteers' status is changed or their data is exported.

Related Use Cases: ViewAList

Steps:

Actor	System
1. Log on to Web site.	2. Ask for id and password.
3. Enter id and password.	4. Verify and display outcome.
5. Identify a period of time.	6. Retrieve shifts for that period.
7. Select an option.	8. Display/export those shifts.
9. Log off Web site.	10. Terminate session.

FIGURE 5.17: Use case **Housecleaning**.

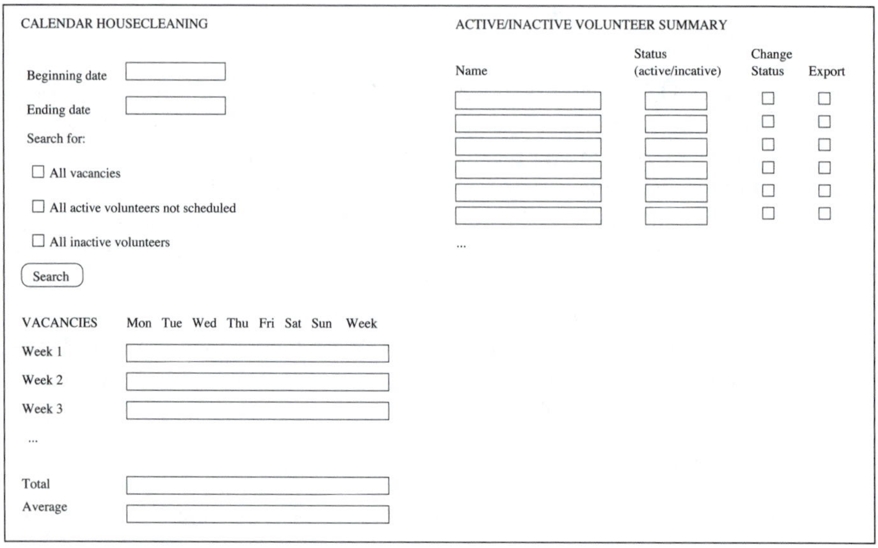

FIGURE 5.18:   A new calendar housecleaning form.

5.5.2.2   Impact on Classes and Modules

To determine which classes and modules are affected for implementing this new use case, we must take a systematic look at the code base. This process is discussed in the next chapter, which provides a broader treatment of the influence of software architecture on development.

But informally, we can easily observe that implementing the main menu change will affect the header.php module. We can also predict that a new user interface module will be required, one that manages the user's entry and retrieval of information while performing the new use case.

All underlying classes and modules that this new module imports will also need to be suitably modified. In particular, it will need to call upon existing and new functionality provided by the Shift, RMHdate, Week, and Person classes, as well as their associated database modules dbShift, dbDates, db-Weeks, and dbPersons.

5.5.2.3   Impact on the Database

When considering the impact of this new use case on the database tables, we ask the question: "Does an implementation of the use case require additional information to be stored permanently in the database tables, beyond what is already stored there?"

If such additional information needs to be added to existing tables, then all functions in the database module that work with that table must also be revised accordingly. If an entirely new table is needed, then we must define a new module to manage that table, including initialization, adding rows, deleting rows, and updating rows.

For the new use case described above, we do not need a new database table or new table columns, since all of the new reports can be fully generated from information already in the tables. Moreover, none of the reports need to be kept permanently after the manager retrieves and views them.

5.5.2.4 System Security

All of the current system's security constraints must be upheld when the new functionality is implemented. In addition, only the House Manager should have access to the functionality described in the new use case.

For this to happen, we must ensure that all code added to the user interface modules occurs "under the umbrella" of `$_SESSION['access_level']==2`, which distinguishes a manager's login privileges from everyone else's.

5.5.2.5 User Help

The development of effective user support is so important that it is covered separately in Chapter 9. For this discussion, we note that the current user help pages for *RMH Homebase*, as summarized in Figure 9.7, will need only minor modifications to document these new features for users.

For the first requirement, the help page "Generating and publishing calendar weeks" should be modified and a new help page "Summarizing Vacant Shifts (Managers Only)" should be added. For the second requirement, the help page "Searching for People" should be changed and a new help page "Summarizing People's Hours (Managers Only)" should be added.

5.5.3 Team Discussions

At this time, the team should be actively discussing the initial development of this new project, including the assignment of tasks, the scheduling of milestones, and a review of design decisions already made (such as those outlined above).

Since the user initiated the development of these new requirements by stating needs that aren't fulfilled by the current software, it is imperative that the user remain in the loop as new classes, modules, security constraints, and user help menus are identified for fulfilling those needs.

These initial discussions should include a review of the user interface (forms) that will be changed or added, the strategy that will be used to ensure security, and the new help menus that will be needed. Discussions about technical details involving new and existing classes, modules, and database tables may require less user participation.

5.6 Summary

This chapter has presented fundamental ideas underlying working with a code base—refactoring, testing, and debugging. Strategies for developing new classes and modules that implement new functionality were introduced as a by-product of reading a new requirements statement and relying on knowledge of the existing code base.

While refactoring and testing are highly individualized activities, debugging and adding new features are highly collaborative activities. Some of the exercises below will help individuals develop basic refactoring and testing skills, and others will help teams to begin working together in reading requirements, reading code, and defining classes and modules for new projects that build upon an existing code base.

Exercises

5.1 Examine the *RMH Homebase* release 1.5 code base and its accompanying documentation in Appendix A. Identify at least one instance of each of the following "bad smells" in the code base.

    a. Long Method

    b. Too Few Comments

    c. Data Clumps

    d. Speculative Generality

5.2 For each of the bad smells identified in the previous exercise, complete a refactoring that will remove it from the code base. Which of these refactorings reduces the size of the code base? Which one(s) improves its readability?

5.3 After completing the previous exercise, rerun the unit tests to be sure that your refactorings have not compromised any of the project's functionality.

5.4 Design a new unit test for the dbSchedules module that tests each function except the `setup_dbschedules` function. Add a call to this unit test from within the AllTests module shown in Figure 5.8; be sure that your call occurs in the correct sequence.

5.5 Design a new unit test for the editMasterSchedule module that tests each of its functions. Add a call to this unit test from within the AllTests module shown in Figure 5.8; be sure that your call occurs in the correct sequence.

5.6 Consider the strategy for sequencing unit tests described in Section 5.3.3, along with the extended layering chart that you developed in Exercise 4.5. Extend that strategy by adding to the sequence unit tests for all the remaining modules in *RMH Homebase*. Be sure that you locate each unit test in its proper place in the sequence.

5.7 The debugging example in Section 5.4.2 suggests an opportunity for refactoring. That is, the determination of whether or not a given shift in the calendar display should show its "notes" field for editing is governed by the question of whether or not today's date follows that shift's date chronologically. If it does, the shift's "notes" field should be displayed for editing; otherwise, it should not.

a. Locate the module in *RMH Homebase* that displays a shift's "notes" field for editing.

b. Locate instances of the code in that module which are similar to the "ugly" code in Figure 5.15. Confirm that those instances perform the same computation as the ugly code.

c. Define a new function called "predates(a, b)" that performs that same computation and returns true or false if a predates b, respectively. Insert that function as a new feature of the Shift class.

d. Replace each instance of the "ugly" code shown in Figure 5.15 by a call to your new function.

e. Test your refactoring by adding a new test case to each of the testCalendar and testeditShift unit tests and rerunning AllTests.

5.8 Examine the *RMH Homebase* requirements in Appendix A and the release 1.5 code base to answer the following questions:

a. Why do some shifts have a "Generate Sub Call List" button and others have a "View Sub Call List" button instead? What does that tell you about the relationship between shifts and sub call lists—does every shift have a sub call list?

b. What is an "archived week" and how does a week become archived? Who does the archiving? How can an archived week be removed from the database? Suggest a different approach for handling this, including its advantages and disadvantages vs the current approach.

5.9 Suppose we want to generalize the *RMH Homebase* software so that it can be more easily adapted for use in other organizations with similar scheduling needs. Typically, another organization's scheduling needs will vary in the following fundamental ways:

- The number of venues for scheduling can vary. For *RMH Homebase*, the number of venues is two, the House and the Family Room.

- The layout of shifts for a typical week on the calendar can vary for each venue.

- The master schedule's shifts and number of slots in each shift will vary for each venue. For *RMH Homebase*, the House schedules four shifts on each weekday (9-12, 12-3, 3-6, and 6-9) and a different layout on the weekends. The Family Room schedules three shifts on each weekday (10-1, 1-4, and 4-7) and no shifts on the weekends.

- The frequency for repeating the master schedule will vary: some organizations will schedule two groups of volunteers, each on a bi-weekly basis, others will rotate four groups on a monthly cycle, and others will schedule the same group every week.

- The individual fields in a volunteer's database entry will vary. In most cases, a person's first name, last name, home address, phone number, and e-mail address are standard fields. For *RMH Homebase*, additional fields include an alternate phone number, a type (volunteer, family room volunteer, etc.), shift availability for each day in the week, and special notes.

What new GUI pages, if any, would be needed for these functions to be effectively added to *RMH Homebase*? What would need to be added to the existing pages and menu items? What new classes would be required for accomplishing this task? What new database tables? What are the security implications of this new feature? Which classes and modules would be affected by this change, and which ones would not?

5.10 Suppose we want to integrate *RMH Homebase* with iCalendar (see http://en.wikipedia.org/wiki/ICalendar), which is a standard file format that allows people to keep personal calendars and exchange meeting times via e-mail. We would like the weekly schedule to be stored in this standard format and thus more easily downloaded, printed, and shared by Volunteers and the House Manager.

What new GUI forms, if any, would be needed for iCalendar to be effectively integrated with *RMH Homebase*? What would need to be added to the existing pages and menu items? What new classes would be required for accomplishing this task? What new database tables? What are the security implications of this new feature? Which classes and modules would be affected by this change, and which ones would not?

Chapter 6

Developing the Domain Classes

> "When in Rome, do as the Romans do."
>
> —*St. Ambrose*

A robust collection of domain classes is fundamental to a sound software system. Whether debugging, refactoring, adding new features to a class, or adding an entirely new class, the developer must always begin by understanding the current system's documentation and code base.

The domain classes are at the heart of a software architecture. Above them sit the user interface modules and below them sit the database modules. All three of these levels utilize the namespace and properties that are initially defined by the domain classes and drawn from the application domain itself.

In this chapter, we explore the principles and practice of reading and understanding the code base, working with the domain classes while adding new features, and developing appropriate unit tests and refactorings.[1]

6.1   Understanding the Current System

In any open source software project, the user's view captures the developer's initial attention. When the project has some form of design documentation, such as user stories or use cases, developers begin by reading that documentation to understand the software in more detail.

In the end, developers must also understand the code base that underlies the software and serves as the basis for adding new features. Ideally, all the classes and modules in the code base are well documented. In the absence

---

[1]To facilitate hands-on engagement with adding new features, readers are encouraged to download and install the *sandbox version* of *RMH Homebase* release 2.0 from the book's Web site myopensoftware.org/textbook. Release 2.0 has some of the code enhancements and refactorings of the release 1.5 domain classes that are needed to support the new features described in Appendix B. Other enhancements and refactorings needed to support these new features are left as team exercises.

of such documentation (which, in practice, *does* happen), the code base must assume the role of its own documentation.

Proponents of agile methods often advocate developing the requirements for a new project simultaneously with developing the code. In this approach, the team starts by evoking stories from users to help sketch an initial design document. We do not advocate this degree of informality, mainly because we think its open-endedness creates uncertainty about the overall scope and limitations of the project. That is, with some form of design document available up front, the development team can be circumspect about the endgame, and thus can more accurately predict and reach specific coding, testing, and other milestones that will be needed to complete the project.

6.1.1   Reading a Design Document

A design document typically contains a domain analysis, a requirements analysis, and a set of use cases. The domain analysis summarizes the setting in which the new software will be used, the types of users (called "roles") who will be accessing the software, and the ways in which the new software will influence the work conducted in that setting.

The *domain analysis* also describes how the *current* application works, including any existing software that may be used to support that application. This description should provide enough detail so that readers can understand the existing system's strengths and weaknesses.

The *requirements analysis* identifies the activities that the new software must support. Emphasis here is on the word *must*—a software product is incomplete if it doesn't fulfill all of its requirements. The requirements statement has two key parts: a collection of *use cases* and a statement about the *platform and other constraints* that will govern running the new software.

A *use case* provides a transformative view, showing how the system should support specific kinds of interactions between types of users (called *user roles*) and the system. It is written in a highly stylized way that identifies actors and roles, preconditions, results, and other details necessary for the implementation to be effective.[2]

For example, the **FindASub** use case shown in Figure A.12 appears in the *RMH Homebase* design document. It describes how a user should interact with the system when adding a Person (called a "Sub") to a shift on the calendar that has a vacancy.

When we read a use case, we need to perform three different kinds of activities in order to understand or add new features to an existing code base.

1. Identify classes and modules.

---

[2]For a detailed discussion of how to develop domain analysis, requirements analysis, and use cases, readers may want to look at Chapter 11.

2. Identify instance variables.

3. Identify methods and functions.

Each of these activities is further discussed below.

6.1.1.1 Identify Classes and Modules

When reading the requirements for a new system, developers look for *"big picture" nouns*, which are those that can be abstracted into *classes* or *modules*— the major elements in the system design. They also look for *"supporting" nouns* that can be abstracted as *instance variables* in a class or module.

For example, a reading of the **FindASub** use case in Figure A.12 suggests a need for the following classes that correspond to "big picture" nouns:

Person — a house manager or a volunteer,

Week — a calendar week (a sequence of 7 days),

Shift — a collection of openings on a particular day and time slot to be populated by volunteers, and

SubCallList — a list of Persons who are available to substitute on a particular shift.

6.1.1.2 Identify Instance Variables

To connect a class's instance variables with a use case, we look for detailed entities in the use case that characterize the state of an object in a class. Consider the Shift class, for example, in the *RMH Homebase* release 1.5 code base alongside the **FindASub** use case. The Shift class contains an array of `Persons` who are currently assigned to the shift, as well as a count of the number of `vacancies` (unfilled slots) in that shift. A shift's capacity is easily computed as the sum of the size of that array and the number of vacancies, so it need not be stored as a separate instance variable.

Other key instance variables for a Shift are the date and time slot when an individual shift occurs. These variables, however, are less apparent from reading the **FindASub** use case than they are from reading other use cases. Thus, identifying all of a class's instance variables is seldom achieved by examining a single use case in isolation.

So answering one question leads to more questions:

What sort of Person can be assigned to a shift?

How do we determine who is available to be assigned to a shift and who is not?

What variables are needed for a SubCallList entry, and how do we keep track of who has been called and who has not?

Answers to these and other questions can only be achieved after reading all the use cases and related discussions in the design document, alongside corresponding elements in the existing code base itself.

6.1.1.3   Identify Methods and Functions

The third kind of information that comes from a use case is information that helps designers specify *actions* — methods or functions — that need to be implemented for each class and module in the new system. These actions are suggested by the *verbs* that appear in the use case.

For instance, the **FindASub** use case identifies at least the following functions: *add* a Person to a shift on the calendar (step 9), *verify* the user logging in as a House Manager or Volunteer (step 4), and *record* an entry in the SubCallList in response to the user making an entry (steps 7 and 8).

One answer leads to more questions here, too:

What additional supporting actions are needed to realize these new functions?

What underlying database functionality is needed to implement these actions so that they are permanently recorded?

Answering these questions requires examining more use cases and discussions in the design document, as well as related sections of the code base itself.

When extracting a new method or function, it is important to determine what class should contain that method (if there's a choice), what to name that method, and what (if any) parameters does it need.

Consider, for example, the process of adding a Person to a shift on the calendar. The method could be called `fill_vacancy` and implemented in the Shift class, with the `id` of the Person to be added supplied as a parameter. Alternatively, the method could be called `schedule_me` and implemented in the Person class, with the `id` of the Shift supplied as a parameter. The former choice was made for *RMH Homebase*, where the method appears in the Shift class as follows:

```
/**
 * fill a vacancy in this shift with a new Person
 * @return false if this shift has no vacancy
 */
   function fill_vacancy($who) {
       if ($this->vacancies > 0) {
           $this->persons[] = $who;
           $this->vacancies=$this->vacancies-1;
           return true;
       }
       return false;
   }
```

The meaning of this method should be clear in light of the foregoing discussion. Notice also that the documentation for this method is written in a standard style, rather than freelance.

A more detailed discussion of the principles of new class design occurs later in this chapter.

6.1.2 Reading Code

Often the design document for an existing code base is unavailable or unrelated to the current version of the software. In this case, developers need to begin by reading and extracting information directly from the code base itself. The code base provides a reliable starting point from which they can launch a new software project. In this setting, reading the code base has three key goals:

1. To understand the overall architecture and functionality of the existing software

2. To learn the vocabulary established by the domain classes

3. To identify the extent to which the code must be refactored before it can be modified to support the functions of the new system

Reading the code base is often accompanied by exercising the software itself, so that developers can understand the relationship between various user actions and the corresponding classes and modules that support those actions.

When reading the code base for the first time, developers are well-advised to keep the following strategies in mind:

- Start from the top

- Look for classes with unique keys

- Avoid the temptation to refactor

Each of these is discussed more fully below.

6.1.2.1 Start from the Top

Reading a code base is a disciplined and orderly activity. The initial reading is usually top-down: it begins at the highest structural level and then works its way down gradually to the details of individual classes, variables, and functions.

Your reading should begin with an examination of the code's overall structure. You should be looking for answers to the following questions:

What are the domain (core) classes, and how do they characterize the principal objects that are active when the software is running?

What are the database modules, and what tables are needed in the database? How do the database modules relate to the domain classes?

What are the graphical user interface (GUI) modules, and how do they relate to the use cases described in the design document?

What particular domain classes and database modules are needed by each GUI module? What are the key methods and functions in these classes and modules that implement individual user actions?

How does the software enforce the client's security requirements?

What other modules are in the code base, and what is their purpose?

It is necessary to have the current version of the code base running during this reading, so that whenever a particular element of the code is read, its run-time role and behavior can be quickly validated. For example, Table A.1 summarizes the directory structure of the *RMH Homebase* code base.

6.1.2.2 Look for Classes with Unique Keys

For every class we examine, it is important to determine whether or not each member of the class has an instance variable that distinguished it from all the other members. Such an instance variable is called a *unique key*, a *unique identifier*, or just an `id` for short.

For example, in *RMH Homebase*, every Person must be distinguishable from every other Person in the database. Each Person's `id` is unique for a variety of reasons, such as protecting system security when a user logs in and accesses their own entry in the database.

Defining the unique key for a Person can be done using various strategies. The strategy used in *RMH Homebase* is to define each Person's `id` as the concatenation of their first name with their 10-digit primary phone number. This pretty much guarantees uniqueness, since it is unlikely that two different Persons will share the same first name and phone number.[3] This strategy also has the advantage that it is easy to remember—few people forget their first name or their phone number.

Similarly, every Shift is distinguishable from every other Shift. When we go searching the database to find which Persons are currently assigned to a particular Shift, we need to be able to uniquely retrieve that Shift from the database and no others. The `id` for a Shift in *RMH Homebase* is a composite of the month, day, year, and time of day for that Shift, written in the following format:

`mm-dd-yy-hh-hh`

---

[3]Unlikely, but not impossible—for example, a parent and child of the same gender may live in the same house and share the same first name and phone number.

For example, the `id` = 09-02-09-6-9 uniquely identifies the 6-9pm shift on September 2, 2009.

6.1.2.3   Avoid the Temptation to Refactor

While reading an existing code base will identify the extent to which refactoring is needed, this activity should avoid the temptation to refactor ugly code when it is first encountered. While it is highly likely that an existing code base will be full of bad smells, succumbing to the temptation to correct them during the initial read is fraught with peril. Why?

- Refactoring must be accompanied by testing, to ensure that the refactored code doesn't introduce new bugs.

- Once refactoring starts, it threatens to never end.

Combined, these two perils can easily bog the project down and divert developers from their primary code-reading goals—to understand the architecture and core vocabulary of the system. *Remember that the purpose of this initial read is to understand the structure and functioning of the existing code base, no more and no less.* There will be plenty of opportunities to refactor later in the development process.

At the same time, developers should not avoid the temptation to add or refine existing documentation. That activity has no effect on the functionality of the code, and it can only improve the quality of the code base. Many elements of an existing code base will not be properly commented when you first encounter them. Whenever you come to a certain understanding of *what* a particular class, module, method, or complicated function does, take a moment to add a brief documentary comment if it is not already there.

Assuming somebody else will reread that code later in the development process, your enhancement will help others avoid rereading the code at the same level of detail. Here's an example from *RMH Homebase*:

```
function remove_availability ($a) {
    $index = array_search($a, $this->availability);
    if ($index !== false)
        array_splice($this->availability, $index, 1);
}
```

This little method in the Person class searches a Person's `availability` array for a certain time slot `$a` and, if present, removes it using the PHP function `array_splice`. This code is a bit technical, requiring readers to remember what is returned by the `array_search` function and also what is accomplished by `array_splice`.

So if you think the title of the method doesn't fully reveal its purpose, you should feel free to add a comment at the top of this method that will help clarify its purpose for the next reader of this code:

```
/**
  * remove $a from a Person's availability if it's there
  */
```

6.1.3   Examining the Domain Classes

The domain classes characterize the central concepts in a software system. That is, they define a "name space" which permeates the entire application and its documentation. The names themselves originate from the user's domain, so that they characterize objects and actions with which the users are already familiar. Table A.1 shows that *RMH Homebase* release 1.5 has five domain classes: Person, Shift, SCL, RMHdate, and Week.

Looking in more detail at the Person class, we see that a Person is either the House Manager, a Volunteer, or an Applicant (visitor). This class's instance variables (see Figure A.15) tell us a lot about the information that the system needs in order to implement all nine use cases.

For example, each Person is uniquely distinguished from every other Person by a unique key, the $id variable. This unique key identifies each Person in the database, and it is used by many other classes and modules throughout the scheduling process.

Importantly, a Person's unique key serves as their "Username" when they log in to *RMH Homebase,* and $password serves as that Person's "Password." In general, the commentary documentation in Figure A.15 tells us a lot about these instance variables and their valid values. Notice, for example, that the default password for a Person is the $id itself. At login time, users are encouraged to change this default password to something more secure.

More insight about a Person can be gained by looking at a few Persons in the database and/or the form that a new applicant fills out when seeking a volunteer position. That is, if we exercise the existing system as a new applicant, we will see the form shown in Figure A.29 when we select **apply**.

"Live" examples of actual Persons in the database can also be viewed by looking at some entries in the dbPersons table. Table 6.1, for example, shows two entries in this table.

Reading this information provides insight into the software design, and it raises more questions as well. For example, we see that a Person's `password` is not identical with their login id, but why and how is it encrypted? To clarify this question, we can examine that part of the code base that handles logins and passwords.

Other classes in *RMH Homebase* are similarly designed and have associated tables in the database:

Shift A Shift (see Figure A.16) is an individual time slot that occurs on a particular day of the year. It has a unique $id that distinguishes it from all other shifts, and it contains a list of the $ids of all the Persons who are scheduled to work at that time.

TABLE 6.1: Two Entries in the dbPersons Table

id	bette2077291234	ellen2077291234
first_name	bette	ellen
last_name	jones	jones
address	14 Way St	14 Way St
city	Harpswell	Harpswell
state	ME	ME
zip	04079	04079
phone1	2077291234	2077291234
phone2		
email	bette@bowdoin.edu	ellen@bowdoin.edu
type	sub,volunteer	volunteer,sub
availability	Thu3-6,Sun2-5	Mon6-9,Thu6-9
schedule	,TwoThu3-6	,TwoThu6-9,OneMon6-9
birthday	02-19-89	02-19-89
start_date	03-14-08	03-14-08
password	4ea40dcbfd...	5be84f62b7...

SCL A SCL (see Figure A.17), or Sub Call List, may be associated with any particular shift. It is a list of the $ids of all the Persons who are available for a particular shift to fill a vacancy on that shift.

RMHdate An RMHdate (see Figure A.18) is a particular date on the calendar for scheduling volunteers. As such, it contains an array of all the shifts that can be scheduled on that date.

Week A Week (see Figure A.19) is an array of seven consecutive dates, from Monday to Sunday. Each such date is an object in the RMHdate class.

For each class, there are a few different ways to understand its elements and interrelationships more fully:

- Read the design document.

- Read the instance variables and their documentation in the code base.

- Look at examples of entries in the class's corresponding database table.

These three sources can provide sufficient detail to answer many questions about the nature of a class and its representative objects.

6.2 Adding New Features

The client or a group of end users of a software system usually provides the catalyst for adding new features to an existing software system. The system's developers should have good communication channels with users, so that when new needs arise they will be quickly transmitted and discussed with the developers.

Such a discussion was initiated by the users of *RMH Homebase* release 1.5. They identified a "wish list" of new features that would be helpful to make the software more useful. Chapter 5 introduced this new project and summarized its impact on the current system, including the code base, the user interface, the database, system security, and user support.

This entire new project is summarized in Appendix B. In this chapter, we want to consider the impact of this project on the current and new domain classes. Here is the initial e-mail from the users, which identifies the "wish list" in detail:

From: Gina
Date: November 9, 2009 10:51:53 AM EST
To: Alex
Subject: Homebase ideas

Alex,

Below is a list of ideas that have come about in using Homebase— if you want to go through them over the phone, please give me a call. Thanks!

1. *Volunteer status—ability to categorize a volunteer as inactive, preventing them from showing up on a sub list. This would be helpful to ensure volunteers on vacation or otherwise unavailable do not get called for shifts.*

2. *Make Active/Inactive—ability to track when a volunteer has last been scheduled for a shift. For example, when a manager logs in a screen pops up showing the names of any volunteer who has not been on a shift for the past month.*

3. *Calendar view—In the current calendar view, shift times are hard to distinguish if the user is unfamiliar with it. For example, 9–12 looks like it could be 9–11. Moreover, sometimes a shift (especially a weekend shift) needs its start or end time to be changed by the user.*

4. *Calendar month view—Is it possible to view one month at a time? This would be simply for convenience and is not a necessity.*

5. *Import/export—possible with Raiser's Edge database?*

6. *Guest Chef—Information is erased if a change is made to the calendar and the date has passed. For example, I have entered info in the guest chef field for 11/9/09. Tomorrow if*

we make a change, Monday's guest chef information will be deleted. I am testing this today and will let you know if it happens when any change is made or only in the guest chef field.

I think the issue is only with the note field in relation to guest chef information being deleted. I just went into the calendar and made a change to the note field under Friday's 3–6 PM shift. After clicking the save button, Monday and Tuesday's guest chef information was deleted. It does not happen when changes are made to shifts-adding/removing a volunteer.

7. *Vacancies and shifts worked—information for the House Manager:*

   a. *Sort the upcoming vacancies on the manager's screen by date*

   b. *The total and average number of vacancies for each day and shift, for any series of weeks in the past*

   c. *The total and average number of shifts worked by any volunteer, for any series of weeks in the past*

8. *Open Applications—sorted by first name and "grayed out" if the interview, background paperwork, or shadow buttons are selected.*

   The inactive feature would be helpful here as well. There are often applicants who submit their information and then they do not complete the application process. Rather than leave them in the open application status they could be marked as inactive and then completely deleted after several months.

9. *Volunteer Application:*

   a. *Allow for spaces in the name field. Example, Jo Ann. Also, remove the "&" from the first name field. Example Jack & Jill. Entries that have "&" are not accessible in the database.*

   b. *Allow for only the month/year field to be completed when selecting a start date.*

   c. *When an applicant fills out their info and clicks submit the screen appears blank. Perhaps an automatic note thanking them for submitting an application.*

   d. *We overlooked this when first submitting information to you: can fields be added such as employer's information and emergency contact?*

10. *Log—I love this feature! Could there be an ability to view additional pages as we can with the "people: view" tab?*

Let me know what I can clarify, and thank you as always!—*Gina*

Thus, the users have asked the developers to add 10 new features to *RMH Homebase* 1.5, creating in effect a new version that we hereafter call *RMH Homebase* 2.0.

This chapter uses this particular list of new features to illustrate the principles of class design and implementation. The next two chapters, in turn, will consider the impact of adding these same new features on the database and user interface modules.

6.2.1   Top-Down Analysis/Bottom-Up Development

When reading the requirements for new system features, we look for opportunities to add new instance variables, methods, and entire classes to the code base. Recall from Section 6.1.1 that new instance variables are triggered by the existence of *"supporting" nouns*, new methods are triggered by *verbs*, and new classes are triggered by *"big picture" nouns* that identify entirely new entities in the requirements statement.

Once these elements are identified, their implementation evolves through the code base from the bottom up. First, the domain classes are revised, then the database modules, and finally the user interface modules. New test cases are developed as the new code appears, either just before (if test-driven development is preferred) or just after. In this chapter, we discuss the impact of adding new features on the domain classes.

As it turns out, only four of the 10 new features in Gina's wish list affect the domain classes. These are:

1 **Volunteer status**—ability to categorize volunteers as inactive, preventing them from showing up on a sub list. This would be helpful to ensure volunteers on vacation or otherwise unavailable do not get called for shifts.
   Impact on the code base:
   Domain classes: Add a new instance variable "status" to the Person class, with appropriate changes to its constructors and other functions.

3 **Calendar view**—Shift times are hard to distinguish if you are unfamiliar with the calendar. For example, 9–12 looks like it could be 9–11. Moreover, sometimes a shift (especially a weekend shift) needs its start or end time to be changed by the user.
   Impact on the code base:
   Domain classes: Shift should be altered so that its start and end time can be changed (within the same day).

4 **Calendar month view**—Is it possible to view one month at a time?
   Impact on the design:
   Domain classes: Add a new class Month, which is a series of RMHdates. This could be organized similarly to the existing class Week.

9d Volunteer Application—We overlooked this when first submitting information to you: can fields be added such as employer's information and emergency contact?
Impact on the code base:
Domain classes: Add new fields and appropriate functions to the Person class.

Our goal here is to analyze the text of these particular features and define more precisely how each one impacts the domain classes. In this exercise, we look for cues that suggest particular changes that must be made to the domain classes in order to implement the new features.

The noun phrase "ability to categorize ... " in Item 1 suggests adding a new instance variable, say $status, to the Person class, and the values of that variable may be "active" or "inactive."

The phrase "start or end time to be changed by the user" in Item 3 suggests adding new instance variables $start_time and $end_time to the Shift class, as well as a function to change the start/end time for a shift dynamically. Currently, a Shift's start and end time are not explicit and cannot vary.

Item 4's phrase "one month at a time" requires a more major change, since the current domain classes only identify time units for Shift, RMHdate, and Week objects. Adding a new class Month to the code base, along with appropriate instance variables and functions, is necessary for implementing this new requirement.

Finally, Item 9d suggests straightforwardly that we add new instance variables for a volunteer's employer and contact information (e.g., name and phone) to the Person class.

6.2.2 Modifying the Domain Classes

The particular modifications to existing domain classes that are suggested in this list range from simple to complex. Let's take them one at a time.

6.2.2.1 Person Class Changes

Adding a $status variable to the Person class (Item 1 above) is simple, as is adding employer and contact information (Item 9d above). A partial listing of the revised Person class with these additions is shown in Figure 6.1.

In conjunction with these new variables, we need to add functions that will set and retrieve their values. We must also modify the constructor that creates a new Person object. For instance, we need to be able to set the value of the $status variable to active or inactive, as well as retrieve the value of that variable. The new functions shown in Figure 6.2 will accomplish that.[4]

---

[4]Notice that the set_status function does not check that the $value passed is valid: either active or inactive. Thus, whatever $value is passed becomes a Person's status.

```
class Person {
private $id;     // id (unique key) = first_name . phone1
private $first_name; // first name as a string
private $last_name;  // last name as a string
...

private $type;        // array of "applicant", "volunteer", ...
private $status;      // a Person may be "active" or "inactive"
private $employer;    // name of current employer
private $contact_person;  // name of a contact Person
private $contact_phone;   // phone of the contact Person
...
```

FIGURE 6.1:   New instance variables for the Person class.

```
function set_status ($value) {
    $this->status = $value;
}
function get_status () {
    return $this->status;
}
```

FIGURE 6.2:   New functions for the Person class.

Similar pairs of functions can be designed to set and retrieve the values of the variables $employer, $contact_person, and $contact_phone. These are left as an exercise.

Addition of new code to the Person constructor should initialize all four of these new variables to the values passed via their respective arguments. The header of the constructor for the Person class should therefore be changed from:

```
function __construct($f, $l, $a, $c, $s, $z, $p1, $p2, $e, $t,
    ... )
```

to:

```
function __construct($f, $l, $a, $c, $s, $z, $p1, $p2, $e, $t,
    $st, $em, $cp, $cph, ... )
```

and four corresponding assignment statements should be added to the constructor. Completion of this change is also left as an exericise.

6.2.2.2   Shift Class Changes

In preparation for adding flexibility to the calendar view (Item 3 above), we need to add functionality to the Shift class that allows its start and end times to vary. *RMH Homebase* release 1.5 builds the start and end times into the shift's $id variable, which also contains the date of the shift. For example, the 3-6pm shift for October 23, 2009 has the following $id variable: 10-23-09-3-6.

The Shift class has another variable $name which isolates the start and end time from the date of the shift. For example, the above shift would have as its $name the value 3-6. Moreover, the $id and $name variables serve "double duty" because they contain information about the venue (House or Family Room) where the shift is scheduled.

For example, a shift with $id = 10-23-09-3-6 and $name = 3-6 indicates a shift on the House calendar, while the shift with $id = 10-23-09-3-6Fam and $name = 3-6Fam indicates a shift on the Family Room calendar. Therefore, allowing a shift's start and/or end time to vary is somewhat tricky, since changing either one also changes the shift's $id and $name.[5]

With these considerations, let's begin by revising the definition of the Shift class so that the start and end times are stored in separate variables using a 24-hour clock. Using a 24-hour clock facilitates comparing two times to see which one precedes the other. (The current system makes no such distinction, so that "9-12" could signify a morning shift or a night shift.) We are also adding a new variable $venue ("" for House and "Fam" for Family Room). These additions to the Shift class are shown in Figure 6.3.

This modification must be accompanied by a revision of the Shift class's functions and constructors, so that the new capabilities for a shift are supported. In particular, the Shift constructor must instantiate the new instance variables properly, and the new function set_start_end_time must be properly implemented.

Figure 6.4 shows how the Shift constructor can be modified to ensure that the new variables $start_time and $end_time are properly initialized. The following function enables resetting a Shift's start and/or end time.

```
function set_start_end_time ($st, $et) {
    $this->start_time = $st;
    $this->end_time = $et;
    $this->id = $this->mm_dd_yy .  "-"  . $this->start_time
        . "-" . $this->end_time . $this->venue;
    $this->name=substr($id, 9);
}
```

Its last two lines are needed so that the Shift's $id and $name remain consistent with its new start and end time. Recall that resetting the start/end time cannot be done in isolation, since the Shift's $id contains the start and

---

[5]The implications of this change on the database are also tricky. For example, an attempt to change a shift's start and/or end time is in error if that change would cause the shift to overlap the start/end time for any other shift in the same venue (House or Family Room) on the same day. We shall return to this issue in Chapter 7.

```
class Shift {
    private $mm_dd_yy;  // String: "mm-dd-yy"
    private $name;   // String: '9-12', '12-3', '3-6', '9-12Fam',
                     // '12-3Fam', '3-6Fam', '6-9', '10-1',
                     // '1-4', '12-2', '2-5', 'night', or 'chef'
    private $start_time; // Integer: e.g. 11 (meaning 11:00am)
    private $end_time;   // Integer: e.g. 13 (meaning 1:00pm)
    private $venue;   // "" or "Fam" (for House or Family Room)
    private $vacancies; // number of vacancies in this shift
    private $persons;   // array of Person ids and names
                     // e.g., "malcom1234567890+Malcom+Jones"
    private $sub_call_list; // "yes" if SCL exists
    private $day;    // string name of day "Monday"...
    private $id;                // "mm-dd-yy-ss-ss" or
               // "mm-dd-yy-ss-ssFam" or "mm-dd-yy-chef"
               // suffix "Fam" designates a family room shift
    private $notes; // notes written by the manager
```

FIGURE 6.3:   Revising the instance variables for the Shift class.

end time as an integral part. So to maintain the integrity of the $id, the last line of this function recomputes it using the new start and end time values.

6.2.3   Documentation and Bulletproofing

Whenever a new function is designed, it should be documented using standard practices and appropriate preconditions and postconditions. This is particularly important for non-trivial (i.e., non-getter and non-setter) functions.

Consider, for example, the function `set_start_end_time` sketched in the foregoing section. There are many opportunities for a call to try to reset these variables incorrectly. For example, setting the new start time to an hour that does not precede the end time, or setting the end time to a value that is not in the range 0–23. The range of values for start and end times should also be clear—using a 24-hour military-style clock is the most effective way to enable validity checking between start and end times.

So the function sketched in the previous section should be "bulletproofed" as shown in Figure 6.5, so that it traps these invalid requests. That is, resetting the start and end times will occur only if the parameter values satisfy the preconditions. Otherwise, the current start and end times will not be changed. A true or false indicator is sent back to the caller so that remedial action can be taken as needed.

A related and important issue for the Shift class is to ensure that, if the shift's $id does change, its corresponding entry in the dbShifts database table is replaced by a clone of this shift that reflects a new $id. A revised dbShifts

```
function __construct (
    $id, $vacancies,$persons,$sub_call_list,$notes) {
    $this->mm_dd_yy=substr($id,0,8);
    $this->vacancies=$vacancies;
    $this->id = $id;
    $this->name=substr($id, 9);
    $i = strpos(substr($id, 9), "-");   // find shift time
    if ($i!==false) {
        $this->start_time = substr($id, 9, $i);
        $this->end_time = substr($id, 9+$i+1);
    }
    $i = strpos($id, "Fam");
    if ($i!==false)
        $this->venue = "Fam";
    else
        $this->venue = "";
    $this->day = date("D", mktime(0, 0, 0,
        substr($this->mm_dd_yy,0,2),
        substr($this->mm_dd_yy,3,2),
        "20".substr($this->mm_dd_yy,6,2)));
    if ($persons==null) {
        $this->persons=array();
        $this->notes="";
        $this->sub_call_list = "no";
    }
    else {
        $this->persons = $persons;
        $this->sub_call_list = $sub_call_list;
        $this->notes=$notes;
    }
}
```

FIGURE 6.4: Revising the constructor for the Shift class.

```
/**
 * This function (re)sets the start and end times for a shift
 * and corrects its $id accordingly
 * Precondition:  0 <= $st && $st < $et && $et < 24
 *     && the shift is not "chef" or "night"
 * Postcondition: $this->start_time == $st
 *     && $this->end_time == $et
 *     && $this->id == $this->mm_dd_yy .  "-"  .
 *     $this->start_time . "-" . $this->end_time . $this->venue
 *     && $this->name == substr($this->id, 9)
 */
function set_start_end_time ($st, $et) {
    if (0 <= $st && $st < $et && $et < 24 &&
            strpos(substr($this->id, 9), "-")!==false) {
        $this->start_time = $st;
        $this->end_time = $et;
        $this->id = $this->mm_dd_yy .  "-" . $this->start_time
                 . "-" . $this->end_time . $this->venue;
        $this->name=substr($this->id, 9);
        return true;
    }
    else return false;
}
```

FIGURE 6.5:   Adding a new function to the Shift class.

module should take further precautions against the newly defined shift over-lapping with another existing shift on the same day. These issues will be addressed in Chapter 7.

A more tricky issue is to determine whether rescheduling a shift by moving its start and/or end time should be done automatically without changing the list $persons of volunteers who are assigned to that shift. We will assume that is the norm, so that any change in a shift's start or end time will not change its $persons list. This issue will be revisited in Chapter 8, where we examine the user interface changes needed to implement these new features in *RMH Homebase*.

There is a special function in the original Shift class that returns a shift name (like "Sunday, February 14, 2010 from 2pm to 5pm") given its id (like "02-14-10-2-5"). That function is called get_shift_name_from_id and its original version is shown in Figure 6.6.

Given the new variability that can occur for a shift's start and/or end time, this function must be modified so that any start or end time between 0 and 23 is translated to an appropriate shift name. However, it should be clear that a simple textual replacement of afternoon time slots by their military time

```
/*
    * Creates the $shift_name of a shift from its id
    *       e.g. "Sunday, February 14, 2010 from 2pm to 5pm"
    *       from "02-14-10-2-5"
    */
function get_shift_name_from_id ($id) {
    $shift_name=date("l, F jS, Y",
        mktime(0,0,0,substr($id,0,2), substr($id,3,2),
            substr($id,6,2)));
    $name=substr($id,9);
    $idnames = array("9-12"=>" from 9am to 12pm",
        "12-3"=>" from 12pm to 3pm",
        "3-6"=>" from 3pm to 6pm",
        "6-9"=>" from 6pm to 9pm",
        "10-1"=>" from 10am to 1pm",
        "1-4"=>" from 1pm to 4pm",
        "2-5"=>" from 2pm to 5pm",
        "5-9"=>" from 5pm to 9pm",
        'night'=>" - night shift",
        "chef"=>" - guest chef",
        "9-12Fam"=>" Family Room from 10am to 1pm",
        "12-3Fam"=>" Family Room from 1pm to 4pm",
        "3-6Fam"=>" Family Room from 4pm to 7pm",
        );
    $shift_name = $shift_name . $idnames[$name];
    return $shift_name;
}
```

FIGURE 6.6: Original function to return a Shift name.

equivalents will not work. That is because a shift's start or end time may not match the particular constants listed in the array `$idnames` in Figure 6.6. For example, changing the time slot from "12-3" to "12-15" in this array is useless if that shift's start/end times are later changed to, say, "12-16."

Moreover, the `get_shift_name_from_id` function is screaming out for refactoring. It has a number of issues. First, there is no need for the parameter `$id` to be passed, since the shift's id can be retrieved directly by the local call `$this->get_id()`.

On the other hand, it may be more useful to keep the parameter `$id` and move this function from the Shift class to the dbShifts module. The rationale for that move comes from noticing that the `$id` field is the unique key that distinguishes one shift from another in the dbShifts table. Moreover, every call to the `get_shift_name_from_id` function comes from a user interface module which needs to display the text of a shift in a readable form.

To confirm this, we used our IDE to conduct a search for all calls to the `get_shift_name_from_id` function from across the code base. Here is the result of that search:

```
dbShifts.php
calendar.inc
editShift.inc (7 matches)
editShift.php
index.php (2 matches)
subCallList.php (2 matches)
```

This result leads to the conclusion that the `get_shift_name_from_id` function should be moved to the dbShifts.php module. Therefore, we shall continue this refactoring discussion in Chapters 7 and 8.

6.3   Class Design Principles and Practice

In Chapter 4, we introduced some principles of software architecture, including the complementary goals of minimizing coupling and maximizing cohesion among classes and modules. When we consider designing an entirely new class, we proceed in a way that supports and extends those principles. In particular, any new class we add should have the following characteristics:

1. **Need** The class must fulfill a need that is not already fulfilled by existing features of the programming language or the existing code base.

2. **Information Hiding** All instance variables should be declared **private**.

3. **Object Integrity** The class constructor should initialize all instance variables whenever a new object is created.

4. **Maximum Cohesion** The class should represent a single kind of object.

5. **Minimum Coupling** The class should be distinct from and complementary to all other classes in the code base.

6. **Accessors** The class should provide an access function (often called a "getter") for every instance variable.

7. **Mutators** The class should provide mutators (often called "setters") only for those instance variables that can be modified.

Other textbooks provide more elaborate discussions about these and other principles of class design. However, we find the above seven principles to be both necessary and sufficient for guiding the development of new classes. We illustrate these principles in the discussion below.

6.3.1   Using What's Already There

Every viable programming language comes with a rich vocabulary of built-in functionality. One of the practical aspects of good software development is to avoid reinventing functionality that already exists (this is **Design Principle 1. Need**). Understanding the breadth and depth of functionality that your programming language already contains is a prerequisite for well-informed functional and class design.

For example, PHP has especially good functional coverage for managing dates, times, and other calendar-related entities.[6] It would be a mistake not to understand and utilize this coverage in any application that depends on dates and times, like *RMH Homebase*.

An "epoch timestamp" is a widely accepted standard for representing time as the 32-bit integer number of seconds elapsed from the beginning of the Unix epoch, which is defined as midnight on January 1, 1970 (GMT). This representation makes it easy to perform common date-time calculations, such as, "How many days will elapse between today and April 15, when my taxes are due?"

Support for working with the epoch timestamp is provided by three important PHP functions: the `time` function, the `mktime` function, and the `date` function. The first returns the epoch timestamp for the current time, the second returns an epoch timestamp for a given date, and the third returns a readable date from a given timestamp. Here's a summary:

time() returns the epoch timestamp for the current date and time when it is called

mktime(hh, mm, ss, MM, DD, YYYY) returns the epoch timestamp `et` corresponding to the date and time specified by the six arguments

date(format, et) returns a readable date, using the `format` specification, that corresponds to the epoch timestamp `et` in the call

The format specification is written as a character string composed from the formatting codes defined in Table 6.2. Punctuation characters can be included inside the format specification to make the date more readable.

For example, if we want to store the date September 1, 2012 as an epoch timestamp, we can say:

```
$et = mktime(0,0,0,9,1,2012);
```

If we then want to display this time in the form "Saturday September 1, 2012" we would write:

```
echo date("l F j, Y", $et);
```

On the other hand, if we want to display it as 09-01-12, we would write:

```
echo date("m-d-y", $et);
```

---

[6]So also does Java. See Java's System, Date, and Calendar classes for more information.

TABLE 6.2:   Formatting Codes Used by the PHP
date Function

Code	Meaning
H	Hour, numeric 00–23 (24-hour clock)
h	Hour, numeric 00–11 (12-hour clock)
A	A.M. or P.M.
i	Minute, numeric 00–59
s	Second, numeric 00–59
d	Day of month, numeric 01–31
j	Day of month, numeric 1–31
w	Day of the week, numeric 0–6 (Sunday = 0)
z	Day of the year, numeric 0–365
l	Full weekday name, text (e.g., "Sunday")
F	Full month name, text (e.g., "September")
m	Month, numeric 01–12
t	Month length in days, numeric 28, 29, 30, or 31
y	Year without century (e.g., 12)
Y	Year with century (e.g., 2012)

A second practical aspect of class design is to recognize an existing class as a good model and to utilize that model as a framework for developing the new class. For example, the class Week in *RMH Homebase* is defined as a series of seven consecutive days. So it would seem appropriate, when designing a new class Month, to use the class Week as a model.

6.3.2   Adding a New Domain Class

To implement the new requirement 4, we need to define a new class Month that contains a series of days that span an entire month on the calendar. Since Month is modeled after the existing class Week, our design can use the instance variables shown in Figure 6.7 as a starting point.

```
class Week {
    private $id;      // the first day of the week, mm-dd-yy
    private $dates;      // array of 7 RMHdates, beginning Monday
    private $name;      // the name of the week
                // (e.g., March 3, 2008 - March 9, 2008)
    private $weekday_group; // 1 or 2
    private $weekend_group; // 1-5
    private $family_room_group; // 1 or 2
    private $status; // "unpublished", "published" or "archived"
    private $end_of_week_timestamp; // the mktime timestamp
```

FIGURE 6.7:   Instance variables for the Week class.

```
class Month {
    private $id;      // the first day of the month, mm-dd-yy
    private $dates;   // array of 28, 29, 30, or 31 RMHdates
    private $name;    // the name of the Month (ie March 2008)
    private $weekday_start; // weekday for the first day
    private $timestamp; // timestamp for the last day
```

FIGURE 6.8: Instance variables for a new Month class.

Thus, a Month can be viewed as a series of days, from the first day of the month to the last. So we can define the instance variables for class Month as shown in Figure 6.8. Notice that **Design Principle 2. Information Hiding** is followed in this definition, since instance variables are declared as private.

There are, of course, some differences between the design of a Month class and the design of a Week class. A Week in *RMH Homebase* is the lynchpin for scheduling groups from the master schedule, while a Month plays no such role. Thus, the instance variables for identifying scheduled groups can be omitted.

The second difference between a Week and a Month is that the first day of the week is always Sunday, while the first day of the Month may be any day of the week. To accommodate this difference, we add a new instance variable $weekday_start whose value identifies the day of the week when the first day of the month occurs. Adding this variable will later facilitate displaying a month in the user interface.

When defining a constructor for class Month, it should be clear that the only parameters needed are the month and year for which that month should be generated. The job of the constructor is to initialize all of its instance variables correctly. A complete constructor for the new Month class is shown in Figure 6.9. Notice that **Design Principle 3. Object Integrity** is followed in this specification.

Designing functions for the new Month class starts with developing a complete set of accessor functions ("getters"), one for each instance variable that can legitimately be accessed. This follows **Design Principle 6. Accessors**. All variables but the $timestamp variable fall into this category. For example, a definition of the get_days() function can be written as follows:

```
function get_days() {
    return $this->days;
}
```

Completion of the remaining accessor functions for the new Month class is left as an exercise.

Designing other functions for the new Month class can be done either now (in anticipation of future use) or later, after the need for such functions has been more accurately determined. We usually choose the latter option, since

```
function __construct($mm, $yy) {
    $this->timestamp = mktime(0,0,0,$mm,1,$yy);
    $this->days = date("t",$this->timestamp);
    $this->dates[0] = new RMHdate(
        $mm."-01-".$yy,null,"","");
    for ($i=1; $i<=8; $i++)
        $this->dates[] = new RMHdate(
            $mm."-0".($i+1)."-".$yy,null,"","");
    for ($i=9; $i<$this->days; $i++)
        $this->dates[] = new RMHdate(
            $mm."-".($i+1)."-".$yy,null,"","");
    $this->name=date("F, Y", $this->timestamp);
    $this->weekday_start=date("w", $this->timestamp);
    $this->id=$this->dates[0]->get_id();
}
```

FIGURE 6.9:   Constructor for the new Month class.

anticipating future use may result in the creation of useless functions, as we shall see below. **Design Principle 7. Mutators** guides this choice.

6.4   Managing the Ripple Effect

Whenever new code is added to an existing code base, its interactions with the existing code must be critically reviewed. This review helps ensure that no new features have accidentally broken existing features. It also helps ensure that redundancy has not crept into the code base.

Ensuring that the changes have not introduced faults in the existing code is largely handled by extending the unit tests to cover the additional features. Ensuring that redundancy has not crept into the code base is the reason why refactoring is needed at this step as well.

In all, the Code–Refactor–Unit Test triangle introduced in Figure 5.1 is very much in play here. That is, every time we add new code, we must unit test and debug that code. In turn, adding and unit testing new code typically unearths new opportunities for refactoring.

6.4.1   Unit Testing the New Code

Adding a new instance variable, adding/modifying a function, or adding an entirely new class or module to the code base requires adding assertions to the unit test base to ensure that the variable, function, class, or module behaves as intended. This must be done at all levels of architecture, beginning with the domain classes.

A suite of unit tests for *RMH Homebase* was inherited from its current release 1.5, and it can be used as a basis for developing version 2.0. Within this suite is a collection of unit tests for the domain classes, the databases modules, and the user interface modules. The unit tests for the domain classes are the following:

```
testPerson.php
testShift.php
testSCL.php
testRMHdate.php
testWeek.php
```

As we add the new features described above (and detailed in Appendix B), some of these unit tests must be augmented with additional tests for the new functionality required by these new features. For example, a new test must be added to cover the functionality of the new Month class. Thus, we can anticipate developing a new test suite that has the following components:

```
testPerson.php*
testShift.php*
testSCL.php
testRMHdate.php
testWeek.php
testMonth.php*
```

In this list, asterisks (*) indicate those unit tests that need to be augmented to test the new features added to the domain classes. Here, it is important to emphasize that a unit test may be modified either prior to, during, or following the writing of the new code itself, depending on how closely we follow the philosophy of test-driven development (TDD). When creating the new Month class, in fact, we developed the new testMonth.php' assertions as we went.

To illustrate how a unit tests changes as a result of adding new functionality to an existing class, consider the new elements that were added to the unit test for the Shift class shown in Figure 6.10. Here, we see the addition of new assertions aimed at checking the validity of the new `set_start_end_time` and `get_name` functions. Three of these provide a valid resetting of the shift's times and the other three provide an erroneous one.

We emphasize that these assertions provide only minimal tests for the new functions. The remaining assertions in this unit test are aimed at testing existing functions in the Shift class. These should continue to succeed whenever other new features are added to the class.[7]

---

[7]Adding new assertions to gain better code coverage for these functions is left as an exercise.

```
class testShift extends UnitTestCase {
 function testShiftModule() {
    $noonshift = new Shift("03-28-08-12-15",3, null, "", "");
    $this->assertEqual($noonshift->get_name(), "12-15");
    $this->assertTrue($noonshift->get_id() == "03-28-08-12-15");
// Test new function for resetting shift's start/end time
    $this->assertTrue($noonshift->set_start_end_time(15,17));
    $this->assertTrue($noonshift->get_id() == "03-28-08-15-17");
    $this->assertTrue($noonshift->get_name() == "15-17");
// Be sure that invalid times are caught.
    $this->assertFalse($noonshift->set_start_end_time(13,12));
    $this->assertTrue($noonshift->get_id() == "03-28-08-15-17");
    $this->assertTrue($noonshift->get_name() == "15-17");
    $this->assertTrue($noonshift->num_vacancies() == 3);
    $this->assertTrue($noonshift->get_day() == "Fri");
    $this->assertFalse($noonshift->has_sub_call_list());
    ...
    echo ("testShift complete");
 }
}
```

FIGURE 6.10: Augmenting the unit test for the Shift class.

To illustrate how unit tests change as a result of adding an entirely new class to the code base, consider the new unit test for the new Month class shown in Figure 6.11. Notice here that there is a unit test included for each of the accessor functions as well as the Month constructor. The Month constructor is somewhat tricky to develop because it generates an individual RMHdate $id for every day in the month. The Week class, on the other hand, assumes that these $ids are generated by the caller.

The key code in the constructor that generates these $ids is shown in Figure 6.12. We actually developed this code after writing down a couple of the assertions shown in Figure 6.11. This is the essence of TDD.

Debugging this code requires care because the PHP array indexes begin at 0, while the days of the month begin at 1. Moreover, the RMHdate's $id field retains leading zeroes in the day number, so that March 1, 2008 has an $id of 03-01-08, not 3-1-08. Thus, we need two loops to sort this out, and each loop must start and stop at the right value.

A good unit test should uncover little issues like these whenever a new function is developed. This creates a high level of trust during development of the database and user interface modules that will need to call that function.

Augmenting the testPerson.php class to test the elements of the Person class added to support new features 1 and 9d is also left as an exercise.

```
class testMonth extends UnitTestCase {
function testMonthModule() {

    $m=new Month("03","08");
    $this->assertEqual($m->get_name(), "March, 2008");
    $this->assertTrue($m->get_id()=="03-01-08");
    $this->assertTrue($m->get_start()==6);
    $dates=$m->get_dates();
    $this->assertTrue($dates[1]->get_id()=="03-02-08");
    $this->assertTrue($m->get_days() == 31);

    echo "testMonth complete";
    }
}
```

FIGURE 6.11: New unit test for the Month class.

```
$this->dates[0] = new RMHdate(
    $mm."-01-".$yy,null,"","");
for ($i=1; $i<=8; $i++)
    $this->dates[] = new RMHdate(
        $mm."-0".($i+1)."-".$yy,null,"","");
for ($i=9; $i<$this->days; $i++)
    $this->dates[] = new RMHdate(
        $mm."-".($i+1)."-".$yy,null,"","");
```

FIGURE 6.12: Generating the dates for a new Month.

6.4.2   Refactoring the New Code Base

Adding new code to the code base creates opportunities for refactoring. Whenever a domain class is modified, the entire class can be reexamined to see if it has any redundant or useless functions or instance variables.

A function is *redundant* if the work that it does can be accomplished by one or more other functions. An instance variable is redundant if the information it contains also appears in other instance variables.

A function is *useless* if it is not called from anywhere else in the code base. An easy way to examine a function for uselessness is to invoke the IDE's search tool to find all references to that function from elsewhere in the code base. If there are no references, that function can be safely deleted from the class.

However, this step must be taken with caution. That is, a new function may have been added with the expectation that it will be called by later additions to the database or user interface modules. Thus, later refactorings, especially after the user interface modules have been changed to support new features, will be necessary.

These considerations notwithstanding, let's take a look at the functions in the Person class to see if there are any useless ones hanging around. Using the Search feature of Eclipse, we select each function in turn and search for all references (calls) to that function from elsewhere in the code base. This activity reveals the following insights:

1. Each of the accessors ("getters") defined for the Person class is called at least once, usually by the personForm.inc script in the user interface. So none of these can be removed.

2. On the other hand, none of the mutators ("setters") in the Person class is called. Thus, all of these can be removed.

3. Not all the other functions are called either. Here are the ones that are not called: is_type, is_available, and is_scheduled.

The second and third items above raise an obvious question and concern. For example, we know that a Person can change her personal information, such as her e-mail, in the database. So why isn't there any call in the code base to the set_email mutator? The answer to this question is tied up in the design of the database and user interface modules. In short, when a Person changes any of his/her personal information on a form, an entirely new object is created using the Person constructor. Changes to individual variables, like email, are therefore not ever made independently of this single overall action.

Is this a good design decision? If so, we can safely remove all the mutators from the Person class. If not, we should not remove these mutators and instead we should consider refactoring the database and user interface classes so that these mutators are better utilized. We return to this question in Chapters 7 and 8. For the time being, it does no harm to leave these functions unchanged in the Person class.

The same question can be raised for the useless functions listed in the third item above. For example, if the function is_type is never called, how does the code base answer questions like, "Is Person x a volunteer?" The answer is again tied up in the design of the database and user interface classes, so we will return to this question in Chapters 7 and 8. For the time being, it does no harm to leave these functions unchanged in the Person class.

However, for every *new* domain class we add to the code base, we can assume for now that all the functions and variables are necessary. Later opportunities for refactoring a new domain class will occur after the new features have been incorporated into the database and user interface modules. In the case of *RMH Homebase*, building the new Month class should not require initial refactoring at this point in the process.

Nevertheless, building a new class can suggest refactoring and simplification of other related classes, especially those after which the new class has been modeled. For example, in *RMH Homebase*, our new Month class causes us to look critically at the existing Week class from which it has been built. We notice that the constructor for a week does not contain code that generates an array of 7 days for that week—instead, that task is left to the caller. The constructor for a Month, on the other hand, does incorporate such code. This refactoring activity is left as an exercise.

6.5   Summary

This chapter has focused on the design and development of the domain classes in a software code base. Seven principles of class design govern this work: need, information hiding, object integrity, cohesion, coupling, accessors, and mutators.

We have illustrated these principles by walking through the process of reading the code base and adding new features to it that respond to new requirements requested by the user. We have learned that adding each new feature is necessarily accompanied by adding new unit tests and refactoring existing code.

The next two chapters continue this discussion by completing the addition of these new features to the database and user interface modules of the same code base. That work will provide opportunities to present and illustrate the principles and practice of database and user interface development.

Exercises

6.1 For the Person class, define a new pair of functions to set and retrieve the value of the variables $employer, $contact_person, and $contact_phone in preparation for implementing new features 1 and 9d in *RMH Homebase*.

6.2 Add four new parameters and corresponding assignments to the constructor for the Person class, so that the status, employer, contact person, and contact person's phone are properly initialized. Use the following prototype for your new constructor:

```
function __construct($f, $l, $a, $c, $s, $z, $p1, $p2, $e,
    $t, $status, $employer, $contact, $contact_phone,
    ... )
```

6.3 The set_status function defined in this chapter does not check that the $value passed is valid: either `active` or `inactive`. Thus, whatever

$value is passed becomes a Person's status. Suggest a modification of this function that would perform that check. What value should it assign to a Person's status when the $value passed is invalid? Discuss the unit testing implications of your design decision.

6.4 Refactor the existing Person class by removing all the mutators that are not called from anywhere in the code base. Be sure to test your changes by rerunning the test suite.

6.5 Refactor the existing Week class using the constructor for the new Month class as an inspiration. That is, change the definition of the first parameter in the constructor so that it takes a single date as an argument (such as "03-01-08") and generates an array of seven dates that include that one. Be sure that the first date in the array is a Sunday and the last date is a Saturday. Now search for all calls to the Week constructor in the code base and modify them so that they pass the correct first argument. Be sure to modify the unit test testWeek.php and test your changes!

6.6 Complete of the remaining accessor functions for the new Month class, using the guidelines suggested in Section 6.3.2.

6.7 Add new elements to the testPerson.php class to test the additional features added to that class by new requirements 1 and 9d.

6.8 If you are working on a community-oriented FOSS project, conduct a careful review and testing of that portion of its code base on which you will be working.

    a. Read the source code and its documentation carefully with the goal of understanding the domain classes and their role in the overall architecture of the system.

    b. Run the software using your IDE and the software stack you implemented for it in the previous chapter.

    c. Identify any bugs you encounter and report them on your project's bug tracker.

    d. Identify any features you think should be improved or added and report them on the bug tracker.

    e. Identify and fix any documentation errors or deficiencies that you discover and submit your suggested improvements as patches to the code base. You'll be graded on the thoroughness of your review, the quality of the patches you contribute, and the helpfulness of your suggestions for improvement.

Chapter 7

Developing the Database Modules

"Errors using inadequate data are much less than
those using no data at all."
—*Charles Babbage*

This chapter continues the discussion of adding new features to a code base by focusing on the database aspects of software development. In this discussion, we assume that readers have more limited experience with principles of database design than they do with those of class design and data structures.

The first two sections introduce principles of database design using MySQL as a basis. This includes notions of tables and normalization, database and table creation, and table searching, insertion, and deletion.[1]

The third section discusses the important topic of software security at the database level, including encrypting user passwords and locating vulnerabilities such as SQL injection. It also identifies how the relationship between the database and the overall software architecture can be isolated into modules to minimize coupling.

The fourth section focuses on adding new features described in Appendix B to the database modules in an existing code base. This process includes developing unit tests and refactoring existing code.[2]

---

[1]MySQL is a widely used open source database platform, and it is also firmly based in mathematics. MySQL's databases are particularly straightforward to set up and maintain, and it provides a lot of tutorial material to support learning at all levels. Moreover, *RMH Homebase* is developed using MySQL, so we have a ready source of examples.

[2]To facilitate hands-on engagement with adding new features, readers are encouraged to download and install the *sandbox version* of *RMH Homebase* release 2.0 from the book's Web site myopensoftware.org/textbook. Release 2.0 has some of the code enhancements and refactorings of the release 1.5 database modules that are needed to support the new features described in Appendix B. Other enhancements and refactorings needed to support these new features are left as team exercises.

7.1   Design Principles and Practice

A *database* is a collection of data organized in a particular way for efficient computerized storage and retrieval. Databases can be simple, as in a collection of flat files, or more complex, as in a relational database, a distributed database, or a hierarchical database.

Databases reside at the heart of most viable software applications. A database differs from a class or object primarily because its data remain in a permanent place, such as a disk partition, outside the memory where the program runs. Often this place is on a different computer from the computer(s) that people use to access it. Such a place is usually called a "server" and, as we discussed in Chapter 4, efficient access to the database requires Internet connectivity and a client-server software design.

The data in a database are distinctive because they live in a time continuum that exceeds the life of the program or programs that access those data. This characteristic is known as *persistence*. In practice, one program may create a database, while others may access its data and still others may modify its data. At the end of the day, the data in a database live on, or "persist," while the different client programs that access them may have come and gone.

There are several different models for representing a database, ranging from simple to complex. A database model that is quite popular and accessible is called the *relational model*. Relational databases are convenient because their data can be stored as a collection of two-dimensional tables, they are reliable,[3] they can be accessed efficiently, and their implementations are well understood throughout the software development community.

An implementation of a database model is called a "database management system" or DBMS for short. A particularly popular DBMS for relational databases is called MySQL (see http://mysql.com/). We shall use MySQL for our examples throughout this chapter and the remainder of this book.[4]

---

[3]In fact, the theory of relational databases is grounded firmly in mathematics (see http://en.wikipedia.org/wiki/Relational_model for more information).

[4]MySQL actually dates back to 1970, when IBM researchers created a simple non-procedural language called Structured English Query Language. or SEQUEL [Cod70]. This was based on a relational model for data storage that included a universal programming language for accessing databases. In the late 1980s ANSI and ISO published a standardized version of SEQUEL called SQL (for Structured Query Language). Several versions of SQL subsequently evolved, and SQL-92 is the current standard. Thus, SQL is a language used to query relational databases and MySQL is a particular DBMS for SQL that has become widely used.

```
CREATE USER 'rmhDB'@'localhost' IDENTIFIED BY '*****';
GRANT ALL PRIVILEGES ON * . * TO 'rmhDB'@'localhost'
    IDENTIFIED BY '*****' WITH GRANT OPTION
    MAX_QUERIES_PER_HOUR 0
    MAX_CONNECTIONS_PER_HOUR 0
    MAX_UPDATES_PER_HOUR 0
    MAX_USER_CONNECTIONS 0 ;

CREATE DATABASE IF NOT EXISTS 'rmhDB' ;
GRANT ALL PRIVILEGES ON 'rmhDB' . * TO 'rmhDB'@'localhost';
```

FIGURE 7.1: MySQL commands to create a new user and database.

7.1.1 Database Creation

Before we can work with the information in a database, the database must first be created and initialized. Initialization establishes certain security constraints, such as the names of users who can access the database, their passwords, and the read/write/update privileges that are available to each user.

Typically, database creation is done at an administrative level separate from the software code base itself. By the time the software needs to access the database, the database should already have been created and at least one username and password by which one can gain read/write access to the database should also have been created.

Setting up a MySQL database is particularly easy when our testing environment is running a LAMP (or WAMP or MAMP, depending on whether you are developing on a Linux, Windows, or Macintosh) server. LAMP is an open source package that bundles Linux, an Apache server, MySQL, and PHP together, and it comes with a very nice user interface that facilitates common tasks like database creation and exploration.[5]

For example, to create a MySQL database called rmhDB, we need to be sure that an xAMP (that is, LAMP, WAMP, or MAMP) server is running on the machine where the database will reside. We also need to have access to the server at an administrative level so that we can create the database along with appropriate usernames and passwords. Figure 7.2 shows the result of creating the database rmhDB and one authenticated user with the MySQL commands shown in Figure 7.1.

This is the first example of MySQL code that you will see in this chapter. This style is used for all MySQL commands that retrieve and update information in the database.[6] It is a rather arcane style, but it is straightforward

---

[5]For more information on setting up a LAMP, WAMP, or MAMP database server on your local machine for development purposes, see the book's Web site myopensoftware.org/textbook.

[6]ALL CAPS are used in our examples, though MySQL is not strictly case sensitive.

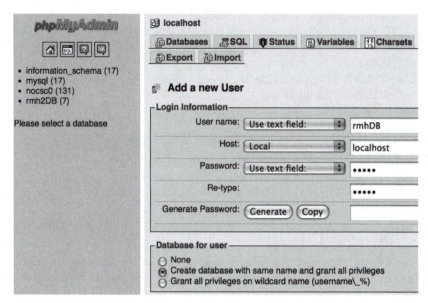

FIGURE 7.2:   Creating a new database using LAMP.

to learn and use. Notice also that the user id and the database name are the same. This is not required by MySQL, but it is required by some Web hosting services that support MySQL databases.

7.1.2   Connecting the Program to the Database

Because of their importance to software development, useful database management systems are well integrated with popular programming languages. This means that one can embed a database query directly within the source code whenever a database action is needed. Table 7.1 lists some popular languages with which MySQL is connected in this way.

TABLE 7.1:   MySQL Language Connections

Programming Language	MySQL Connector
Java	Connector/J
C++	Connector/C++
C	Connector/C
PHP	mysqli
Perl	DBD::mysql
Python	MySQLdb
Ruby	ruby-mysql

```
function connect() {
    $host = "localhost";
    $database = "rmhDB";
    $user = "rmhDB";
    $password = "rmhDB";
    $connected = mysql_connect($host, $user, $password);
    if (!$connected) return mysql_error();
    $selected = mysql_select_db($database, $connected);
    if (!$selected) return mysql_error();
    else return true;
}
```

FIGURE 7.3: Connecting to the *RMH Homebase* database.

Since we are working with PHP in this book, let's look at the key commands
that enable a PHP program to work with a MySQL database.

mysql_connect($host, $user, $password) connects the program with the
    database server $host, submitting $user and $password access infor-
    mation. No other database actions can be performed until a connection
    to the database has been established. The command returns false if the
    connection is not established.

mysql_select_db($database, $connected) After a connection is estab-
    lished, a particular $database must be selected. The $connected pa-
    rameter is set to false if this command fails.

mysql_error() returns the particular MySQL error message that accompa-
    nies the most recent database command.

mysql_close() disconnects the program from the server and the database.

mysql_query($query) A $query can either create or drop a table from the
    database, or else it can select, insert, update, or delete rows from a
    table. We discuss queries in more detail below.

Since establishing a connection with a database is such a frequent activity,
it is useful to write a separate PHP function that accomplishes that. For
example, Figure 7.3 shows the function used to connect RMH Homebase to
its database.

Establishing a connection to a database is thus a two-step process. First,
a connection to the server, or host, must be made. Second, the particular
database must be selected. Either one of these may fail, in which the call
returns the mysql_error() function call that delivers information about what
went wrong. Otherwise, the function in Figure 7.3 returns true.

id	month	day	year	shifts	chef_notes	mgr_notes
02-22-10	02	22	10	02-22-10-9-12*02-22-10-12-3*02-22-10-3-6*02-22-10-...		
02-23-10	02	23	10	02-23-10-9-12*02-23-10-12-3*02-23-10-3-6*02-23-10-...		
02-24-10	02	24	10	02-24-10-9-12*02-24-10-12-3*02-24-10-3-6*02-24-10-...		
02-25-10	02	25	10	02-25-10-9-12*02-25-10-12-3*02-25-10-3-6*02-25-10-...		
02-26-10	02	26	10	02-26-10-9-12*02-26-10-12-3*02-26-10-3-6*02-26-10-...		
02-27-10	02	27	10	02-27-10-10-1*02-27-10-1-4*02-27-10-night		
02-28-10	02	28	10	02-28-10-9-12*02-28-10-2-5*02-28-10-5-9		

FIGURE 7.4:   A view of the dbDates table.

7.1.3   Tables

A database is a collection of tables, and each table has a distinct name, a fixed number of columns, and a varying number of rows. The *RMH Homebase* 1.5 database, for example, has seven tables, named dbDates, dbLog, dbPersons, dbSchedules, dbSCL, dbShifts, and dbWeeks. All tables but the dbLog and dbSchedules tables correspond to a particular domain class, as their names suggest.

All the permanent data for *RMH Homebase* are stored in these seven tables. Any change to a schedule, a calendar, or a personnel entry requires that one or more of these tables be modified. Database modification is a discipline whose principles are the focus of this chapter.

Each column (called an *attribute*) of a table has a unique name and a data type. So, in a sense, a table column is like a variable. Each row of a table designates a particular instantiation of the values for these variables. For example, a row of the dbDates table contains the information corresponding to a single RMHdate, while each row of the dbPersons table has information for a particular Person.

For example, let's look at the seven attributes of the dbDates table that are shown in Figure 7.4. These are named id, month, day, year, shifts, chef_notes, and mgr_notes. Each row identifies a particular object from the RMHdate class, so that attributes in the dbDates table have corresponding instance variables in the RMHdate class. As a matter of good naming practice, we try to keep the names of a table's attributes identical with the names of the instance variables (absent the leading $) of its corresponding class.

Each row of the dbDates table has a unique *key*, designating a distinct date on the *RMH Homebase* calendar. Each row, and hence each date, identifies a collection of shifts to be filled, designated by an asterisk-separated list of Shift id's. For example, the date 02-28-10 has three shifts with ids 02-28-10-9-12, 02-28-10-2-5, and 02-28-10-5-9.[7]

---

[7]Remember, we are working with version 1.5 of *RMH Homebase*, so that shift times are not yet represented on a 24-hour continuum as they will be in version 2.0. We return to this problem later in the chapter, when we modify the database modules to support the new features in version 2.0.

7.1.3.1   Table Naming Conventions

The foregoing discussion, along with Chapter 4, suggests an important design principle that helps immensely as we read and modify the database modules inside a code base. This principle is based on the idea that each of the domain classes in a software architecture usually has a related database table. In such cases, the class's instance variables correspond with the column headings in its related database table, and a row in the table can easily be viewed as an object in the class.

This relationship suggests an important naming convention for developers: *use names that unify classes and instance variables with their corresponding database tables and column headings.* For instance, the following naming convention is used throughout the design of *RMH Homebase*:

- If a class has name C, then its corresponding database table is named dbCs. While class C represents a type of object, its corresponding database table dbCs contains several occurrences of such objects.

- Each instance variable V in class C has a corresponding column heading named V in table dbCs.

- Each database table dbCs has a corresponding module dbCs.php (assuming the programming language is PHP) in the code base.

For example, each Shift (see Figure A.16) has a unique $id that distinguishes it from all the other shifts on the calendar. The instance variables in the Shift class are:

```
private $mm_dd_yy; // String: "mm-dd-yy".
private $name;   // String: '9-12', '12-3', '3-6', '9-12Fam',
                 // '12-3Fam', '3-6Fam', '6-9', '10-1',
                 // '1-4', '12-2', '2-5', 'night', or 'chef'
private $vacancies;   // number of vacancies in this shift
private $persons;     // array of persons,
                 // eg "max1234567890+Max+Jones"
private $sub_call_list; // "yes"  if SCL exists
private $day;         // string name of month "Monday"...
private $id;       // unique key "mm-dd-yy-ss-ss"
                 // or "mm-dd-yy-ss-ssFam"  or "mm-dd-yy-chef"
private $notes;   // notes written by the manager
```

The Shift class has a corresponding database table called dbShifts. A single row in this table represents a single shift, and it has the following columns:

```
id      mm-dd-yy-ss-ss or mm-dd-yy-ss-ssFam or mm-dd-yy-chef
vacancies    # of vacancies for this shift
persons      list of persons, eg "max1234567890+Max+Jones"
sub_call_list "yes" if shift has a SCL
notes        shift notes
```

To gain more insight into this correspondence, we can examine a few entries in the dbShifts table directly. For example, four entries in the dbShifts table for Wednesday September 2, 2009 are shown in Figure 7.5.

```
id            vacancies persons                             sub_call_list
09-02-09-6-9   2        jerome2077291234+jerome+jones          yes
09-02-09-3-6   1        esther2077291234+esther+jones
09-02-09-12-3  0        mary2077291234+mary+jones*meg207...
09-02-09-9-12  0        linda2077291234+linda+jones*orminia207...
```

FIGURE 7.5: Shifts in the database for September 2, 2009.

We can learn a lot by examining a small sample of data such as this. Notice that each shift's $id is different from all the others, distinguished by a unique date-time value. Notice also that the number of vacancies in a shift is explicit, and related to the length of the list of volunteers who are scheduled for that shift. Notice finally that only one shift has a Sub Call List generated for it, the 6-9 shift.

Some database modules and their tables may not have a corresponding domain class. For example, *RMH Homebase* has the following additional database tables:

dbLog stores a series of entries that keep track of individual calendar changes when they occur and who made them. Individual calendar changes can be made by any volunteer, for example to remove themselves from a shift or to add a person to fill a vacancy on a shift after obtaining their agreement. This log is accessible only to the House Manager.

dbSchedules stores the Master Schedule, which is the basis from which individual weeks on the calendar are generated and populated with volunteers, in accordance with their availability.

To learn more about these tables and their uses, look at some sample entries and read their corresponding modules in the *RMH Homebase* release 1.5 code base.

7.1.4 Normalization and Keys

In database design, *normalization* refers to a strategy for designing tables so that they support general-purpose querying and ensure data integrity. E. F. Codd, inventor of the relational model, introduced the idea of normalization in 1970.[8] A major goal of normalization is to allow tables to be queried using

---

[8]For more details, see http://en.wikipedia.org/wiki/Database_normalization

a standarized language, like MySQL, that is grounded in mathematical logic.

Informally, a relational database table is "normalized" if it satisfies the following criteria:

1. The rows can be rearranged without changing the meaning of the table (i.e., there's no implicit ordering or functional interdependency among the rows).

2. The columns can be rearranged without changing the meaning of the table (i.e., there's no implicit ordering or functional interdependency among the columns).

3. No two rows of a table are identical. This is often accomplished by defining one column whose values are mutually unique. This column is known as the table's *primary key*.

4. No row has any hidden components, such as an object id or a timestamp.

5. Every entry in the table has exactly one value of the appropriate type.

6. No attribute in the table is redundant with (i.e., appears as an explicit substring of) the *primary key*.

There are several disadvantages to working with unnormalized tables. For example, querying an unnormalized table can create more complexity than is needed, or else unanticipated side effects (known as "anomalies") may occur.

For example, when a table does not satisfy criterion 3 above, it permits the creation of two or more identical (redundant) rows. Updating an entry in one such row, without doing the same for its identical twin, may introduce an inconsistency into the table.

Another type of anomaly can occur when information cannot be recorded in the table at all. This situation arises when trying to insert a row for which only some of the entries are known (violating criterion 5 above). One way to circumvent this anomaly is to agree that absence of information in a row will be recorded as the `null` value, or equivalently the empty string.

Thus, normalization is good database design practice. While the tables in *RMH Homebase* satisfy most of the criteria listed above, they are not all fully normalized. For example, the dbDates table shown in Figure 7.4 violates both criteria 5 and 6. That is, a date can contain a series of shifts (not just one), and the month, day, and year attributes are redundant with the primary key (id).

7.1.5 Backup and Recovery

A major administrative concern for databases is to ensure that they retain their integrity in the event of an unexpected catastrophe. A database usually contains millions of individual data items, far too many to recover one-by-one

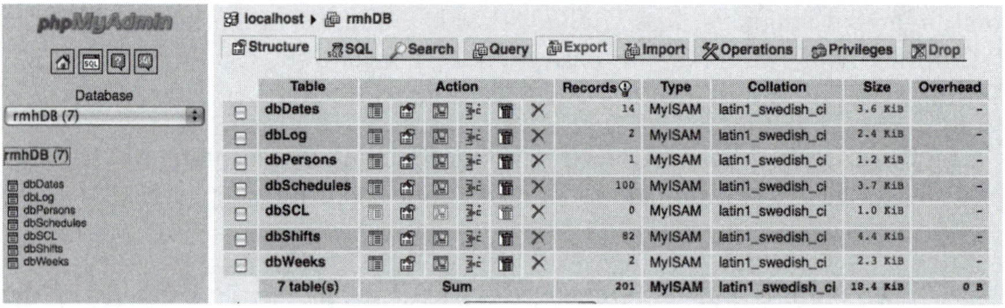

FIGURE 7.6: Backing up a database using LAMP.

if they are suddenly lost. Rather than think about recovering the data in this way, a common strategy is to create a backup copy of the entire database on a regular basis.

Therefore, a fundamental requirement for designing databases is to understand conventional backup and recovery techniques and to build a backup schedule to take effect as soon as the database goes into "live" operation.

Modern DBMS systems provide useful tools for backing up a database. For example, a MySQL database can be backed up in a single step using an "export" command. This command can create a backup copy of the database, or even a single table, in the form of a flat text file (either compressed or uncompressed). The "import" command provides the reverse action—it is used to recover all the tables in a database from a backup copy.

The LAMP user interface provides direct backup and restore capabilities through its user interface. For example, the rmhDB database can be backed up and recovered using the "Export" tab and the "Import" tab shown in Figure 7.6, respectively.

7.2 Working with a Database

Three important types of actions are used when maintaining a table in a MySQL database.

1. The table must first be created.

2. Individual rows of the table can then be retrieved, added, deleted, or changed (updated).

3. The table can be removed from the database, or *dropped*, in which case all its data are also lost.

Correspondingly, every table in a database should provide developers with functions to *C*reate it, *R*etrieve information from it, *U*pdate it, and *D*elete it (affectionately called *CRUD* for short).[9] These four CRUD functions are supported in various ways by different database management systems.

In MySQL, each CRUD function is accomplished by executing a particular type of *query*.[10] Here is a summary of these queries and their uses.[11]

`CREATE TABLE tablename (attribute type, attribute type, ...,`
`PRIMARY KEY attribute)` creates a new table in the database with one column for each attribute-type pair listed. The `PRIMARY KEY` clause identifies that attribute which distinguishes one row from all other rows in the table.

`DROP TABLE IF EXISTS tablename` removes a table from the database.

`SELECT * FROM tablename WHERE relation` returns either a non-empty array of rows or false, depending on whether or not any rows in the table satisfy the given relation.

`INSERT INTO tablename VALUES (value, value, ...)` inserts a new row into the table associating each of the values with the columns defined in the `CREATE` command for that table, from left to right.

`DELETE FROM tablename WHERE relation` removes all rows from the table that satisfy the given relation.

`UPDATE tablename SET attribute = value, attribute = value, ...`
`WHERE relation` changes the attributes' values in the table for all rows that satisfy the given relation.

Execution of a MySQL query relies on the presence of a "current database." Thus, a database connection must be established prior to executing any of these queries on a particular table.

When used in this context, `relation` denotes any Boolean-valued expression that defines the criteria by which a row is included in the result of the query. This relation uses common relational operators, AND, OR, constants, and the names of table attributes as arguments. Table 7.2 summarizes some of the common relations and their meanings. Several examples of using relations in MySQL queries are given in the discussion below.

---

[9]Other more-or-less flattering acronyms have also been used. For a discussion, see http://en.wikipedia.org/wiki/Create,_read,_update_and_delete.

[10]The term *query* is somewhat of a misnomer, since queries not only retrieve information from tables but they also insert, update, and delete individual rows as well as create and drop entire tables.

[11]More complete introductions to the MySQL query types can be found at many Web sites; a particularly good one is http://www.mysqltutorial.org.

TABLE 7.2:   Common Relations Used in a MySQL Query

Relation	Meaning
attribute = v	the attribute's value is v
attribute <> v	the attribute's value is not v
attribute IS NOT NULL	the attribute's value is not NULL
attribute LIKE pattern	the attribute's value matches the pattern
expression AND expression	both expressions are true
expression OR expression	either one or both expressions are true
NOT (expression)	expression is false

7.2.1   Table Creation

Table creation is a one-time event, serving only to establish the table's name, column names, and associated column types within the database. Table creation can be done using the template shown in Figure 7.7.

To use this template, the programmer should replace the phrases "table-name" and "list of attributes and their types" by an actual table name and list of attributes and types.

The `connect()` command opens a connection to the database by calling the function defined in Figure 7.3. Once a connection is established, the second command ensures that any earlier version of the table is dropped from the database. The `IF EXISTS` clause acts like a conditional statement—if the table doesn't exist, no attempt will be made to drop it.

The third command in this sequence creates the table in the database with a unique `tablename`. Following this is a list of arguments that define the names and types of the attributes (columns) that define the table. The next three lines check to be sure the table was created successfully by interrogating the `$result` variable. If not, a MySQL error is reported. In either case, the last line closes the connection to the database.

The types of values that can be stored in a MySQL table are many and varied. A summary of the most common ones is given in Table 7.3. When an attribute has the `NOT NULL` phrase appended, this means that the `NULL`

```
function setup_tablename() {
    connect();
    mysql_query("DROP TABLE IF EXISTS tablename");
    $result=mysql_query("CREATE TABLE tablename" .
        "(list of attributes and their types)");
    if(!$result)
        echo mysql_error();
    mysql_close();
}
```

FIGURE 7.7:   Template for MySQL table creation.

TABLE 7.3: Common Attribute Types in MySQL Tables

Type	Meaning
INT	an integer in the range $-2^{31} \ldots 2^{31-1}$
TIMESTAMP	a timestamp in the form yyyymmddhhmmss
CHAR (m)	a fixed-length string of m characters ($0 < m < 255$)
VARCHAR (m)	a string of up to m characters ($0 < m < 255$)
TEXT	a string of up to 65,535 characters

value is not permitted in any row for that attribute. The list of attributes can also contain the expression PRIMARY KEY (attribute), which means the given attribute serves as the primary key for the table.

To illustrate these ideas, Figure 7.8 shows the function that creates the dbDates table in the *RMH Homebase* database using the protocol shown in Figure 7.7. This definition of the dbDates table requires that no row's id attribute be NULL and that the id attribute also serves as the table's primary key (guaranteeing that every row must have a unique id).

7.2.2 Table Searching

Normalized tables are suitable for general purpose searching. This means any queries against these tables, including future queries whose details cannot be anticipated, return reasonable results.

The query SELECT * FROM tablename WHERE relation searches the table named tablename and returns a so-called "resource" that contains all rows that satisfy relation. The latter is a relational expression describing attributes and values that can satisfy the search.

Omission of the WHERE clause causes this query to return the entire table as the resource. For example, if we want to return all rows in the dbDates table, we would say:

```
function setup_dbDates() {
   connect();
   mysql_query("DROP TABLE IF EXISTS dbDates");
   $result=mysql_query("CREATE TABLE dbDates (id CHAR(8) " .
      "NOT NULL, month TEXT, day TEXT, year TEXT, " .
      "shifts TEXT, chef_notes TEXT, mgr_notes TEXT, " .
      "PRIMARY KEY (id))");
   if(!$result)
      echo mysql_error();
   mysql_close();
}
```

FIGURE 7.8: Creating the dbDates table in the rmhDB database.

```
$result = mysql_query("SELECT * FROM dbDates");
```

On the other hand, if we want to return a particular date from the dbDates table whose id is "02-22-10" (there can be no more than one, since id is the table's PRIMARY KEY), we can use the following pair of PHP functions to issue a MySQL query and then parse the result into an array.[12]

```
$result = mysql_query(
    "SELECT * FROM dbDates WHERE id = '02-22-10'");
if ($result !== false)
    $result_row = mysql_fetch_row($result);
```

The resource returned by the query in the first line will be either a series of rows from the dbDates table that have this particular primary key, or else false (if there are no such rows). To separate a single row into its individual fields, we can use the function that appears in the third line. This function returns the first row of the result as an array of values, in the order in which the columns of the table are defined, with indexes beginning at 0.

If we are not sure that only one row will be returned by a query, we can use a loop to process each row of the resource individually.

```
$result = mysql_query("SELECT * FROM dbDates " .
    "WHERE month = 2 AND day < 10");
while ($result_row = mysql_fetch_array($result))
    // process $result_row
```

Here, each call to the function mysql_fetch_array returns one row at a time from $result until there are no more left. At that point, null is returned, which causes the while loop to terminate. Thus, this loop will process each of the first 9 days in February, assuming they are in the dbDates table.[13]

Pattern matching is often useful when selecting rows from a table that satisfy a particular criterion. For example, if we want to find all persons in dbPersons table whose type contains the string "sub" (in general, a person can be an applicant, volunteer, sub, chef, or manager, or various combinations of these). Here is a query that returns a resource containing all such persons from the dbPersons table.

---

[12] A note about quotes: a MySQL query is treated as a character string by the PHP/MySQL connector. Thus, every call to mysql_query must pass a quoted string as an argument. This becomes tricky when the query itself has a character string embedded inside it, as in the current example. To keep one level of quotes distinct from the other, we can use a double quote character (") to encapsulate the query itself and a single quote character (') to encapsulate any string that is embedded inside the query.

[13] The mysql_fetch_array function has an optional second argument, MYSQL_ASSOC, which allows the result to be returned as an associative array. In this case, the indexes are the names of the attributes defined for the table. In our example, for instance, the reference $result_row['id'] is equivalent to the reference $result_row[0] if the second argument MYSQL_ASSOC had been included in the mysql_fetch_array function call.

```
$result = mysql_query("SELECT * FROM dbPersons WHERE " .
    "type LIKE '%sub%'");
```

Finally, we should mention the useful clause `ORDER BY attributes`. When used in a `SELECT` query, this clause will return the resource with its rows sorted into ascending order according to the attributes listed. For example, the following query returns a list of all persons in the dbPersons table who are volunteers, arranged into alphabetical order by last name and first name.

```
$query = "SELECT * FROM dbPersons WHERE " .
    "type LIKE '%volunteer%'  ORDER BY last_name, first_name";
$result = mysql_query($query);
```

7.2.3   Table Insertion, Deletion, and Updating

The query `INSERT INTO tablename VALUES (value, value, ...)` inserts a new row into the table associating each of the values with the columns defined in the `CREATE` command for that table, from left to right. It returns true or false, respectively, depending on whether the insertion was successful. For example, the following query inserts a row into the dbDates table corresponding to February 28, 2010, which has three shifts and no chef or manager notes, as shown in the last row of Figure 7.4.

```
$query = "INSERT INTO dbDates VALUES ('02-28-10', 2, 28, 10, " .
    "'02-28-10-9-12*02-28-10-2-5*02-28-10-5-9', '', '')";
$result = mysql_query($query);
```

Since the id attribute is the table's primary key, this query will fail (return false) if the table already has a row with id = "02-28-10." Otherwise, it will return true. The PHP variable $result can be used to check the success or failure of the query.

The query `DELETE FROM tablename WHERE relation` removes all rows from the table that satisfy the given relation. It returns true or false, respectively, depending on whether the deletion was successful. For example, the following query removes the row in the dbDates table corresponding to February 28, 2010 (if it is there).

```
$query = "DELETE FROM dbDates WHERE id = '02-28-10'";
$result = mysql_query($query);
```

Since id is the `PRIMARY KEY` for dbDates, there can be no more than one row with id = "02-28-10." The variable $result will be true or false, depending on whether that row was deleted from the table or not.

The query `UPDATE tablename SET attribute=value,attribute=value, ... WHERE relation` changes the attributes' values in the table for all rows that satisfy the given relation. It returns true or false, respectively, depending on whether the update was successful.

Suppose we want to change the arrangement of shift id's for the February 28, 2010 row in the dbDates table so that the 2–5pm shift becomes the 12–5pm shift instead. We can do this in either of two ways; change only the shifts attribute in the row corresponding to February 28, 2010 using the UPDATE query, or completely remove and re-insert that row in the dbDates table using DELETE and INSERT queries. Here is the UPDATE query that would accomplish this change:

```
$query = "UPDATE dbDates " .
    "SET shifts = '02-28-10-9-12*02-28-10-12-5*02-28-10-5-9' " .
    "WHERE id = '02-28-10'";
$result = mysql_query($query);
```

Here, we expect the $result variable to become true or false depending on whether the UPDATE is successful. The UPDATE will fail if there is no row in the dbDates table with id = "02-28-10."

7.3   Database Security and Integrity

As suggested in Chapter 4, a *secure* database is one that accomplishes all of the following goals:

- It prevents unauthorized or accidental disclosure, alteration, or destruction of data.

- It prevents unauthorized or accidental access to data considered confidential to the organization or individual who owns the data.

- It ensures *data integrity*, so that the data stored in the database are always valid and accurate.

To help ensure security, access to all tables must be properly controlled. This can be done by granting privileges that limit individual users to see only those portions of the data to which they should have access. For data that need to be very secure, implementation of an encryption strategy for individual table attributes or individual users may also be required.

In general, definition and enforcement of a security policy for a database requires careful consideration for the types of users and their different levels of access to the database that are permitted by the software system itself. For example, some types of users may be granted access to parts of the database, while others should have access to all of it. Moreover, some users should have read-only access to the data while others should have read-write access.

An additional element of database security is the importance of protecting the database against malicious attacks, as summarized in Chapter 4. Since many of these attacks originate at the user interface level, we shall discuss and illustrate these security issues in Chapter 8.

7.3.1 Database-Level Permissions

A DBMS comes with a built-in permission model, which allows the owner to specify which users have access and what level of access each user has. In the case of MySQL, permissions are controlled via the GRANT and REVOKE commands. Four levels of access can be controlled:

1. Server level: privileges that apply to all databases on the server

2. Database level: privileges that apply to all tables in a particular database on the server

3. Table level: privileges that apply to all columns of a particular table in the database

4. Column level: privileges that apply to an individual column of a table in the database.

The types of privileges that can be granted/revoked at each of these levels are directly aligned with the individual types of MySQL queries that were discussed earlier—Create, Drop, Select, Alter (Insert), Delete, and Update.

For example, the database administrator may assign privileges to individual users who connect to the database, depending on their roles. Alternatively, the administrator may simply assign all privileges to a single user. In turn, that user inherits the responsibility of limiting database access privileges to individual users of the software that interacts with the database.

In the case of *RMH Homebase*, this latter strategy is used (see Figure 7.1). That is, whenever a database connection is made during an individual user's session, the connection grants all the privileges listed above to that user's session. The session, in turn, knows the particular access level that any particular user has (a visitor has access level 1, a volunteer has 2, and a manager has 3), and regulates their access to the database accordingly. A discussion of how this strategy is implemented appears in Chapter 8.

7.3.2 User-Level Permissions

A software development strategy that ensures database security and integrity must adhere to all the constraints discussed in the foregoing sections.

In particular, the strategy must define the tables in such a way that they are normalized to the extent possible. It must limit user access to the database via secure login, so that each user session can be assigned an appropriate access level and thus be restricted from seeing/modifying parts of the database to which they should not have access. Finally, it must minimize the likelihood of deadlocks or other errors occurring when two or more sessions try to access the same table simultaneously.

In *RMH Homebase*, security and integrity are ensured by first defining the following access levels.

1. Each user's password is encrypted in the dbPersons table of the rmhDB database, so that it cannot be casually read by anyone who has access to the database. Password encryption is managed at the user interface level, and its mechanics are discussed in Chapter 8.

2. No user has read access to the dbPersons or dbSchedules table unless their "type" is coded as "manager," which is equivalent to session access level 3. Thus, managers can access all the personnel data in dbPersons. Also, only managers have write access to the dbWeeks and dbDates tables, which underlie the generation of each new calendar week and the initial scheduling of volunteers for that week.

3. No user has read access to the dbWeeks and dbShifts tables unless their "type" is "volunteer" (session access level 2) or "manager" (session access level 3). This allows them to view the weekly calendar schedule and update any shift for which they are scheduled. An individual volunteer also has read/write access to their own entry in the dbPersons table, so that they can update their own data whenever changes occur.

4. Site visitors (session access level 1) have read access only to the volunteer application form, which allows them restricted access to the dbPersons table (for inserting a single entry corresponding to their own personnel data). Visitors must login as "guest," and they have access to no other information in the database.

Second, *RMH Homebase* defines a separate module for each table, ensuring that every CRUD function for that table is implemented within that module. For example, the dbDates table has an associated module dbDates.php, which encapsulates all the functions that create, retrieve, update, and delete information from the dbDates table. All actions on the dbDates table should thus call an appropriate function in the dbDates module.

Third, to control concurrency and ensure the integrity of each CRUD function, each function is implemented in a way that enforces the following step-by-step protocol.

1. Connect to the database.

2. Perform the create, retrieve, update, or delete function.

3. Close the connection to the database.

4. Return a result that reflects the success or failure of the function.

```
/**
 * deletes a date from the dbDates table
 */
function delete_dbDates($d) {
    if (! $d instanceof RMHdate)
        die ("Invalid argument for dbShifts->remove_date call");
    connect();
    $query="DELETE FROM dbDates WHERE id=\"".$d->get_id()."\"";
    $result=mysql_query($query);
    if (!$result) {
        echo ("unable to delete from dbDates: ".
            $d->get_id(). mysql_error());
        mysql_close();
        return false;
    }
    mysql_close();
    $shifts=$d->get_shifts();
    foreach ($shifts as $key => $value) {
        $s = $d->get_shift($key);
        delete_dbShifts($s);
    }
    return true;
}
```

FIGURE 7.9:   Deleting a date from the dbDates table.

This protocol arises from the fact that the bare MySQL functions CREATE, SELECT, INSERT, DELETE, and UPDATE are not adequate by themselves to minimize the likelihood of deadlocks or ensure integrity of the result. For example, it would be naive to assume that whenever an INSERT query is executed a new row will always be inserted into the table. Things can and do go wrong. For example, if a row with the same primary key is already there, the INSERT will fail. If the arguments passed in an INSERT query are in any way invalid (e.g., there are too many arguments or one of them is not of the correct type), the INSERT will also fail.

Therefore, the implementation of each CRUD function inside a database module must be encapsulated inside a functional wrapper that reflects the above protocol. One example of this encapsulation appears in Figure 7.8. A second example of this encapsulation appears in Figure 7.9, which encapsulates the deletion of a row from the dbDates table.

This is an interesting example because it illustrates some of the various abnormal event checking that must be made to ensure that the caller knows exactly what happened when the DELETE query was issued. This example also illustrates a vulnerability that occurs if the database happens to crash just after a row is deleted from the dbDates table and just before its corresponding shifts are deleted from the dbShifts table.[14]

More illustrative examples of this encapsulation strategy appear throughout the database modules in the *RMH Homebase* code base, which can be directly examined at the book's Web site myopensoftware.org/textbook.

Finally, to enforce this protocol, all database actions that are required by non-database modules in the software system, especially the user interface modules, should accomplish those actions by calling an appropriate function defined inside that table's corresponding module rather than issuing MySQL queries from outside the database modules. This issue will be illustrated more fully in Chapter 8, where we will find refactoring opportunities among the *RMH Homebase* user interface modules.

7.3.3   Controlling Concurrency

MySQL uses *table locking* (instead of page, row, or column locking) to ensure database integrity when several users (sessions) are accessing the database at the same time.[15] This means that whenever a particular table in a database is accessed (via CREATE, SELECT, INSERT, DELETE, or UPDATE) by a particular user/session, that table becomes unavailable to all other users/sessions that are currently accessing the same database.

In most cases, table locking is a satisfactory vehicle for controlling concurrency, but there are some drawbacks:

- Table locking enables many sessions to read from (SELECT) a table at the same time, but if a session wants to write (INSERT, DELETE, or UPDATE) to a table, it must gain exclusive access. During a write, all other sessions that want to access this particular table must wait until the write is complete.

- Table locking can cause problems when a session is waiting because the disk is full and free space needs to become available before the session can proceed. In this event, all sessions that want to access the table are put in a waiting state until more disk space is made available.

- Table locking is also disadvantageous when a session issues a SELECT that takes a long time to run. If another session wants to issue an UPDATE on the same table, the new session must wait until the SELECT is finished.

---

[14]A more thorough treatment of this issue might use the concept of *rollback* to help the database gracefully recover from such an event. Interested readers should look at a database textbook for a more careful discussion.

[15]This discussion applies only to MySQL implementations that use the MyISAM storage engine. For the InnoDB and BDB engines, MySQL uses table locking only if the table is locked by a LOCK TABLES query. Otherwise, these engines use automatic row-level locking or page-level locking to ensure query isolation.

There are a variety of database design strategies for reducing contention among sessions when table locking is involved. Perhaps the most important ones are the following[16]:

1. Perform only one or two SELECT, INSERT, DELETE, or UPDATE queries during any single connection to the database; disconnect from the database at all times when no queries are being executed.

2. Try to ensure that each SELECT, INSERT, DELETE, or UPDATE query runs fast so that it locks a table for a minimum amount of time.

Of course, there is a performance price to be paid when these strategies are used. Ensuring high query speed might compromise the power of the MySQL query system to retrieve data, while limiting the number of queries per connection can compromise overall system performance in order to ensure concurrency control.

7.4 Adding New Software Features: Database Impact

In Chapter 6, we considered the impact of adding new features to a software system on the domain classes. As an example, we discussed how to incorporate the addition of a particular set of features presented in Appendix B into the domain classes of the existing code base for *RMH Homebase*.

All changes to the domain classes to incorporate new features have an inevitable ripple effect on the database modules and the user interface modules as well. Since the database modules are closely aligned with the domain classes, any change to the instance variables in the latter will immediately affect the column structure of the corresponding database tables. Other changes to the database modules or tables may be indicated by other new requirements that don't affect the domain classes.

Here is a summary of all the new features that affect the database modules (notice that only features 1, 3, 4, and 9d affect both the domain classes and database modules, while features 5 and 7 affect only the database modules).

1 Volunteer status—ability to categorize a volunteer as inactive preventing him or her from showing up on a sub list. This would be helpful to ensure volunteers on vacation or otherwise unavailable do not get called for shifts.
Impact on the code base:
Domain classes: Add a new instance variable "status" to the Person

---

[16]For other strategies, see http://dev.mysql.com/doc/refman/5.0/en/table-locking.html.

class, with appropriate changes to its constructors and other functions. *Database modules:* Add a new column "status" to the dbPersons table, with appropriate changes to the setup and other related functions.

3 **Calendar view**—In the current calendar view, shift times are hard to distinguish if the user is unfamiliar with it. For example, 9-12 looks like it could be 9-11. Moreover, sometimes a shift (especially a weekend shift) needs its start or end time to be changed by the user.
Impact on the code base:
Domain classes: Shift should be altered so that its start and end time can be changed (within the same day).
Database modules: dbShifts should be altered so that the start and end time of any shift in the database can be changed (within the same day).

4 **Calendar month view**—Is it possible to view one month at a time?
Nature: new feature
Impact on the code base:
Domain classes: Add a new class Month, which is a series of RMHdates. This could be organized similarly to the existing class Week.
Database modules: Add a new module dbMonths which has one row for each active or archived month. It would be organized similarly to the existing class dbWeeks.

5 **Import/export**—Can a person's data be exported to a comma-separated list for importing into an Excel-type of spreadsheet? Data so formatted could be imported to create a new Person in the database.
Impact on the code base:
Domain classes: none
Database modules: dbPersons needs a new function that would export an entry in the database into a text that could be downloaded by the user. Another new function should be added that imports a person and creates a new entry in the database.

7 **Vacancies and shifts worked**—information for the House Manager:

- A list of the upcoming vacancies on the manager's screen, ordered by date.

- The total and average number of vacancies for each day and shift, for any series of weeks in the past.

- The total and average number of shifts worked by any volunteer, for any series of weeks in the past.

Impact on the code base:

Domain classes: none

Database modules: Add functions to dbShifts and dbDates that accumulate the total and average numbers of vacancies for each shift and date over any series of weeks.

9d Volunteer application—We overlooked this when first submitting information to you: can fields be added such as employer's information and emergency contact?

Impact on the code base:

Domain classes: Add new fields and appropriate functions to the Person class.

Database modules: Add new fields and appropriate functions to the dbPersons module.

Once the database tables are appropriately modified, their associated CRUD functions must also be examined and modified, and then unit tested. Existing unit tests must be augmented in a way that tests the changes in the CRUD functions. Finally a refactoring of the database modules is particulary important at this point; we need to pay special attention to ensure that each table is normalized to the extent possible, and that its related CRUD functions will be appropriate to fulfill the needs of the augmented user interface modules.

To illustrate these activities, this discussion shows the changes required to implement the following new features in *RMH Homebase*, moving it forward from version 1.5 toward version 2.0. In this discussion, we assume that the changes discussed in Chapter 6 have already been applied to the domain classes and unit tested.

Each of the following sections considers one of these activities in isolation by discussing the new code it requires, along with the new unit tests and refactorings that are suggested by that new code.[17]

7.4.1   Items 1 and 9d: Volunteer Status and Application

This change requires us to modify the dbPersons table and associated module dbPersons.php by adding four new attributes. The model for this change is found in the modified instance variables for the Person class: $status, $employer, $contact_person, and $contact_phone (recall Figure 6.1). To be systematic about this activity, we review in turn each of the CRUD (create,

---

[17]Since much of these discussions refer to significant parts of the code base, we suggest that readers have the code base for versions 1.5 and 2.0 of *RMH Homebase* available for review as they read. These versions can be downloaded from the book's Web site myopensoftware.org/textbook.

```
function setup_dbPersons() {
    connect();
    mysql_query("DROP TABLE IF EXISTS dbPersons");
    mysql_query("CREATE TABLE dbPersons(id TEXT NOT NULL, ...
    ...
    " email TEXT, type TEXT, status TEXT, employer TEXT, " .
    " contact_person TEXT, contact_phone VARCHAR(12), " .
    " background_check TEXT, interview TEXT, shadow TEXT, " .
    ...
    " birthday TEXT, start_date TEXT, public_notes TEXT,  " .
    " my_notes TEXT, private_notes TEXT, password TEXT)");
    ...
    mysql_close();
}
```

FIGURE 7.10: New attributes defined in dbPersons table creation. (Unchanged lines are ellipsed.)

retrieve, update, and delete) functions that comprise the dbPersons.php module and modify the ones that are redundant with these four new attributes.

First, we see that the function that creates the dbPersons table must be modified so that four new column attributes are added to accommodate the new instance variables in the Person class. These new attributes are accordingly called status, employer, contact_person, and contact_phone. This modification is summarized in Figure 7.10, where unchanged lines are ellipsed.

Second, we see that the function that adds a person to the dbPersons table must accommodate these four new variables. The changes to this function are straightforward and they are summarized in Figure 7.11 (again, unchanged lines are ellipsed).

No other changes to the dbPersons module are needed to implement this new requirement. That is, none of the other retrieval, update, and delete functions in this module have dependencies on the four new attributes added to the table.

7.4.1.1   Unit Testing

To unit test these changes, we add assertions to the testdbPersons script that assures that the four new attributes are properly stored and retrieved from a person's entry in the database. These new assertions are summarized in Figure 7.12.

These new tests, alongside the existing ones, confirm that the new functionality for dbPersons is properly implemented and that existing functionality has not been interrupted by the changes.

```
function add_person($person){
    if(! $person instanceof Person)
        die("Error: add_person type mismatch");
    connect();
    $query = "SELECT * FROM dbPersons WHERE id = '".
        $person->get_id()."'";
    $result = mysql_query($query);
    //if there's no entry for this id, add it
    if($result==null || mysql_num_rows($result) == 0) {
        mysql_query('INSERT INTO dbPersons VALUES("'.
        $person->get_id().'","'.

        ...

        implode(',', $person->get_type()).'","'.
        $person->get_status().'","'.
        $person->get_employer().'","'.
        $person->get_contact_person().'","'.
        $person->get_contact_phone().'","'.

        ...

        $person->get_password().
        '");');
        mysql_close();
        return true;
    }
    mysql_close();
    return false;
}
```

FIGURE 7.11: Inserting a new person into the dbPersons table.
(Unchanged lines are ellipsed.)

Notice the use of the MYSQL_ASSOC argument in the mysql_fetch_array
call just before the last four assertions in Figure 7.12. This allows us to
reference the values of individual attributes in the array $p by their names
rather than by indexes, adding significant readability to the program code.

7.4.1.2 Refactoring

Once the changes to dbPersons are unit tested, it is advisable to revisit the
Person class to see if there are any new refactoring opportunities remaining to
be done there. For example, recall the discussion in Chapter 6 about useless
mutators and other functions that were defined in the Person class. At that
time, we determined that all the mutators and other useless functions could
be eliminated, but we left that decision open until after the dbPersons table
and module had been modified to accommodate the new features.

```
class testdbPersons extends UnitTestCase {
    function testdbPersonsModule() {
    //add a manager
    $m = new Person("ted", "jones", "14 Way St",  " .
    "Harpswell", "ME", "04079",
    2074415902, 2072654046,"ted@bowdoin.edu","volunteer",
    "active", "Apple", "Steve", 2071234567,"","","","","","",
    "","","Mon9-12,Tue9-12","","",
    "02-19-89", "03-14-08","","","","ted2074415902");
    $this->assertTrue(add_person($m));

    $p = get_person("Taylor2074415902");
    $this->assertTrue($p!==null);

    $p = mysql_fetch_array($p, MYSQL_ASSOC);
    $this->assertTrue($p['status'] == "active");
    $this->assertTrue($p['employer'] == "Apple");
    $this->assertTrue($p['contact_person']=="Steve");
    $this->assertTrue($p['contact_phone']==2071234567);
    ...
    echo("testdbPersons complete");
    }
}
```

FIGURE 7.12:   Testing modifications in the dbPersons.php module.

Now we have done that modification, and we conclude that the useless mutators and other functions can be safely removed from version 2.0 of the Person class. If, when we begin incorporating these new features into the user interface modules, we need to add one or more mutators back into the Person class, we can revisit this question at that time (see Chapter 8 for a continuation of this discussion). In the meantime, we have just removed about 20 useless functions from the Person class, and that is an important gain.

7.4.2   Item 3: Calendar View

For this feature, we need to modify the dbShifts table and associated module dbShifts.php so that shift start and end times are variable. Adding support for this new feature began in Chapter 6 with additions to the Shift class (see Figures 6.3 and 6.5). There, we created the important function set_start_end_time that would allow a shift's start and end time to vary.

Now we want to create the ability to move a shift that is already in the dbShifts table to a different start-end time on the same day and venue, but with the following additional caveats:

- The volunteers currently scheduled for the shift to be moved will be retained for the new start or end time. (Users can later modify the volunteer list for that shift by using other tools on the shift form at the user interface.)

- The new shift should not overlap with an existing shift on the same day and venue. If an attempt is made to change a shift's start or end time in a way that would overlap with an existing shift, the function that performs this change should not make this change.

To support this feature, three new functions, called `move_shift`, `selectDateVenue_dbShifts`, and `timeslots_overlap`, can be added to the dbShifts.php module. Here's a brief description of each one:

`move_shift ($s, $new_start, $new_end)` moves a shift to a new start and end time on the same date and venue, but only if the new start and end times do not overlap with any other shift. If there's an overlap, no change is made and the function returns `false`.

`selectDateVenue_dbShifts ($date, $venue)` selects all shifts from the dbShifts table for a given date and venue. This is a helper function for `move_shift`.

`timeslots_overlap ($s1_start, $s1_end, $s2_start, $s2_end)` determines whether two time slots overlap and returns `true` or `false` accordingly.

A complete rendering of the code for these functions is included in the *RMH Homebase* 2.0 code base.

This new feature has an interesting side effect on the process that finds all volunteers who are available within a given shift's start and end times. That is, a volunteer's availability is stored as an array of date-timeslot pairs (like "Mon12-3"). So the following question arises: "How do we match a volunteer's availability that is expressed in this form with a shift's new start and end times, which are stored as a pair of integers?" We shall return to this question in Chapter 8, where we implement the user interface component of this feature.

7.4.2.1 Refactoring

In reviewing the database tables affected by this new feature, recall that the dbDates table (see Figure 7.4) is not fully normalized because some of its attributes are redundant with its primary key. This anomaly can be removed by refactoring. That is, we can eliminate the month, day, and year attributes, since they are redundant with the id attribute.

A search for references to the month, day, and year attributes within the dbDates table yields nothing. So we first eliminate them from the dbDates.php

```
function setup_dbDates() {
   connect();
   mysql_query("DROP TABLE IF EXISTS dbDates");
   $result=mysql_query(
      "CREATE TABLE dbDates (id CHAR(8) NOT NULL,
      shifts TEXT, chef_notes TEXT, mgr_notes TEXT,
      PRIMARY KEY (id))");
   if(!$result)
      echo mysql_error();
   mysql_close();
}
```

FIGURE 7.13:   New `setup_dbDates` function in dbDates.php refactoring.

module and then reinstall the database and the sandbox using the redefined dbDates table.

Eliminating these attributes from the dbDates.php module requires modifying the functions `setup_dbDates`, `insert_dbDates`, and `select_dbDates` functions in that module. The new `setup_dbDates` function is shown in Figure 7.13.

Following this refactoring and reinstallation of the database and sandbox, the test suite must be rerun to make sure no new errors are introduced. If this run reveals no errors, we gain confidence that the refactored dbDates.php module has not upset the system's integrity in any unforeseen way.

A second refactoring activity is carried over from the previous chapter, where we decided to move the get_shift_name_from_id function from the Shift class to the dbShifts.php module. In doing this, we must correct the rigidity of possible start and end times that is built into the original function (see Figure 6.6). These needs lead to the revised function shown in Figure 7.14.

This new `get_shift_name_from_id` function now generates a full shift name, like "Sunday, February 14, 2010 from 2pm to 5pm" from its unique id field. No other attributes of a shift are needed for this function to perform its task.

After this move is completed, we must also change all calls to the old version of this function, of the form `$shift->get_shift_name_from_id($id)`, to the simpler form `get_shift_name_from_id($id)`, since the function no longer resides inside the Shift class.

Finally, notice that the new `get_shift_name_from_id` function calls five different helper functions, like `get_shift_month($id)`, to extract individual pieces out of a shift's $id. Implementation of these five functions is left as an exercise.

```
function get_shift_name_from_id($id) {
    $shift_name=date("l, F jS, Y",
        mktime(0,0,0,get_shift_month($id),get_shift_day($id),
            get_shift_year($id)));
    $special_cases = array (
        "night" => " night shift", "chef" => " guest chef");
    if (array_key_exists(substr($id, 9), $special_cases))
        $shift_name = $shift_name .
            $special_cases[substr($id, 9)];
    else {
        if (strpos($id, "Fam") !== false)
            $shift_name = $shift_name . " Family Room ";
        $shift_name = $shift_name . " from ";
        $st = get_shift_start($id);
        $et = get_shift_end($id);
        $st = $st <12 ? $st . "am" : $st - 12 . "pm";
        if ($st == "0pm")
            $st = "12pm";
        $et = $et <12 ? $et . "am" : $et - 12 . "pm";
        if ($et == "0pm") $et = "12pm";
        $shift_name = $shift_name . $st . " to " . $et;
    }
    return $shift_name;
}
```

FIGURE 7.14: New `get_shift_name_from_id` function for dbShifts.php.

7.4.2.2 Unit Testing

The unit test for the dbShifts.php module should be expanded to test all these new functions. A minimal approach to this is shown in Figure 7.15.

Here, we have added two new tests for the function `move_shift`—one for a move that should succeed and the other for a move that should fail. We have also added a couple of assertions to test the new `get_shift_name_from_id` functon. The remaining lines in this unit test carry over from the testing of *RMH Homebase* version 1.5; of course all these should be retained.

7.5 Summary

This chapter has introduced the fundamentals of database design and its importance in software development. Database creation, retrieval, update, and

```
class testdbShifts extends UnitTestCase {
  function testdbShiftsModule() {
    $s1=new Shift("02-25-08-night",3, null, "", "");
    $this->assertTrue(insert_dbShifts($s1));
    $this->assertTrue(delete_dbShifts($s1));
    $s2=new Shift("02-25-08-15-18",3, null, "", "");
    $this->assertTrue(insert_dbShifts($s2));
    $this->assertTrue(select_dbShifts("02-25-08-15-18")!==null);
    $s2=new Shift("02-25-08-15-18",2, null, "", "");
    $this->assertTrue(update_dbShifts($s2));
    $this->assertTrue(get_shift_name_from_id($s2->get_id())==
        "Monday, February 25th, 2008 from 3pm to 6pm");

// test moving a shift around
    $s3 = new Shift("02-25-08-12-15",2, null, "", "");
    $this->assertTrue(insert_dbShifts($s3));
    $this->assertTrue(move_shift($s3, 9, 12));
    $this->assertTrue($s3->get_start_time()==9);
    $this->assertTrue(get_shift_name_from_id($s3->get_id())==
        "Monday, February 25th, 2008 from 9am to 12pm");
    $this->assertFalse(move_shift($s3, 12, 16));
    $s3->set_start_end_time(9, 12);
    $this->assertTrue(delete_dbShifts($s3));
    $this->assertTrue(delete_dbShifts($s2));

    echo ("testdbShifts complete");
  }
}
```

FIGURE 7.15:   Upgraded unit test for the dbShifts module

delete (CRUD) operations are studied using examples from *RMH Homebase*.

Database tables should be designed in a way that facilitates concurrent access by many clients and ensures database security. Strategies for effective design and refactoring are guided by the principle of normalization.

Exercises

Some of these exercises are best completed by teams of two or more persons working together, using the *RMH Homebase* release 2.0 code base as a starting point.

7.1 Not all the tables in *RMH Homebase* satisfy all six database normalization criteria. For example, dbDates doesn't satisfy either criterion 5 or criterion 6. Give another example of how a *RMH Homebase* table violates normalization criterion 5. Give another example of how a table violates criterion 6. Explain why either of these anomalies can cause a problem—create more programming work or introduce an error—when updating one of these tables.

7.2 Develop and unit test the functions `get_shift_month`, `get_shift_day`, `get_shift_year`, `get_shift_start`, and `get_shift_end` for the db-Shifts.php module that are called by the new `get_shift_name_from_id` function shown in Figure 7.14.

7.3 Design, implement, and unit test the changes to the database modules required by the new feature **Item 4: Calendar month view** in the "wish list" described in Appendix B.

This new feature requires the addition of a new dbMonths table and associated module dbMonths.php so that an entire month can be retrieved from the database and passed to a user interface module for display. The model for this change is found in the new Month class and constructor developed in Chapter 6 (see Figures 6.8 and 6.9).

Unit testing this new feature will require that you develop a new unit test `testdbMonths` that contains assertions to exercise the constructor and each of the new functions in the dbMonths.php module. New code for creation of your dbMonths table should be added to the dbInstall.php script, which must be run before any unit testing begins.

7.4 Design, implement, and unit test the changes to the database modules required by the new feature **Item 5: Import/export** in the "wish list" described in Appendix B.

This feature can be implemented by adding functions to the dbPersons.php module that export/import a person's information in the form of a comma-separated list for use in a spreadsheet or other external database application. The export function should be tailorable so that only a subset of the columns in the dbPersons table are retrieved, rather than all of them.

Unit testing this new feature will require that you augment the unit test `testdbPersons` with assertions to exercise the new functions you added to the dbPersons.php module.

7.5 Does the previous exercise reveal any new refactorings that could be done in the dbPersons.php module? Why or why not?

7.6 Design, implement, and unit test the changes to the database modules required by the new feature **Item 7: Vacancies and shifts worked** in the "wish list" described in Appendix B.

This new requirement is asking the dbDates.php and dbShifts.php modules to search their respective tables and summarize particular information. It will be important in this exercise to look further into the capabilities of MySQL so that summarization functions already provided in standard queries are not duplicated in PHP code.

Unit testing this new feature will require that you augment the unit test `testdbDates` and `testdbShifts` with assertions to exercise the new functions you added to the dbPersons.php module.

7.7 Does the previous exercise reveal any new refactorings that could be done in the dbDates.php or dbShifts.php module? Why or why not?

Chapter 8

Developing the User Interface

> "What you see is what you get."
> —*Flip Wilson*

The user interface of an open source software product is the main point of interaction between the user and the software. The interface provides the glue that holds all the other elements together—not only in the code base but also during the development process. That is, all developer-user discussions about a particular functionality, bug, or new feature begin and end at the user interface.

The user interface is also the place where system integrity and usability are established and maintained. Any Web-based software artifact that has a clumsy user interface, fails to enforce restrictions on access to sensitive data, or prevents different users from exercising the system simultaneously, is relatively useless.

This chapter introduces both the principles of user interface design and the practice of user interface development. Our main source of examples is again the code base for the *RMH Homebase* software. However, the principles and practice discussed here apply to all open source software projects, both client-oriented and community-oriented.[1]

8.1 Design Principles and Practice

The design and development of a good user interface is special art that requires both skill and experience. Being a good programmer is a necessary but not sufficient requirement for becoming a good user interface designer. A

---

[1]To facilitate hands-on engagement with adding new user interface features, readers are encouraged to download and install the *sandbox version* of *RMH Homebase* release 2.0 from the book's Web site myopensoftware.org/textbook. Release 2.0 has some of the code enhancements and refactorings of the release 1.5 user interface modules that are needed to support the new features described in Appendix B. Other enhancements and refactorings needed to support these new features are left as team exercises.

good user interface design follows several aesthetic and functional principles that guide the development process.

Many books and articles have been written about user interface design (e.g., see [Tid05]). The Web contains many examples of excellent user interfaces, but unfortunately it also contains many more examples of bad user interfaces. For the remainder of this chapter, we shall use the following principles as our guide for what we mean by a *good user interface.*

1. **Completeness** All the steps of every use case in the design must appear on a page or group of related pages in the user interface, but no more.

2. **Language** The language of the interface must be consistent with the language of the domain and the user. All labels and user options that appear on individual pages must be consistent with their counterparts in the design document and the application's domain.

3. **Simplicity** No page should contain too much information or too little. Each page should be pleasant to view, yet its functionality should not be buried by excessive detail or elaborate stylistics.

4. **Navigability** Navigation within a page and among different pages should be simple, explicit, and intuitive.

5. **Feedback and recovery** Each page must provide the user with a clear indication of what has just been done, what can be done next, and how to undo what has just been done.

6. **Data integrity** The types and valid values for individual user data entries must be clearly indicated. The software should validity-check all data at the time of entry and the user should be required to correct errors before the data are kept in the database.

7. **Client-server integrity** The activities of several different users who happen to be using the system at the same time must be kept separate and independent.

8. **Security** An individual user should have access to the system's functionality, but only that functionality for which he/she is authorized.

9. **Documentation** Every page or group of pages in the user interface should be linked to a step-by-step on-line instruction that teaches a user how that page can be used to accomplish a task.

When designing an individual element of the user interface, for example a menu or a form that displays and receives information from the user, developers must ensure that all these principles are followed. If an element of the user interface cannot provide that assurance, the software that underlies the entire user interface is potentially compromised.

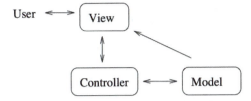

FIGURE 8.1:   The Model-View-Controller pattern.

The following three sections introduce design strategies that, when used together, can help developers achieve the first eight of these principles.[2]

8.1.1   The Model-View-Controller Pattern

The code underlying a user interface is both complex and loaded with details. It may contain a mix of HTML and additional programming elements called *scripts* that combine to render a user interface that is simultaneously pleasant to view and responsive to users' needs. Breaking the user interface design into separate conceptual components can help the developer manage this inherent complexity.

A widely used strategy for separating the user interface design into conceptual components is known as the *Model-View-Controller (MVC)* pattern of software architecture (see Figure 8.1).

The MVC pattern separates a user interface into three distinct conceptual components—the application's logic (the *model*), the user interface presentation (the *view*), and the user input/output and navigational functionality (the *controller*). This separation permits independent development, testing, and maintenance of each component.

The *model* contains the session-specific representation of the data, or *state* of the system, during user-system interactions. The model thus contains the active variables in the current user session as well as the database tables themselves. When information in the database changes, the model can provide this information to the view and controller.

The *view* renders the model in a way that supports user interaction. This rendering is typically a collection of user interface forms, including graphics, text, and various widgets that enable information to be easily transmitted by the controller between the user and the model. In Web-based applications, the view can be created using HTML and an embedded scripting language, like PHP, that displays information and facilitates user interactions. The view plays a major role in enforcing design principles 2, 3, 4, and 5 listed above.

---

[2]The last principle, **documentation**, requires so much discussion that it is covered separately in Chapter 9.

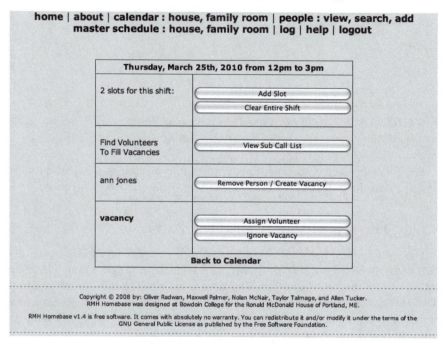

FIGURE 8.2:   The Shift view in *RMH Homebase*.

The *controller* receives user input via the view and initiates a response by making transformations on the data in the underlying model. In this sense, the controller maintains and interprets the current *state* of an interaction between the user and the system. To accomplish this, the controller maintains SESSION, GET, and POST information; verifies user input; and updates other appropriate model elements. In this sense, the controller contains the logic that underlies the sequences of steps in individual use cases.

A user interface for a complete software product is often organized as a collection of MVC triplets, each triplet responsible for a distinct user activity (for example, rendering a use case as a related collection of pages) within the entire system.

To illustrate these concepts, let's look at the *view* that appears when a user edits a particular shift in *RMH Homebase*, as shown in Figure 8.2. The *model* that underlies this view includes all the active variables in the current session along with the contents of the dbShifts table itself.

The *view* shown in Figure 8.2 is rendered by a mix of HTML and PHP code that is activated by the query string `editShift.php?shift=03-25-10-12-3`. Thus, this view is rendered with the argument `shift=03-25-10-12-3`, using functionality provided by the editShift.php, editShift.inc, header.php, footer.inc, and styles.css controller modules.

The *controller* for this view includes all the code within those modules that specifically handles $_GET and $_POST information and passes that information back and forth to update other variables and database tables within the model.[3] The controller also includes code that determines what particular form is displayed to the user—that is, the controller supports user navigation by transferring control between different modules in the user interface.

When user interactions are implemented by embedding a PHP script inside the HTML code, the controller and view functions are intermingled with each other. In this case, these two parts cannot be neatly separated.[4]

Figure 8.3 provides a summary overview of the HTML and PHP script in the editShift.php module.[5] The HTML code that shows this entire view is bounded by the tags <html> and </html>. Inside these tags, the entire form for editing a shift is rendered as an HTML table (denoted by the tag pair <table> and </table>) that encloses a series of rows and columns (denoted by the tag pairs <tr> and </tr> and <td> and </td>).

Embedded inside this HTML code are PHP scripts (which are enclosed inside the tag pairs <?PHP and ?>) that implement much of the view and all of the controller elements needed for supporting user-system interaction when a particular shift is edited.

- Two included PHP modules, header.php and footer.inc, control the display of the main menu at the top of the view and the copyright notice at the bottom of the view in Figure 8.2. These are activated by the two PHP include calls that appear near the top and bottom of the the the editShift.php module, respectively.

- The arrays $_GET and $_POST contain variable-value pairs used by the controller to share information with the view and the model. For example, the assignment $shiftid=$_GET['shift'] retrieves the id of the particular shift to be displayed in this view, which is the string '03-25-10-12-3' passed via the URL query string to the $_GET array.

- A number of auxiliary functions, such as process_fill_vacancy, help implement parts of this view, and thus receive information from the user via the $_POST array in order to function properly. These functions are all grouped together in the editShift.inc auxiliary module.

---

[3]In PHP, $_GET is an array of variables passed to the current script via URL parameters, while $_POST is an array of variables passed to the current script via the HTTP POST method, which stores user input from forms.

[4]In other settings, such as an Android/Java API, the view can be described declaratively using XML. In this case, the controller supplies the content for the view by pulling it out of the model. Similarly, a clean separation of the model—the interface's state variables—from the controller can also be made. More discussion of these alternatives appears at the book's Web site myopensoftware.org/textbook.

[5]Readers are encouraged to look at the entire editShift.php module and its supporting modules in order to see the details of how every piece of the view in Figure 8.2 is implemented.

The PHP code is interpreted on the server and generates HTML code that is then sent to the browser, which renders it for the user.[6] The header.php code is executed first and rendered, then the shift form is rendered, and finally the footer.inc code is executed and rendered. The first two of these three renderings appear in Figure 8.2, while the footer does not appear.

8.1.2   Sessions, Query Strings, and Global Variables

Distinguishing the activities of several different simultaneous users is aided by the notion of a *session*. Each individual user who logs in to the system initiates a unique session. Associated with that user's login is a set of *session variables* stored on the server that distinguishes that user from all other user sessions that are active at the same time. Here's how it works.

An individual user's session is created by a call to the `session_start()` function. If a session is already active for that user (that is, the user hadn't logged out) when a new page is loaded, then `session_start()` simply resumes it. When the `session_cache_expire(minutes)` function is called, it extends the time available to the user before the session expires. For example, when the pair:

```
session_start();
session_cache_expire(30);
```

appears at the beginning of a PHP user interface script, it 1) ensures that the session is running and 2) extends the run time for the session by 30 minutes.

During the life of a session, its session variables are stored on the server in a global array named `$_SESSION`. A session is officially terminated when the session_unset() function is called or the session times out. The session_unset() function is called when the user logs out of the system (e.g., see the logout.php script in *RMH Homebase*).

Each separate user login is assigned a unique value stored in his/her own session variable `$_SESSION['id']`. Other domain-dependent variables can be added to that `$_SESSION` array at the time the user logs in. For example, in *RMH Homebase*, execution of the login_form script causes the following domain-dependent variables to be established in that particular user's `$_SESSION` array.

`$_SESSION['_id']` gives the user's id as stored in the dbPersons database table. A visitor to the site can login as "guest," which becomes his/her id for the duration of that session.

`$_SESSION['access_level']` defines the level of access this particular user has to various functions and data.

---

[6]Note that the browser plays no role with PHP. This is different from Javascript, for example, which is interpreted on the client side (i.e., on the browser).

```php
<?PHP
    session_start();
    session_cache_expire(30);
?>
<html>
    ...
    <div id="container">
        <?PHP include('header.php');?>
        <div id="content">
            <?php
            include_once('editShift.inc');
            $shiftid=$_GET['shift'];
            $shift=select_dbShifts($shiftid);
            ...
            if (!process_fill_vacancy($_POST,$shift,$fam) &&
                !process_add_volunteer($_POST,$shift,$fam)) {
                if (process_unfill_shift($_POST,$shift,$fam))
                    $shift=select_dbShifts($shiftid);
                ...
                $persons=$shift->get_persons();
                echo ("<br><br><table align=\"center\">"
                    ."<tr><td align=\"center\" colspan=\"2\"><b>"
                    .$shift->get_shift_name_from_id($shiftid)
                    ."</b></td></tr><tr><td valign=\"top\">"
                    ."<br> ".do_slot_num($shift)."</td><td>");
                // ONLY A MANAGER CAN ADD SLOTS OR CLEAR A SHIFT
                ...
                echo "<br></td></tr>";
                // LIST ALL VOLUNTEERS AVAILABLE FOR THIS SHIFT
                ...
                echo (display_filled_slots($persons)
                    .display_vacant_slots($shift->num_vacancies()));
                echo "<tr><td colspan=\"2\" align=\"center\">
                     <a href=\"calendar".$fam.".php?id="
                    .substr($shiftid,0,8)."&edit=true\">
                    Back to Calendar</a></td></tr></table>";
            }
            ?>
            <?PHP include('footer.inc');?>
        </div>
    </div>
    ...
</html>
```

FIGURE 8.3: Overview of the editShift.php module.

`$_SESSION['f_name']` gives the user's first name.

`$_SESSION['l_name']` gives the user's last name.

User navigation among the various pages in a user interface uses two primary vehicles: the links in the main menu and various application-dependent links that are embedded within the rest of the user interface. The underlying controller transitions that occur among the PHP scripts that support the various forms are enabled by URL query strings.

The HTML *form* provides the vehicle through which users can initiate such navigation and enter data for the controller to pass to the system. Underlying the form is the `$_POST` array, whose individual variables define the current values of variables entered by the user.

To illustrate these ideas, look again at the shift view displayed in Figure 8.2. The main menu is shown at the top of the view, followed by a table that provides several options for editing a particular shift—adding or removing a volunteer, for example—on a particular day. As mentioned above, this view is achieved when the user selected this shift on a calendar display, which in turn executes the query string `editShift.php?shift=03-25-10-12-3`.

The HTML for this view is generated by the editShift.php module, but only after it has retrieved the shift value `03-25-10-12-3` from the `$_GET` array and all the information for that particular shift from the dbShifts database table. So now the editShift,php module can show the user that the shift has two slots—one is a vacancy and the other is occupied by the volunteer **ann jones**—and has an active sub call list.

This view also provides several user options: adding a third (vacant) slot, clearing the shift, viewing the shift's sub call list, removing **ann jones** from the shift, assigning another volunteer to the vacant slot, or ignoring (removing) the vacant slot from the shift. Selecting one of these options causes a new query string to be generated and control to pass to a corresponding PHP script.

For example, look at the code snippet in Figure 8.4 (which had been elided in the editShift.php script shown in Figure 8.3). This code is executed only if the shift has one or more vacancies. In that case, it adds a row to the shift view that allows the user to find volunteers to fill those vacancies, which is initiated by the lines beginning:

```
echo("<tr><td valign=\"top\"><br> Find Volunteers<br> 
...
```

The phrase `action="subCallList.php"` inside the code in Figure 8.4 is the device for transferring control to the subCallList.php module when the user selects the button "Find Volunteers to Fill Vacancies."

Depending on whether or not the shift already has a sub call list, the nature of the button on the right will vary ("View Sub Call List" or "Generate Sub Call List," respectively), as will the nature of the value added to the `$_POST`

```
//    LIST ALL VOLUNTEERS AVAILABLE FOR THIS SHIFT
if($shift->num_vacancies()>0) {
    echo("<tr><td valign=\"top\"><br> Find Volunteers<br>
         To Fill Vacancies</td><td><form method=\"POST\"
        action=\"subCallList.php\" style=\"margin-bottom:0;\">
        <input type=\"hidden\" name=\"_shiftid\"
        value=\"".$shiftid."\">");
    if (!$shift->has_sub_call_list() ||
        !(select_dbSCL($shift->get_id()) instanceof SCL)) {
        echo "<input type=\"hidden\" name=\"_submit_generate_scl\"
            value=\"1\"><br><input type=\"submit\"
            value=\"Generate Sub Call List\" name=\"submit\"
            style=\"width: 250px\">";
    }
    else {
        echo "<input type=\"hidden\" name=\"_submit_view_scl\"
            value=\"1\"><br><input type=\"submit\"
            value=\"View Sub Call List\" name=\"submit\"
            style=\"width: 250px\">";
    }
    echo "</form><br></td></tr>";
}
```

FIGURE 8.4: Controlling navigation via $_POST variables.

global array (`_submit_generate_scl` or `_submit_view_scl` respectively). In either case, the variable `_shiftid` is also added to the $_POST global array.

This information is all that is needed for the subCallList.php script to respond by (generating and) displaying the current sub call list for this shift.

8.1.3   Ensuring Security at the User Interface

Here, we discuss four different types of security concerns that can be addressed at the user interface level: enforcing levels of user access, password encryption, protecting against SQL injection attacks, and protecting against cross-site scripting attacks.

While this is by no means a complete or thorough treatment of security in software development, it should make readers aware of the importance of security in software development.

8.1.3.1   Enforcing Levels of User Access

Ensuring system security so that each user has access only to the functions and data to which he/she is entitled is aided by the $_SESSION variable access_level together with a system-wide convention for authenticating all system users.

Recall from Chapter 4 that the value of the $_SESSION['access_level'] variable is established at the time the user first accesses the system via the index.php script. At that time, the header.php script is executed, which in turn displays a login form (see Figure 4.5) via the login_form.php script (see Figure 4.6). Here's how that script works:

> The login_form script checks the User id entered by the user. If it is guest, the $_SESSION['access_level'] global variable is set to 0. Otherwise, the User id and Password are checked for a matching entry in the dbPersons table. If there is one, that entry provides information about the type of user who has just logged in—manager, volunteer, or applicant. Accordingly, the $_SES-SION['access_level'] global variable is set to 2, 1, or 0, respectively.

Once the user has logged in, they will see a main menu that is matched with their personal access level, which is summarized in Figure 4.7. The essential code that underlies these menu displays is shown in Figure 4.8. Notice how that code uses the $_SESSION['access_level'] variable to control the level of menu access that appears for each type of user.

The $_SESSION['access_level'] global variable is referenced throughout the user interface modules whenever they need to ensure that only persons logged in as managers can perform certain functions. For instance, if a person is logged in with access level 1 (i.e., a volunteer), they will never even see the option to add a slot or to clear a shift.

If a manager is logged in, however, he or she will have the option of adding a new slot or removing all volunteers from a particular shift. The code that controls this activity is shown in Figure 8.5, which is part of the overall edit-Shift.php module shown in Figure 8.3.

If the manager selects one of these options, either _submit_add_slot or _submit_clear_shift will be added to the $_POST array accordingly. These variables are used later to control what action the model will perform in response to the manager's selection.

8.1.3.2 Password Encryption

It is conventional to store a user's password in the database in an encrypted form. The reason for this is that someone else gaining access to the database (independently from the application) won't have the password—the other person only sees the encryption. The encryption principle is simply that only the password owner knows his/her password.

In *RMH Homebase*, each user's password is stored in the dbPerson's table in encrypted form, using the so-called "md5" encryption algorithm. When the user enters his/her password, it is sent to the server, encrypted, and compared

```
//  ONLY A MANAGER CAN ADD SLOTS OR CLEAR THIS SHIFT
if($_SESSION['access_level']>=2) {
   echo ("<form method=\"POST\" style=\"margin-bottom:0;\">
      <input type=\"hidden\" name=\"_submit_add_slot\"
      value=\"1\"><br><input type=\"submit\" value=\"Add Slot\"
      style=\"width: 250px\" name=\"submit\" ></form>");
   echo ("<form method=\"POST\" style=\"margin-bottom:0;\">
      <input type=\"hidden\" name=\"_submit_clear_shift\"
      value=\"1\"><input type=\"submit\"
      value=\"Clear Entire Shift\"
      style=\"width: 250px\" name=\"submit\" ></form>");
}
```

FIGURE 8.5: Ensuring security via $_POST and $_SESSION variables.

with the encrypted value stored in that person's database entry.[7] A match allows login to succeed, while a mismatch prevents the user from accessing any of the *RMH Homebase* scheduling functions.

The PHP code for password verification appears in the login_form.php script at the *RMH Homebase* user interface level. The essential logic in this code is shown in Figure 8.6.

```
$db_pass = md5($_POST['pass']);
$db_id = $_POST['user'];
$password_query_result = get_person($db_id);
if ($password_query_result){ //avoids null results
    $person = mysql_fetch_array(
        $password_query_result, MYSQL_ASSOC);
    if ($person['password']==$db_pass){
    // the passwords match, login
      ...
    else {
        echo('Error: invalid username/password<br />' .
          'if you cannot remember your password,' .
          'ask a house manager to reset it for you.</p>');
      ...
```

FIGURE 8.6: Password checking during *RMH Homebase* login.

---

[7]Note the security vulnerability revealed by this approach, since the password is transmitted from the client to the server in plain text before it is encrypted on the server side.

Here, we see that the user's password and login name are retrieved from the user's POST, the password is md5-encrypted, the person's record is retrieved from the database, and the encrypted password is compared with the value stored in the database record. From this, the login either succeeds or fails with a message suggesting that the user can request that his/her password be reset. The house manager is the only one who can reset a person's password.

The downside of password encryption is, of course, that nobody besides the password owner knows the owner's password. So if a user forgets his/her password, it will need to be reset by some algorithm and e-mailed to the user. No other person, such as a help desk support person, can read or create a new password, since that would compromise the encryption principle.

8.1.3.3 SQL Injection Attacks

SQL injection was identified in Chapter 4 as one of the common vulnerabilities of a software system. Recall that SQL injection is a code injection technique that exploits a security vulnerability to corrupt or destroy information stored in the database layer of a software architecture. The vulnerability is present when user input is inadequately filtered for string literal escape characters embedded inside database queries.

For example, by reading the *RMH Homebase* function in Figure 7.3 a malicious hacker immediately learns the name of the database, the root user, and the root password. Thus, if the following MySQL code were "injected" into another query, it would remove the entire rmhDB database from the server:

```
DROP DATABASE rmhDB;
```

How can MySQL code such as this be injected into another query? The main avenue for this activity is the user interface, where a user is either logging in (entering a username and password) or filling out an HTML form. If user input is not properly screened, it can contain an embedded snippet of malicious MySQL code. Here's an example:

> Consder the following PHP code, which is used in an authentication procedure to validate a user logging in as userName:
>
> ```
> mysql_query("SELECT * FROM users WHERE name = '" .
>     userName . "';")
> ```
>
> Now suppose that the user logs in by entering ' or '1'='1 as the userName. Now the above mysql_query call will actually execute the following query:
>
> ```
> SELECT * FROM users WHERE name = '' OR '1'='1';
> ```
>
> This query will retrieve all entries from the users table because its WHERE clause is always true.

Fortunately, measures can be taken to help prevent such an attack. First, user input data can be filtered by the function `mysql_real_escape_string()`, so that single quotes will be escaped to prevent them from being "injected" into the text of a MySQL query. In the above example, the following rewriting of the call will escape all instances of single quotes from the user's input before executing the query.

```
mysql_query("SELECT * FROM users where name='" .
    mysql_real_escape_string($userName) . "' ;")
```

Second, the PHP `mysql_query` function does not allow more than one MySQL query to be executed in a single call. Thus, injecting the above DROP query into another query as the argument of a `mysql_query` call would not drop the database.

8.1.3.4 Cross-Site Scripting Attacks

Cross-site scripting was identified in Chapter 4 as another of the common vulnerabilities of a software system. This is a technique that injects external information into Web pages viewed by other users. This vulnerability is present when input from an external source is inadequately filtered.

To help prevent such an attack, the code should filter all external data coming in from users. It should assume that such data are invalid until they can be proven valid. If a user is supplying his/her last name, the code should check that it contains only alphabetic characters, hyphens, and spaces.

For example, the PHP function htmlentities() helps screen user input to prevent cross-site scripting attacks. Several instances of these functions, such as the following, occur throughout the personEdit.php user interface script in *RMH Homebase*:

```
$last_name = trim(str_replace('\\\'','\''
    htmlentities($_POST['last_name']))) ;
```

This particular assignment replaces all HTML special characters by their HTML encodings (e.g., '<' is replaced by '<'), and escapes each single quote (') using a `str_replace` function call.

We conclude this section with an observation. That is, a fundamental distinction of FOSS is that the source code can be read by anyone, friend or foe. Does this make FOSS more likely than proprietary software to be attacked by cross-site scripting or SQL injection?

Definitely not. The entry point for these types of attacks is the user interface. Thus, the attack can be carried out with or without any specific knowledge of the source code, as long as that code itself has security vulnerabilities.

In fact, some proponents of proprietary software have argued that hiding the source code is one way of making a software system secure. However, most security experts conclude that this "security by obscurity" argument is false. For example, a study of Diebold's leaked proprietary voting software found a very large number of security vulnerabilities, which shows that this argument is false. For more information, see **avirubin.com/vote/response.html**.

Thus, it is always prudent to understand and use best practices for security when developing software, whether it is open source or proprietary. Taking defensive measures such as the ones suggested above is not a waste of time for any software developer.

8.2   Working with Code

Collectively, the user interface modules provide the main point of contact between the user and the system. They are the easiest to read and understand, since each one corresponds to a particular form on the screen when the user is exercising the system. Moreover, there should be a strong correspondence between the user interface modules and the original use cases that underly the original design.

Reading the user interface code helps explain the relationships among the domain classes, the corresponding database module, and the user interface.

For example, Figure 8.7 shows a snippet of code from the subCallList.php module that implements the use case **FindASub**. It is the main logic that responds to a user's request for finding a sub using a SubCallList (SCL).

A reading of this code reveals a simple structure, which calls one or another function depending on what the user has just requested:

1. generating a new SCL,

2. viewing an existing SCL, or

3. saving changes to the current SCL.

Such a call returns the $id of the resulting SCL or not, in which case the program will either display the new SCL or display a list of all SCLs.

To gain more insight into this code, we should exercise that part of the GUI where the user is working with a Sub Call List. In particular, we should start by viewing the form shown in Figure 8.8.

Looking at this form, we can see that it directly supports only the third user action, saving changes to the current SCL. However, digging deeper, we notice that this form provides a link to the Shift form, so maybe we can understand the other two actions by looking at the Shift form, shown in Figure 8.9.

On the Shift form, which is displayed by the editShift.php module, we see that this Shift's Sub Call List can be viewed by selecting "Generate Sub Call List" (Figure 8.9).

```
include_once('database/dbSCL.php');
include_once('database/dbShifts.php');
include_once('database/dbLog.php');
$id=$_GET['shift'];
if (array_key_exists('_submit_generate_scl',$_POST)){
    generate_scl($_POST['_shiftid']);
    $id=$_POST['_shiftid'];
}
else if (array_key_exists('_submit_view_scl',$_POST)){
    $id=$_POST['_shiftid'];
}
else if (array_key_exists('_submit_save_scl_changes',$_POST)){
    $id=process_edit_scl($_POST);
}
if ($id) {
    $id=view_scl($id);
}
if (!$id) {
    do_scl_index();
}
```

FIGURE 8.7: Part of the code base for handling a SubCallList.

Once a Shift's SCL has been generated, it can be later viewed from the same Shift form, where we now see the message "View Sub Call List" instead. Mystery solved.

So this little investigation of the code and its run-time behavior provides an initial understanding of the subCallList.php code and a starting point for exploring other related modules.

8.2.1 Reading Deeply

The above exercise with the subCallList.php and editShift.php code revealed some information about how the user interface relates to the GUI modules. However, it did not reveal anything about how specific functions in the underlying domain classes and database modules support a user activity.

To begin understanding these deeper relationships that occur during a user session, we can start with a specific user action and explore how the user interface and database modules implement that action. To illustrate, let's take another look at the Shift form for September 2, 2009 6–9pm, shown in Figure 8.9.

Now let's assume we want to remove "jerome jones" from that shift, creating a third vacancy. If we are running software inside an Eclipse environment, we should be able to see exactly what module is active at the time this form

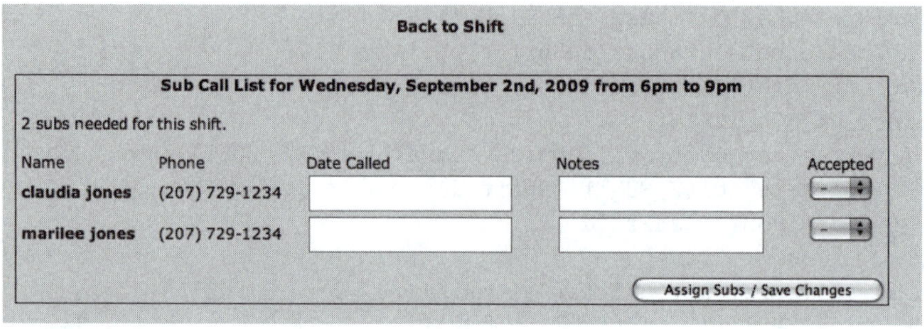

FIGURE 8.8:   Using the SubCallList form.

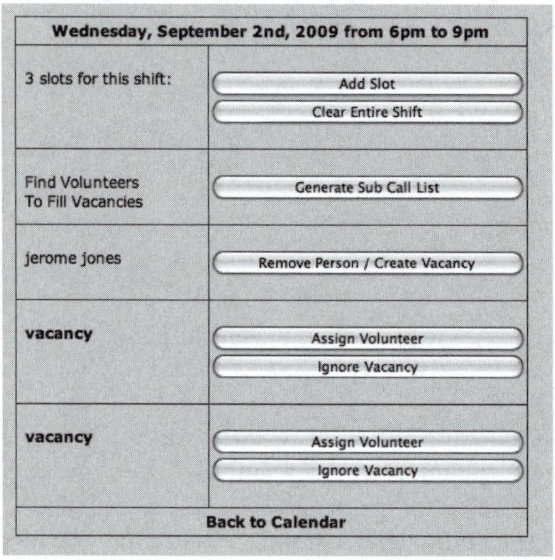

FIGURE 8.9:   Using the Shift form to generate an SCL.

appears in the browser: the `editShift.php` module. So we select "Remove Person / Create Vacancy" on this form, and the form reappears with three vacancies rather than two. What happened to cause this?

Our first look at the editShift.php code reveals a large module, though it appears to be well organized. It is organized into the following major sections:

A main section, which is a block of HTML code defining the layout of the Shift form.

A series of supporting functions—do_slot_num, display_filled_slots, and display_vacant_slots—that assist with the display of a shift.

A series of functions that govern the management of vacancies in a shift—process_fill_vacancy, process_unfill_shift, process_clear_shift, process_add_slot, and process_ignore_slot. Notice significantly that each of these functions returns `true` or `false` depending on whether or not it succeeds or fails. Success depends on the presence of a user request to perform that action and a successful completion of that action.

Some more supporting functions that assist with the identification and selection of a volunteer to fill a vacancy—get_available_volunteer_options, get_all_volunteer_options, and process_add_volunteer.

A helper function, fix_SCL, which brings a shift's SCL into agreement with its number of vacancies after a vacancy has been filled or created.

Notice also that editShift.php uses modules dbShifts.php, dbPersons.php, db-SCL.php, and dbLog.php in order to carry out its various functions.

So removing "jerome jones" from the 6–9pm shift on September 2, 2009 is triggered in the main section of code in editShift.php, where the code is determining whether or not the user has requested that action:

```
if (process_unfill_shift($_POST,$shift,$fam))
    $shift=select_dbShifts($shiftid);
else if (process_clear_shift($_POST,$shift,$fam))
    $shift = select_dbShifts($shiftid);
else if(process_add_slot($_POST,$shift,$fam))
    $shift=select_dbShifts($shiftid);
else if(process_ignore_slot($_POST,$shift,$fam))
    $shift=select_dbShifts($shiftid);
```

This code makes four tests. The first test calls `process_unfill_shift` to determine whether or not the user has requested removal of a person from a slot in this shift. The arguments `$_POST` and `$shift` are passed in this call.[8]

The first argument is an array of current user actions, including the action '_submit_filled_slot_0', and the second is the Shift object itself, which includes the id = "09-02-09-6-9". Recall that the persons scheduled for a shift are stored as an array, so "jerome jones" occupies slot 0 in that array.

Figure 8.10 shows a code snippet from the function `process_unfill_shift` where the removal of "jerome jones" takes place. In this code, we see that the outer loop is searching through the array of slots in the shift to find out if the user has selected any person for removal (line 2). Since "jerome jones" is in slot 0, _submit_filled_slot_0 should appear in the `$post` array.

At that point, the inner loop (line 3) builds the new array `$p2` that contains everyone who had been in the shift except "jerome jones." Finally, this new array is reassigned to the `$shift` (line 11), which also has its vacancy count incremented by 1 (line 12). This change is permanently recorded in the

---

[8]The third argument discriminates the venue for this shift—House or Family Room—but we shall ignore it in this discussion.

```
line code
 1   for($i=0;$i<count($persons);++$i) {
 2       if (array_key_exists('_submit_filled_slot_'.$i, $post)){
 3           for ($j=0;$j<count($persons);++$j) {
 4               if ($i!=$j)
 5                   $p2[]=$persons[$j];
 6               else
 7                   $name=$persons[$j];
 8           }
 9           if (count($p2)==0)
10               $p2=array();
11           $shift->assign_persons($p2);
12           $shift->add_vacancy();
13           fix_SCL($shift);
14           if ($name)
15               $name=explode("+",$name);
16           update_dbShifts($shift);
17           add_log_entry('<a href=\"viewPerson.php?id='...
18           return true;
19       }
20   }
```

FIGURE 8.10:   Code snippet for removing a person from a Shift.

dbShifts database table (line 16) and recorded in the Manager's log (line 17) before the function returns `true`.

The odd little function `$fix_SCL` adjusts the shift's SCL indicator depending on whether the last action has filled the shift (in which the shift's SCL becomes "closed") or created a first vacancy (in which the shift's SCL becomes "open"). It also updates the dbSCL table in the database in order to permanently record this change.

To understand the underlying database modules and their corresponding tables, we dig further into this example. In particular, let's look at the dbShifts.php module, where the function `update_dbShifts` function resides. Table 8.1 summarizes the principal modules in dbShifts.php and their purpose.

It is important to remember that a row in the table corresponds to a single Shift object, in the sense that the values in that row correspond to individual instance variables.

How, in particular, does an individual row in the database table get updated? The code for `update_dbShifts` is deceptively simple, having a pair of calls that removes the row whose key matches that of shift $s and then inserts a new row using $s again:

```
delete_dbShifts($s);
insert_dbShifts($s);
```

TABLE 8.1: Functions in the dbShifts.php Module

Function	Purpose
setup_dbShifts	Creates a new dbShifts table in the database and gives labels to its columns
insert_dbShifts($s)	Inserts Shift $s into dbShifts as a new row
delete_dbShifts($s)	Removes the row corresponding to Shift $s from dbShifts
update_dbShifts($s)	Replaces the row corresponding to the id of Shift $s by $s itself
select_dbShifts($id)	Returns the Shift with id = $id from dbShifts

So to get to the bottom of an update, we need to examine the code for `delete_dbShifts` and `insert_dbShifts` in succession. We shall persist with this example because it contains some principles that are also useful for a wide range of database design problems.

First, the code for `delete_dbShifts` has the following essential steps:

```
line code
 1    connect();
 2    $query="DELETE FROM dbShifts WHERE id=\"".$s->get_id()."\"";
 3    $result=mysql_query($query);
 4    if (!$result)
 5        echo "unable to delete from dbShifts ".
 6             $s->get_id().mysql_error();
 7    mysql_close();
```

Line 1 establishes a connection to the database, while line 2 executes a MySQL query that deletes a line from the dbShifts table whose id is identical with the id in Shift $s. Lines 3-6 check to see if this deletion has been completed successfully (the query returned one line). A `null` result would have indicated failure to find the given Shift in the dbShifts table, which would be an unusual event. Line 7 disconnects the call from the database.

Second, the code for `insert_dbShifts` has the following essential steps:

```
line code
 1    connect();
 2    $query =
 3        "SELECT * FROM dbShifts WHERE id =\"".$s->get_id()."\"";
 4    $result = mysql_query ($query);
 5    if (mysql_num_rows($result)!=0) {
 6        delete_dbShifts($s);
 7        connect();
 8    }
 9    $query="INSERT INTO dbShifts VALUES
10        (\"".$s->get_id()."\",".$s->num_vacancies().",\"".
```

```
11      implode("*",$s->get_persons())."\",\"".
12      $s->get_sub_call_list()."\",\"".$s->get_notes()."\")";
13  $result=mysql_query($query);
14  if (!$result)
15      echo "unable to insert into dbShifts ".
16          $s->get_id().mysql_error();
17  mysql_close();
```

This is a bit more detailed, since before making an insertion the function must check to see if a Shift with the same id as that of $s is already in the database. If so, that Shift is removed (lines 2–8). The insertion of a new row with id == $s->get_id() is done on lines 9–12, and then a check is made on lines 13–16 to be sure that the insertion was made. Lines 1 and 17 open and close the connection to the database in the same way that was done in lines 1 and 7 of the previous example.

8.2.2 Debugging as a Community Activity

Most bugs appear during the time a user is working with the system through a user interface module. Thus, the starting point for correcting a software error often begins with a discussion between the user and the developer. Without smooth communication between the user and the developer, debugging in an open source environment may not be effective.

To illustrate this communication in detail, we trace the activities of an actual debugging episode that occurred with the *RMH Homebase* software. It is listed as Item **9a** in the list of bugs and new features summarized in Appendix B.

When this episode takes place, almost two years have gone by since *RMH Homebase* was initially installed. By now, one developer, Alex, is maintaining the code base and another, Ellis, is maintaining the Web site and server where *RMH Homebase* is running. Gina, one of the original clients, is still the primary user of the software. The entire episode has a distinctive workflow in which all three parties play essential roles.

8.2.2.1 User-Developer Discussion

The episode begins when the user discovers a problem when trying to search and edit an entry in the personnel database.

From: Gina
Date: Friday, March 5, 2010 12:08 PM
To: Alex

Hi Alex-

Hope you are doing well.

View Entries in the Personnel Database
To find a specific volunteer, **search the database!**

Viewing results 1-25. Showing <u>25</u> **50 100** people per page.

| admin, admin | **view edit** |
| applicant, a & b | **view edit** |

FIGURE 8.11:   Reproducing the bug.

Homebase question: I now have three separate applications that have been submitted and were entered with two names separated by &. I am unable to open them and therefore cannot contact the applicants to let them know they need to resubmit without the "&" symbol. Is there any way to permanently remove these? They sit under the Open Applications.

Heading off on vacation for a week so no hurry on responding.

Best,
Gina

8.2.2.2   Debugging Activities

The next step in this episode involves a series of developer activities to identify the bug, correct it and test the correction.

To identify and fix this bug, the developer must first reproduce it using the "sandbox" version of the code base. This involves navigating to the **people : add** menu in the user interface and adding a new person to the "sandbox" database whose first name contains an ampersand, such as "a & b applicant." The result of this step is shown in Figure 8.11, using the **people: view** menu to list all persons in the database.

The next step in fixing the bug is to locate where the software fails when working with this particular data. If the developer selects the **edit** button beside the entry for "a & b applicant," the error message shown in Figure 8.12 is raised. This message provides some important information:

- The module that is running when this error occurs is `personEdit.php`, as indicated by the URL in Figure 8.12.

- That URL also shows the query string being passed to this particular call contains `id=a%20&%20b1234567890`.[9]

- The user interface module initiating the call is viewPerson.php.

The solution is exposed by the developer's knowledge about how an HTML query string is formed and punctuated. Specifically, the "&" character is

---

[9]Recall that a user id is the concatenation of the user's first name and phone number.

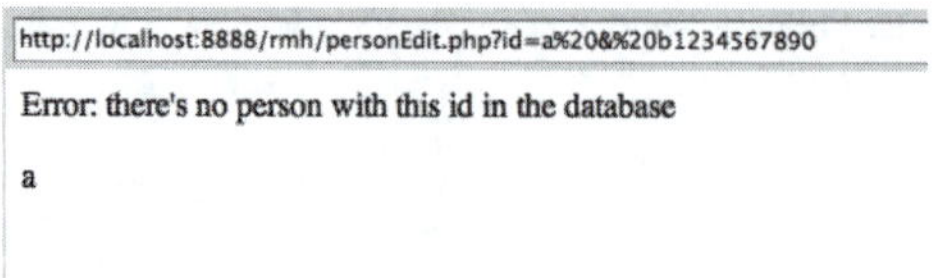

```
http://localhost:8888/rmh/personEdit.php?id=a%20&%20b1234567890
```

Error: there's no person with this id in the database

a

FIGURE 8.12: Locating the defect.

used to separate individual arguments in the query. Thus, this query string is parsed by the system as two arguments, "a " and " b1234567890" rather than the single argument "a & b1234567890".

There are a couple of options for fixing this bug, each of which involves tightening the requirements for storing the first name of a new Person in the database. Since each row in the dbPersons table has a unique key formed by concatenating the first_name with the primary phone number (phone1), neither of these two fields should contain any special character, especially "&."

Thus, when a user enters a first name like "a & b," all instances of "&" in that entry should be replaced by a reasonable substitute, like "and." The user interface module where this correction should be made is of course the point where the "&" is first entered, which is the personEdit.php module.

The function within that module that processes new Person entries is called process_form, and the first line of that function reads:

```
$first_name = trim(str_replace('\\\'','',
    htmlentities($_POST['first_name'])));
```

Literally, this line retrieves the first_name value (typed by the user and stored in the $_POST array), replaces special characters by their equivalent HTML representations (e.g., a blank is replaced by %20;), removes all single quotes, and trims all leading and trailing blanks. The result is assigned to the $first_name variable, which is later part of a new entry stored in the dbPersons table.

Thus, the developer should modify this line so that it additionally replaces all instances of "&" by "and" before assigning the result to $first_name. The following replacement line of code seems to be appropriate:

```
$first_name = trim(str_replace('\\\'','',
    htmlentities(str_replace('&','and',$_POST['first_name'])))));
```

To test this modification, the developer should take two steps.

First, a new assertion should be added to the testeditPerson.php module in the test suite. This step is left as an exercise.

Second, the use case **UpdateVolunteerList** should be exercised by running the editPerson.php and adding a person to the database who has "&" in their first name, like "a & d." If all goes well, a new view of the persons list should show that new person's first name with "&" replaced by "and." This result is confirmed in Figure 8.13.

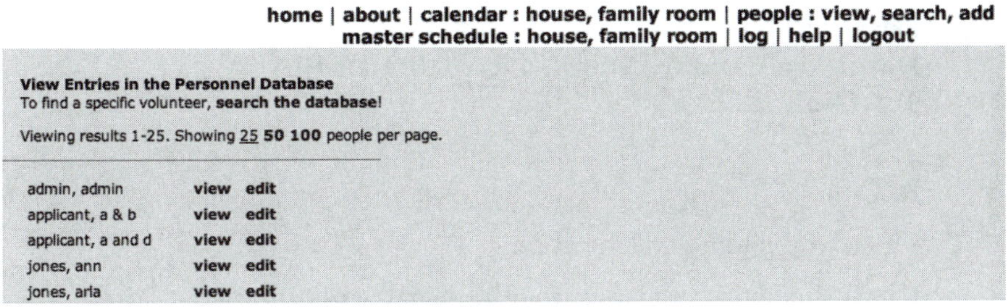

FIGURE 8.13: Designing the fix.

To complete testing the fix, the developer must be sure that selecting "view" or "edit" for a person with "and" in their first name (e.g., "a and d" in Figure 8.13) now navigates successfully. This is confirmed in the two displays of Figure 8.14.

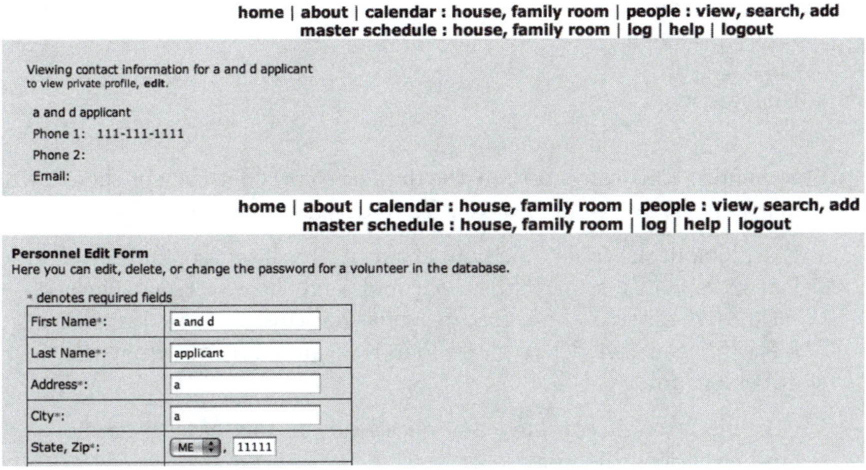

FIGURE 8.14: Testing the fix: viewing a person and editing a person.

8.2.2.3 Developer-Developer Discussion

Once the fix has been made and tested, a series of conversations now take place in order to transfer the fix into the production version of the software. In the e-mail below, Alex is passing the corrected module (editPerson.php) to the the developer, Ellis, who is maintaining the live version of the system. He also warns the user that current entries in the database with "&" in their first names must be corrected manually.

From: Alex
Date: Wednesday, March 17, 2010 4:16 PM
To: Gina, Ellis

Hi Gina,

I hope you had a good vacation.

I have finally figured out your problem with the "&." I have changed the software so that if anyone enters "&" as part of their first name, like "Jack & Jill," it will store the name as "Jack and Jill" instead.

Attached is the file personEdit.php that Ellis can upload to the software to fix this problem when he has a chance.

Unfortunately, this doesn't fix any database entry that already has "&" in its first name. I used the **people: search** function looking for "&" in the first name and found the following four entries:

Amos & Andy
Romeo & Juliet
Mutt & Jeff
Ding & Dong

Hopefully, Ellis can print out the database entry for each of these four persons and send it to you for re-entry.

Ellis, look in the table called dbPersons in the database, find these four rows, and just print them out and send them to Gina. Once she has re-entered these four persons' data using the corrected software, you can delete these four rows permanently from the dbPersons table.

Give me a call if you have any questions. In any case, keep me posted on how this works out.

Best,
Alex

In reply to this e-mail, Ellis offers to correct these entries directly in the database, a rather risky step but less time consuming than the alternative.

From: Ellis
Date: Wednesday, March 17, 2010 4:39 PM
To: Alex

Can I just edit these four rows in the table itself?

From: Alex
Date: Wednesday, March 17, 2010 7:00 PM
To: Ellis

Good idea, Ellis. If you want try that, it can save Gina from reentering all the data.

There are two columns in the table that need the "&" replaced by "and," one named "id" and the other named "last_name." Let me know when that's done and I'll fix the rest. (For example, the passwords will need to be reset for these four persons.)

Thanks, Alex

From: Ellis
Date: Thursday, March 18, 2010 6:54 AM
To: Alex

I've uploaded the new file and have changed the four rows in the database.

Ellis

8.2.2.4 Closure

Now that the fix has been completed and installed, the developers wait for a reply from the user, who will exercise the new code. The episode ends with a final exchange between the developers and the user.

From: Alex
Date: Thursday, March 18, 2010 7:49 AM
To: Ellis, Gina

Thanks, Ellis. Everything looks okay.

Gina, let me know if you have problems accessing these four persons' information. In the future, there will be nobody in the database with "&" in their first name. It will show as "and" instead.

Alex

From: Gina
Date: Thursday, March 18, 2010 8:56 AM
To: Alex, Ellis

Thank you both so very much! Everything is working perfectly — you're good!

Gina

All's well that ends well.

8.3   Adding New Features: User Interface Impact

Adding a new feature to an existing software system almost always has an impact on the user interface. After the domain and database modules have been revised to accommodate the new feature, the user interface modules can be extended to complete that addition.

When considering the user interface impact of adding a new feature to a software product, developers can focus on answering two questions:

1. How should the *view be changed* so that the user can naturally identify this new feature?

2. How should the *controller be changed* so that the user can naturally use this new feature?

Answering the first question should produce a new and enhanced view, while answering the second should produce new functionality that enables users to respond to the view and utilize the new feature effectively.

Notice that these two questions ignore the *model*. Changes to the model should have been substantially completed during the earlier process of incorporating the new feature into the domain classes and database modules.

To illustrate this process in detail, the next few sections revisit several of the new features outlined in Appendix B for *RMH Homebase* and explore their impact on the user interface modules.[10] These discussions revise both the user interface modules and the unit tests that help validify those revisions. New refactoring opportunities introduced by these activities are also discussed.

All changes discussed in these next few sections are implemented in version 2.0 of the *RMH Homebase* code base, which already contains the domain class and database module changes discussed in Chapters 6 and 7.

8.3.1   Item 1: Volunteer Status

This new feature allows the system to categorize a volunteer as inactive, thus preventing his or her name from showing up on a sub call list. This will ensure that volunteers who are unavailable do not get scheduled for shifts.

In previous chapters, we prepared for this new feature by adding a "status" field for each volunteer, with value "active" or "inactive." There, we modified the Persons domain class and the dbPersons.php database module accordingly.

Now at the user interface level, we must make the following view and controller changes to complete the addition of this new feature:

---

[10]Implementation of the rest of these new features is left for the exercises at the end of the chapter. Each one provides a substantial opportunity for readers to collaborate and enhance an actual software system at the user interface level.

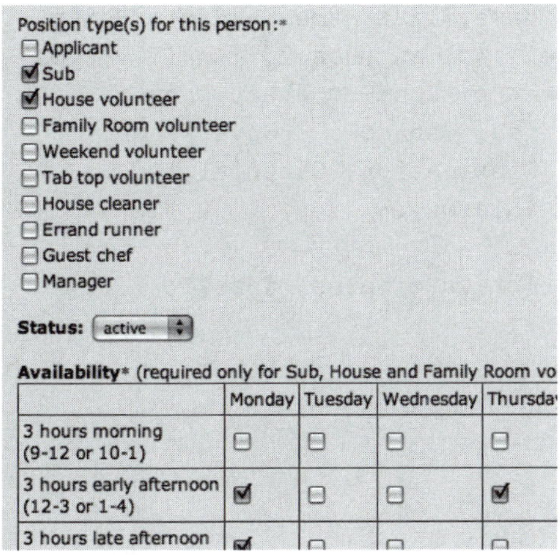

FIGURE 8.15: Showing a person's status.

1. Changing personEdit so that it displays and allows changing the new "status" field,

2. Changing viewPerson so that the person's status appears in the view,

3. Changing searchPeople so that "status" is a field to search on,

4. Changing editMasterSchedule.php and editShift.php so only "active" volunteers are listed for filling a vacancy, and

5. Changing subCallList so that it lists only "active" volunteers.

The impact of the first of these changes on the view for editing a person is shown in Figure 8.15. In between the **Type** and **Availability** areas, we see a new selection labeled **Status:**, with options "active" and "inactive." The display of this selection is implemented by the code shown in Figure 8.16.

```
echo('<p><strong>Status: </strong> <select name="status">');
echo ('<option value="active"');
if ($person->get_status()=="active") echo (" SELECTED");
echo ('>active</option>');
echo ('<option value="inactive"');
if ($person->get_status()=="inactive") echo (" SELECTED");
echo ('>inactive</option></select>');
```

FIGURE 8.16: Changing personForm.php to show a person's status.

```
$newperson = new Person($first_name,$last_name,$address,$city,
    $state, $zip, $clean_phone1, $clean_phone2, $email, $type,
    $status, $employer, $contact_person, $contact_phone,
    $background_check, $interview, $shadow, $convictions,
    $wherelived, $experience, $motivation, $specialties,
    $availability, $schedule, $history,
    $birthday, $start_date,
    $public_notes, $my_notes, $private_notes, $pass);
$result = add_person($newperson);
```

FIGURE 8.17: Updating a person's database entry.

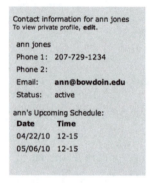

FIGURE 8.18: Showing a person's status in the view.

When the user selects "inactive" or "active," the controller records that information in the $_POST['status'] variable. When the user hits "Submit" at the bottom of the form, all user changes on the form are recorded in that person's entry in the dbPersons table.

The personEdit.php module must be changed in a number of places to accommodate the four new fields (status, employer, contact_person, and contact_phone) that have been added to the dbPersons database table. For example, Figure 8.17 shows how the construction of a new person is done before that person's table entry is updated. The third line in this constructor call includes these four new variables as they have been set by the user editing the person's form. The last line updates the table entry by calling the add_person function in the dbPersons.php module.

Showing the status of a person in the view is a simpler matter. That is, all we need to do is add a line that contains a label and the current value of the person's status, which has been retrieved from the dbPersons table. The user's view of that activity is shown in Figure 8.18. The new code in viewPerson.php that creates this view is shown in Figure 8.19.

Searching for volunteers who are "inactive" can be implemented by modifying the view that allows searching for people by last name. Such a modifica-

```
echo("<tr><td class=\"searchResults\">Email:</td>
  <td class=\"searchResults\">
  <a href=\"mailto:".$person['email']."\">".$person['email'].
  "</a></td></tr>");
echo("<tr><td class=\"searchResults\">Status:</td>
  <td class=\"searchResults\">".$person['status']."</td></tr>");
```

FIGURE 8.19: Changing viewPerson.php to show a person's status.

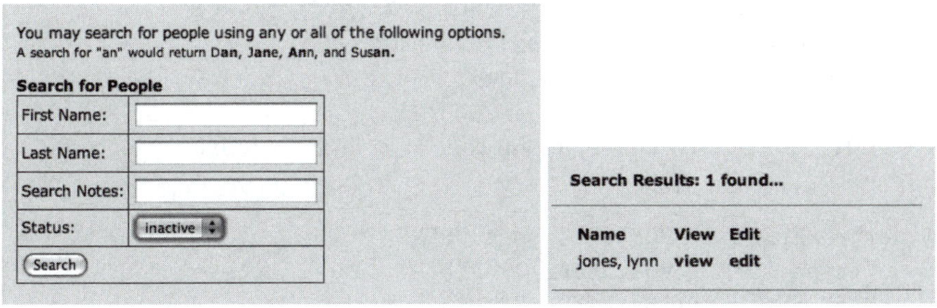

FIGURE 8.20: Searching for "inactive" volunteers and results.

tion is shown in Figure 8.20, where the new selection titled **Status:** has been added. The code that adds this option is shown in Figure 8.21, along with the code that initiates the query to find all inactive people in the database. The result shows "lynn jones" as the only "inactive" volunteer in the database.

Changing editMasterSchedule.php so that only "active" volunteers are listed as candidates for filling a vacancy requires modifying the query that retrieves all volunteers who are available on that particular day and time. This is shown in Figure 8.22, where the second line ensures that only active volunteers are retrieved by the query. Assuming again that "lynne jones" is inactive, we see in Figure 8.23 that she no longer appears on the list of available persons even though she would be available for that particular time slot.

Changing editShift.php and subCallList.php so that only "active" volunteers can be scheduled for a shift is left as an exercise.

8.3.1.1   Unit Testing and Refactoring

The foregoing discussion shows how a new user interface feature is initially tested at the time it is implemented. That test exercises the user interface for this particular feature to be sure that it functions as expected.

To complete the testing for this new feature, we must add assertions to the unit tests for personEdit, viewPerson, editMasterSchedule, editShift, subCal-lList, and searchPeople. Those additions assure us that when future coding changes are made, this particular feature will continue to be viable.

```
echo('<tr><td>Status:</td><td><select name="s_status">' .
  '<option value="active">active</option>' .
  '<option value="inactive">inactive</option>' .
  '</select></td></tr>');
  ...
$query = "SELECT * FROM dbPersons WHERE " .
  "first_name LIKE '%". $fns .
  "%' AND last_name LIKE '%".$lns."%' ".
  "AND (private_notes LIKE '%". $pns .
  "%' OR public_notes LIKE '%".$pns."%') " .
  "AND status = '".$_POST['s_status']."' " .
  "ORDER BY last_name,first_name";
```

FIGURE 8.21: searchPeople.php code that finds "inactive" volunteers.

```
$query="SELECT * FROM dbPersons WHERE  " .
  "(type LIKE '%volunteer%') AND status = 'active' " .
  "AND availability LIKE '%". $day.$time .
  "%' ORDER BY last_name,first_name";
```

FIGURE 8.22: Changing editMasterSchedule.php to list only "active" volunteers.

Recall the discussion of the layering principle in Chapters 4 and 7. That principle encourages that all modules in the user interface requiring a CRUD function on a database table should do so by calling functions in the database module rather than directly accessing the MySQL table itself.

The user interface modules contain several violations of the layering principle. At the time they were written, these modules were very much in a prototype stage of development, but now that the software has been in use for a while, it is a good time to correct these violations. For example, one opportunity for refactoring appears in Figure 8.21, where a MySQL query is issued directly from the searchPeople.php user interface module.

FIGURE 8.23: Listing only "active" volunteers when filling a vacancy.

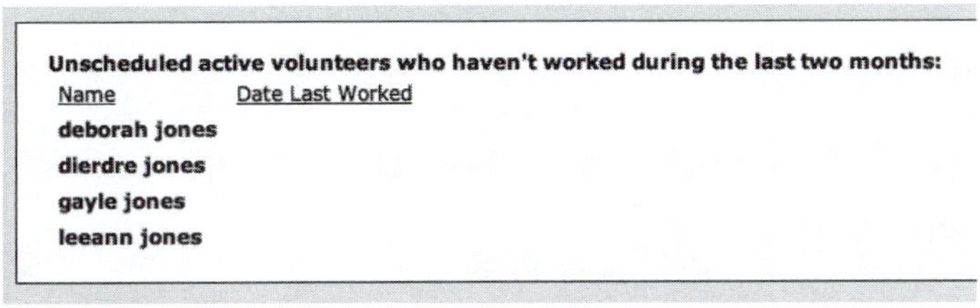

FIGURE 8.24: Listing volunteers who have not worked recently.

8.3.2 Item 2: Make Active/Inactive

This new feature will help the manager track when a volunteer has last been scheduled for a shift. For example, when a manager logs in, her screen should show the names of all "active" volunteers who have not worked a shift for the past two months. Optionally, the manager should be able to make any such volunteer "inactive."

A design for this feature is shown in Figure 8.24. To implement this feature, we need to modify the index.php module to show a list of volunteers who have not worked for the past 2 months, with links to their forms so that the manager can make any of them "inactive." The code for this feature is summarized in Figure 8.25. A full listing appears in the *RMH Homebase* 2.0 code base.

This code has two nested loops. The outer loop traverses all the volunteers in the dbPersons table, while the inner loop traverses all the shifts worked by each volunteer. PHP's date functions provide an easy computation for the key variables $today and $two_months_ago. Notice that the shifts worked by a volunteer are ordered chronologically, so that the most recent shift worked appears last. Notice finally that each person listed has a link to his/her individual form, so that the manager can easily change their status to "inactive."

8.3.2.1 Refactoring

The module index.php contains several violations of the layering principle, for example when it directly accesses the dbPersons table in the database (see Figure 8.25). The MySQL queries that appear there suggest that additional functions need to be added to the dbPersons.php and dbShifts.php modules so that these queries can be relocated to their proper layer. Once such functions are added, these queries can be replaced by appropriate function calls in the index.php module itself.

For example, consider the two MySQL queries that appear in Figure 8.25. The first query retrieves the id, first name, and last name of every active volunteer in the dbPersons table. It can be replaced by a call to the new function shown in Figure 8.26, to be added to the dbPersons.php module.

The second query retrieves the id and persons values for all shifts in the dbShifts table that were worked by a particular person, who is identified by the variable $thisRow['id']. It can be replaced by a call to an existing

```
$everyone = mysql_query(
    "SELECT id,first_name,last_name FROM dbPersons " .
        "WHERE status = 'active' AND type LIKE '%volunteer%'");
...
$two_months_ago = $today - 60*86400;
...
while($thisRow = mysql_fetch_array($everyone, MYSQL_ASSOC)){
   $shift_query= mysql_query("SELECT id,persons FROM dbShifts " .
      "WHERE persons LIKE '%".$thisRow['id']."%' ORDER BY id");
   ...
   $havent_worked = true;
   $last_worked = "";
   if(mysql_num_rows($shift_query)>0){
      while ($havent_worked &&
         $shifts_worked = mysql_fetch_array(
             $shift_query, MYSQL_ASSOC)){
         $date_worked = mktime(
             0,0,0,get_shift_month($shifts_worked['id']),
             get_shift_day($shifts_worked['id']),
             get_shift_year($shifts_worked['id']));
         $last_worked = substr($shifts_worked['id'],0,8);
         if ($date_worked > $two_months_ago)
             $havent_worked = false;
      }
   }
   if ($havent_worked)
      echo('<tr><td class="searchResults">'
         .'<a href="personEdit.php?id='.$thisRow['id'].'">'
         .$thisRow['first_name'].' '.$thisRow['last_name']
         .'</a></td><td class="searchResults">'
         .$last_worked.'</td></tr>');
   }
   echo('</table></p></div><br>');
}
```

FIGURE 8.25: Code for listing volunteers who have not worked recently.

```
function getall_names($status) {
    connect();
    $result = mysql_query(
        "SELECT id,first_name,last_name FROM dbPersons " .
            "WHERE status = '". $status .
            "' AND type LIKE '%volunteer%'");
    mysql_close();
    return $result;
}
```

FIGURE 8.26:   New function to search for active or inactive persons.

function `selectScheduled_dbShifts($person_id)`, which was added to the dbShifts.php module in an earlier refactoring exercise. That function returns an array of shift id's, and so the code that follows the call also needs to be adjusted to accommodate this change. That adjustment is left as an exercise.

8.3.3   Item 3: Calendar View

In the current calendar view, shift times are hard to distinguish if the user is unfamiliar with it. For example, 9-12 looks like it could be 9-11. Moreover, sometimes a shift (especially a weekend shift) needs its start or end time to be changed by the user.

In Chapters 6 and 7, we altered the Shift class and the dbShifts module so that a shift's start and end time can be changed (within the same day and venue). To complete the implementation of this new feature, we need to make three significant alterations at the user interface level:

1. Alter the calendar.php and masterSchedule.php modules so that the functions that display a week of the calendar can accommodate the flexibility that is built into each shift's start and end time—currently, the calendar.php module is "brittle" in this regard.

2. Alter the editShift.php and editMasterSchedule.php modules so that they properly locate all persons who are available for a given shift, now that its start and end times can vary.

3. Alter the editShift.php module so that it allows the manager to change the start and/or end times of a shift on a given day, without changing the volunteers who are scheduled to work that shift.

For the first alteration, the calendar.php module can be greatly simplified when it uses a shift's start and end times for displaying each day of the week. The code now becomes a nest of two loops, one running across the hours of a day and the other running across the days of the week (see calendar.php in

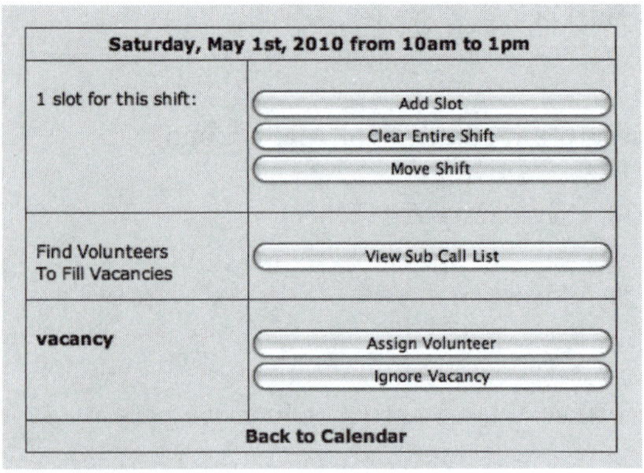

FIGURE 8.27:   A view of the new Move Shift feature.

the code base at the book's Web site myopensoftware.org/textbook for more details). Properly displaying hours that are not scheduled for any shift is accommodated by the auxiliary array $free_hour.

For the second alteration, recall that a volunteer's availability is stored as an array of date-time pairs (like "Mon12-3"). Now we need to match a volunteer's availability that is expressed in this form with a shift's new start and end times, which are stored as a pair of integers, in order to answer the question, "Does this volunteer's availability overlap with this shift's start and end times?" If so, the program concludes that the volunteer is available for this particular shift.

For the third alteration, we can define the following functions inside the dbShifts.php module:

move_shift ($s, $new_start, $new_end) moves a shift to a new start and end time on the same date and venue, but only if the new start and end times do not overlap with any other shift. If there's an overlap, no change is made and the function returns false.

timeslots_overlap($s1_start, $s1_end, $s2_start, $s2_end) decides whether two time slots overlap and returns true or false accordingly.

A full rendering of the code for these functions is included in the *RMH Homebase* 2.0 code base.

The user interface changes required to implement this alteration originate at the editShift.php module. There, a new option called "Move Shift" can be added to the manager's view (see Figure 8.27) so that she can change either the start or end time of an individual shift on the calendar.

Selection of that option leads to a new form, where the manager can set either the start time or the end time for the shift. This is shown in Figure 8.28.

Discussion of the coding details for this change would be long and tedious. To summarize, the editShift.inc module required two new functions that re-

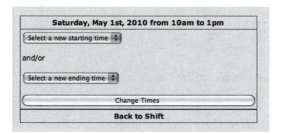

FIGURE 8.28:   Selecting new start and end times for a Shift.

spond to user posts when either the start or end time of a shift is changed. The editShift.php module, in turn, must enable the activation of these two functions when the user actually selects "Move Shift" or "Change Times." For more details, readers are encouraged to visit the *RMH Homebase* 2.0 code base at the book's Web site myopensoftware.org/textbook.

8.3.3.1   Unit Testing and Refactoring

These new features provide a number of opportunities for developing new unit tests and refactoring existing code. It is important to be sure that the new features are fully unit tested before any refactoring is considered. Failure to separate these two concerns can lead to confusion during debugging.

8.4   Summary

This chapter has studied the principles and practice of user interface development in the context of an active open source software project. It exposes the value of design principles like model-view-controller, session management, and software security. It also describes the impact of adding new features to software upon the user interface modules in the code base.

Because all the levels of a software architecture are interrelated, we have seen that adding new features to a user interface usually has a ripple effect on the underlying domain classes and database modules. Moreover, refactoring and debugging activities that begin with a user interface module also migrate to modules and classes at all other levels.

Finally, this discussion leads naturally to the development and proper maintenance of good developer and user documentation. The principles and practices of maintaining good user documentation provide a focal point for the next chapter.

Exercises

Many of these exercises are best completed by teams of two or more persons working together.

8.1 Password recovery in *RMH Homebase* uses the idea that the person's default password is identical to his login id. This is inherently insecure unless every person changes his password as soon as he logs in—an unlikely scenario for a database of 200 or more persons. Moreover, the convention for resetting a forgotten password is for the House Manager to reset it to the default value and then rely on the user to change it the next time he logs in.

    a. Suggest a more secure definition for default password assignment in *RMH Homebase*.

    b. When a person forgets his password, suggest a way by which the person can recover it without bothering the House Manager.

    c. Revise login_form.php and other related modules so that your suggestions are implemented in *RMH Homebase*. Be sure to test this revision to ensure that it works in all cases.

8.2 Change the editShift.php and subCallList modules in *RMH Homebase* so that only "active" volunteers can be scheduled or included on a sub call list for any particular shift on the calendar.

8.3 When we refactored index.php by replacing a MySQL query by a call to the function `selectScheduled_dbShifts($person_id)`, we noted that the code following that call must be adjusted to accommodate the value returned. Complete this adjustment, using the code in Figure 8.25 as a starting point.

8.4 Design, implement, and unit test the changes to the user interface modules required by the new feature **Item 4: Calendar month view** in the "wish list" described in Appendix B.

This feature should allow an entire month to be viewed. The user should be able to click any day of that view to activate that particular week's display. In previous chapters, we added the new class Month and a new database table dbMonths that will support this new feature.

To complete the implementation of this feature, we can add the following user interface functionality:

    a. A new button "View Month" at the top of the current calendar view should link to a new page that displays an entire month.

b. Each day on the month view should be white or gray depending on whether or not it has a shift with a vacancy.

c. Selecting any day of the month should bring the user back to the calendar week view which shows all the week's shifts in detail (as it does now).

Unit testing this new feature will require adding new assertions to the unit tests for the user interface modules affected.

8.5 Design, implement, and unit test the changes to the user interface modules required by the new feature **Item 5: Import/export** in the "wish list" described in Appendix B.

This feature should provide managers with the option to export any person's data into a comma-separated list for importing into an Excel-type of spreadsheet. An import option should allow managers to retrieve any suitable comma-separated list and add it to the dbPersons table.

Chapter 7 discussed the addition of new functions import and export to the dbPersons.php database module to support this feature. Now we need to add user interface options to selectively activate these functions, ensuring that any new data added to the dbPersons table have been screened for validity as if they had been entered using the on-line application form.

Unit testing this new feature will require adding new assertions to the unit tests for the user interface modules affected.

8.6 Design, implement, and unit test the changes to the user interface modules required by the new feature **Item 7: Vacancies and shifts worked** in the "wish list" described in Appendix B. The House Manager should see the following information supported by a new search function:

a. Sort the upcoming vacancies on the manager's screen by date.

b. Compute the total and average number of vacancies for each day and shift, for any series of weeks in the past.

c. Compute the total and average number of shifts worked by any volunteer, for any series of weeks in the past.

These new capabilities augment the current system's listing of upcoming vacancies (in no particular order) on the House Manager's screen. The database modules dbShifs and dbDates have been augmented so that they can accumulate the total and average numbers of vacancies for each shift and date over any series of weeks.

Now the user interface modules view.php and index.php should be modified to provide the new functionality and to ensure that upcoming vacancies are ordered by date.

8.7 The previous exercise provides an opportunity to refactor the index.php code to remove violations of the layering principle. Perform that refactoring, and run the unit test suite to ensure that your changes have not had any adverse side effects.

8.8 Design, implement, and unit test the changes to the user interface modules required by the new feature **Item 8: Open applications** in the "wish list" described in Appendix B.

On the manager's home page, open applications should be sorted by last name and "grayed out" if any of the interview, background check, or shadow buttons are selected. Also, if an application remains open for more than a month, it should be marked inactive and also grayed out in this list.

The domain and database changes have already been made to support this change. Now, the index.php module should be modified to enable this change at the user interface.

8.9 Design, implement, and unit test the changes to the user interface modules required by the new features **Item 9b,c,d: Volunteer application** in the "wish list" described in Appendix B. These three new features should be added to the personEdit.php module so that the user can:

Item 9b Enter a start date by selecting only the month and year fields

Item 9c Receive an acknowledgment (rather than a blank page) when the user submits an application form

Item 9d Enter new information: employer, contact name, and contact phone

The domain and database classes have been changed to support the addition of this new feature. Now we need to modify the personEdit and searchPeople forms to accommodate them as well.

8.10 Design, implement, and unit test the changes to the user interface modules required by the new features **Item 10: Log** in the "wish list" described in Appendix B. This feature should allow the manager to view up to 50 entries at a time and provide a pager at the bottom for scrolling. Adding this feature will impact only the log.php user interface module.

Chapter 9

User Support

> "The skill of writing is to create a context
> in which other people can think."
> —*Edwin Schlossberg*

When working with a code base, developers maintain good *developer documentation*, so that future developers can understand the functioning of every module and function in the code base. Earlier chapters have identified techniques for establishing and using good developer documentation.

However, software development also requires maintaining good *user documentation*. Such documentation connects the software to its users. It can be viewed as a technical (reference) manual of "how to's" for using the software to perform each of the tasks that the system supports. User documentation can also act as a tutorial for beginners when they encounter the software for the first time.

User support is not only about documentation; it is also about feedback and responsiveness. A variety of tools are available today for maintaining communication channels between developers and users. The effectiveness with which these channels are used follows directly from how well they are set up and supported by the developers.

This chapter begins by reviewing principles of good writing, especially as they apply to writing user documentation. Next, we discuss ways of integrating written documentation within the code base, so that users will have immediate support when they interact with the software. Third, we cover other ways of maintaining user support, including user training, forums, and feedback surveys.

9.1 Technical Writing

Technical writing is a special kind of writing. As such, it follows stylistic and other standards that ensure good writing quality. This section summarizes the principles and practice of good technical writing.

When we think about technical writing for user documentation, we must first determine how the documentation will be presented. Here are the main elements of presentation:

Organization is the way the document is arranged. Organization also includes navigability and access. That is, how easily can the user navigate among related sections of the document? For an on-line document, how easily can a relevant section of the document be accessed from a related element of the user interface for the software itself?

Illustration is the interplay between text, images, and other media. Appropriate selection and placement of images, for example, can do a lot to clarify a written description for the reader.

Style is the way we use words and media to describe a software feature or user activity. It includes word order, sentence length, use of examples, grammar, punctuation, spelling, and various media presentation options.

Tone shows the attitude of the writer toward the reader. For example, a peer-to-peer tone suggests using a level of language and subject matter understanding that the writer and reader share in common. A mentor-student tone, on the other hand, requires that the writer adapt to a level of language and understanding that is appropriate for the user.

Thus, effective software documentation takes into account the characteristics of the audience of users for whom it is written. In addition, effective software documentation must follow the detailed principles of good writing in general. These two subjects are considered in more detail below.

9.1.1   Knowing Your Audience

The audience of users who read and utilize a software document typically varies from one software artifact to another. Even within the same artifact, some users will be more familiar with the application domain, better educated, more fluent in the native language of the application (typically English), more adept at using computers, and/or more familiar with the artifact itself than others. A well-written software document tries to address the diverse perspectives of all users who need the software—this is not a simple task.

To help address different users' levels of experience, two separate kinds of user documents can be developed: one that initiates *new users* to the software and another that provides *experienced users* with "how to's" on every aspect of using the software. The former document is sometimes called a *tutorial* while the latter is sometimes called a *reference manual*. A third type of document, an *open discussion forum*, tends to address the needs of both novice and advanced users. Further discussions of these three forms of user documentation appear in Section 9.2.

Typically, Web-based software comes with a "Help" tab on the main menu that facilitates convenient keyword-based searching for reference material. There are many examples of good reference manuals on the Web. Look at your browser's main menu, for example, and check out its Help tab.

Whether they are beginners or experienced, users access documentation because they want answers. That is:

Good documentation *directly answers any question* that a user asks, no more and no less. For example, there is no point in showing an experienced user all the screens that may appear when logging in to use the software. On the other hand, a novice user will need precisely this detailed level of information.

Good documentation *covers all the situations* that users may encounter when using the software. For this reason, it is desirable for the document to be organized along the same lines that the software's use cases are organized. That is, we may start organizing a user manual by identifying one chapter with each use case, beginning with the login and logout procedures.

Organizationally, it is often desirable to present an on-line help manual in a way that parallels the way the user interacts with the software. That is, each of the software's main menu items typically initiates a series of steps that the user must perform to accomplish a task. Thus, a corresponding help page for that menu item can describe each of those steps, along with a screen shot that the user can expect to encounter as each step is completed.

A hard copy by-product of an on-line help manual may also be desirable. Many users prefer having a hard copy nearby while using the software, so that they can refer to it when they have a question about what to do next. Other users may prefer to "fiddle" with the software in order to become familiar with the nuances of each activity as it is needed.

For some applications, not all users may be native speakers of English. Thus, keeping documentation as simple as possible is very important. To this end, some technical fields have adopted a "Simplified English" that contains about 1,000 words, each with just one meaning. Being aware of any relevant Simplified English for your software's application domain will help you write text that users are likely to understand. For more information, see http://en.wikipedia.org/wiki/Simplified_English.

When significant populations of users speak a different language from English, it may be necessary to produce the documentation in two or more different languages. This is called "localization," and it is a particularly common feature of community-oriented software products such as *Sahana* or Drupal (see http://sahanafoundation.org or http://drupal.org) that have a worldwide user community.

On a different note, some users may have reading disorders or cognitive disabilities. Others may just read poorly. Text content will always pose problems for these users. Some of the ways in which documentation can be responsive to people with cognitive disabilities are:

1. Supplement the text with illustrations. The most drastic, and yet perhaps the most useful, solution for these audiences is to provide graphics instead of text. In other words, do everything possible to clarify and simplify the text, and then go one step further by supplementing the text with a redundant graphic.

2. Reduce the text to a bare minimum on each page. Pages with a large amount of text can intimidate users with reading difficulties.

3. Be as literal as possible—avoid using metaphor or humor to illustrate a point. Some people with cognitive disabilities cannot distinguish between the literal meaning of an idea and its implied meaning.

Overall, good documentation assumes that readers are intelligent, but it does not assume that readers know the subject matter as well as the author. Therefore, explaining and illustrating basic concepts of the software is more helpful than insulting, as long as the explanations show respect for the reader.[1]

Surely, no collection of user documentation for a software artifact can please everyone. However, knowing and being sensitive to users' preferences will take the writer a long way toward producing documentation that will satisfy most users' needs.

9.1.2   Principles of Good Writing

Overall, good writing requires that the document be clear and simple. The task of writing clearly and simply can be one of the most difficult of all writing tasks. Clear and simple writing is a skill to which many aspire and few achieve. In the words of Ernest Hemingway:

> "My aim is to put down on paper what I see and what I feel in the best and simplest way."

In particular, the development of useful software documentation depends critically upon clear and simple writing. Unclear or complex documentation will surely deflate the user's enthusiasm for the software, and it can be especially off-putting for people with reading disorders or cognitive disabilities.

The following guidelines provide a detailed definition of what we mean by "clear and simple" as they apply to writing good software documentation:

---

[1]Some experts say writers should aim for "eighth grade level" when writing user documentation. For instance, many popular magazines are written at about eighth grade level. News sources such as *Newsweek* are written at a slightly higher level, say 10th grade.

Organize your topic into a logical outline before you begin writing. This may be the most important guideline of all. You must think clearly about a topic in order to communicate it clearly.

The organizing process is ongoing, starting before any words are written and continuing throughout the entire development process. In this sense, documentation writing is like code refactoring.

Put summary information first. Describe the purpose of each section before laying out its details.

Use the language of the domain. Users will relate more quickly to documentation if it contains words and phrases that are familiar and (in some cases) unique to the domain where the software is being used. The instance variables and names of the domain classes in the code base provide a good beginning vocabulary.

Be precise. Use precise words as opposed to more general variants. Provide enough detail so as not to keep the reader in the dark. Avoid using ambiguous words.

Use the present tense. Software use has no past or future. Everything happens in the moment as a direct result of some event, usually initiated by the user. As soon as another event occurs, the computer has another reaction. So good technical writing uses the present tense almost exclusively.

Be direct. Use the second person and the imperative mood. That is, use "you" and phrases like "do this and then do that." The result is usually more precise, concise, and clear. Direct instructions can increase comprehension and place more of a sense of responsibility on the user.

Be concise. Avoid stating the obvious or using unnecessary padding, repetition, verbosity, or pomposity. Software users are not looking at the style of your prose; they are only looking for guidance that helps them perform a task. Wordiness is not a virtue in technical writing.

For example, the sentence "The unwise leaving their login or password on their workspace may result in a dangerous breach of software security and therefore it is recommended that one retain their password in a safe and secure location in order to ensure data integrity" can be rewritten as "Keep your password secure."

Use simple and short sentence structure. Avoid compound sentences and long phrases. Some suggest that a good average sentence length for technical documentation is somewhere between 15 and 20 words.

Use parallel sentence construction. Make sure that sentence construction is internally consistent. Consider the inconsistent sentence "This algorithm is correct, improves memory usage and efficiency." It can be correctly rewritten as "This algorithm is correct, improves memory usage and improves efficiency." Alternatively, it can be rewritten as "This algorithm is correct and improves both memory usage and efficiency."

Use the active voice. The active voice works better than the passive in technical writing because the focus of the sentence is the user's action rather than the object being acted upon.

Use positive terms. It is always best to use phrases that don't contain a negative element like "no" or "not." For example, "impossible" is a positive construction as opposed to "not possible." Emphasize the way things are, rather than what they are not.

Punctuate properly. Use complete sentences terminated by a period. Use other punctuation appropriately and sparingly.

Check your spelling. Use an automated spell checker, but don't rely on it completely. Proofread the document to find correctly spelled words that are used incorrectly. For example, the spelling error in "For score and seven years ago..." will not typically be picked up by a spell checker.

Use computer terms as needed, but only ones that are commonly known. For example, click, double-click, select, type, mouse, touchpad, browser, button, window, and file are all okay.

Avoid specifying gender. For example, using "he/she" rather than "he" or "she" alone creates reading comfort among diverse groups of users that typically include both genders.

Clarify acronyms and abbreviations. Unfamiliar acronyms and abbreviations mean nothing to users. Expanding acronyms when they first appear allows users to learn their meaning.

Avoid slang and jargon. Slang and jargon can be useful to people who understand it, but confusing to people who don't.

Avoid weak verbs. Don't use a form of the verb "to be" (is, are, was, were) when a more active verb would be more appropriate. Over-use of "to be" often forces writers to use the passive voice more than necessary.

Write cohesive paragraphs constructed around a single major idea. All of the ideas in a paragraph should relate back to the main point. Typically, the main point belongs in the first sentence.

Use two columns to describe the steps of a user-computer interaction. Label one column "User" and the other "System." Number the steps serially, which clearly indicates their order.

Use short numbered lists (3–9 items) to list a sequence of steps. Lists are useful because they break up long sentences and they identify easy-to-digest information chunks.

When making a list of steps, use the same form in each step. Start with a verb to establish the imperative mood. For example:

1. Open the file you want to rename.
2. Select Rename from the Edit menu.
3. Type the file's new name.
4. Click Save.

Add a graphic whenever it will help visualize a point. A picture is worth a thousand words. Many users will prefer a visual clue over a textual one. If practical, write instructions with both visual and textual content.

So there you have it: an explicit list of guidelines that, when followed carefully, can ensure that written user documentation is concise and clear. The examples in later sections will illustrate these guidelines in greater detail.

9.2 Types of User Support

This section provides guidance on how to organize different types of user support, along with some detailed examples. We consider four different genres: on-line help, reference manuals, open discussion forums, and training tutorials. All four genres require that the author follow the principles and guidelines for good writing presented in the foregoing section.

On-line help is aimed at novice and occasional users, while reference manuals are aimed at experienced and frequent users. Open discussion forums are accessible to novices and expert users alike. Thus, individual users must filter their level of access depending on their level of familiarity with the software. Tutorial training is designed to be used off-line, especially by novice users who need extra time to experiment with the software before using it in a production environment.

9.2.1 On-Line Help

On-line help is usually organized so that it can be followed from beginning to end, starting with the assumption that the user has never seen that particular feature before. A table of contents provides a road map of the major features that the tutorial covers, so that users can anticipate what topics will occur and in what order.

On-line help is typically available instantaneously and is integrated with the software itself. It can be accessed by simply selecting the "Help" item in the software's main menu. As such, it provides the first point of assistance when a user becomes confused about some particular aspect of the software.

The quality of an on-line help session is enhanced when the writer follows these organizational guidelines:

User access and navigation Most software systems provide users with a main menu, which identifies each of the major functions that users can perform. The organization of this menu often provides a basis for organizing the on-line help support itself.

That is, allocating one help section to each entry in the main menu identifies the major sections of the help document. Moreover, the online help should have a header page containing a table organized like the software's main menu and linked to each of the help sections.

This table, and every help section, should open in a separate window from the user's screen, so as not to interrupt the user's interaction with the software itself while he/she is reading the related help page. The correspondence between table entries and the software's main menu entries should be obvious to the user.

Step-by-step guidance Each on-line help page should address a single user task from beginning to end. Typically, a user task is accomplished as a series of steps (as in the task's original use case). Thus, it makes sense to organize each task's on-line help page as a series of steps to be carried out in order.

Each step should be described as a simple English-language command, using the principles of good writing introduced in the foregoing section. A step may often be accompanied by a visual picture (screen shot) that describes how that step is carried out.

Screen shots and thumbnails Each screen shot that accompanies an individual step in an on-line help page should be captured from a "live" software session by the help page writer. However, it is important that this screen shot reveal only hypothetical data, so as not to reveal information that must be kept confidential.

Because most users will not need to look at the full screen shot for each step on the help page, a "thumbnail" image (rendered at about 10% of the screen shot's full size) should appear by default. Thereby, only those users (maybe novice users) who need to view the full screen shot can click on the thumbnail to take a look at the full image, while others will be satisfied by reading the text alone.

9.2.2 Reference Manuals

Reference manuals are best organized so that discussions about individual topics, called "chunks," can be accessed randomly. This allows experienced users to search for any topic whenever the need arises and read about it directly. To facilitate this activity, a reference manual must be well indexed. On-line reference manuals typically include a search feature that leads users directly to the topic of interest, as well as internal links that facilitate navigation between major sections.

A reference manual should describe every feature of a software artifact. It should also provide relevant examples that assist users who want to exercise those features to accomplish useful tasks. A good reference manual can also provide troubleshooting assistance. It is very important for a reference manual to be kept up to date. In this sense, the manual can be viewed as a contract specifying what the software will do.

While a reference manual need not be organized in any particular way, it should always have a thorough and searchable index. It is also useful to provide a "Frequently Asked Questions" (FAQ) section at or near the front. So an overall organizational scheme for a reference manual may have the following main elements:

Table of Contents This is like a table of contents in a textbook. However, it should also provide direct links to each of the sections so that users don't need to navigate manually.

Frequently Asked Questions This provides answers to questions that occur so often that an average user is likely to find help here rather than diving more deeply into the manual. Typically, the length of a FAQ list is rather short. The list shows each question in **boldface** so as to make it easy to locate with a quick visual scan. A longer FAQ list is usually accompanied by a "search box" which can assist users to locate relevant questions more quickly.

Chapter Layout Each chapter in a reference manual should be short and address a particular function of the software. If the topic of a chapter requires more length, the chapter should be divided into shorter sections that are focussed on individual sub-topics. Hyperlinks among chapters and sections should be abundant, so that users can easily navigate among related topics as they read.

Examples and Illustrations Each topic discussed should be accompanied by a brief, illustrative example. Good examples always help to clarify abstract ideas.

Indexing and Searching A thorough index is also a necessity. The search box allows users to find information about topics that do not appear explicitly in the index.

FIGURE 9.1: First page of the *Firefox manual*, including Help and FAQs.

Below are two examples of particularly effective and useful on-line reference manuals and FAQs.

9.2.2.1   Example: Firefox Reference Manual

The first page of the Firefox browser reference manual is shown in Figure 9.1 (see http://support.mozilla.com/en-US/kb/). Its prominent features are a search tab and a short list of links to articles that are most frequently accessed. Thus, the Firefox manual tries to head the user in the right direction right from the get-go, without any fanfare.

However, looking at the entire index of the Firefox reference manual is a somewhat more daunting task. That index contains about 250 topics, arranged in random (non-alphabetical) order, and is very difficult to browse.

A familiar search box appears at the top of the index, and this is really the only practical avenue for entry into the manual's content. A complete overview of the manual's content is impossible to obtain, since (at this writing) there appears to be no accessible table of contents at the Firefox help site.

9.2.2.2   Example: Sahana FAQs

Figure 9.2 shows a snapshot of the *Sahana* FAQ that was taken in June 2010. Each entry in the list is a particular question that was raised by a user;

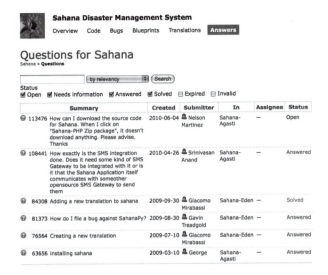

FIGURE 9.2: Accessing the *Sahana* FAQ list.

the last column indicates the *Status* of that question (open, answered, solved, etc.) as of that particular date.

Notice that the questions can be sorted by relevancy to the user's own search query, which would be entered in the Search box near the top of the page. Notice also that the questions can be filtered by Status, so that if a user wants to see only questions that have been answered, all others can be filtered out.

9.2.3 Open Discussion Forums

Open discussion forums are widely used by community-oriented software projects. They are organized by topic, and individual topics are initiated by developers and users themselves. Anyone can access an open forum, and anyone can post a question or a response as well. Most forums are *moderated*, so that useless questions and answers can be filtered out before they are made available for general public access.

An open discussion forum is designed to capture and publish user questions "as is," and then provide an open channel through which more experienced users or developers can address each question directly. In general, forums tend to be more up to date than tutorials or reference manuals.

On the other hand, the quality of information in forums can be more spotty compared with that found in tutorials and reference manuals; a forum is only as good (or bad) as the quality of questions and answers provided by its volunteer participants. Forum moderation can help retain good quality, and a certain level of "filtering skill" on behalf of the forum user can also help

FIGURE 9.3:   Point of access to the *Sahana* forums.

establish usefulness.

9.2.3.1   Example: Sahana Forums

Figure 9.3 shows the point at which users can access the *Sahana* discussion forums. There, we see a main menu at the top through which users can navigate to the bug reports, answers to FAQs, and so forth. The right-hand margin provides suggestions that enable users to get involved with *Sahana*: by reporting a bug, asking a question, or helping to translate the application into a different language.

Figure 9.4 suggests how people can contribute to the *Sahana* bug tracking system. It provides a list of all active bugs, their status, and other information that will help users relate current bugs to their particular issues. Developers can use this same list for guidance if they want to help fix a particular bug. The search box at the top of the page allows users to specify their particular issues in more detail.

9.2.3.2   Example: Drupal Forums

Drupal (see http://drupal.org) is an open source software platform that supports the development of content-management Web sites. Begun about 10 years ago by Dries Buytaert, Drupal has grown dramatically so that it now has a very large developer and user community. At this writing, Drupal has several hundred developers and hundreds of thousands of users (Web site developers) worldwide.

To keep developers and users up to date with its rapid growth, Drupal

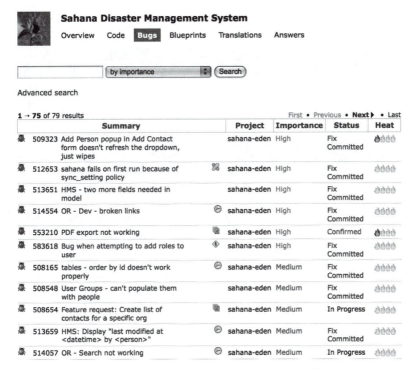

FIGURE 9.4: Accessing the *Sahana* bug tracking list.

maintains several developer and user forums. These are called "Support," "General," "Services," "Newsletters," and "Deprecated." The first three threads in the Support forum are shown in Figure 9.5.

The presentation of posts can be filtered in a number of ways, especially by specifying a Search criterion. As the numbers in columns 2 and 3 of Figure 9.5 show, these posts have a very high level of activity and reach a very large number of users.

9.2.3.3   Example: Firefox Forum

Like Drupal, Firefox (see http://support.mozilla.com/en-US/kb) has several active user forums that provide useful guidance for new and experienced users. The main Firefox forum is called "Support," while there is also a separate "Contributors forum" and an "Off-topic forum." Figure 9.6 shows the main page that opens when the Firefox Support forum is accessed.

The threads in this forum are shown in order beginning with the most recent. Also shown is a snippet of each thread's discussion topic, its author, and the number of replies received to date. To narrow the search, users are encouraged to "Ask a New Question" right at the top of the forum. This will provide a Google-like list of discussion threads that are most relevant to the

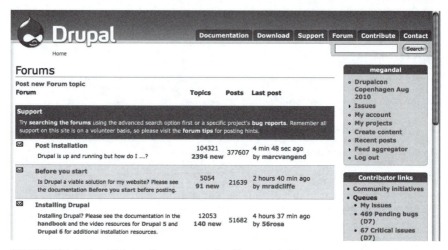

FIGURE 9.5:   Point of access to the Drupal forums.

FIGURE 9.6:   Accessing the Firefox user forum.

user's topic of interest.

For example, if a user wants to learn about printing Web pages, they would type, "How do I print a Web page?" In reply, the Support forum would likely retrieve the second item in Figure 9.6 but not the other three.

9.2.4 User Training and Feedback

For a new client-oriented system, it may be desirable to organize live user training sessions in which developers work directly with users and teach them about each function in the system. The goal of such a session is not only to train new users but also to further troubleshoot the new system for errors and other usability issues that had not occurred before.

At the end of the training session, it is often helpful to ask new users to provide feedback on the new system, the training experience itself, and their opinion about the general value of the new software in their working environment. Users usually provide frank and insightful advice, not only for debugging purposes but also in regard to the overall utility of the system and the possibilities for adding new functionality in the future.

When *RMH Homebase* was completed and ready to install, only the House Manager was familiar with the software. At that time, the need to establish RMH staff buy-in had become an important goal. To that end, two training sessions were organized and the student developers used the on-line help pages to initiate other RMH staff members and volunteers to using the software.

Eleven persons attended the two workshops: four RMH staff members and seven volunteers. Workshop attendees completed a questionnaire where they rated the quality of the software and the chances that they would use it and be able to teach it to other volunteers in the future. The responses from all 11 participants are summarized in Table 9.1.

All 11 participants uniformly agreed that the software was "extremely user friendly" and that they could see themselves "easily teaching another volunteer" how to use the system. Several commented that the software should be useful at many other Ronald McDonald Houses and similar organizations in the future.

For a community-oriented project, organizing live user training sessions is not usually feasible, since the user community is large and diverse. For this need, some software projects provide tutorial Web casts, which can be used either freely or at a cost low enough not to deter interested users. Web casts can often be downloaded individually and played by users at their own convenience and pace. A good example of such a tutorial is the introduction to Drupal is available at http://learnbythedrop.com.

TABLE 9.1: *RMH Homebase* User Questionnaire and Results

Question	Average Response (1 = poor, ... 5 = excellent)
Evaluate *RMH Homebase* with regard to:	
1. Logging in	4.7
2. Headings and logo	4.9
3. Searching for volunteers	5.0
4. Adding, deleting, and changing volunteers	4.7
5. Viewing the calendar	5.0
6. Changing the calendar (sub call lists)	5.0
7. Managing the calendar (generating weeks)	5.0
8. Editing and managing the master schedule	5.0
9. Understanding the on-line help	5.0
10. Logging out	5.0
11. Workshop effectiveness	5.0
12. Quality of client/developer collaboration	5.0

9.3   Example: RMH Homebase On-Line Help

The following discussion highlights the on-line help documentation that is incorporated into *RMH Homebase.* Readers should consult the code base at the book's Web site myopensoftware.org/textbookto obtain more detailed information.

9.3.1   Help and the Code Base

In addition to its core, database, and GUI modules, a software system usually has additional supporting modules that provide on-line help pages for users to access while they are working with the software.

These user help pages should be collected in a separate directory and should be associated directly with each of the forms in the user interface. It is a good habit to write user help pages in tandem with each such form as it is being developed, since testing each form involves mimicking sequences of actions that users will perform to accomplish its related use case.

For *RMH Homebase*, the help page modules are all stored in the directory `tutorial`. Help pages can be accessed directly by authenticated users when they select "help" on the main menu (see Figure 4.7). Help pages appear in a separate window, so as not to interfere with the page that the user is currently viewing.

To ensure that the appropriate help instructions are displayed, the code in Figure 4.8 invokes the PHP module `help.php` along with a parameter that identifies the particular page for which help has been sought. If more than

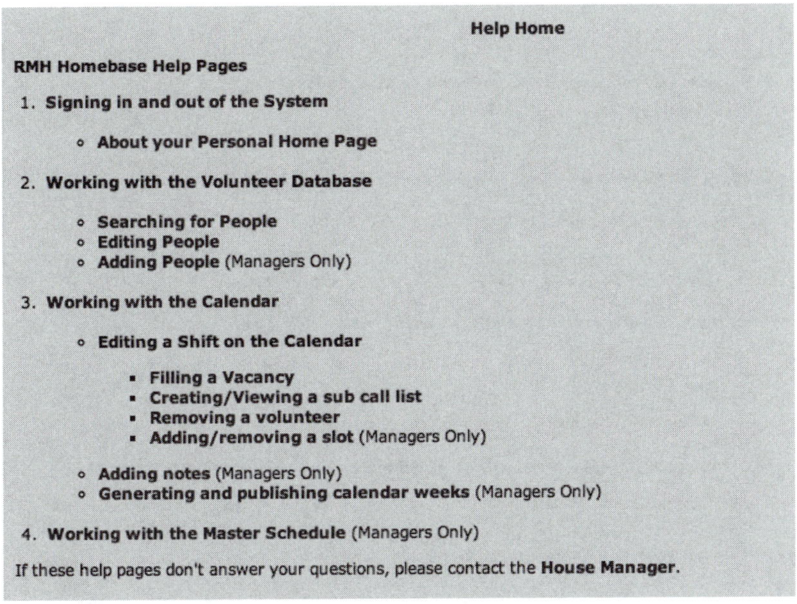

Help Home

RMH Homebase Help Pages

1. **Signing in and out of the System**

   ○ **About your Personal Home Page**

2. **Working with the Volunteer Database**

   ○ **Searching for People**
   ○ **Editing People**
   ○ **Adding People** (Managers Only)

3. **Working with the Calendar**

   ○ **Editing a Shift on the Calendar**

     ▪ **Filling a Vacancy**
     ▪ **Creating/Viewing a sub call list**
     ▪ **Removing a volunteer**
     ▪ **Adding/removing a slot** (Managers Only)

   ○ **Adding notes** (Managers Only)
   ○ **Generating and publishing calendar weeks** (Managers Only)

4. **Working with the Master Schedule** (Managers Only)

If these help pages don't answer your questions, please contact the **House Manager**.

FIGURE 9.7:   The main help menu in *RMH Homebase*.

one help page would be useful for the current form, an index of all help pages is displayed and the user can choose one.

9.3.1.1   User Access and Navigation

Organization of the main help page in *RMH Homebase* follows directly from the main menu, which we recall from Figure 4.7. Notice that direct access to the main help page is provided by the "help" link in the main menu. Notice also that the main menu has four separate parts, one for the user's "home" page, one for the calendar, one for people, and one for the master schedule.

Correspondingly, the main help page has four major parts, as shown in Figure 9.7. Among these parts are links to individual help pages, about 11 in number. Recall that the original design of *RMH Homebase* (see Appendix A) has about the same number of use cases, and so there is a nearly one-to-one correspondence between these individual help pages and the use cases themselves.

9.3.1.2   Step-by-Step Guidance

Each help page contains step-by-step guidance on how to complete a particular task (in other words, how to accomplish a particular use case) using the software. An example is shown in Figure 9.8 for the task of filling a vacancy for a shift on the calendar.

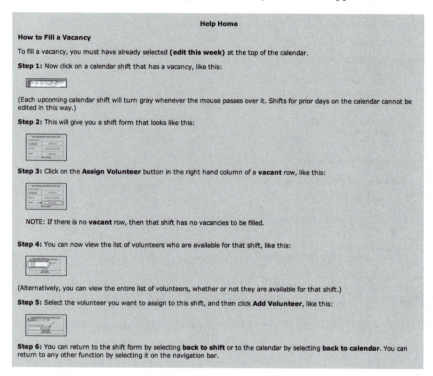

FIGURE 9.8:   Stepping through the task of filling a vacancy.

This help page opens in a separate page from where the user is working, so that by following these steps the user can accomplish some useful work with the software. These steps begin by ensuring that the user is at the right place to fill a vacancy. Specifically, the user must be editing a particular week of the calendar where the vacancy occurs.

When followed one-by-one, these steps will result in a vacancy being filled in the shift. Step 1 brings the particular shift into focus, while Step 2 shows what that will look like. Step 3 brings the particular vacancy into focus, while Step 4 shows the options that become available for that vacancy (a list of the volunteers who are available to work that shift). Step 5 then shows how to complete the assignment of a volunteer, while Step 6 suggests how to navigate back to the shift or the calendar after the assignment is complete.

Filling a vacancy is a pretty straightforward task overall, but it can be daunting for someone who has never worked with the software before. This help page thus gracefully initiates a new user into the process of assigning a volunteer to a shift. Performing this task two or three times should enable the user to fill a vacancy independently, without the need to refer to the help page in the future.

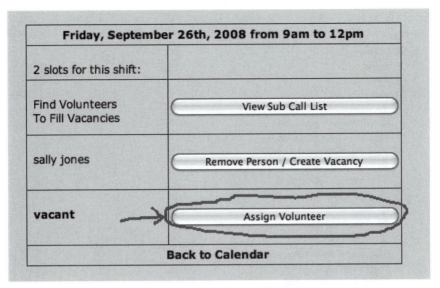

FIGURE 9.9: Showing a screen shot by selecting its thumbnail.

9.3.1.3 Screen Shots and Thumbnails

Often a visual clue can reinforce the textual description of a particular step in a help page. Such a clue helps the user to relate the text to a specific visual situation that is occurring at the time the user asks for help.

An easy way to provide a visual clue for an individual step is to add a screen shot below the text, in thumbnail form, so that some users can view that screen shot when they need further clarification. An example of such a screen shot appears in Figure 9.9, which corresponds to the thumbnail in Step 3 of the foregoing example.

This screen shot will be useful for users who can't find the "Assign Volunteer" button beside the **vacant** slot in the shift form. Other users who find that button can skip over that screen shot by simply not clicking on its thumbnail.

9.3.1.4 Integration with the Code Base

On-line help should be integrated within the code base, alongside the domain classes, database modules, GUI modules, and test suite. Such integration provides motivation for developers to treat the user documentation with the same respect that they treat the rest of the code base.

For example, in *RMH Homebase*, the on-line help pages are kept in a separate folder "tutorial" within the code base, as shown in Figure 9.10. Each file within that folder contains the HTML code for one help page. Figure 9.11 shows the beginning of the HTML code for the help page for filling a vacancy.

```
▼ 🗂 rmh1.5
    ▶ 📂 database
    ▶ 📂 images
    ▶ 📂 tests
    ▼ 📂 tutorial
        ▶ 📂 screenshots
          📄 addPersonHelp.inc.php
          📄 addSlotToShiftHelp.inc.php
          📄 assignToShiftHelp.inc.php
          📄 calendarNotesHelp.inc.php
          📄 editPersonHelp.inc.php
          📄 generateWeekHelp.inc.php
          📄 index.inc.php
          📄 indexHelp.inc.php
          📄 login.inc.php
          📄 manageCalendarHelp.inc.php
          📄 removeFromShiftHelp.inc.php
          📄 schedulingHelp.inc.php
          📄 searchPersonHelp.inc.php
          📄 styles.css
          📄 subCallListHelp.inc.php
          📄 viewCalendarHelp.inc.php
```

FIGURE 9.10:   Integrating help pages within the code base.

```
<p> <strong>How to Fill a Vacancy</strong>
<p>  To fill a vacancy, you must have already selected <strong>
     (edit this week)</strong> at the top of the calendar.
<p>  <B>Step 1:</B> Now click on a calendar shift that has a
     vacancy, like this:<BR><BR>
     <a href="tutorial/screenshots/assigntoshiftstep1.gif"
     class="image" title="assigntoshiftstep1.png"
     horizontalalign="center"
     target="tutorial/screenshots/assigntoshiftstep1.gif">
         
     <img src="tutorial/screenshots/assigntoshiftstep1.gif"
     width="10\%" border="1px" align="center"></a>
     <br><br> (Each upcoming calendar shift will turn gray
     whenever the mouse passes over it.  Shifts for prior days
     on the calendar cannot be edited in this way.)
     ...
```

FIGURE 9.11:   HTML code for Step 1 of the help page for filling a vacancy.

As you can see, this HTML is a straightforward encoding of the text written to help a user with this task. The code that includes a graphic image is particularly interesting, since it gives a clue about how to display a thumbnail using HTML.

It also reveals that all the images are stored together in a separate subfolder "screenshots" within the tutorial folder. This is a common organizational strategy for images.

9.4 Summary

This chapter has discussed the principles and practices of developing and maintaining good user support for an open source software project.

Since it is a published work, good user documentation must be well written. Thus, it must use principles of good (technical) writing. It must be clear, concise, and sensitive to a variety of user reading and skill levels.

Four prominent types of user documentation are particularly valuable—on-line help, reference manuals, open discussion forums, and tutorials. This chapter has discussed the organization and usefulness of each one, along with some illustrative examples.

Exercises

9.1 Read the written user documentation for the software project on which you are working.

    a. Write a brief critique of that documentation vis-a-vis the principles of good writing introduced in this chapter.

    b. Briefly characterize the wider audience of people who use the software produced by your project. Include in your characterization factors like reading level, cognitive skills, native language, and education level.

    c. Evaluate the quality of your project's written documentation with respect to how well it matches the characteristics of its wider audience of users.

9.2 Review the on-line documentation for *RMH Homebase* release 1.5. Find three specific instances where the documentation does not agree with the actual software when it is running. Why do you suspect that this disagreement exists? Who should be responsible for updating the documentation to correct this mismatch? Explain.

9.3 Update the on-line user documentation for calendar editing on *RMH Homebase* release 2.0 so that it reflects the new functionality for moving a shift to a new start-end time (see Chapter 8 and Appendix B Item 3 for the implementation details).

9.4 Add a completely new on-line documentation page that explains to the user how to exercise the new Month view in *RMH Homebase* release 2.0.

9.5 If you are working on a client-oriented project, sketch the design of a training session that will introduce users to the new features that your software will have. Include a survey form that asks users to evaluate your new features.

9.6 If you are working on a community-oriented project, briefly evaluate the quality of its on-line user support. Does it provide good functional documentation for using the software? Does it provide training for new users? Do its discussion forums seem to be welcoming to answering (naive) questions about how to use the system? Does it provide an avenue for users or new developers to improve its user support?

Chapter 10

Project Governance

> "Empowerment of individuals is what makes open source work,
> since innovations tend to come from small groups,
> not from large, structured efforts."
> —*Tim O'Reilly*

The leadership and organizational dynamics for an open source project is sometimes called "project governance." This term suggests a collaborative process that is driven by factors other than cost and profit.

Open source projects are gift economies. The organization that runs an open source software project differs in fundamental ways from that which oversees a proprietary project. Eric Raymond's book *The Cathedral and the Bazaar* [Ray01] was a landmark publication describing the organizational differences between these two extremes.

However, many shades of gray have evolved as open source has become popular, even among projects that originated as proprietary software. An open source community in its most mature form is quite diverse. It includes not only individual volunteers, but also corporations with paid contributors, academics, and practitioners. Governing such a diverse group is fundamentally democratic, in the sense that one's citizenship is determined by one's contributions to the project.

Within the open source spectrum, project governance varies depending on the type and maturity of the project. These variations are due to the fundamental differences in community size, ownership models, and diversity of the user community.

In this chapter, we study the important elements of project governance for an open source project.

10.1 Origins and Evolution

Open source projects do not often originate with a democratic process. A project's governance gradually evolves based on the diversity and maturity of its community of contributors. An open source project may have any one of the following starting points:

- A client-oriented project,

- A lone developer or small group of developers "scratching an itch,"

- A proprietary product released into the open source arena, or

- A fork of an existing project.

Surprisingly quite a few of the large open source projects began not as client-oriented projects, but as proprietary projects. This seems to be an increasing trend as more and more software companies start adopting open source development strategies.

Recall from Chapter 1 the origins of Mozilla Firefox. This is a good example of a project that originated as a proprietary product called Netscape, originally developed at Sun Microsystems. When Sun started losing market share to Microsoft's Internet Explorer, Sun adopted an open source strategy and released the Netscape code base as the Mozilla browser. Thus, Netscape provided the code base that spawned the now-diverse community that supports the Firefox browser.

A project's transition from proprietary to open source, whether it be within a company or a small group of owners, is typically isolated and has little community involvement. This is mainly because there is no tangible product that people can get interested in—only a vision—which makes it hard to form any sizable developer or user community at the outset.

The second phase of an open source project is what we might lightheartedly call the *benevolent dictator* phase. In this phase, the project has a tangible product that is of some value to users and has a community developing around it. However, despite the community's contributions, all real decisions are made by the benevolent dictator or a core team that includes the original system's developers.

Linux is a good example of a lone-developer project that remained in the benevolent dictator phase for a long time. Linux had a large number of contributions from the community, but Linus Torvalds was the benevolent dictator who had the final call on what contributions went into the code base.

A significant number of projects do not move out of the benevolent dictator phase, and in some cases that might be the right outcome. That is, the next phase involves a lot of investment in time and new governance processes, which a project might not be able to afford.

If the original developers desire that the project remain in its original phase, that is acceptable since they are the ones who have the most risk and investment in the project. In that event, anyone else has the right to fork the project (because of its FOSS license) and create a new branch with a different vision, as long as they do not violate the terms of the original license.

10.1.1   Starting a Client-Oriented Project

Starting an open source project to develop an entirely new product is often done with a small core team of developers and clients. The client-oriented approach begins by identifying a key stakeholder that will provide direct feedback on the project. If successful, the project can provide a springboard for developers to participate in other open source projects in the future.

Client-oriented projects can use any of a variety of development methodologies and programming environments. For small teams, a highly recommended methodology is agile, as found in *extreme programming* (see the Web site http://en.wikipedia.org/wiki/Extreme_Programming) or *scrum* (see the site http://en.wikipedia.org/wiki/Scrum_(development)).

Below is a summary of the other key start-up ingredients.

10.1.1.1   Communication

Developers and clients should establish short, rich communication paths. These may include a discussion forum, working in the same room (or at least using some form of synchronized communication like Skype), and an agreed-upon schedule of availability for team meetings.

Team meetings should be conducted on a weekly basis, both to confirm the achievement of goals and to set new tasks and goals for the upcoming week. Failure to complete one or more tasks in a given week is not sufficient cause for canceling or even delaying a meeting.

10.1.1.2   Release Plan

An automated unit testing and build process should be established, and the development platform (stack) and version control system should be established. Developers should synchronize their choices of IDE and protocol for accessing the VCS.

A first task for a new team is to develop an initial release plan, in which each iteration contains new integrated and tested code. Each release should be delivered to real users, after which a review session should be conducted to reflect on the outcome and recalibrate goals for the next iteration.

10.1.1.3   Staging Server and Live Server

While the use of a code synchronization repository facilitates communication among developers in a small project, it is not much use to the other members of the project team: the users.

To facilitate interaction among all team members, the team needs a vehicle to allow users and developers to instantly experiment with the current version of the software so that they can see what's working and provide informed feedback on that version's strengths and weaknesses. This is particularly important when the user interface components are being developed.

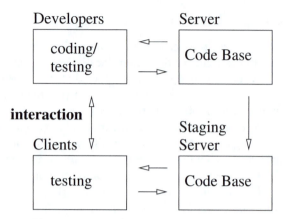

FIGURE 10.1:   The staging server: Client-Developer interaction.

The use of a *staging server* can support this kind of interaction.[1] Typically, the staging server has a current copy of the project's code base, along with some sample data and Web-based tools for clients to easily interact with the code's functional elements.

The staging server's functionality naturally grows with each new release. At the end of the project, the staging server provides a complete user interface for the software product being developed, implementing all the use cases that appear in the design document. This client-developer interaction is illustrated in Figure 10.1.

Typically, the staging server is set up by the IT support person on the development team. The staging server is a temporary tool, since it will go out of business when a client-oriented project reaches completion. At that point, the completed software is installed on a *live server* where it can be permanently accessed by clients. Eventually, the new software may be integrated within the client's main Web site.

A sample staging server for *RMH Homebase* development is at the book's Web site myopensoftware.org/textbook. A staging server provides a vehicle through which clients/users can easily access the current version of the software throughout the life of the project. When the *RMH Homebase* project was completed, release 1.0 of the software was installed on the House's live server in May 2008 at http://rmhportland.org/volunteers/homebase.[2]

---

[1]An equivalent term for staging server is *sandbox*.

[2]As of this writing, the software has seen four additional releases. Releases 1.5 and 2.0 are discussed more thoroughly in earlier chapters of this book.

10.1.1.4   Membership Levels and Meritocracy

Different team members assume different levels of team membership in a new project, depending on their prior experience and their experience with the client's application domain. Cockburn (e.g., [Coc05], p 9) equates the three levels of team participation—novice, apprentice, and expert—with the three levels of mastery in *Shuhari*, a Japanese martial art concept.[3]

The initial team for a new project must include at least one real user, one key sponsor (client), and one lead developer. Each member of this core group must understand his/her own particular role within the project. Novices may participate, but their contributions are initially on the periphery.

Achieving different levels of contribution—novice, apprentice, expert—is defined by meritocracy, in which merit is measured by the quality and quantity of an individual's contributions to the code base. What constitutes merit varies among projects, but it can include any of the following elements in combination:

- Code contributions

- Infrastructure support contributions

- Mentorship contributions

- Documentation contributions

- Testing and bug reports

10.1.1.5   Task Assignment

Once the project, team, and delivery cycle are identified, a collection of initial tasks should emerge. These tasks must be matched with the skills of individual team members. This process usually occurs by consensus, allowing each team member to self-select (volunteer) to complete a specific task. Workload balancing among team members is also negotiated from the outset.

At the beginning of a new client-oriented project, it is important to start with relatively easy task assignments, allowing team members to get used to working together and find early success in the first iteration of the delivery cycle ([Coc05], p. 48).

Another initial task for a new software project is to build what Cockburn calls a "walking skeleton" ([Coc05] p. 49), so that all layers (user interface, domain, and database) of the architecture are exercised to complete a simple artifact. For example, that task could be to implement a login and password validation script, using a database table to validate the password.

---

[3]In Shuhari, "shu" means *follow tradition*, "ha" means *break with tradition*, and "ri" means *leave tradition behind*. For more information, see http://en.wikipedia.org/wiki/Shuhari.

The requirements document's use cases play a major role in the scheduling, partitioning and assignment of developer tasks. For example, implementing a single use case early in the development process provides a way to demonstrate viability of the project to the client.

10.1.1.6   Making Progress and Resolving Conflicts

Progress on a new project can be measured concretely by counting such artifacts as lines of code written, tests written, use cases (user stories) implemented, domain classes completed, and database modules completed. Information provided by the VCS can assist with this bookkeeping.

Each weekly team meeting should be both retrospective and prospective. Looking backward, assigned tasks should be checked for completion. Looking forward, the next week's agenda should be set and tasks assigned to team members.

In this exercise, it is important not to "overdrive your headlights." That is, add features in small enough increments that will favor short-term success over long-term completeness ([Coc05], pp. 51, 73).

Conflicts will occur on small projects where the team members are all familiar with each other and the tasks to be completed. When conflicts arise, it is important for the lead developer to play the role of mediator, or benevolent dictator.

Preference for face-to-face discussions and consensus building on thorny issues tends to mitigate against conflicts. Agendas, for example, should be set jointly, emphasizing clarity about roles and task boundaries and taking into account sensitivity among developers about workload balancing.

In any team project, team members will disagree from time to time on strategies, schedules, or task assignments. In these events, one team member must step back and moderate a discussion that resolves the conflict and moves the project forward.

Task assignment is a clear area where disagreements may arise. Sometimes team members will disagree with the task assignments initially made by the team leader and suggest changes. At other times, two or more team members will want to perform the same task, or else no team members want to perform that task.

In these cases, (re)assignment of team members to tasks can occur with the team leader playing the role of "benevolent dictator." That is, the team leader must resolve the issue in a way that steps on the fewest toes but avoids the risk of compromising the project schedule because some team members cannot agree on who does what tasks.

10.1.2   Quality Assessment

Several different models for measuring the maturity of an emerging open source project have been proposed.[4] Maturity models provide clear quantifiable measures for evaluating a project.

Several areas must be considered when evaluating the maturity of an open source project and its community. Most of these are no different from those used for measuring the maturity of a proprietary project such as quality assurance, scalability, security, performance, adoption, and support. However, some measures are specific to open source projects, such as community strength, community governance, support, and IT management.

The first measure of an open source project's success is the strength of the community that surrounds it. A strong community can provide a wealth of diverse input from the best minds around the world. In comparison, a proprietary product can only benefit from the input of its employees.

A second measure of success is the licensing terms and intellectual property management policies and controls in the project. As we saw in Chapter 1, several popular open source licenses have proven to be effective.

Fine-grained methodologies that can be used for assessing an open source software product are defined in products like QSOS (Qualification and Selection of Open Source Software, see http://atosorigin.com) and OpenBRR (Open Business Readiness Rating, developed by Carnegie Mellon University West http://cmu.edu/silicon-valley/ and others).

These assessment methodologies have three basic parts:

- evaluation criteria,

- requirements weightings (which allow the evaluator to assign weights according to the importance of each criterion), and

- final scores.

The following list provides a summary of several key open source software characteristics and how they are measured in an assessment activity for a particular software product.

Functionality: The domain and expected features of the application. Measured by a weighted criteria on the typical features expected of an eqivalent application in this domain.

Usability: The overall user interface experience and ease of interaction, especially by non-technical users. Measured by the time it takes to interact and perform key activities (use cases).

---

[4]Maturity models are not new in the software engineering industry. The Capability Maturity Model Integration (CMMI) is one such example [cmm]. CMMI covers best-practices for planning, engineering, and managing product development and maintenance.

Quality: The stability of the product and the overall efficiency of its bug-fixing process. Measured by the number of open bugs, the number of releases made, and the average age of a bug.

Community: The size, activity, and diversity of the community that controls the project roadmap. Measured by the number of messages to the mailing lists, the number of active contributors, and the number of organizations involved in the community.

Documentation: A detailed description of use of a system. Measured by availability/access to users, administrators, and installation.

Security: How well security vulnerabilities in the system are handled by the project, especially for mission-critical applications. Measured by the number of distinct security vulnerabilities and how they are maintained.

Support: How well the community supports its users, especially the availability and diversity of immediate help. Measured by the level of activity in user forums and the quality of the service level agreement (SLA) provided by professional support vendors.

Scalability and Performance: The efficiency with which the product executes and its ability to scale up to higher usage and data levels. Measured by various performance test results and benchmarks.

Architecture: How well the system architecture supports third-party add-ons/plugins, along with the availability of an API for integration. Measured by the number of third-party add-ons or plugins available and usage levels of the APIs.

Adoption: The size of the installed user base. Measured by the number of referenced deployments.

Governance: Quality and professional integrity of governance. Measured by the type of organization driving the project and how the core team is selected.

So we can assess the quality of an open source project using a number of detailed criteria and related quantitative measures. However, a simpler way to make a quick judgment about project quality is to ask whether each core developer has at least 2–3 months experience on the project, the project has many more users than developers, and the following actions have been taken:

- the source code has been placed in a repository for public download,

- the project has established a public forum where users can post bug reports and queries about the system's adaptability to new users, and

- the development team is open to taking on new members who may volunteer.

For a new project, it may take a few months to measure how many downloads have occurred, how many users have participated in the public forum, how many new developers have joined the team, and how many user posts have been made in bug and feature discussions. The results of these measures can provide good indicators about the future viability of the project.

Mitigating against these quality measures are measures of the risks involved in continuing a new software project, as opposed to the alternative of simply letting the project go dormant. Questions that help assess the risk of continuing a project include:

- Does the project have the (human and material) capital to go on?

- Does it have the need/demand for new features or applications?

- Are its developer and user communities sustainable for the projected life of the project?

- Does the project have a stable and adaptable code base?

- Is the code base running on a platform that is likely to remain stable for the foreseeable future?

Whatever approach is used, each one requires careful research and evaluation. Moreover, these different measures must be weighted according to the priorities of the organization for which the assessment is being made.

Before joining a project, a developer should also use these sorts of assessment criteria. If the project is well rated in all these areas, it may be more attractive to join and make meaningful contributions.

10.2 Evolving into a Democratic Meritocracy

Some new open source projects that promise to have broader impact may experience community pressure to expand. These projects can transition to a more mature phase which might be called the *democratic meritocracy* phase. This transition cannot be made without having a strong community and an accepted development process in place.

The democratic meritocracy phase is an ideal form of governance for a FOSS project, in the sense that the project is governed by a democratic process whose participants are representatives from the meritocracy of contributors. Typically, the sponsors of these types of projects are non-profit foundations, where the board of directors is also selected by the membership.

Any democratic process involves politics. A project that makes this transition has to invest a lot of time bringing transparency to the governing process so that the majority of citizens are happy. Probably the best example of such a community is the Debian community, which has thousands of voluntary developers and a very mature process of voting and selecting project leaders.

However, the Debian 100% voluntary model and maturity level are not easy to replicate. A lot of time is required to manage the political process, and it takes years to get this right. A more expedient alternative for reaching a high level of rigor and maturity for a project would be to fund a core development group that is selected from the leading core contributors (based again on merit).

In this section, we explore the transition of a young open source project with benevolent dictator governance into a mature community-oriented project. In doing so, we address the basic question, "How can a community-oriented open source software project escape the threat of total chaos and be rationally governed?"

10.2.1   Incubation

The formation of an active, vibrant community of users and developers marks a critical stage in an open source project's life that we call *incubation.* An open source project that fails to incubate risks becoming inactive and dying. This section discusses the process of incubation and what it takes for an open source project to pass successfully through the incubation stage into a mature and democratic meritocracy.

The purpose of incubation is to establish a self-sustaining open-source project. Both the Eclipse project and the Apache Software Foundation have established *incubators* that invite open source projects with complementary goals to become members.

Both of these incubators accept new projects, provide guidance and support to help new projects develop their own collaborative communities, educate new developers in the principles of collaborative development, and propose to their boards the promotion of such products to "mature" status. (This is a paraphrase of the Apache policy for project incubation, found at the Web site http://incubator.apache.org/incubation/Incubation_Policy.html.)

However, membership in either of these two incubators is appropriate only for open source projects that develop middle-level software—that is, software for software developers, rather than non-technical persons, as end users. These biases exclude many important software projects, especially those which are developed for humanitarian organizations as end users.

So in this discussion, we use the term *incubation* in a more general sense, rather than implying membership in either the Eclipse or the Apache incubation process. Two key activities govern how successfully an open source project can pass through its incubation phase and become healthy and sustainable for the long run: building a vibrant community and establishing a viable bug tracking process.

Essential to successful project incubation is the development of strong and sustainable communities of developers and users. At its beginning, a project has only a single (lead) developer, a sponsoring client, and a single user. As the code base evolves, a core group of developers emerges and a handful of "bleeding edge" users become actively involved.

How does the project transform this fragile community into one that has a significant number of developers and users, in which many users are actively reporting issues and developers are contributing bug fixes as the product evolves into productive use?

The development of three inter-related communities seems to be a vital part of this transition: users, contributors, and developers. Communication among contributors and committers should be open and transparent, and it should encourage inclusiveness and diversity of opinion (separate from the influence of any one company or sponsoring organization).

Attracting new contributors and committers to the project requires active recruiting, not just passive "openness." For example, a certain amount of professional and social networking must be directly associated with the project. The lead developers especially must make reasonable efforts to recruit promising new contributors.

An active and engaged user community is also an essential measure of successful project incubation. (Absence of such a community suggests that the software has been developed for the entertainment of the developers alone.) Growing such a user community takes time, of course, but once it is established, the user community tends to be self-sustaining.

An active Web presence, including easily accessible developer and user forums and project wiki, are valuable catalysts that encourage the growth of sustainable committer, contributor, and user communities.

10.2.1.1 FOSS Project Foundations

An open source software project can either be a free-standing entity or seek membership in a larger (umbrella) organization to ensure continuity and sustenance.

As a free-standing entity, the project has complete autonomy over all its activities. For example, it may incorporate as a not-for-profit foundation or simply maintain a project Web site as a point of contact for all its community members. As a free-standing entity, it may choose from among several alternative open source licensing arrangements for distribution and development of its code base.

For example, the Sahana Software Foundation promotes free and open source software solutions for disaster and emergency management. The Foundation took over the governance and management of the *Sahana* software project from the Lanka Software Foundation in October 2009. By that time,

Sahana had become the leading open source disaster management system worldwide, having been used by dozens of countries following natural and man-made disasters.

However, remaining as a free-standing entity comes with certain risks. Perhaps the most significant risk is that the project may become dormant and eventually die from inactivity. This can occur, for example, when the number of contributors and committers becomes too low in relation to the number of "free-riding" users. Other risks include legal exposure and financial stress.

As an alternative, an open source software project may become part of a larger umbrella organization that is dedicated to sustaining such projects over the long term. For example, the Apache Software Foundation:

> provides organizational, legal, and financial support for a broad range of open source software projects. The Foundation provides an established framework for intellectual property and financial contributions that simultaneously limits the potential legal exposure for the contributors.
>
> Through a collaborative and meritocratic development process, Apache projects deliver enterprise-grade, freely available software products that attract large communities of users. The pragmatic Apache License makes it easy for all users, commercial and individual, to deploy Apache products.

For details, see http://en.wikipedia.org/wiki/Apache_Software_Foundation.

10.2.1.2   Developer and User Forums

A most critical element of community building for a young open source software project is the establishment of effective on-line forums in which users and developers can discuss issues related to the development and effective use of the software.

These forums provide an immediate avenue of expression through which a user can report a bug or other technical problem related to using the software. They also provide timely information to developers about the status of all active bugs and other new features that are being considered for the next release of the software.

Finally, these forums provide documentary evidence that can be used when a contributor is being considered for "promotion" to committer status—that person's contributions are all retrievable from the forum's discussion threads and they can be used by project leaders to evaluate the merits of that person's contributions.

Thus, the user and developer forums play a vital role in ensuring that a healthy open source project remains healthy and the community of contributors and other users remains up to date with the latest news about the project's progress.

For example, here is an actual excerpt from a recent EasyEclipse user forum discussion thread (the names are changed to ensure privacy):

Comment by Arlo 2009-09-08 03:37:37
EasyEclipse for PHP doesn't start under Mac OS X Snow Leopard?please Update Eclipse ...

Comment by Woody 2009-09-30 08:57:55
Hello, I have got the same problem under Mac OS X Snow Leopard. Please fix the problem. I will be grateful eternally. Thank you

Comment by Tom 2009-12-10 01:22:38
Will the problem with snowleopard be fixed or not? Please let me know. Thanks, tom

Comment by Denise 2010-01-07 07:32:55
Hi: I ran into the same error as the others reported with Snow Leopard. Certainly would like a fix soon. Thanks, Denise

Comment by Rondelle 2010-02-02 13:31:41
Hi, I have the answer for you Snow Leopard people. The problem with Snow Leopard 1.6 is that java 5 is not installed and there are symbolic links pointing java 5 to java 1.6. You can fix it by going here: wiki.oneswarm.org/index.php/OS_X_10.6_Snow_Leopard. Follow this and it should start working fine. Cheers, Rondelle

Comment by Horace 2010-02-18 01:28:19
Thanks A LOT for your link. Great help. hm

This thread illustrates the utility of user forums for reporting problems to developers and developers responding to the problem. Note that this particular issue was resolved not in the form of a bug fix, but simply by referring users to a resource that would allow them to correct the problem themselves.

Note also the amount of time that elapsed between the first instance of this particular problem and its final resolution—more than four months! Typically, an issue is more or less quickly resolved depending on the volume and intensity with which users express their concerns.

10.2.2 Organization

Abstractly, Jensen [JS10] characterizes FOSS project organization as a socio-technical interaction network, or *STIN* for short. STINs are always in flux; they are self-organizing networks of activities, people, and tools, and often all these parts are geographically distributed around the world.

More concretely, community-oriented FOSS projects tend to have three main organizational distinctions from proprietary projects. These are:

1. **Self-organizing** Community-oriented FOSS projects allow participants to find their own level and project activity with which to become engaged, based on their interests and skills. Proprietary project leaders assign each participant to a project activity.

2. **Egalitarian** Community-oriented FOSS projects openly invite contributions from everyone. Proprietary projects are hierarchically organized and closed in this regard.

3. **Meritocratic** Community-oriented FOSS projects organize their work around public discussions, and decisions about future directions are based on merit. Proprietary projects organize around the results of private discussions among project leaders, and decisions about future directions are highly influenced by cost and profit.

A community-oriented FOSS project is also organized in a way that recognizes three distinct roles that community members can play:

Users know and use the software actively. They provide feedback to developers (contributors and committers) when they find bugs or other difficulties when using the software. They also suggest new features that could improve the software's usability or applicability.

Contributors are users who also contribute bug fixes and minor features to the software, but don't have the right to alter the code base itself. Contributions can also be in the form of documentation, administative support, and testing.

Committers are developers who review user contributions and install them in the code base. In this activity, the committer ensures that the code base keeps its integrity—i.e., that the new features are correctly implemented and that the bugs are actually fixed.

A FOSS community itself is quite fluid—most users of a software artifact are, in fact, passive users. Jensen [JS10] calls these users "free-riders," since they give nothing back in return for the privilege of using the software.

Users who do provide feedback to the developers do so in an entirely voluntary spirit. Feedback typically occurs through the software's user forum, which is prominently accessible at the project's Web site.

Some users may actually go a step further by providing bug fixes or suggestions for new features in the form of code patches. A user who is also a programmer can, in fact, do this since the open source code base is freely available for anyone to read. Engaging in this activity self-promotes the user to *contributor* status. Whether or not a contributor's suggestions are accepted and become part of the code base, however, is decided by a committer.

Promotion to *committer* status is done on the merits of a person's collected contributions to the project over time. In this sense, the contributions become a portfolio of work that can be evaluated to assess the merits of that person's case for assuming the responsibilities of a committer.

Who decides on the promotion of a contributor to committer status? This is often done by a core project leadership group. In Apache this is the *Project Management Committee* (*PMC* for short), which is a group of committers that oversees the project's organization. The PMC promotes a contributor to the role of committer strictly on the merits of his/her contributions to the project. This certification process is thus peer-to-peer and publicly documented (rather than closed).

The overall role of the PMC is to ensure that the community is behaving and governing itself in a manner that is consistent with the objectives of making the project successful. This includes operational, legal, and procedural oversight on all software releases.

While users and contributors are most likely volunteers, many committers are paid employees of the project. What particular skills are required to attain committer status? Generally, an applicant's portfolio contains two types of contributions: those that illustrate technical competence and those that exhibit social skills.

- On the technical side, a portfolio should demonstrate that the applicant has programming and software architecture skills, documentation writing skills, and a general understanding of how software systems are built and maintained.

- On the social skills side, a portfolio should demonstrate successful collaboration, good reading and writing skills (e.g., effective use of e-mail and discussion forums), leadership skills, and an understanding and adaptability to various peer and sub-culture behaviors.

Finally, research [JS10] has shown that successful FOSS projects must maintain a critical mass of contributors and committers, in relation to "free-riding" users, in order to remain vibrant over the long run. If there are too many free-riders, they will kill the project.

10.2.2.1 Task-Specific Roles

In addition to maintaining the code base, the participants in a FOSS project play roles that accomplish a number of other important project tasks. Those who play these roles are all committers, and many are members of the PMC. Here is a summary of these roles and their respective activities:

- The **project leader** maintains the project's release plan and current status, and moderates the developer forum.

- The **expert user** maintains the software's actors, use cases, requirements, and user roles.

- The **lead developer** maintains the software architecture.

- Other **developers** maintain the user interface design, domain classes, database design, code base, unit test suite, build package, and build schedule.

- **Testers** maintain bug reports and the user forum.

- **Writers** maintain on-line help text.

- **Bug Marshalls** overlook opened bugs and filters them and pass them on to developers.

- **Release Managers** overlook the packaging and releasing of new versions of the software for general public consumption.

We also note that it is not unusual for an individual to play two or more of these roles simultaneously, depending on his/her particular skills and interests.

The FOSS project usually publishes detailed guidelines for each of these tasks.

### 10.2.2.2	Oversight

The relationships among these four levels of partipation in a community-oriented FOSS project are summarized in Figure 10.2. These four levels address the organization of a single community-oriented FOSS project, outlining the various roles that people play during the life of the project. This organization is very loose, and membership at any level is based solely on the merits of a person's contributions to the project.

However, a successful FOSS project eventually reaches a point in its life where an additional level of oversight and goal-setting is required. This level often emerges as the project becomes (part of) a non-profit organization whose investors play a role in setting future directions for the project.

Figure 10.2 shows this fifth level in the form of a Board of Directors. Unlike other levels, the Board is populated mainly by persons outside the community of developers, as indicated by the arrow in the upper-right corner of the figure.

The Board's role is to promote the adoption and growth of the software that the project is developing. The Board actively engages with partners from the private sector, academic institutions, and the public sector. The Board also establishes mechanisms for supporting the project, evaluating its success, making licensing decisions, and addressing general development and implementation issues.

Some FOSS projects are sponsored by non-profit foundations, while others are sponsored by for-profit corporations. An example of the former is *Sahana*, which is sponsored by the Sahana Foundation. An example of the latter is NetBeans, which is sponsored by Oracle/Sun. This difference has some influence over the degree of openness and autonomy from the Board that the four lower levels enjoy.

Organization Level   Individual Role

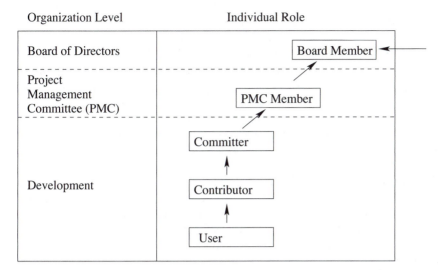

FIGURE 10.2: Organizational levels in the *Sahana* project.

For example, the *Sahana* project is placed in the humanitarian sector which has a lot of non-governmental and non-profit organizations. Thus, *Sahana* has a natural alignment to be run by a non-profit foundation. Through its Board of Directors, the Sahana Foundation engages with private sector, academic institutions, and public sector partners in promoting the adoption and support of *Sahana*. In most cases it is simply a legal entity established to manage the finances, legal issues and expense reimbursements for its core developers.

NetBeans, on the other hand, is an open source project run by Oracle/Sun, a for-profit organization. Its Board has three members, one of whom is appointed by Sun. The Board ensures that the netbeans.org project is being run in a fair and open manner. The Board also resolves disputes and grievances, although most of those are ideally resolved at the community level.

10.2.3 Decision Making and Conflict Resolution

The developers in a community-oriented FOSS project are highly motivated and skilled individuals. Inevitably, rivalries and conflicts will arise because of individual differences in values and priorities. It is healthy for a high level of rivalry to occur among developers, as long as individuals' needs are diverse (e.g., they are working on different parts of the code base). If individuals' needs are similar, however, rivalry must be kept low in order to keep the project vibrant.

Policy, procedural, and technical decision making in an open source project aims to be fully transparent to all community members. Absence of transparency, for example by way of off-line decisions by Board members, can lead to demoralization among other community members—especially those who have invested heavily in the collaborative process.

When a complex policy, procedural, or technical issue arises, a member of the PMC typically posts the issue on a public discussion forum, where it is debated and either ratified or rejected by consensus or majority vote. Here, *consensus* means that at least two other developers support a particular solution and no other developers post strong disagreements.

For example, *Sahana* uses a *lazy consensus* process. Voting is done with +1 denoting "for a motion," -1 denoting "against to a motion," and 0 denoting abstention. With a lazy consensus process, a 72-hour time frame is given for a decision. If there are no negative votes during that period, the motion passes.

A lazy consensus process is practical in a voluntary community where only a fraction of the participants actively contribute to any particular vote. Depending on the nature of the decision, the vote is made at either the committer, the PMC, or the Board level. For Board or PMC decisions, a poll is first run to gather community feedback, and this serves as additional input for the final decision.

Sometimes, of course, achieving consensus on a contentious issue is not possible. Often conflicts arise during discussions about community infrastructure, technical direction, expectations about developer roles, or interrelationships among roles.

These kinds of *conflicts* can be resolved by a process involving a small PMC made up of prominent members of the community. The PMC has the job of ensuring fairness throughout the community by solving persistent disputes.

The reputation of the individual PMC members carries some weight in conflict resolution, even though they may not vote unanimously on any single issue. Thus, the role of this Board is more that of a mediator that assists community members to resolve conflicts among themselves.

10.2.4 Domain Constraints

It is also important to understand the domain that the project is serving. Different domains can force additional constraints and priorities.

Sometimes the application domain places special constraints on the governance of a community-oriented FOSS project. Consider, for example, the humanitarian area, where the software is targeted to help people recover from a disaster or longer-term condition that is debilitating to a significant population.

These systems often operate in a constrained setting—one that is not experienced in other FOSS or proprietary software development situations. For example, *Sahana* works in the domain of humanitarian response and disaster management. In this domain the following considerations must be factored into the software development process:

- Telecoms and Internet access is either down or intermittently available.

- Bandwidth is often at a premium so every character counts.

- Power can go out at any time or not be available.

- Any central data center or infrastructure might have been affected by the disaster.

- People have little time to get familiar with new systems.

- Off-the-shelf systems often have to be customized for the requirement or risk not capturing aspects of gathered data.

- Local developers have very little time to learn and support the system.

- There are many existing legacy systems and loads of spreadsheets with valuable data.

- Data will come to you with different levels of granularity, validity, and redundancy. Such data often need to be cleaned up.

Because of these constraints, the governance of a humanitarian FOSS project must follow some additional conventions that do not usually apply to other types of projects. Designers need to be sure that their project has a clear purpose and applicability, avoids complex user workflows, is debuggable, and depends on operating system and database architectures that ensure scalability. In particular:

- Designers should avoid introducing excessive functionality, especially without considering how much their contributions are costing in terms of throughput. A lot can be said for abstraction, but the more a developer is in close contact with the cost of his/her contribution the better. For example, *Sahana* allows developers to use PHP without much abstraction except in the form of template helper if needed.

- Designers should avoid introducing complex workflows, security and dependencies that require people to approve. When a disaster hits, most people are overwhelmed; if a system dictates that person X should approve person Y before he can do action Z, most likely person X will become a bottleneck or will end up wasting his time having to monitor approvals. It is better to design software that is open by default and has minimal workflows, in order to deliver effective responses. The risk of volunteers not having access to good information on the ground is a more serious problem than the risk of unauthorized access.

- Designers need to depend on proven operating systems and database management platforms for their robustness and scalability. For example, the LAMP stack, which includes PHP and MySQL, is an architecture that was designed that way to be scalable. This stack is one of the most popular stacks for horizontally scaling large portals and is widely used by organizations such as Yahoo! and Google.

10.3   Releasing Code

The process of packaging, releasing, and distributing code is different for a client-oriented project than for a community-oriented project.

In the first case, the code base is in its infancy and relatively small, and the users are also few in number and in close communication with the developers. Two central questions that the project team must address are, "Which open source license should govern its distribution and use?" and "Where should we publish the first release?" In the second case, a much more circumspect process accompanies decisions about releasing and distributing the code base.

The following sections address the needs of these two different types of projects in more detail.

10.3.1   Licensing

Once the project begins evolving into a broader venture, the question of licensing must be carefully addressed. That is, which FOSS license should be chosen for the project? Most open source projects are licensed under the GNU General Public License (GPL). As we learned in Chapter 1, this license requires that derivatives of the software must also be licensed under the GPL—in particular, the work cannot be relicensed under a proprietary license. Licenses that include this requirement are called "copyleft."

In cases where a FOSS product is likely to be incorporated into an established proprietary product, it can be licensed under the LGPL (Library or Lesser GPL). Although a weaker version of the GPL in terms of the copyleft principle, the LGPL protects the FOSS nature of the software while permitting its use in proprietary products.

Non-copyleft licenses like BSD and Apache allow developers to relicense derivatives of the software under a different license, including under a proprietary license. They are, however, still considered FOSS licenses because they protect users' freedom to use, study, share, and modify the software.

The issue of FOSS licensing is a broad and complex one. For details and discussions of the various licenses, readers should consult the appropriate pages of the FSF and OSI Web sites. Red Hat also maintains a comprehensive description and comparison of the various licenses on its Web site.

Not surprisingly, some of the philosophical and political differences between the free software and open source software camps are played out here. For an example, see Stallman's discussion of when it is appropriate or not to use the LGPL, according to the free software philosophy (http://gnu.org/philosophy/why-not-lgpl.html).

10.3.2   Finding a Project Host

Early in the life of a viable client-oriented FOSS project, a decision should be made to use a Web-based hosting site for managing releases and encouraging communication among developers and users. Such a site should provide all the communication and code development tools and services that a FOSS project needs.

Three popular hosting sites are Sourceforge (sourceforge.net), Launchpad (launchpad.net), and Google Code (code.google.com). Other notable hosting sites include RubyForge, which hosts open source Ruby projects; Tigris.org, which is supported by the sponsors of Subversion; JavaForge, which provides services for open source Java projects; and GNU Savannah, which is sponsored by the Free Software Foundation (FSF).

While all hosting sites provide a similar range of services, some distinguish themselves by the particular focus of their projects—e.g., Ruby Projects or Java Projects. The GNU Savannah site has two sub-domains, one that is officially part of the GNU Project and the other for non-GNU projects, both of which support only free software projects as defined by the FSF—it maintains a ban on the use of non-free formats such as Macromedia Flash.

Both Sourceforge and Google Code are general purpose services that host a wide range of projects spanning many different programming languages and many varieties of free and open source licenses.

10.3.2.1   Sourceforge

As a case study, let's take a more careful look at Sourceforge, which began in 2000. At that time, it was known as the Open Source Development Network (OSDN), a division of VA Linux Systems. Sourceforge was supported by several computer and software companies, including IBM, Sun Microsystems, Hewlett-Packard, Intel, and others. It was set up to serve as a gateway for collaborative software development.

At this writing, the Web site http://sourceforge.net reports hosting more than 230,000 open source development projects and has more than 2 million registered users, although only a fraction of the projects and users are active. Over the past 10 years Sourceforge has hosted and supported a number of successful software projects, including MySQL, Python, JRuby, and others.

Currently, the most popular Sourceforge projects are eMule (over 526 billion downloads), Azureus/Vuze (nearly 500 billion downloads), Ares Galaxy (222 billion), 7-Zip (over 91 billion), and FileZilla (over 81 billion), all of which are open source file sharing programs. Among its most active projects today are Pidgig, an instant messaging application for Windows and Unix; JEdit, a programmer's text editor written in Java; and Python, the programming language.

Sourceforge provides the following broad services:

- *Search*: Sourceforge contains thousands of open source software products for a wide variety of applications.

- *Community Building*: Projects hosted on Sourceforge are always looking for developers to join in their effort. Users can create a developer account and participate in fixing bugs, providing patches with one of the existing projects.

- *Project Hosting*: Registered users can create their own development project. The registration process is open and accessible and provides a wide range of tools and services to support project development.

Among the services provided to the projects hosted by Sourceforge are the following:

- *Code Hosting*: The project's source code can be hosted on one or more of Sourceforge's versioning servers, SVN, CVS, Git, Mercurial, and Bazaar.

- *Web Hosting*: Sourceforge will host the project's Web site as a sub-domain—i.e., with the URL myproject.sourceforge.net. It provides shell access for Web sites as well as traffic analytics.

- *Application Hosting*: Sourceforge hosts a wide range of open source applications ranging from blogging (Wordpress) to bug tracking (Trac) to wiki software (Mediawiki).

- *Software Distribution*: Sourceforge provides easy-to-use tools to package your software for download and distribution. Its servers can detect the user's platform (Mac, Windows, Linux) and direct users to the appropriate version. Downloads are supported by a mirror network that spans five continents.

- *Bug Tracking*: Sourceforge provides extensive bug tracking and issue reporting services for the project. Software tools are available to manage the reporting and handling of bugs in the software as well as requests for enhancements and new features. There are a variety of stand-alone tools available for this process, including BugZilla and Trac.

- *Communication Services*: Forums, mailing lists, wikis, blogs, and other forms of project communication services can be hosted on Sourceforge.

Once a client-oriented project is uploaded to a hosting site, it is positioned to evolve and grow into a larger, community-oriented project. That is, the hosting site provides the project with the necessary exposure for other developers and clients to learn about it and study its code base in detail.

10.3.3 Release Strategies

The convention followed by most community-oriented FOSS projects is agile—that is, *release early and release often*. This approach exemplifies the openness and transparency that characterizes the open source philosophy. It stands in sharp contrast to the secrecy and infrequency with which proprietary software is released.

The release early and often philosophy was first articulated by Eric Raymond in his classic monograph *The Cathedral and the Bazaar* [Ray01]. Raymond attributes the inspiration behind this approach to Linus Torvalds's Linux development model:

> Early and frequent releases are a critical part of the Linux development model. ...Linus's open development policy was the very opposite of cathedral-building. Linux's Internet archives were burgeoning, multiple distributions were being floated. And all of this was driven by an unheard-of frequency of core system releases. Linus was treating his users as co-developers in the most effective possible way: Release early. Release often. And listen to your customers.

As this suggests, an important element of this release strategy is the bond it creates between a software's users and its developers.

It is difficult to generalize about release strategies because they differ among different community-oriented projects.[5] For proprietary software developed in a hierarchical, top-down fashion, the decision to release a new version is made by management which has the authority to focus the entire enterprise's attention on the release objective. This approach might also be appropriate for small-scale development teams where the team leader or a consensus of team members arrives at a decision to produce a new release.

Once the release decision is made, the entire team focuses on preparing the release. Work on new development stops, or nearly so; the software's features are frozen; and development focuses on fixing known bugs, preparing documentation, and packing the software for release.

By contrast, FOSS projects rely on contributions from volunteers, so it may be difficult or impossible to get the entire community focused on producing a release. Instead, as Fogel suggests, the process more nearly resembles a highway construction project that closes a couple of lanes at a time (the release branch) while other lanes continue to serve traffic (the main development effort continues). This strategy is less disruptive than a total shutdown of the highway, which is more closely analogous to corporate release strategy.

In addition to the decision of how often and when to release new software versions, a project must also decide on a numbering scheme. The approach

---

[5]This section is based on the discussion in Chapter 7 of Fogel's book, *Producing Open Source Software* [Fog09].

used by the Apache Portable Runtime (APR) project, one of the simpler numbering schemes, uses three numbers: a *major*, *minor*, and *micro* number. For example, versions 1.2.4 would be major version 1, minor version 2, micro version 4.

Fogel [Fog09] describes this scheme as follows:

1. Changes to the micro number only (that is, changes within the same minor line) must be both forward and backward compatible. That is, the changes should be bug fixes only, or very small enhancements to existing features. New features should not be introduced in a micro release.

2. Changes to the minor number (that is, within the same major line) must be backward compatible, but not necessarily forward compatible. It's normal to introduce new features in a minor release, but usually not too many new features at once.

3. Changes to the major number mark compatibility boundaries. A new major release can be forward and backward incompatible. A major release is expected to have new features, and may even have entirely new feature sets.

Another important feature of a release is its *alpha* or *beta* status. As Fogel [Fog09] describes it:

> The term *alpha* usually means a first release, with which users can get real work done and which has all the intended functionality, but which also has known bugs. The main purpose of alpha software is to generate feedback, so the developers know what to work on.
>
> The next stage, *beta*, means the software has had all the serious bugs fixed, but has not yet been tested enough to certify for release. The purpose of beta software is to either become the official release, assuming no bugs are found, or provide detailed feedback to the developers so they can reach the official release quickly. The difference between alpha and beta is very much a matter of judgment.

10.3.3.1   Release Branches

An important element of the release process is the need to separate the release code from the ongoing development code. Those developers not participating in the release process need a way to keep working on the code. But their efforts should not get mixed up with the code that will make up the release.

A good strategy is the create a *release branch* in the VCS where the release code can be segregated from the main part of the repository—where development can continue. To create a new release, a copy of the trunk can be made and named something like *release_ 1.0.x*—the *x* here, in the three-number scheme, reflects the fact that micro changes (bug fixes) will be made within this same branch.

10.3.3.2 Managing the Release

Once the decision to produce a new release is made, it is important that the process be managed by a single individual within the community, the so-called *release manager*. Even though decisions about what features and what fixes will go into the release may be made by community or team consensus, it is important that the responsibility for managing the release fall to one person. This person's job is to serve as a gatekeeper, making sure that only the agreed upon features go into the release, and to keep the tasks required to produce the release on track.

What should go into a new release? Fogel [Fog09] provides the following list:

- Severe bug repairs

- Documentation updates

- Error message corrections (except those that belong to the user interface and need to remain stable)

- Certain other low-risk changes

Because individual developers often want to see their work incorporated into the new version, managing what gets into the release can be difficult. In an open source project, resolving such issues often requires much discussion before a consensus is reached. Otherwise, the release manager has to make the call.

10.4 Summary

In this chapter, we have discussed the major elements of governance for open source software projects. Measuring the quality of a FOSS project is a different activity from measuring the quality of a proprietary project, where cost and profitability play a large role.

Nevertheless, concrete measures such as the size of the developer community and the level of activity in the bug forums provide important metrics for assessing the quality and future status of a FOSS project.

The governance of a community-oriented project comes with special considerations. These include sustaining motivation among community members who are driving the project forward, resolving conflicts in philosophy or methodology, and making decisions about project hosting, licensing and releasing code.

Exercises

10.1 After browsing through the projects registered on a project hosting service, such as Sourceforge, identify one project in each of the following categories and briefly explain why you categorized it that way:

    a. Dormant, client-oriented

    b. Vibrant, client-oriented

    c. Incubating

    d. Vibrant, community-oriented

    e. Dormant, community-oriented

10.2 Use one of the maturity models discussed in this chapter to assess a particular community-oriented FOSS project (different from the one you are working on). Does your assessment suggest that the project is one that you would enjoy working on? Why or why not?

10.3 If you are working on an unreleased (new) client-oriented project, discuss the steps required to register it on Sourceforge, establish its first release, and begin to grow a larger developer and user community.

10.4 If your project is already registered on Sourceforge (or another project hosting service), assess its maturity by measuring the size of its user and developer community, the frequency and currency of its bug reporting, and other criteria suggested in this chapter.

10.5 For the project you are working on, discuss its licensing type (LGPL or other) and the reasons why that particular licensing type was chosen. If your project is a new client-oriented project, choose a licensing type that it should have, and the reasons why you are making that choice.

Chapter 11

New Project Conception

> "The most important single aspect of software development is
> to be clear about what you are trying to build."
>
> —*Bjarne Stroustrup*

In the traditional scheme of a software engineering course, this chapter would be titled "Requirements Analysis" and would probably occur at or near the beginning of the text. Such a course focuses on the development of a software product whose requirements are fully specified at the outset. As such, they can be analyzed all at once, before the design and coding phases begin.

In an open source software project, however, the situation is quite different. Because the development process is agile, the project's requirements are far from static. From day 1, requirements evolve alongside the code base itself. Due to the vibrancy of its developer and user community, an open source project has new requirements emerge even after the first release of the code base.

Because of the dynamic nature of open source requirements, this chapter takes a different perspective on requirements analysis. We call this perspective *New Project Conception*. The idea here is to capture the spirit of how a new open source software artifact is initially conceived and defined. This name change notwithstanding, we shall see that many traditional requirements analysis tools remain quite valuable when a new open source project is first conceived.

As a case study, we illustrate how the requirements for a new open source software product are developed using a new project which we shall call *RMH Homeroom*.[1] This project is presented in the first section of this chapter. The remaining sections describe the elements of requirements gathering and initial design of a new system, using this case study as an example.

---

[1] For information about the current status of this project, see the book's Web site myopen-software.org/textbook.

11.1   Requirements Gathering

This section discusses the process of gathering an initial set of requirements from the client in preparation for developing a new open source software system. This process includes meeting face-to-face with users, learning about the domain and the applications, eliciting user stories, and then developing an initial set of use cases from those stories.

As a case study, we use the development of an actual new software system that has been requested by the Ronald McDonald House in Portland, Maine. This system is relatively simple, yet it is interesting enough to provide a rich set of information from which a new software project can be launched.

The Ronald McDonald House of Portland, Maine (RMH) serves the community by providing lodging and meals for families of children who are patients at nearby hospitals. Its services are particularly valuable for families who travel a long distance from their homes to the Maine Medical Center or other Portland area hospitals and whose children are hospitalized for more than one night. The RMH Web site (see http://www.rmhportlandme.org/) provides a good overview of the House and its services.

RMH has 21 rooms that, on a typical night, are almost fully booked. The House is run by a full-time staff of five—an Executive Director, a House Manager, an Office Manager, a Night Manager, and a Community Manager. The House is operated with the help of dozens of volunteers. RMH staff work closely with social workers at the Maine Medical Center to help identify families who need a place to stay while their children are in the hospital.

Room scheduling for RMH guests is currently a completely manual process. RMH wants to replace this process by one that is fully supported by software. This new project is called *RMH Homeroom*.[2]

11.1.1   Domain Analysis

In short, the process of *domain analysis* creates a non-technical description of how the current system functions. This description must be written at a sufficient level of detail to provide developers with an initial level of familiarity with the application domain. It must also be written using a vocabulary with which people who need the software are familiar.

A good domain analysis introduces developers to the professional setting in which the software will be used, as well as all the individual artifacts—both digital and manual—that are in use to support the current system that the software will eventually replace or enhance. Here is the domain analysis for *RMH Homeroom*:

---

[2]RMH Homeroom is conceived as an entirely independent project from *RMH Homebase*.

Prior to installation of the new software, guests are normally referred to the House Manager by a Social Worker in a local hospital, using the guest referral form shown in Figure 11.1.

Once a room is located for the required dates, the House Manager fills out a guest registration card for the family (see Figure 11.2). If the family has stayed at RMH in the past, their previous guest registration card is retrieved from a Rolodex-style file and the information for their new stay is entered onto that card.

At the same time, the House Manager "reserves" the room by placing a "sticky" on the room schedule for the date requested (see Figure 11.3). On the day of their arrival, the family must call to confirm their reservation, the number of guests who will be staying in the room, and the time of their arrival. When they arrive, the House Manager checks them in by removing the "sticky" from that entry on the schedule and writing in the names of the guests.

In addition to the names of the persons staying in a room, the following information is recorded:

- the room's capacity

- whether or not there's a refrigerator in the room

- whether or not the family has borrowed an air bed

- the number of the garage remote door opener loaned to the family

- whether or not the room has been cleaned

- the name of a "linked" room

A room is "linked" to another room if members of the same family are staying in both rooms. For example, in Figure 11.3 room 152 is linked with room 254.

At 9am each morning, a new day's room schedule is generated by manually copying the previous day's schedule. When a family "checks out" of a room, their name is erased from the new day's room schedule and the room becomes a candidate for cleaning. While guests stay at RMH for free, some choose to make a nominal contribution to RMH to help offset the cost of their stay.

Because the same family may return to the RMH at a later date, the House Manager maintains a Rolodex file of all guests who have stayed there in the past. Because the process requires that confidentiality be maintained, only the House Manager and the Social Worker have access to this Rolodex file.

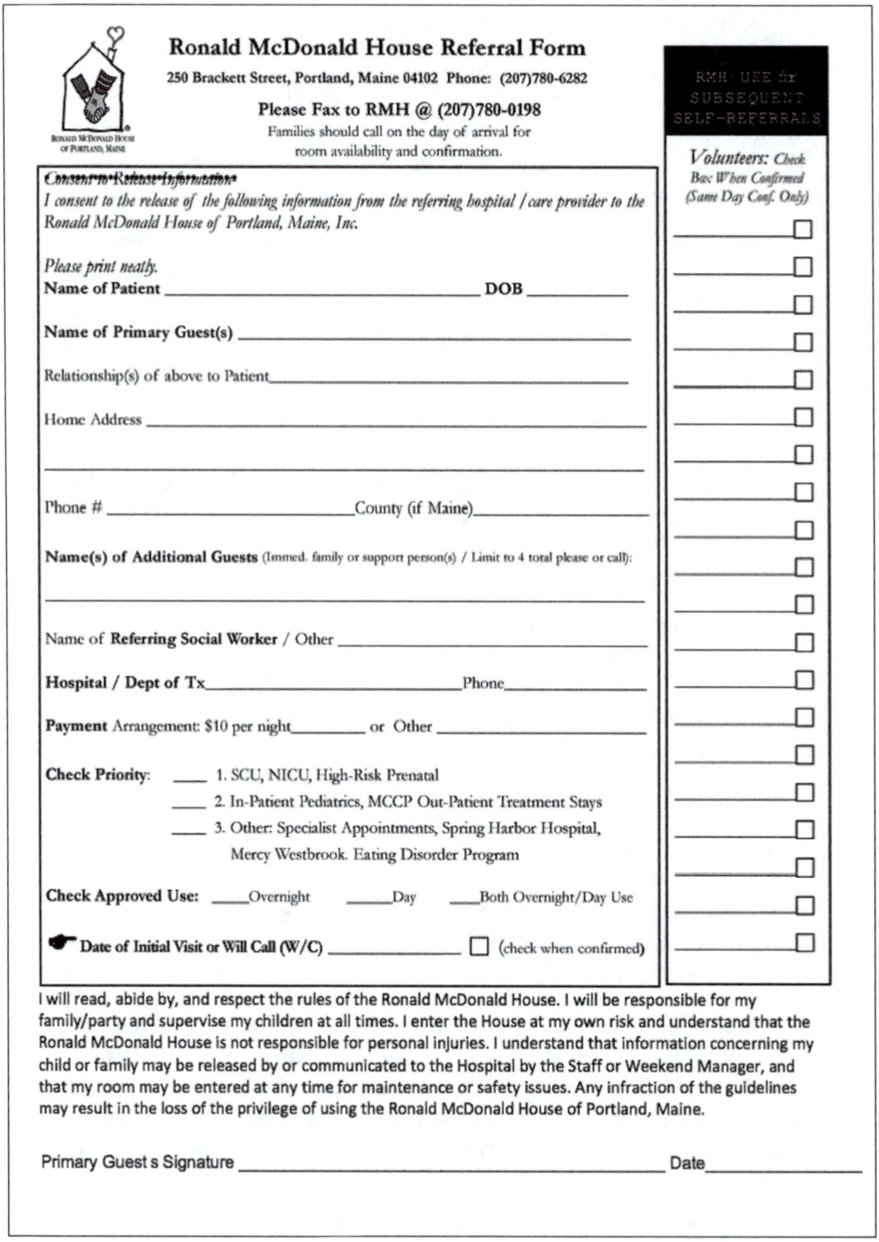

Ronald McDonald House Referral Form

250 Brackett Street, Portland, Maine 04102 Phone: (207)780-6282

Please Fax to RMH @ (207)780-0198

Families should call on the day of arrival for room availability and confirmation.

Ronald McDonald House of Portland, Maine

RMH USE for SUBSEQUENT SELF-REFERRALS

Volunteers: Check Box When Confirmed (Same Day Conf. Only)

~~Consent to Release Information~~

I consent to the release of the following information from the referring hospital / care provider to the Ronald McDonald House of Portland, Maine, Inc.

Please print neatly.

Name of Patient ____________________ **DOB** __________

Name of Primary Guest(s) ____________________

Relationship(s) of above to Patient____________________

Home Address ____________________

____

Phone # ____________________County (if Maine)____________________

Name(s) of Additional Guests (Immed. family or support person(s) / Limit to 4 total please or call):

____

Name of **Referring Social Worker** / Other ____________________

Hospital / Dept of Tx____________________Phone__________

Payment Arrangement: $10 per night________ or Other ____________________

Check Priority: ____ 1. SCU, NICU, High-Risk Prenatal

____ 2. In-Patient Pediatrics, MCCP Out-Patient Treatment Stays

____ 3. Other: Specialist Appointments, Spring Harbor Hospital, Mercy Westbrook. Eating Disorder Program

Check Approved Use: ____Overnight ____Day ____Both Overnight/Day Use

Date of Initial Visit or Will Call (W/C) __________ ☐ (check when confirmed)

I will read, abide by, and respect the rules of the Ronald McDonald House. I will be responsible for my family/party and supervise my children at all times. I enter the House at my own risk and understand that the Ronald McDonald House is not responsible for personal injuries. I understand that information concerning my child or family may be released by or communicated to the Hospital by the Staff or Weekend Manager, and that my room may be entered at any time for maintenance or safety issues. Any infraction of the guidelines may result in the loss of the privilege of using the Ronald McDonald House of Portland, Maine.

Primary Guest s Signature ____________________ Date__________

FIGURE 11.1: RMH guest referral form.

GUEST REGISTRATION CARD   RE#_____

Names of Guests _____

_____

Relationship(s) to Patient_____

Patient's Name_____

Primary Guest's Address_____

City_____**State**_____**Zip**_____**County**_____

Primary Guest's Phone (Cell)_____(Home)_____

***Automobile Make/Color/State_____

Would you like to receive our newsletter? Email_____

REFERRAL INFORMATION

Hospital_____**Dept. Of Treatment**_____

Social Worker or Referring Individual_____

Room #								
Date In								
Date Out								
# Guests								

FIGURE 11.2:   RMH guest registration card.

11.1.2   User Stories

Before the use cases for a new project can be defined, developers must elicit from users their "stories" about particular functionalities they would like to see in the new software artifact.

According to Wikipedia (http://en.wikipedia.org/wiki/User_story, June 26, 2010):

> A *user story* is a software system requirement formulated as one or more sentences in the everyday or business language of the user. User stories are used with Agile software development methodologies for the specification of requirements (together with acceptance tests). Each user story is limited, so it fits on a small paper note card—usually a 3 x 5 inch card—to ensure that it does not grow too large. The user stories should be written by the clients themselves, and they are the main instrument to influence the development of the software.

A good user story has several key characteristics:

1. It should be written in a client-focused style, ideally by the client herself. If the client doesn't write the story, the developer must write it in the language and style of the application domain. Technical jargon should be avoided at all costs, so that the story can be understood by everyone on the team.

2. It should be brief, so that it can be fully expressed in less than a minute. In other words, the story should be no more than three sentences long

DATE: *Thurs 11/18/10*

2010 GUEST ROOM LOG

Write firmly in pencil for nightly copying of room log

125 2T/PB	128 1Q/3T/ PB 4+ guests ✓	151 2T/PB ✓	152 2T/PB	214 Q ✓	215 2T ✓	218 Q/PB
Meghan Jordan		Richard Sarah	Crystal (with #254) Aaron extra pillows +sheets	2 adults 1 child 1:30-2:00pm	Mike	Annabel
223 Q	224 3T 3+Guests ✓	231 2T/PB	232 2T	233 3T 3+ guests	243 3T/1Q/PB 4+ guests	244 Q
		Jennifer Christopher Tyler- Remote #5 Fan #4 Airbed		Kim Jeff	Glenda Timothy	Katie Kenneth 1 Remote
245 2T ✓	250 2T/PB	251 2T/PB	252 Q/PB	253 Q/PB	254 2T/PB	255 2T/PB
Jon	Jim Penny	Andy Jeannie Air bed	Teresa Robert	Jason Brittany (with #152) Air bed	Lynne Brittany	

T = Twin   Q = Queen   PB = Private Bath   R = Remote-Garage   F = Fan   AB = Air Bed

3+guests = given out to families with 3 or more overnight guests

FIGURE 11.3: RMH guest room schedule.

and focus on a single activity. In this sense, a story is just a place-holder for more detailed conversations later on, not a specification or requirements document.

3. It should discuss a modest-sized activity by a single user role, requiring a short time to carry out. An example of such a user story is "Capture name and contact information from a client needing a room."

4. It should be testable. That is, when the story is implemented, it should be clear how to go about testing whether it has been properly implemented. This helps clarify acceptance testing goals, especially when the stories themselves appear ambiguous. For example, "Name and contact information should be captured and entered into the system in no more than 5–10 minutes (e.g., by completing an on-line form)."

So user stories provide a quick way of developing requirements without becoming bogged down in too much formality. The intention of the user story is to be able to respond quickly and with less overhead to rapidly changing real-world requirements. Acceptance testing procedures accompany user stories to provide a measure by which the goals of the user story have been fulfilled.

Here are a few more examples of user stories for each of the principal user roles for *RMH Homeroom*:

- House Manager

    - Determine if there are rooms that are off-line and arrange for repairs to be made.

    - Check a guest out of a room and note that the room needs to be cleaned.

    - Review a pending referral.

    - Book a room on a particular date.

- Social Worker

    - Determine whether or not there's a vacant room for a particular date.

    - Refer a family to the House Manager to stay at the House on a particular date.

    - Fill out a referral form.

- Volunteer

    - Determine if there are any rooms needing to be cleaned.

    - Record the status of a room as "clean."

Thus, user stories provide small-scale and easy-to-use pieces of information. They are written in the everyday language of the user and contain little detail, thus remaining open to interpretation. Stories thus should help the reader understand what it is the software should accomplish, rather than how it can be accomplished.

11.1.3 Use Cases

A *use case*, on the other hand, describes a user activity in detail, and it contains substantially more technical information than does a user story. That is, a use case describes a series of interactions between the new system and a user for accomplishing a particular task.

While user stories are different from use cases, they provide the fodder from which use cases are built. That is, we may view a use case as an elaboration and combining of user stories that fits within the setting of an overall system design.

Development of use cases is a highly interactive process. Cockburn ([Coc05], pp. 81–88) suggests conducting a workshop in which the key users tell their stories. That is, they talk about their roles and activities at a somewhat detailed level. The developers in the room do a lot of listening and note-taking.

Out of these discussions, user tasks and roles emerge, and a model of these tasks and their interactions can be derived. This task model, in fact, identifies the individual use cases that need to be written.

In the case of a loosely specified open source project, these task descriptions, and the use cases themselves, should be written so that they can be modified and expanded as more and more features are added to the software.

The task model also identifies individual user roles. For example, here are the roles that we have identified for *RMH Homeroom*:

House Manager The house manager generates and maintains the daily room schedule, keeps a record of all families who have stayed at RMH in the past, reviews applications for future bookings, and oversees the regular cleaning and maintenance of all guest rooms.

Social Worker A social worker at a hospital identifies families who need a place to stay and generates a referral for these families to the House Manager.

Volunteer A volunteer reviews the room schedule to see what rooms are vacant and need cleaning or laundry services, and provides support for guests who are staying in the other rooms.

The House Manager oversees the room scheduling process. The Social Worker provides input by entering referrals, and so must also use the system for this purpose. The Volunteer uses the system to learn about the status of a room and update that status once a room has been cleaned. Once the new software is installed, a technical person will be responsible for maintaining the integrity of the software and the data. However, the technical person does not fulfill a role because he/she does not interact with the software as a user.

For each user role, the task model describes each of the different tasks a user must perform using the software. The following specific tasks are associated with the *RMH Homeroom* software project.

The House Manager should be able to see the status of each room on any day's schedule. A room's *status* can be "clean and non-reserved," "dirty," "occupied," "reserved," or "off-line." An off-line room is one that cannot be occupied because it requires maintenance beyond a normal cleaning. One way to indicate status on a room display is to color-code the room display in the user interface according to its status (green = "clean and non-reserved," red = "dirty," white = "occupied," yellow = "reserved," and gray = "off-line").

The House Manager should be able to change the status of a room (e.g., from "green" to "white"), as well as identify the number and names of the guests, and all other details related to the occupancy of the room. If the room is linked to another room, a visual symbol (e.g., a teddy bear) can be used in both rooms' displays to help visualize that link.

The House Manager should be able to generate the next day's schedule from the previous day's schedule, and then update the status of the room(s) for any guest who will be checking out the next day. In general, the room schedule should be viewable in a daily, weekly, or monthly format, and the details for any particular room on any particular date should also be viewable. Here is a summary of the four different views and their interactions:

Room view should show all the detailed information about a single room, including its room number, capacity, status, and other details describing the room (that is, a single block in Figure 11.3). A House Manager or Social Worker should be able to determine from this description whether a particular room is available and its suitability for a new family to occupy.

Daily view should show the date and a summary of all rooms on the screen at once. Each room should appear with its room number and status (that is, all the blocks in Figure 11.3, but without all the details shown there). The daily view should be linked to the **room view** whenever the user selects a particular room.

Weekly view should show at a glance the date range and the room numbers of all non-reserved rooms for each day of that week. The weekly view should be linked to the **daily view** by selecting any particular day.

Monthly view should show at a glance a complete month and the number of non-reserved rooms for each day of that month. The monthly view should be linked to the **weekly view** by selecting any particular day.

The House Manager should also be able to keep track of all clients using an on-line database associated with the system. The relevant data for each client should be that which appears on the guest registration card (Figure 11.2).

Finally, the House Manager should be able to view statistical reports on room occupancy—by room, for all rooms, and by room type (capacity, private bath, etc.)—for any day, week, or month on the calendar. An on-line guest survey form would also be useful for the House Manager to receive feedback directly from guests.

Volunteers should be able to view the status of all rooms on the schedule (but not the names of the occupants, since that is confidential information), so that they can clean any dirty rooms in preparation for new occupancy. After cleaning a room, a volunteer should be able to change the status of a room from "red" to "green."

Social Workers should be able to view the status of all rooms on the schedule, in order to tell whether there are any vacancies available on dates when the client's child is scheduled to be hospitalized. While room scheduling is done by the House Manager, this view can help facilitate the referral activity. Social workers should also be able to fill out a referral form on-line, and all pending referrals should be accessible to the House Manager (but not to the Volunteers, since confidential information is present).

11.1.3.1   Unified Modeling Language

The task model described above can be presented in the form of a *use case diagram*, which is part of the Unified Modeling Language (UML) [uml]. UML is a formalization designed to help software developers graphically express the elements of a new software system in sufficient detail that the software can actually be developed using those expressions as a guide.

UML includes a set of graphic notation techniques to create visual models of object-oriented software designs. To display visual models, UML provides 14 different types of diagrams that can capture both the static and the dynamic aspects of the software and its use. The major UML diagram types are summarized as follows:

Class diagram shows the system's classes, their attributes, and their interrelationships.

Component diagram shows how the system is split into components and their interdependencies.

Use case diagram summarizes the system's actors and use cases and their interactions.

Sequence diagram shows the sequence of events that occur during the execution of a use case.

In practice, only a few of the 14 UML diagram types are widely used, especially in the open source development arena. Often the requirements of a new software product are so fluid that to encapsulate them into a rigid diagram can make the diagram prematurely obsolete.

Nevertheless, we have found that certain UML diagram types, especially the ones identified above, provide useful tools for grounding the details of an initial design and expressing them rather precisely. For example, Figure 11.4 shows an initial use case diagram for the new *RMH Homeroom* software.

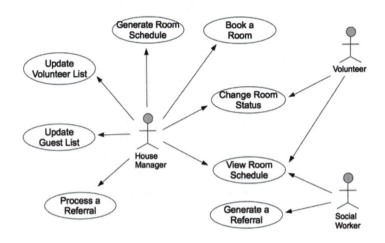

FIGURE 11.4: *RMH Homeroom* use cases.

This use case diagram delineates eight distinct activities that *RMH Homeroom* must support in order to fulfill its requirements. The House Manager has access to all eight, while the Volunteer and Social Worker have access to two each.

For example, all three user roles need to view the room schedule. However, only the Social Worker can generate a referral, while only the House Manager can process a referral. These distinctions are made very clear by the use case diagram. The use case diagram can thus stand as an important information resource throughout the early stages of a project's incubation.

11.1.3.2 Writing an Effective Use Case

In general, a use case must convey certain information in order for it be useful in a software design. This information is presented in a stylized form, so that readers don't have to do too much digging to find the information they need. As we have seen in Chapter 5 and Appendix A, a use case conveys the following information about a specific user-system interaction:

Use Case Name is a unique and meaningful name for the use case—a name that will be familiar to users and developers alike. For instance, in *RMH Homeroom*, we have given the use cases names like "Generate Room Schedule" and "Process a Referral," which provide initial clues about the kind of interaction that will be described.

Description is a brief summary of how this use case will support the overall goals of the application. For instance, we might write the following to describe the "Process a Referral" use case:

> All the information on the referral form should be entered into the system, and an attempt should be made to book a room for this referral on the requested dates.

Actors identifies the roles who are authorized to perform this use case. For instance, for "Process a Referral," the lone actor is the House Manager.

Goals describes the general outcome that will occur when the actor completes this use case. For instance, the "Process a Referral" has the goal of either approving or disapproving a referral, and possibly booking a room as well. A reason for disapproving a referral might be unavailability of any suitable room at the House for the requested dates.

Preconditions describes what must be true before this use case can be started. For instance, "Process a Referral" must have a referral available for processing.

Postconditions describes what must be true after this use case is completed. For instance, "Process a Referral" will leave the referral either approved or disapproved, and possibly a new room booking completed as well.

Related Use Cases describes any other use cases that are directly related to this use case. For example, "Process a Referral" is related to both "View Room Schedule" and "Book a Room."

Steps is a step-by-step description of how the actor will interact with the system to accomplish the goals of the use case. This is usually written as a two–column table, one column for the user's actions and the other for the system's responses. This is the most critical and intricate part of the use case to write, since it holds the key to the eventual design of user-system interactions in the user interface itself. In the case of "Process a Referral," the steps might look like this.

Actor	System
1. Log on to Web site	2. Ask for id and password
3. Enter id and password	4. Verify; Display outcome
5. Obtain a referral for the requested date.	6. Display the next available referral
7. Request week view for the requested date	8. Display week view
9. If there is a suitable room available for the requested date, book the room	10. Execute the booking and confirm the outcome
11. Notify client of the outcome	12. Issue notification to the client
13. Log off Web site	14. Terminate session

Steps 1-4 ensure client privacy and system security: only the House Manager should be able to process a referral. Steps 5-12 describe the essence of the interaction, while Steps 13-14 terminate the interaction.

Notice that the style of writing here reflects the language of the domain and doesn't force any technicalities of user interaction or any specific user interface design on the reader; it only indicates what must be accomplished to complete the use case. This is important; over-specifying the user-system interaction at this early stage can tie developers' hands prematurely.

11.2 Initial Design

With a reasonably complete set of use cases in hand, the design of the code base can thus begin. Design starts with a clear and crisp statement of the software's overall design goals. For example, the general design goals for *RMH Homeroom* are the following:

1. Develop a complete, correct, reusable, and well-documented software system for guest room scheduling.

2. Provide a fully functional and intuitive user interface that implements all the use cases, with on-line help immediately accessible for each function.

3. Provide secure user access to the system via a Web browser.

11.2.1 Domain Classes

One area in which UML is particularly useful is to assist with the initial domain class design for a new software system. There are a few open source UML tools available that can be helpful with this drawing and visualization task, especially if you are not particularly keen on drawing diagrams by hand.

One useful open source tool is ArgoUML (see http://tigris.org). Figure 11.5 shows the result of using ArgoUML to sketch some of the initial domain classes and their instance variables for *RMH Homeroom*.

Once the classes and their key instance variables and methods are sketched, the UML tool can automatically generate a new project with these classes embedded. The classes can be generated in any current object-oriented language (e.g., Java, C++, PHP, Python, or Ruby). This step establishes an initial namespace for the code base that is consistent with the one that underlies the user stories and use cases.

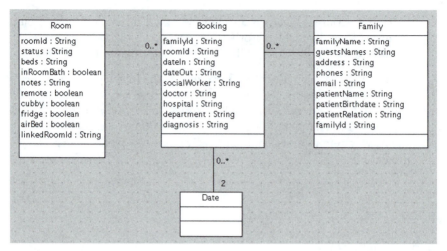

FIGURE 11.5: Some of the initial domain classes for *RMH Homeroom.*

11.2.2   User Interface

User interface design, on the other hand, is not particularly amenable to UML diagramming techniques. Instead, a series of sketches tends to help express the elements of an initial user interface and their interrelationships. Cockburn refers to these as "screen drafts" in the following way ([Coc05], p. 181):

> Screen drafts are low-cost renditions of the way screens will look, used to explore the ways that users might interact with the system, and invent better ways for them to get their goals accomplished. Very often they are just drawings on paper.

The team may also use a simple graphical drawing tool to generate screen drafts rapidly.

For *RMH Homeroom*, several screen drafts are needed to help design the user interface. For example, each one of the different views of the room schedule (room view, day view, etc.) requires a screen draft, clearly showing the points of navigation that allow users to switch from one to another.

Figure 11.6 shows a screen draft of what the room view can look like. It was drawn using *xfig*, a well-known open source drawing tool (see http://xfig.org for download information).

In this screen draft, the simple notational convention is for existing information to be indicated by underscores, user-entered information to be indicated by text areas, and buttons (for links to other views) to be indicated by named ovals. The development of other screen drafts for *RMH Homeroom* is left as an exercise.

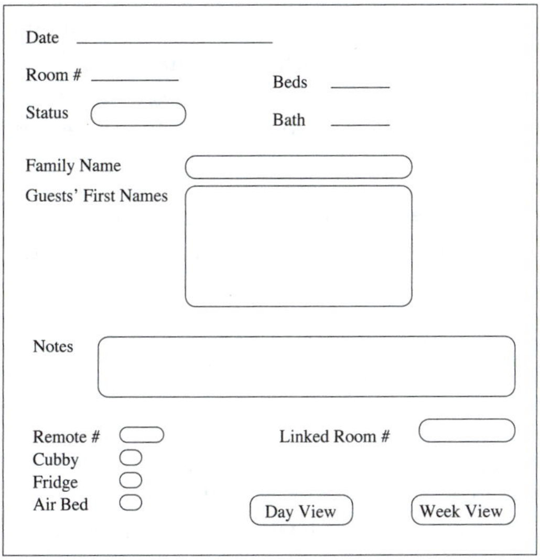

FIGURE 11.6: Room view screen draft for *RMH Homeroom*.

11.2.3 Performance and Platform

A number of initial design decisions must be made for a new sofware project before any development begins. This section identifies those decisions in the form of performance, platform, and process requirements. While many of these may seem to be "obvious," it is good to gain developer and user consensus about these choices by writing them into the initial design.

Easy to learn and use: The user interface should be consistent with modern calendar and address book applications. It should be easy to learn by persons with a variety of backgrounds and minimum technical training.

Web-based: The system should have aclear and consistent Web-based user interface, with full functionality and help screen tutorial support.

Secure and protective of privacy: Information about clients should be accessible on a strict need-to-know basis. Information in the database should also be protected from inadvertent corruption.

Efficient: The user interface should be responsive and the entire system should use computing resources efficiently.

Reliable: The system should run correctly; all user interactions should be reversible and repeatable.

Available: The system should be available 24/7 and accessible from any Web browser connected to the Internet.

Supportive of backup and recovery: Performing system backup should be possible by the system administrator or the House Manager. If the system fails or the database is lost, recovery to a reasonably recent checkpoint (e.g., the previous day or the previous hour) should be possible.

Maintainable: The system's architecture and documentation should be designed to facilitate efficient correction of minor defects as well as the development of major future enhancements.

Open source: The system and its source code should be freely available and adaptable by any other organization that has a similar need for room scheduling.

Interoperability: The system should run on Windows, Mac, and Linux (and mobile) platforms. For instance, the database may be hosted on a Linux system and users may access it from any Windows, Mac, or mobile device through its Web browser.

System, language, and database technology: The system should be designed and implemented using programming language, database system, and Web server technologies that support interoperability, for example Apache/Java/MySQL or Apache/PHP/MySQL.

Staging server and version control: The system will be developed using a server at the developer's site, which will support the programming environment, database and version control system selected for the project. The software and database will be designed so that they can eventually be relocated to the client's computing environment.

Development team: The system will be designed and implemented by a group of initial developers, users, and support persons using agile techniques.

Development timeline: The project will begin on a particular starting and ending date, at which time a working prototype will be completed for public demonstration. Several intermediate milestones will be set so that users and developers can exchange ideas about partially completed system components, especially at the user interface level, and adjustments to initial design features and use cases.

Sources of support: The project may draw ideas and code from other open source projects, whose goals and/or technical elements may overlap with those of the current project.

Collaboration: Collaboration will be supported by the use of specific collaboration and code management tools, for example Google Groups and Subversion.

Delivery: The software developed by this project will be designed so that it can eventually be placed in the public domain with an open source software license, such as GPL, and downloaded from a widely used open source repository, such as Sourceforge.

11.2.4 System Architecture

Open source software is often modeled using a client-server architecture, as discussed in Chapter 4. That is because such software often allows several users to simultaneously access the software's services and underlying database.

For example, both *Sahana* and *RMH Homebase* have client-server architectures. For the same reasons of multiple user access, *RMH Homeroom* should also have a client-server architecture.

Moreover, open source software artifacts are often designed using frameworks that allow different developer groups to work independently and contribute new features in the form of *plug-ins* to the original code base. These are sometimes called "pluggable architectures."

For example, Drupal (http://drupal.org) has a pluggable architecture. Drupal is an open-source software product that allows users to create content-rich Web sites for a wide range of applications.

Drupal's developer community has several quasi-independent sub-groups, each working on a separate feature that users can add to their Drupal Web sites. These features are called Drupal *modules.* Users can choose to add any particular module by simply downloading it, plugging it into the Drupal site, and activating it. For example, a particular user developing an e-commerce site may download and plug in a module that implements e-commerce. Other Drupal sites may have no interest in e-commerce, so they would not need that particular module.

Many other popular software artifacts, such as Firefox and Eclipse, also have pluggable architectures. Frameworks for adding plug-in capabilities to a software artifact exist for many programming languages, including C++, Java, and Python. For more information, see http://en.wikipedia.org/wiki/Plug-in_(computing).

Since this system is open source software, an appropriate copyright and reuse notice should appear at the beginning of each module and at the bottom of each page in the software's user interface. For example, the GNU General Public License notice would look like this:

```
/* Copyright 2008 by <names of copyright holders>. This
 * program is part of <name of software artifact>, which is free
 * software. It comes with absolutely no warranty. You can
 * redistribute ormodify it under the terms of the GNU General
 * Public License as published by the Free Software Foundation
 * (For more  information, see <http://www.gnu.org/licenses/).
 */
```

11.2.5   Design Alternatives

A newly conceived open source software project should consider and resolve its design alternatives before coding actually begins. Some of the obvious alternatives have already been covered in Section 11.2.3.

In addition to these, open source developers should think about alternative strategies for including particular features in a software architecture. Often, a feature can be implemented by downloading a pre-written software component and adapting it to "fit" within the new system's architecture.

An obvious benefit of adapting a pre-written component to fit the new application is that it can save time vs the alternative of developing that feature from scratch. Another benefit of this choice is that the resulting feature may be more "bulletproof" (since it's already been used elsewhere) and user friendly than what would be developed from scratch. That is, adapting an existing component brings with it the collected benefits of the open source philosophy.

For example, one design alternative that faces many software projects is that of developing a good calendar interface. This was a need in *RMH Homebase*, and it is also a need in *RMH Homeroom*.

Any application that has a scheduling function should consider adapting the iCalendar standard, a file format that allows Internet users to share calendar data across most platforms and common applications. iCalendar support packages are available for most common programming languages, including Java, PHP, C++, and Python. For more information about iCalendar, see http://en.wikipedia.org/wiki/ICalendar.

RMH Homebase does not currently use the iCalendar standard for displaying volunteer schedules—instead, its PHP code for calendar display and updating was written from scratch. For the reasons suggested above, it would be a good idea to adapt *RMH Homebase* to use the iCalendar standard. For the same reasons, any new development project for *RMH Homeroom* should consider iCalendar integration as a priority.

11.2.6   Design Document

A newly conceived software project should establish clear and open communication at the outset. Much of that communication reflects initial design elements that require continual review and refinement.

Clearly, the use cases and initial class design are two key elements of a good design document. Other key elements of a complete design document include a description of the system's performance and platform requirements and overall software architecture. Finally, a discussion of design alternatives and the rationale for making a particular set of choices should be included.

The design document should be on-line and editable by all developers who have commit privileges for the code base itself. That will ensure that the design details keep pace with progress in the code base itself. These developers should regularly review and update those parts of the design document that are affected by their work with the code base. A useful tool for achieving this goal and keeping the design document up to date would be to set up a project wiki, to which all developers and users have secure access for reading and writing.

11.3 Summary

This chapter discusses the first steps needed to conceive and begin developing an open source software artifact from scratch. Many of these steps are found in the requirements analysis phase that begins a traditional software process. Thus, some of the traditional tools, such as UML use case and class diagrams, are also useful in this setting.

However, the conception of an open source development project differs fundamentally from the requirements analysis step in a traditional software process. That is mainly because open source development is agile and fluid. New open source project requirements, therefore, must be developed and implemented with the idea that they will change throughout the development process.

A new project, called *RMH Homeroom*, is introduced in this chapter to illustrate the process of new project conception. This introduction also provides a basis for conceiving an interesting new open source product. The exercises below are presented with that activity in mind.

Exercises

Most of these exercises are best carried out by a development team working together. For each exercise, the work should be divided equitably among the team members.

11.1 Develop the remaining use cases for *RMH Homeroom*.

11.2 Develop screen drafts for all the user interface screens identified for *RMH Homeroom*.

11.3 Develop a complete class diagram for all the domain classes identified for *RMH Homeroom*.

11.4 Complete the design for *RMH Homeroom* by selecting a language and platform and completing the design document using the guidelines in this chapter.

11.5 Start a new project for *RMH Homeroom*. Identify team membership and roles, and set up the code base, version control system, and a project Web site.

11.6 Add a project wiki to your new *RMH Homeroom* project.

11.7 Add developer and user forums to your new *RMH Homeroom* project.

11.8 Add Bugzilla bug tracking to your new *RMH Homeroom* project.

11.9 Extend the domain class design and the code base for *RMH Homebase* so that it integrates the iCalendar standard for displaying and updating the room scheduling calendar.

Appendix A

Details of the Case Study

This Appendix describes in some detail the requirements and design for *RMH Homebase*. This software has had four modifications since release 1.0 was initially placed on Sourceforge in May 2008. Release 1.4 is the version currently in productive use at http://rmhportland.org/Volunteers/homebase.

Releases 1.5 and 2.0 are discussed most heavily in the middle chapters of this textbook. Since this software is open source, any of these three releases can be downloaded as a .zip file and installed, from the Sourceforge site http://sourceforge.net/projects/rmhhomebase. Detailed installation instructions and other supporting information are also available at that Web site.

The requirements described in Section A.1 are for release 1.0, while the design and code base described in Section A.2 are for release 1.4. While these requirements have not been kept up to date with the functionality found in later releases, they do provide a good introduction to the general capabilities of the software.

A.1 Requirements

This section provides a background description of the prior (manual) system that was replaced by the new software *RMH Homebase*. It also provides detailed descriptions of the specific ways in which users will interact with the new system—these are called *use cases*.

This analysis also describes the system requirements for the new software—information about platform, database, and other technical details and constraints. Finally, it provides a preliminary description of the system's core classes, database tables, and user interface elements that need to be implemented in order to enable the software to be implemented.

Examples of all these elements are an important part of the design document, since they allow readers to quickly visualize the key components of the new system and how it can be used.

A.1.1   Domain Analysis

The Ronald McDonald House (RMH) in Portland, Maine serves the community by providing nearby lodging and meals for families of children who are patients at nearby hospitals. Its services are particularly valuable for families who travel a long distance from their homes to the Maine Medical Center or other Portland area hospitals and whose children are hospitalized for more than one night. The RMH Web site (see http://www.rmhportlandme.org/) provides a good overview of the House and its services.

RMH has 21 rooms that, on a typical night, are almost fully booked. The House is run by a full-time staff of five—an Executive Director, a House Manager, an Office Manager, a Night Manager, and a Community Manager. The House is operated with the help of dozens of Volunteers. RMH staff work closely with social workers at the Maine Medical Center to help identify families who need a place to stay while their children are in the hospital.

A.1.1.1   Background Information

Volunteer scheduling is a central activity of the RMH. The purpose of Volunteer scheduling is to manage the House calendar so that house coverage is maintained on a daily basis. Volunteers help support the House operation in many ways: they cover the front desk and welcome visitors, clean rooms, cook meals, and run errands. The House Manager oversees the scheduling of Volunteers for all these tasks. Whenever a Volunteer has to cancel his/her shift, a Substitute must be found to cover that shift.

Volunteer scheduling is coordinated by the House Manager. It is done mainly by hand, using worksheets and desk calendars. Many people assist the House Manager with this scheduling task, especially when a Substitute must be found to fill in for a cancellation. The system works well because of the good spirit of teamwork that exists among the House staff and its Volunteers.

However, because it is the product of many hands, Volunteer scheduling is tedious and sometimes error prone. In the worst case, a scheduling mistake can have a Volunteer show up for a shift and not be needed. Most importantly, the scheduling task requires a lot of effort and coordination.

This scheduling activity presents an opportunity to design software that could assist the House Manager and staff to schedule House activities and keep track of Volunteers in a less cumbersome way. If done right, such software should help eliminate errors and facilitate the task of scheduling for everyone involved.

It is important to note that this type of scheduling problem is not well solved for the general case. Current software solutions tend be tailored to narrow requirements, are often tied to corporate payroll systems, and are proprietary (costly). By contrast, an effective software solution for Volunteer scheduling at the RMH could be designed so that it can be adapted to address the Volunteer scheduling problem at other RMHs as well as many other non-profit organizations throughout the country.

A central goal of this project is to engage the skills of undergraduate computer science students at Bowdoin College to create free and open source software for Volunteer scheduling at the RMH. If successful, this software can be freely adapted by any organization with similar needs.

As an initial model for this design effort we will use the open source Volunteer Management system for the *Sahana* project (see http://sahanaproject.org), which was developed to help manage the 2004 tsunami relief effort. Trinity College students and faculty helped design and implement the Sahana Volunteer Management software. The idea of undergraduate students and faculty developing humanitarian free and open source software is the theme of a project at Trinity College called HFOSS (see http://hfoss.org) which is sponsored by an NSF grant. The outcome of this project will help determine how well the HFOSS concept will transport to Bowdoin College computer science faculty and students.

A.1.1.2 System Users

We envision a new Volunteer scheduling system at RMH to be managed by four different types of users.

House Manager The House Manager creates and maintains all Volunteer lists, creates the schedule and the monthly calendars, fills vacancies as they occur, and screens new applicants for Volunteer positions.

Volunteers The regular Volunteers staff the front desk, welcome new visitors, and help fill vacancies in the calendar as they occur. This includes receiving phone call cancellations from other Volunteers, managing a "sub call list" for that new vacancy, and calling other Volunteers on this list until the vacancy is filled.

Applicants Applicants interested in volunteering at the RMH should be able to log in to the system and fill out an application form that will be automatically transmitted to the House Manager.

Technical Person The Technical Person will oversee the smooth running of the software, including its integration with the RMH Web site.

The House Manager and the Volunteers oversee the scheduling process. Once the new software is installed, a Technical Person will be responsible for maintaining the integrity of the software and the data.

A.1.1.3 Overview of the Current System

Prior to installation of the new software, people could apply for a Volunteer position at the RMH by filling out a form that they downloaded from the House Web site. This form is shown in Figure A.29.

RONALD MCDONALD HOUSE OF PORTLAND, MAINE, INC.
VOLUNTEER APPLICATION FORM

Name:_____

Address:_____ City: _____

State, Zip Code:_____ Home Phone:_____

Work /Cell Phone:_____ E-mail Address:_____

Employer: _____

Employer's Address:_____

Emergency Contact:_____

Relationship:_____ Phone:_____

The Ronald McDonald House requires volunteers under the age of 18 to be accompanied by an adult.

What volunteer positions are you interested in?

   ____   Three-hour shift: Weekday 3-hour shifts are scheduled weekly or every other week. Weekend shifts are typically scheduled once per month (i.e., 2ⁿᵈ Saturday, 10-1).

Please check the days and times you are available for shift volunteering below:

	Mon	Tues	Wed	Thurs	Fri			Sat		Sun
9 to 12							2-3 hours morning		2-3 hours morning	
12 to 3							2-3 hours afternoon		2-3 hours afternoon	
3 to 6									5 - 9 p.m.	
6 to 9										

   ____   Weekend Managers (need a pair, from Friday 5 p.m. to Sunday 3 p.m., typically twice a year)

   ____   Guest Chef (dinners, weekend brunches or holiday dinners)

   ____   House Cleaner (weekdays or weekends)

~ see reverse side

Ronald McDonald House • 250 Brackett Street • Portland, Maine 04102 • 207.780.6282
www.rmhportland.org

FIGURE A.1: RMH Volunteer application form: 12/2007.

DATE>>> TIME	12-Nov 26-Nov 10-Dec 24-Dec	13-Nov 27-Nov 11-Dec 25-Dec	14-Nov 28-Nov 12-Dec 26-Dec	15-Nov 29-Nov 13-Dec 27-Dec	16-Nov 30-Nov 14-Dec 28-Dec
	Monday	Tuesday	Wednesday	Thursday	Friday
9:00-12:00					
12:00-3:00					
3:00-6:00					
6:00-9:00					
Sub Only	Temporary Opening	Permanent Opening	Notes-		

RMH	Volunteer Schedule	Group One

FIGURE A.2: RMH master schedule—Group One.

When an Applicant is accepted for a position, his/her contact information is saved in a Rolodex file. The new Volunteer is scheduled according to his/her interests and current House needs. The main positions available are:

Volunteer working a normal 3-hour weekday shift on alternate weeks

Weekend Volunteer working a normal Friday 5pm—Sunday 3pm shift (usually a two-person team that covers two or more weekends per year)

Substitute on-call for a normal shift when another Volunteer cancels

Guest Chef providing weekday dinners, brunches, and holiday dinners

Other house cleaning, pick-up/delivery, errand running

The House Manager keeps a master schedule for Volunteers working normal shifts. The schedule has three parts: Group One and Group Two (weekdays on alternate weeks) and Group Weekend. For example, the master schedule for Group One is shown in Figure A.2.

Each daytime shift requires two Volunteers, while 6–9pm shifts usually require three. All shifts are filled either by Volunteers or by Substitutes.

MONDAY	TUESDAY	WEDNESDAY	THURSDAY	FRIDAY	SATURDAY	SUNDAY

FIGURE A.3: Typical handwritten monthly Volunteer calendar.

From the master schedule, the House Manager generates the next 2 months' Volunteer calendars by hand on a desktop calendar. A typical month's handwritten calendar is shown in Figure A.3.

Each weekday on the calendar has four shifts (9am–12pm, 12–3pm, 3–6pm, and 6–9pm) and each shift usually has two Volunteers scheduled. A vacant shift shows as a blank space and it can be filled by locating a Substitute. A typical day's shift schedule on the handwritten calendar is shown enlarged in Figure A.4.

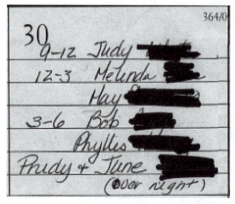

FIGURE A.4: Typical scheduled day on the handwritten calendar.

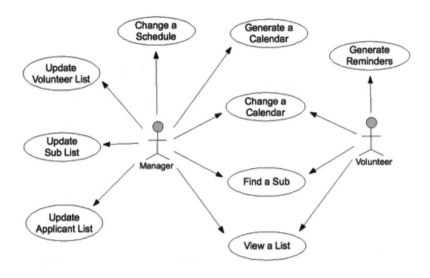

FIGURE A.5: RMH use case diagram.

A.1.2 Use Cases

To be useful, software support for the scheduling process must support user interaction in specific ways. This support is described below as a collection of use cases, which together characterize how the House Manager and a Volunteer can the use software to facilitate the scheduling tasks described above.

The diagram in Figure A.5 identifies nine specific use cases. The nine use cases are carefully described in Figures A.6 through A.14. These descriptions explain how each of these nine activities can be carried out using an on-line system. They make frequent references to specific information in lists, schedules, and calendars as if that information were available electronically in an on-line database.

The two main players in Volunteer scheduling are the House Manager and the Volunteer working at the front desk. The House Manager interviews and tracks Applicants, and she keeps the Applicant list, the Volunteer list, the Substitute list, and the master schedule up to date. The House Manager also prepares each month's Volunteer and Guest Chef calendars. The Volunteer and the House Manager can later make changes to the calendars, recruit Substitutes, and send reminders to Volunteers who are scheduled for certain shifts.

UpdateApplicantList

Description: The House Manager tracks an Applicant by arranging for the Applicant to shadow another Volunteer working at the House to learn about the duties that he/she will perform. This use case provides a way to record an Applicant's progress and add him/her to the Volunteer List or the Sub Call List at the end of the tracking process.

Actor: The House Manager

Goals: To keep the Applicant list, Substitute list, and Volunteer list up to date.

Preconditions: 1. An application has been received.
2. The Applicant has been interviewed and background-checked.

Postconditions: 1. The Applicant's information is entered or updated in the Applicant List.
2. If the Applicant's tracking is complete, add him/her to the Sub List or the Volunteer List.

Related Use Cases: ViewAList, UpdateSubList, UpdateVolunteerList

Steps:

Actor	System
1. Log on to Web site.	2. Ask for id and password.
3. Enter id and password.	4. Verify; Display outcome.
5. View an Applicant's status (use case ViewAList).	6. Execute the action. Display results.
7. If the Applicant is not in the Applicant List, add him/her to the list. Otherwise, update Applicant's status.	8. Execute the action. Display results.
9. If tracking is complete, add Applicant to Sub List and/or Volunteer List and remove Applicant from Applicant List (use cases UpdateSubList and UpdateVolunteerList).	10. Execute the actions and confirm the outcome.
11. Log off Web site.	12. Terminate session.

FIGURE A.6: Use case **UpdateApplicantList**.

UpdateSubList

Description: The House Manager may add people to the Sub List, remove people from the Sub List, or change information about people in the Sub List.

Actor: The House Manager

Goals: To add, remove, or change information about people in the Sub List

Preconditions: 1. Information to be added, removed, or changed is available.
2. Each new person being added is in the Applicant List and not yet in the Sub List. Each person whose information is being changed or deleted is already in the Sub List.

Postconditions: 1. Entries in the Sub List are added, changed, or removed.

Related Use Cases: ViewAList, UpdateApplicantList, UpdateVolunterList

Steps:

Actor	System
1. Log on to Web site.	2. Ask for id and password.
3. Enter id and password.	4. Verify and display outcome.
5. Repeat steps 6–9 for each update to be made.	
6. Select Add, Change, or Remove, along with the person's name and phone.	7. Find person in Applicant List or Sub List. Display outcome.
8. If Add, get details from Applicant List and submit them. If Change, make changes and submit. If Delete, signal deletion.	9. If Add, validate and add to Sub List. If Change, validate changes and replace entry in Sub List. If Delete, remove entry from Sub List. Display outcome.
10. Log off Web site.	11. Terminate session.

FIGURE A.7: Use case **UpdateSubList**.

UpdateVolunteerList

Description: The House Manager may add persons to the Volunteer List, remove persons from the Volunteer List, or change information about Volunteers.

Actor: The House Manager

Goals: To add, remove, or change information about people in the Volunteer List

Preconditions: 1. Information to be added, removed, or changed is available

2. Each person being added is in the Applicant List and not in the Volunteer List.

3. Each person whose information is being changed or deleted is in the Volunteer List.

Postconditions: 1. Entries in the Volunteer List are added, changed, or removed.

Related Use Cases: ViewAList, UpdateApplicantList, UpdateSubList

Steps:

Actor	System
1. Log on to Web site.	2. Ask for id and password.
3. Enter id and password.	4. Verify and display outcome.
5. Repeat steps 6–9 for each update to be made.	
6. Select Add, Change, or Remove, along with the person's name and phone.	7. Find person in Applicant List or Volunteer List. Display outcome.
8. If Add, get details from Applicant List and submit them. If Change, make changes and submit. If Delete, signal deletion.	9. If Add, validate and add to Volunteer List. If Change, validate changes and replace entry in Volunteer List. If Delete, remove entry from Volunteer List. Display outcome.
10. Log off Web site.	11. Terminate session.

FIGURE A.8: Use case **UpdateVolunteerList**.

GenerateACalendar

Description: The House Manager should complete this activity before the beginning of the month for which the calendar is being generated. Other use cases involving that month's calendar can be initiated only if it is accessible on line.

Actor: The House Manager

Goals: To generate a monthly calendar and make it accessible on-line for viewing or updating

Preconditions: 1. The Volunteer list exists.
2. The master schedule (Group One, Group Two, and Group Weekend) exists.

Postconditions: 1. A new month's calendar is generated and made available on-line for viewing and updating.

Related Use Cases: ChangeACalendar

Steps:

Actor	System
1. Log on to Web site.	2. Ask for id and password.
3. Enter id and password.	4. Verify and display outcome.
5. Access the Schedules and the Volunteer list.	6. Confirm.
7 Generate a new calendar from the master schedule.	8. Confirm.
9. Repeat steps 10–11 as many times as needed. Signal when done.	
10. Change a calendar entry using the Volunteer List and Sub List (use case ChangeACalendar).	11. Confirm validity of the change; issue an error message if not valid.
12. Log out.	13. Make calendar available on-line and terminate the session.

FIGURE A.9: Use case **GenerateACalendar**.

ChangeASchedule

Description: The House Manager may add, remove, or change persons on any shift on the schedule.

Actor: The House Manager

Goals: To add, remove, or change an entry on the Group One, Group Two, or Group Weekend schedule

Preconditions: 1. Information to be added, removed, or changed is available.
2. Each person being added is in the Volunteer List and available for that shift.
3. Each person whose information is being changed or deleted is on the schedule.

Postconditions: 1. Entries in the schedule are added, changed, or removed.

Related Use Cases: ViewAList

Steps:

Actor	System
1. Log on to Web site.	2. Ask for id and password.
3. Enter id and password	4. Verify and display outcome.
5. Identify group schedule to change.	6. Display the schedule.
7. Repeat steps 8–9 for each change to be made.	
8. Identify a shift on the schedule to be changed. If Change or Remove, select the entry to be changed or removed. If Add or Change, enter the new person's name and phone.	9. If Add or Change, check availability for that shift. Perform Add, Change, or Remove. Display outcome.
10. Log off Web site.	11. Terminate session.

FIGURE A.10: Use case **ChangeASchedule**.

ChangeACalendar

Description: The House Manager or a Volunteer may change persons scheduled for individual shifts on the calendar whenever a vacancy appears or a person cancels his/her scheduled shift. They may also add notes to any individual shift or day of the week. The primary sources of information for this activity are the list of Volunteers and their availability, as well as each individual shift's SubCallList.

Actor: The House Manager or a Volunteer

Goals: To fill vacant shifts on the calendar or the Chef's calendar

Preconditions: 1. The Volunteer list and the SubCallList are available. 2. There are shifts on the calendar to be changed or vacancies to be filled.

Postconditions: 1. Shifts are changed and vacancies are filled.

Related Use Cases: FindASub

Steps:

Actor	System
1. Log on to Web site.	2. Ask for id and password.
3. Enter id and password	4. Verify and display outcome.
5. Repeat steps 6–11 for each vacant shift.	
6. Identify a shift to be changed and remove the person who has cancelled.	7. Display outcome.
8. Identify a vacancy in a shift and create or retrieve the SubCallList for that shift (use case FindASub).	9. Display outcome
10. If the SubCallList has a "Yes!" on it, schedule the Volunteer into the vacant shift and retire the SubCallList.	11. Confirm the change and display the new calendar.
12. Log off Web site.	13. Terminate session.

FIGURE A.11: Use case **ChangeACalendar**.

FindASub

Description: The House Manager or a Volunteer on duty may fill a vacancy on the Calendar by calling people on the SubCallList.

Actor: The House Manager or a Volunteer

Goals: To locate a Substitute to fill a vacancy in the calendar.

Preconditions: 1. There is a vacancy on the calendar.
2. There is a SubCallList for that vacancy.

Postconditions: 1. The vacancy is filled.

Related Use Cases: ViewAList, ChangeACalendar

Steps:

Actor	System
1. Log on to Web site.	2. Ask for id and password.
3. Enter id and password.	4. Verify and display outcome.
5. Locate a vacancy on the calendar and access the SubCallList for that vacancy.	6. Display outcome.
7. If there is no "Yes!" on the SubCallList, view all Substitutes available on the list for that vacancy. Call as many of these as time permits and enter result of each call on the SubCallList.	8. Validate each entry and display outcome.
9. If there's a "Yes!" on the SubCallList, add that Substitute to the calendar (ChangeACalendar).	10. Validate the replacement and display outcome.
11. Log off Web site.	12. Terminate session.

FIGURE A.12:   Use case **FindASub**.

GenerateReminders

Description: The actor may, while viewing a calendar, decide to send a reminder to a person scheduled for an upcoming shift. That reminder may be sent out by phone, mail, or e-mail. (This use case was not implemented in *RMH Homebase*. Instead, a Volunteer can directly view his/her upcoming shifts by logging in to the system from any Web browser.)

Actor: The House Manager or the Manager's Assistant

Goals: To print a reminder for mailing (e-mailing) to a Volunteer who is scheduled for an upcoming shift

Preconditions: none

Postconditions: 1. Reminders are generated.

Related Use Cases: ViewAList

Steps:

Actor	System
1. Log on to Web site.	2. Ask for id and password.
3. Enter id and password.	4. Verify and display outcome.
5. Identify a scheduled shift on the calendar for which a reminder needs to be sent.	6. Display outcome: name, address, phone, and e-mail of the persons scheduled for that shift.
7. If the reminder is an e-mail reminder or a mail reminder, generate the reminder message and send it.	8. Complete the sending by printing a postcard or sending an e-mail.
9. If it is a phone call, make the call.	
10. Log off Web site.	11. Terminate session.

FIGURE A.13: Use case **GenerateReminders**.

ViewAList

Description: In updating a list, schedule, or calendar, the actor needs to know who fulfills certain constraints, such as availability for a particular shift or having a particular skill. That information is specified, along with the list to be searched, and the system provides the names and phones of all persons satisfying those constraints.

Actor: The House Manager or a Volunteer

Goals: To view entries in the Applicant List, the Volunteer List, the Sub List, a Schedule, or a Calendar. Different selections should be possible, such as:

"view all Substitutes available on Mondays from 12–3,"

"view all Volunteers who have not worked since last July,"

"view all Volunteers and Substitutes who have been scheduled fewer than three times this fall," or

"view all Applicants who have been background-checked and interviewed."

Preconditions: 1. A list, schedule, or calendar and a search criterion are specified

Postconditions: 1. All persons on the designated list who satisfy that criterion are displayed.

Related Use Cases: UpdateApplicantList, UpdateSubList, UpdateVolunteerList, GenerateACalendar, ChangeACalendar, FindASub

Steps:

Actor	System
1. Log on to Web site.	2. Ask for id and password.
3. Enter id and password.	4. Verify and display outcome.
5. Identify a list, schedule, or calendar to be searched.	6. Display outcome.
7. Select search criteria.	8. Perform the search and display the outcome.
9. Log off Web site.	10. Terminate session.

FIGURE A.14: Use case **ViewAList**.

A.1.3 System Requirements

In addition to implementing the application described in the use cases, the software should also fill certain performance, platform, and process requirements. These requirements are outlined in the sections below.

A.1.3.1 Performance Requirements

Whenever the system is used, it should have the following characteristics.

Easy to learn and use: The user interface should be consistent with modern Web-based calendar and address book applications. It should be easy to learn by persons with a variety of backgrounds and minimum technical training.

Web-based: The system should have clear and consistent Web-based interfaces, with full functionality and help screen tutorial support.

Secure and protective of privacy: Information about individual Volunteers should be accessible on a strict need-to-know basis. Information in the database should also be protected from inadvertent corruption.

Efficient: The user interface should be responsive and the entire system should use computing resources efficiently.

Reliable: The system should run correctly; all transactions should be reversible and repeatable.

Available: The system should be available 24/7 and accessible from any Web browser connected to the Internet.

Supportive of backup and recovery: System backup should be executable by the system administrator or the House Manager. If the system fails or the database is lost, recovery should be performable by either of these persons.

Maintainable: The system should be designed and documented so as to facilitate quick correction of minor defects as well as major future enhancements.

Open source: The system and its source code should be freely available and adaptable by any other organization that has a similar need for personnel database and calendar scheduling.

A.1.3.2   Platform Requirements

The software should also be implemented for a wide range of platforms.

Interoperability: The system should run on a Windows, Mac, or Linux system or any mix of these. For instance, the database may be hosted on a Linux system and users may access it from any Windows or Mac machine.

System, language, and database technology: The system should be designed and implemented using an open source programming language, database system, and Web server technology that support interoperability. Possibilities are Apache/Java/MySQL and Apache/PHP/MySQL.

Staging server and version control: The database will be developed using a server at Bowdoin College that will support the database and a CVS-like version control system for the software development. The software and database will be designed so that they can eventually be relocated to the RMH computers.

A.1.3.3   Process Requirements

The system will be developed using the following general process.

Development team: The system will be designed and implemented by Bowdoin students, faculty, and IT staff, in collaboration with RMH staff throughout the life of the project.

Development timeline: The project will begin in January 2008 and a working prototype will be developed for demonstration by May 2008.

Sources of support: The project will draw ideas from HFOSS open source software developed at Trinity College, principally the Volunteer Management system (VMOSS) that evolved out of the Sahana project.

Collaboration: Collaboration will be supported by the use of Basecamp tools at Bowdoin College and Web-based Skype teleconferencing.

Delivery: The software developed by this project will be designed so that it can eventually be placed in the public domain as a new open source software product.

A.2   Design

This section describes the overall design characteristics of *RMH Homebase*. In this sense, it is a retrospective of the project's outcomes when the development period ended in May 2008.

TABLE A.1: Overall Structure of the *RMH Homebase* Code Base

Domain Classes	Person Shift SCL RMHdate Week
Database Modules	dbPersons dbShifts dbSCL dbDates dbWeeks dbInfo dbInstall dbLog dbSchedules
User Interface	about addWeek calendar calendarFam editMasterSchedule editShift header help index log login_form logout masterSchedule masterScheduleFam personEdit searchPeople subCallList tutorialHeader view viewPerson
On-Line Tutorial	addPersonHelp addSlotToShiftHelp assignToShiftHelp calendarNotesHelp editPersonHelp editShiftHelp generateWeekHelp index indexHelp manageCalendarHelp removeFromShiftHelp schedulingHelp searchPersonHelp subCallListHelp viewCalendarHelp
Unit Tests	testWeeksGUI testWeek testShift testRMHdate test-Person testDBWeeks testDBShifts testDBSCL test-DBSchedules testDBPersons testDBLog testDBDates

A.2.1 Goals

The general design goals for *RMH Homebase* are

1. To develop a correct, reusable, and well-documented software system for Volunteer scheduling,

2. To provide a fully functional and intuitive user interface with on-line help for each function, and

3. To develop a complete system for productive use by the end of spring semester 2008.

A.2.2 Software Architecture

The *RMH Homebase* code base has five groups of PHP modules. The project Web site http://sourceforge.net/projects/rmhhomebase has several different releases. Release 1.0 is the one described in Section A.1, while Release 1.4 has more functionality and many bug fixes and refactorings.

Table A.1 reflects the module structure in Release 1.4; unless otherwise noted, these modules appear as examples throughout the text.

Since this system is open source software, the following copyright and reuse notice appears in the programs and the user interface:

```
/* Copyright 2008 by Orville, Malcom, Ted, Nat, and Alex. This
 * program is part of RMH Homebase, which is free software. It
```

A.2.3   Domain Classes

The central (domain) classes for this application are identified in Figures A.15, A.16, A.17, A.18, and A.19, along with their key instance variables. These classes establish a namespace for defining the database and user interface.

```
class Person {
    private $id;            // id (unique key) = first_name . phone1
    private $first_name;    // first name as a string
    private $last_name;     // last name as a string
    private $address;       // address - string
    private $city;          // city - string
    private $state;         // state - string
    private $zip;           // zip code - integer
    private $phone1;        // main phone
    private $phone2;        // alternate phone
    private $email;         // email address as a string
    private $type;          // array of "applicant", "volunteer",
            // "sub", "guestchef", "manager"
    private $availability;  // array of day-time pairs; eg Mon9-12
    private $birthday;      // format: 03-12-08
    private $start_date;    // format: 03-12-08
    private $public_notes;  // notes a person can see but not edit
    private $my_notes;      // notes a person can see and edit
    private $private_notes; // notes managers can see and edit
    private $password;      // password for access: default = $id
```

FIGURE A.15:   Key instance variables for the Person class.

A.2.4   Database Design

The first five modules in the Database list are implemented as MySQL tables. Each table is a collection of rows of individuals from the Domain classes.

For example, dbPersons is a table in which each row is a Person. Similarly, dbWeeks is a table in which each row is a Week (from Mon to Sun), dbDates is

```
class Shift {
    private $mm_dd_yy; // String: "mm-dd-yy".
    private $name;     // String: '9-12','12-3','3-6','9-12Fam',
                       // '12-3Fam', '3-6Fam', '6-9', '10-1',
                       // '1-4','12-2','2-5','night', or 'chef'
    private $vacancies;    // number of vacancies in this shift
    private $persons;      // array of persons: id+first+last
    private $sub_call_list; // "yes" or "no" for if SCL exists
    private $day;          // string name of month "Monday"...
    private $id;   // unique key "mm-dd-yy-ss-ss"
                   // or "mm-dd-yy-ss-ssFam" or "mm-dd-yy-chef"
    private $notes;  // notes written by the manager
```

FIGURE A.16:   Key instance variables for the Shift class.

```
class SCL {
    private $id;       // unique key "mm-dd-yy-ss-ss"
                       // or "mm-dd-yy-ss-ssFam"
    private $persons; // array of person information arrays
        // person[i]=array(personid, first_name, last_name,
        //      phone1, phone2, date_called, result, accepted);
    private $status;    // open, closed
    private $vacancies; // number of slots to fill
    private $time;      // YYYYMMDD#, # is shift order
```

FIGURE A.17:   Key instance variables for the SCL class.

a table in which each row is an RMHdate, dbShifts is a table in which each row is a Shift, and dbSCL is a table in which each row is an SCL (SubCallList).

The next two modules in the database list are dbInstall and dbLog. dbInstall clears all the tables and enters a single manager called "admin" with password "admin" into the dbPersons table: it should be used infrequently.

Running dbInstall can be followed by running testDBSchedules (in RMH Homebase 2.0, this is renamed dbInstallSandbox), which populates the dbPersons and dbSchedules tables with a group of hypothetical people who all have the last name "jones." This is useful for system testing and demonstrations.

The last module in the database list is called dbSchedules. It initializes and maintains the master schedule, which the House Manager uses as a basis for generating new weeks on the calendar. Each row in dbSchedules represents a single shift in the master schedule. A shift has the following elements:

```
group = "One", "Two", or "Wkd"
day = "Mon", "Tue", ... "Sun"
time = "9-12","12-3","3-6","6-9","10-1","1-4","2-5, or "5-9"
slots = number of slots to be filled for this shift
```

```
class RMHdate {
    private $id;  // "mm-dd-yy" form of this date: used as a key
    private $month;      // Textual month of the year (e.g., Jan)
    private $day;        // Textual day of the week (Mon - Sun)
    private $dom;        // Numerical day of month
    private $month_num;  // Numerical month
    private $day_of_week; // Numerical day of week (1-7, Mon=1)
    private $day_of_year; // Numerical day of year (1-366)
    private $year;       // Numerical year (e.g., 2008)
    private $shifts;     // array of Shifts
    private $chef_notes; // text field for guest chef notes
    private $mgr_notes;  // notes on night/weekend manager
```

FIGURE A.18:   Key instance variables for the RMHdate class.

```
class Week {
    private $id;        // the first day of the week, mm-dd-yy
    private $dates;     // array of 7 RMHdates, beginning Monday
    private $name;      // the name of the week
                        (eg March 7, 2008 - March 14, 2008)
    private $weekday_group;    // 1 or 2
    private $weekend_group;    // 1-5
    private $family_room_group; // 1 or 2
    private $status;  // "unpublished","published" or "archived"
    private $end_of_week_timestamp; // the mktime timestamp
```

FIGURE A.19:   Key instance variables for the Week class.

```
persons = list of ids, like "alex2077291234", for this shift
notes = notes to be displayed for this shift on the calendar
```

The master schedule has three groups called Group One, Group Two, and Group Weekend. The first two groups cover weekday shifts for alternating weeks, while the third covers weekend shifts. These schedules are created by the House Manager using information from the dbPersons table. Each shift is scheduled with one or more Volunteers.

An example Group One master schedule is shown in Figure A.20, populated with persons from the hypothetical Volunteer database. The Group Weekend master schedule has five parts, one for each weekend of the month: the first Sat and Sun, the second Sat and Sun, and so forth. The first weekend's Group Weekend master schedule is shown in Figure A.21.

Two additional groups define the master schedule for the Family Room, which is a separate venue in the hospital where RMH Volunteers are also scheduled. These two groups are called FamOne and FamTwo, which represent alternating weeks.

Group One				
Monday	**Tuesday**	**Wednesday**	**Thursday**	**Friday**
9am 10am 11am	jane jones linda jones	lynne jones arla jones	linda jones orminia jones	dottie jones joy jones	becky jones sally jones
12pm 1pm 2pm	mary jones gerry jones	judy jones jenny jones	mary jones meg jones	ann jones **Vacancies (1)**	pat jones evelyn jones
3pm 4pm 5pm	sharon jones laura jones	becky jones betsy jones	esther jones **Vacancies (1)**	jane jones nancy jones	phyllis jones bob jones
6pm 7pm 8pm	ellen jones kelly jones meghan jones	cathy jones joan jones carol jones	claudia jones marilee jones **Vacancies (1)**	ron jones derek jones **Vacancies (1)**	**Vacancies (3)**

FIGURE A.20:   Group One master schedule.

A.2.5   GUI Design

Three basic views are central to the user interface: the Calendar View, the Shift View, and the SubCallList View.

The Calendar View shows a single week's calendar, with each day showing the Volunteers scheduled for each shift, as shown in the example of Figure A.22. There, for example, the 12–3pm shift on May 1 has "ann jones" scheduled and one Vacancy. While a calendar is displayed one week at a time, navigation bars at the top facilitate viewing the next week or the previous week.

The House Manager initially generates each week of the calendar from the master schedule. "Publishing" a week's calendar means that any shift entry can be changed whenever a Volunteer cancels a shift for which she is scheduled and a Substitute is found to cover that shift on a one-time basis. The House Manager or a Volunteer can cancel or repopulate any shift in this way.

Any single day on the calendar can be selected for editing, for instance when a shift needs to be rescheduled because a Volunteer cancels or needs to be added to a vacant shift. This creates a Shift view, as shown in Figure A.23 for 12-3pm on May 1. In this view, either "ann jones" can be removed from the shift (if she has cancelled) or an additional person can be added to fill the vacancy on the shift.

To fill a vacancy, one can access the SubCallList view for that shift, which is a list of all persons available to fill that shift, as shown in Figure A.24. This list allows several people to be called until the vacancy is filled; records are kept in the database of calls already made to people on the list, so as to avoid duplication.

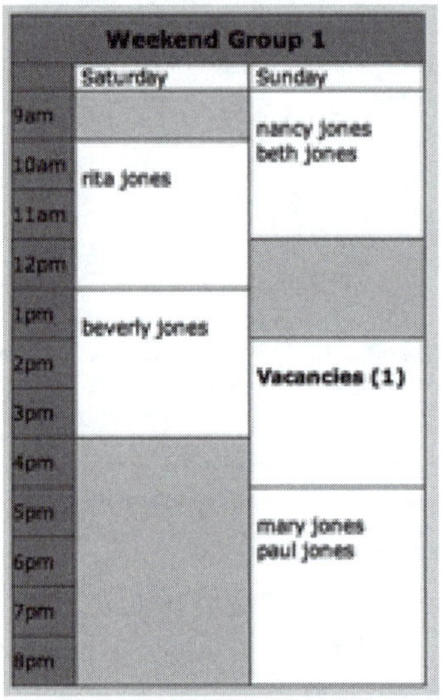

FIGURE A.21:   First weekend's master schedule.

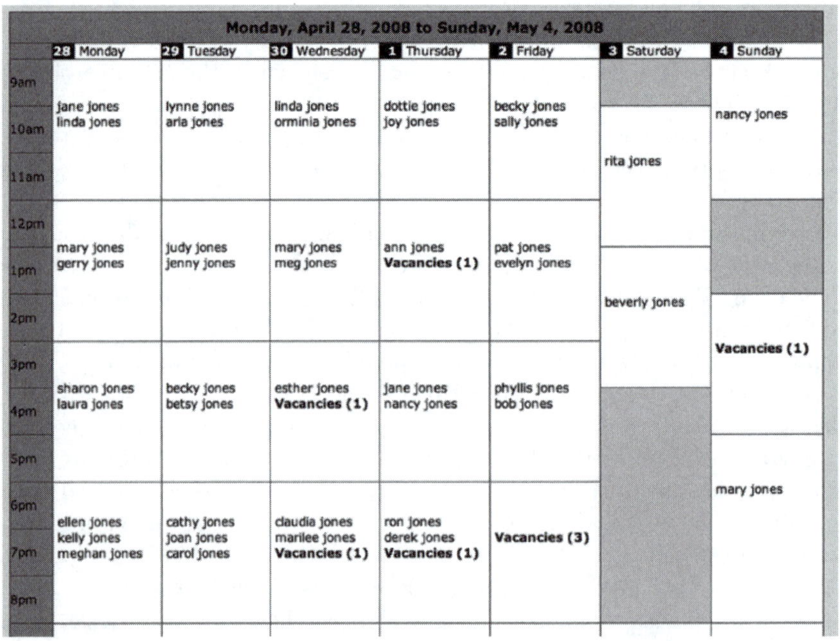

FIGURE A.22:   Example calendar view.

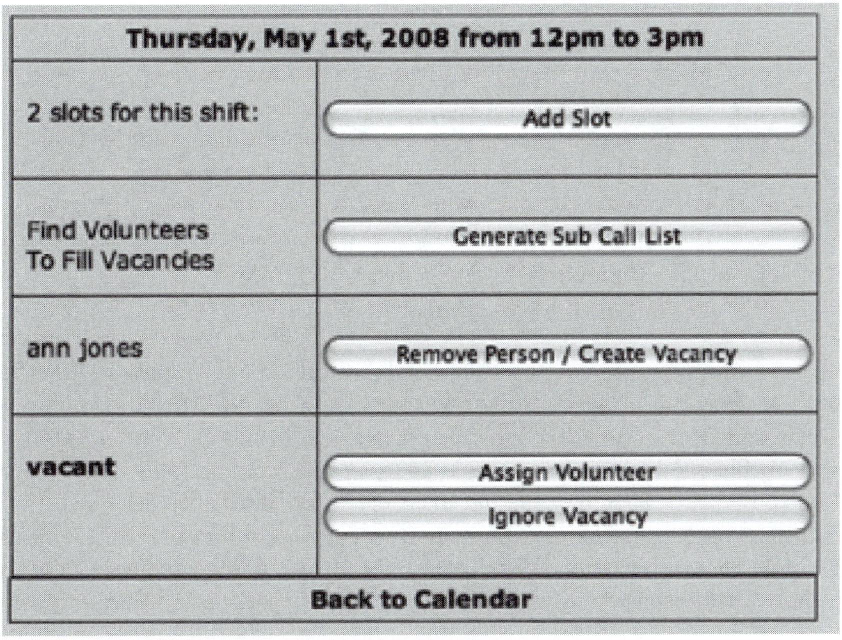

Thursday, May 1st, 2008 from 12pm to 3pm	
2 slots for this shift:	Add Slot
Find Volunteers To Fill Vacancies	Generate Sub Call List
ann jones	Remove Person / Create Vacancy
vacant	Assign Volunteer
	Ignore Vacancy
Back to Calendar	

FIGURE A.23: Shift view for 12–3 pm on May 1.

Thursday, May 1st, 2008 from 12pm to 3pm

1 sub needed for this shift.

Name	Phone	Date Called	Notes	Accepted
barbara jones	(207) 729-1234			
tenny jones	(207) 729-1234			
			Assign Subs / Save Changes	

FIGURE A.24: SubCallList view for 12–3 pm on May 1.

Monday, April 28, 2008 to Sunday, May 4, 2008

	28 Monday	29 Tuesday	30 Wednesday	1 Thursday	2 Friday	3 Saturday	4 Sunday
9am							
10am	jane jones linda jones	lynne jones arla jones	linda jones orminia jones	dottie jones joy jones	becky jones sally jones		nancy jones
11am						rita jones	
12pm							
1pm	mary jones gerry jones	judy jones jenny jones	mary jones meg jones	ann jones barbara jones	pat jones evelyn jones		
2pm						beverly jones	
3pm							Vacancies (1)

FIGURE A.25: Filling the 12–3 pm vacancy on May 1.

Once a vacancy is filled, the calendar is automatically updated with the choice, as shown in Figure A.25 for "barbara jones" in our May 1 example.

Given sufficient access privileges, additional details about a potential Volunteer to fill a shift can be obtained by selecting that person's name. For instance, Figure A.26 shows the database entry for "barbara jones."

Editing this information can be done by the House Manager, which causes the Volunteer's database entry to be updated. Closing this window reverts to the short form display, which only shows the person's contact information.

A.2.6   Implementation Schedule

The schedule followed by this project is similar to the first sample syllabus given in the Preface for a one-semester course. The project had four major milestones, each one requiring about 3 weeks to complete. The first draft of the requirements document (Section A.1) was available to the team members at the beginning of the semester. Weekly videoconferences among the developers reviewed the prior week's progress and set the agenda for the upcoming week.

A.2.7   User-System Interaction

The system has three different kinds of users—the House Manager, the Volunteer, and the Applicant. Each kind has a different level of access to the system and its functionality, as described in the following sections.

A.2.7.1   House Manager Interaction

The House Manager can access and modify all information in the database, master schedule, and calendar from any Web browser. When logging in, a Manager has a personal home page with a lot of useful information, as shown in Figure A.27.

Personnel Edit Form
Here you can edit or delete entries in the database.

*:denotes required fields

First Name*:	barbara
Last Name*:	jones
Address*:	14 Way St
City*:	Harpswell
State, Zip*:	ME ⬍ , 04079
Primary Phone*:	2077291234
Alternate Phone:	
Email:	barbara@bowdoin.edu
Birthday:	Feb ⬍ 19 ⬍ 1989 ⬍
Volunteer Start Date:	Mar ⬍ 14 ⬍ 2008 ⬍

This Person is a*:
- ☐ Applicant
- ☑ Sub
- ☑ Volunteer
- ☐ Guest Chef
- ☐ Manager

Availability*

Weekday Shifts

	Monday	Tuesday	Wednesday	Thursday	Friday
9 to 12	☐	☐	☐	☐	☐
12 to 3	☐	☐	☐	☑	☐
3 to 6	☐	☐	☐	☐	☐
6 to 9	☐	☐	☐	☐	

Weekend Shifts

	Saturday	Sunday
3 hours morning	☐	☐
3 hours afternoon	☐	☐
5-9 pm		☐

FIGURE A.26:   Display of a Volunteer in the database.

A Manager can view or generate new calendar weeks; edit the master schedule; and view, edit, or add people in the Volunteer database. Tutorials that teach how to use these House Manager's functions are available on-line by selecting **help** in the menu bar, which appears at the top of Figure A.27.

A.2.7.2   Volunteer Interaction

Any Volunteer can access and modify her own information in the database, as well as make changes to the calendar, from any Web browser. When logging in, a Volunteer sees a personal home page with information telling about his/her upcoming scheduled shifts, as shown in Figure A.28.

Volunteers have a more restricted level of access to the system than Managers. They can only view their own database entry, and they can view, remove, and add people to shifts on the calendar. Tutorials that assist with these functions are available on-line by selecting **help** in the menu bar, which appears at the top of Figure A.28.

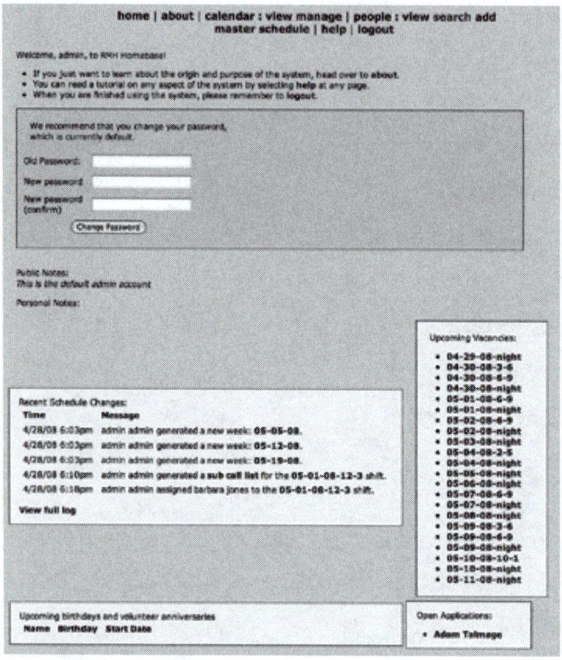

FIGURE A.27: Manager home page.

More information about using this system as a Volunteer can be found at the book's Web site myopensoftware.org/textbook.

A.2.7.3 Applicant Interaction

Anyone who visits the RMH Home Page (http://rmhportlandme.org) can apply for a Volunteer position by filling out and submitting the on-line application form, shown in Figure A.29. The completed form is automatically transmitted to the House Manager, who call follow up with the new Applicant.

Note in the menu bar that no other functionality is available to persons logging in from the outside. This is an important aspect of how the system protects its own security and individual Volunteer privacy.

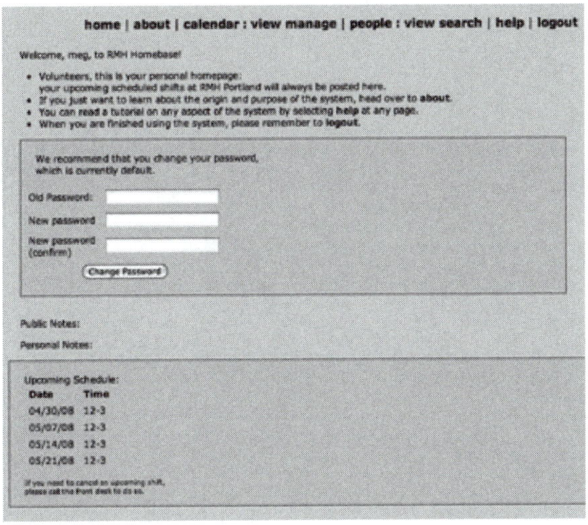

FIGURE A.28: Volunteer home page.

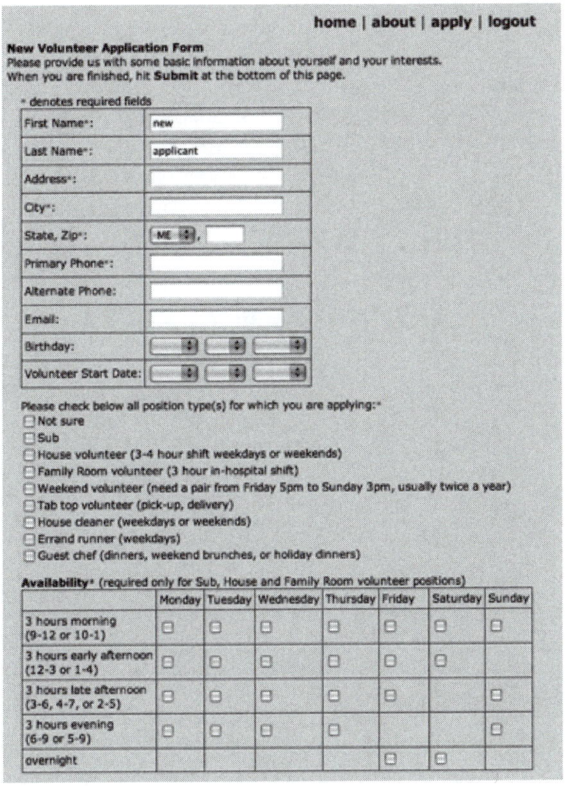

FIGURE A.29: On-line Volunteer application form.

Appendix B

New Features for an Existing Code Base

This Appendix summarizes the origins and motivation for adding new features to *RMH Homebase*. These new features originate directly from the client, who at the time had been using *RMH Homebase* release 1.4 for over a year.

The actual implementation of these new features is discussed in Chapters 5–9 of the text. The working code base referenced in these chapters for illustrating the development of these new features is release 2.0, which can be downloaded from the book's Web site myopensoftware.org/textbook.

B.1 Starting with a Request from the Client

The e-mail below came from the client to the lead developer. It outlines a series of features that would be desirable to add to *RMH Homebase*. From this e-mail, a set of new requirements can be developed, their impact on the existing code base can be estimated, and a plan for implementation of these new features can be developed.

These steps are outlined later in this Appendix, and they become the basis for the examples and exercises in Chapters 4–9.

> **From: Gina**
> **Date: November 9, 2009 10:51 AM**
> **To: Alex**
> **Subject: Homebase ideas**
>
> *Alex,*
>
> *Below is a list of ideas that have come about in using Homebase— if you want to go through them over the phone, please give me a call. Thanks!*
>
> *1. Volunteer status—ability to categorize volunteers as inactive preventing them from showing up on a sub list. This would*

be helpful to ensure volunteers on vacation or otherwise un-available do not get called for shifts.

2. *Make active/inactive*—ability to track when a volunteer has last been scheduled for a shift. For example, when a manager logs in a screen pops up showing the names of any volunteer who has not been on a shift for the past month.

3. *Calendar view*—In the current calendar view, shift times are hard to distinguish if the user is unfamiliar with it. For ex-ample, 9–12 looks like it could be 9–11. Moreover, sometimes a shift (especially a weekend shift) needs its start or end time to be changed by the user.

4. *Calendar month view*—Is it possible to view one month at a time? This would be simply for convenience and is not a necessity.

5. *Import/export*—possible with Raiser's Edge database?

6. *Guest Chef*—Information is erased if a change is made to the calendar and the date has passed. For example, I have entered info in the guest chef field for 11/9/09. Tomorrow if we make a change, Monday's guest chef information will be deleted. I am testing this today and will let you know if it happens when any change is made or only in the guest chef field.
   I think the issue is only with the note field in relation to guest chef information being deleted. I just went into the calendar and made a change to the note field under Friday's 3-6 PM shift. After clicking the save button, Monday and Tuesday's guest chef information was deleted. It does not happen when changes are made to shifts—adding/removing a volunteer.

7. *Vacancies and shifts worked*—information for the House Man-ager:

   a. Sort the upcoming vacancies on the manager's screen by date.

   b. The total and average number of vacancies for each day and shift, for any series of weeks in the past.

   c. The total and average number of shifts worked by any volunteer, for any series of weeks in the past.

8. *Open applications*—sorted by first name and "grayed out" if the interview, background paperwork, or shadow buttons are selected.

   The inactive feature would be helpful here as well. There are often applicants who submit their information and then they do not complete the application process. Rather than leave them in the open application status they could be marked as inactive and then completely deleted after several months.

9. *Volunteer application:*

   a. *Allow for spaces in the name field. Example, Jo Ann. Also, remove the "&" from the first name field. Example: Jack & Jill. Entries that have "&" are not accessible in the database.*

   b. *Allow for only the month/year field to be completed when selecting a start date.*

   c. *When an applicant fills out their info and clicks submit the screen appears blank. Perhaps an automatic note thanking them for submitting an application.*

   d. *We overlooked this when first submitting information to you: can fields be added such as employer's information and emergency contact?*

10. *Log—I love this feature! Could there be an ability to view additional pages as we can with the "people: view" tab?*

Let me know what I can clarify, and thank you as always!—Gina

---

B.2   Impact on the Design and the Code Base

Some of the items in this list are really "bugs," and so they should be treated differently from the ones which are genuinely new features. Others impact the user interface modules, while still others go deeper and impact the domain classes and corresponding database modules.

Some of these items also need more clarification, such as the request for an "import/export" feature (item #5 in the list). Here, we may ask what should be imported/exported—a volunteer's data, a calendar week, or other information? Would the import/export use a comma-separated list that could be copied and pasted into a spreadsheet? Or would it use a series of MySQL database queries that can be used to build tables in an external database? An examination of Raiser's Edge software could help answer some of these questions, but the most important step here would be to talk with Gina to obtain more clarification.

1. **Volunteer status**—ability to categorize a volunteer as inactive preventing them from showing up on a sub list. This would be helpful to ensure volunteers on vacation or otherwise unavailable do not get called for shifts.

Nature: new feature.

Impact on the design: The current system assumes all volunteers are "active" and hence are eligible to be scheduled for shifts. Supporting this feature would require adding a "status" field for each volunteer, with values "active" or "inactive."

Impact on the code base:

Domain classes: Add a new instance variable "status" to the Person class, with appropriate changes to its constructors and other functions.

Database modules: Add a new column "status" to the dbPersons table, with appropriate changes to the setup and other related functions.

User interface modules: Every user interface module that involves a person should be updated to accommodate the new "status" field. These include: editMasterSchedule and editShift (listing only "active" volunteers when filling a vacancy), personEdit (adding a "status" field), sub-CallList (listing only "active" volunteers), searchPeople (add "status" as a field to search on), and viewPerson (adding the person's status to the view).

User documentation: No modifications are needed.

2. **Make active/inactive**—ability to track when a volunteer has last been scheduled for a shift. For example, when a manager logs in a screen pops up showing the names of any volunteer who has not been on a shift for the past month.

Nature: new feature.

Impact on the design: The current system does no such tracking. This feature could be added to the manager's home page, giving her the option of marking each such volunteer as "inactive".

Impact on the code base:

Domain classes: none (beyond #1 above).

Database modules: none (beyond #1 above).

User interface modules: index.php would need to be modified to include a list of volunteers who had not been scheduled for at least a month, and an option to mark each one "inactive." personEdit.php should also be changed to allow a volunteer's status to be changed between "active" and "inactive."

User documentation: indexHelp.inc.php must be modified to describe this new function.

3. **Calendar view**—In the current calendar view, shift times are hard to distinguish if the user is unfamiliar with it. For example, 9–12 looks like it could be 9–11. Moreover, sometimes a shift (especially a weekend shift) needs its start or end time to be changed by the user.

Nature: new feature.

Impact on the design: This is a more complex request for a new feature. It raises the question of whether or not to scrap the current approach taken by *RMH Homebase* to managing the calendar and replace it with an integrated iCalendar-compatible module.

Impact on the code base: Scrapping the current approach to the calendar would impact almost all components of the code base. Keeping the approach would require significant alterations to some of the user interface modules so that the House Manager can dynamically redefine the start/end time of any shift. We will favor the latter approach in this text.

Domain classes: Shift should be altered so that its start and end time can be changed (within the same day).

Database modules: dbShifts should be altered so that the start and end time of any shift in the database can be changed (within the same day).

User interface modules: calendar.php should be modified so that the functions that display a week of the calendar can work with the new definition of a shift.

User documentation: manageCalendarHelp.inc.php would need significant new sections.

4. **Calendar month view**—Is it possible to view one month at a time?

Nature: new feature.

Impact on the design: A new class and database table would be needed to store all the days in each month.

Domain classes: Add a new class Month, which is a series of RMHdates. This could be organized similarly to the existing class Week.

Database modules: Add a new module dbMonths which has one row for each active or archived month. It would be organized similarly to the existing class dbWeeks.

User interface modules: At the top of the calendar view, add a button "View Month" that shows an entire month. Each day on the month view would be either white or gray depending on whether it has a shift with a vacancy or not. Clicking the mouse on that day brings you back to a calendar week view, which shows that week's vacancies in detail (as it does now).

User documentation: manageCalendarHelp.inc.php would need a new section to describe how to use this new feature.

5. **Import/export**—possible with Raiser's Edge database?

Nature: new feature.

Impact on the design: any person's data could be exported into a comma-separated list for importing into an Excel-type of spreadsheet. Data so formatted could be imported to create a new Person in the database.

Impact on the code base:

Domain classes: none.

Database modules: dbPersons needs a new function that would export an entry in the database into a text that could be downloaded by the user. Another new function should be added that imports a person and creates a new entry in the database.

User interface modules: This export function would be added to the personEdit module and be accessible only to the House Manager.

User documentation: The editPersonHelp.php should be modified to describe how to use this new function.

6. **Guest Chef**—information is erased if a change is made to the calendar and the date has passed. For example, I have entered info in the guest chef field for 11/9/09. Tomorrow if we make a change, Monday's guest chef information will be deleted. I am testing this today and will let you know if it happens when any change is made or only in the guest chef field.

   I think the issue is only with the note field in relation to guest chef information being deleted. I just went into the calendar and made a change to the note field under Friday's 3-6 PM shift. After clicking the save button, Monday and Tuesday's guest chef information was deleted. It does not happen when changes are made to shifts—adding/removing a volunteer.

   Nature: bug.

   Impact on the design: none.

   Impact on the code base: minor.

   Domain classes: none.

   Database modules: none.

   User interface modules: calendar.php is where this problem arises, particularly when the "Save changes to all notes" button is selected.

   User documentation: none.

7. **Vacancies and shifts worked**—information for the House Manager:

   a. Sort the upcoming vacancies on the manager's screen by date.

   b. The total and average number of vacancies for each day and shift, for any series of weeks in the past.

   c. The total and average number of shifts worked by any volunteer, for any series of weeks in the past.

   Nature: new feature.

   Impact on the design: the current system lists upcoming vacancies in no particular order. It does not report any statics like the ones desired. A new use case should be defined that describes the user-system interaction for this activity. Such a use case would include the import/export feature described earlier.

   Impact on the code base: significant.

   Domain classes: no changes.

   Database modules: Add functions to dbShifs and dbDates that accumulate the total and average numbers of vacancies for each shift and date over any series of weeks.

User interface modules: Add to the view.php module. Refactor the index.php and ensure that the upcoming vacancies are ordered by date. Here also is an opportunity to refactor the index.php code to remove violations of the layering principle. This would require adding a new search function to dbShifts.

User documentation: no changes

8. **Open applications**—sorted by first name and "grayed out" if the interview, background paperwork, or shadow buttons are selected.

   The inactive feature would be helpful here as well. There are often applicants who submit their information and then they do not complete the application process. Rather than leave them in the open application status they could be marked as inactive and then completely deleted after several months.

   Nature: new feature

   Impact on the design: The House Manager's applicant list would show applicants "grayed out" when their processing has begun.

   Impact on the code base:

   Domain classes: none.

   Database modules: none.

   User interface modules: Change index.php so that it grays out every applicant who has begun processing or who has been marked as "inactive" for lack of activity in the last month.

   User documentation: No changes are needed.

9. **Volunteer application**

   a. Allow for spaces in the name field. Example: Jo Ann. Also, remove the "&" from the first name field. Example: Jack & Jill. Entries that have "&" are not accessible in the database.

   b. Allow for only the month/year field to be completed when selecting a start date.

   c. When an applicant fills out their info and clicks submit the screen appears blank. Perhaps an automatic note thanking them for submitting an application.

   d. We overlooked this when first submitting information to you: can fields be added such as employer's information and emergency contact?

   Nature: Item **a** is a bug and the other three are features.

   Impact on the design: Add fields to each person's entry to contain employer's name and an emergency contact name and phone number.

   Impact on the code base:

   Domain classes: Add new fields and appropriate functions to the Person class.

Database modules: Add new fields and appropriate functions to the dbPersons module.

User interface modules: Modify the personEdit form to accommodate these new fields and fix these bugs. Fix the searchPeople.php module so that it finds persons with blanks in their first name.

User documentation: No changes are needed.

10. **Log**—I love this feature! Could there be an ability to view additional pages as we can with the "people: view" tab?

Nature: new feature.

Impact on the design: none.

Impact on the code base: minor.

Domain classes: none.

Database modules: none.

User interface modules: fix log.php so that it displays 50 entries at a time (as does view.php for viewing persons), and provides a pager at the bottom for navigation.

User documentation: No changes are needed.

Figure B.1 describes the use case **Housecleaning** that is suggested by combining several of the items (1, 2, 5, and 7) above.

Housecleaning

Description: Occasionally, the House Manager needs to view the total
and average number of vacancies for each shift and each day, over a
period of weeks in the recent past. Various other information about
volunteer schedules should also be retrievable, such as the total and
average number of shifts worked by any particular volunteer for any
such period, a list of active volunteers who have not been scheduled
during that period, and a list of all the inactive volunteers. The ac-
tive/inactive status of any person on such a list should be reversible.
The database entries for any group of volunteers should be exportable
as a comma-separated list so that they can be imported into a spreadsheet or another application.

Actor: the House Manager

Goals: Different selections should be possible, in particular:

"View the total and average number of vacancies for each day and
shift, over any period of time in the past."

"View the total and average number of shifts worked by any volunteer, over any period of time in the past."

"View all active volunteers who have not been scheduled for a shift
over any period of time (change their status to inactive)."

"View all inactive volunteers (change anyone's status to active)."

"Export the database entries for any group of volunteers in the list."

Preconditions: 1. A beginning and ending date for the period of time
has been specified.
2. One of the above selections has been made.

Postconditions: 1. The desired list is displayed, and some volunteers'
status is changed or their data is exported.

Related Use Cases: ViewAList

Steps:

Actor	System
1. Log on to Web site.	2. Ask for id and password.
3. Enter id and password.	4. Verify and display outcome.
5. Identify a period of time.	6. Retrieve shifts for that period.
7. Select an option.	8. Display/export those shifts.
9. Log off Web site.	10. Terminate session.

FIGURE B.1: Use case **Housecleaning**.

B.3   Defining a Project that Implements these Features

Now that we have a clear idea of the requirements and their impact on the code base, here is a process that will implement these requirements and develop a new version 2.0 of *RMH Homebase*, starting with the code base for the current version 1.5.

1. Address the debugging and refactoring requirements, as discussed in Chapter 5.

2. Complete the development of the new elements of the domain classes that are needed to implement these new requirments, extend the unit tests, and then unit-test the domain classes. This is discussed as a detailed example in Chapter 6.

3. Complete the development of the new elements of the database modules that are needed to implement these new requirements, extend the unit tests appropriately, and then unit-test all the database modules. This is discussed as a detailed example in Chapter 7.

4. Complete the development of the new elements of the user interface modules that are needed to implement these new requirements, extend the unit tests appropriately, and then unit-test all the user interface modules. This is discussed as a detailed example in Chapter 8.

5. Complete the development of the revisions of the on-line help that are needed to support effective utilization of these new features, and then implement them. This is discussed as a detailed example in Chapter 9.

References

[ACM08] ACM. *Computing Curricula 2008: Computer Science*. ACM/IEEE Joint Task Force on Computing Curricula, 2008.

[BBC09] BBC. UK government backs open source. *Online*, February 2009.

[CD07] Samir Chopra and Scott D. Dexter. *Decoding Liberation: The Promise of Free and Open Source Software*. Routledge Studies in New Media and Cyberculture. Routledge, 2007.

[cmm] http://en.wikipedia.org/wiki/capability_maturity_model_integration.

[Coc05] Alistair Cockburn. *Crystal Clear: A Human-Powered Methodology for Small Teams*. Addison-Wesley, 2005.

[Cod70] E. F. Codd. A relational model of data for large shared data banks. *Communications of the ACM*, 13(6):377–387, June 1970.

[Com05] President's Information Technology Advisory Committee. *Cyber Security: A Crisis of Prioritization*. National Coordination Office for Information Technology, Arlington, VA, February 2005.

[Com06] European Commission. Economic impact of open source software on innovation and the competitiveness of the information and communication technologies (ict) sector in the EU. *Online*, November 2006.

[Con07] Liberal Arts Computer Science Consortium. A 2007 model curriculum for a liberal arts degree in computer science. *Journal on Educational Resources in Computing (JERIC)*, 7(2), June 2007.

[dIdSL] Festival Latinoamericano de Instalación de Software Libre. http://www.installfest.net/flisol2010.

[dSdSC$^+$06] Chamindra de Silva, R. de Silva, Mifan Careem, Louiqa Raschid, and S. Weerawarana. Sahana: Overview of a disaster management system. *Proceedings of the IEEE International Conference on Information and Automation*, 2006.

[Fog09] Karl Fogel. *Producing Open Source Software: How to Run a Successful Free Software Project*. O'Reilly, 2009.

[Foua] Apache Software Foundation. http://www.apache.org/.

[Foub] Free Software Foundation. http://www.fsf.org/licensing/licenses/.

[Fouc] Free Software Foundation. http://www.gnu.org/copyleft/gpl.html.

[Foud] Free Software Foundation. http://www.gnu.org/philosophy/
        free-sw.html.

[Foue] Mozilla Foundation. http://www.mozilla.org/about/.

[Fow00] Martin Fowler. *Refactoring: Improving the Design of Existing
        Code.* Addison-Wesley, 2000.

[GNU]   GNU. http://www.gnu.org/gnu/initial-announcement.html.

[Groa] Standish Group. http://www.standishgroup.com/newsroom/
        chaos_2009.php.

[Grob] Standish Group. http://www.standishgroup.com/newsroom/
        open_source.php.

[Hil09a] Gijs Hillenius. Amsterdam to make OpenOffice and FireFox
        default on city desktops. *Online*, April 2009.

[Hil09b] Gijs Hillenius. Fr: Gendarmerie saves millions with open desktop
        and web applications. *Online*, 2009.

[HPW99] Jim Hamerly, Tom Paquin, and Susan Walton. Freeing the
        source: The story of Mozilla. *Open Sources: Voices from the
        Open Source*, pages 197–206, 1999.

[JS10] Chris Jensen and Walt Scacchi. Governance in open source soft-
        ware development projects. In Pär Ågerfalk, Cornelia Boldyreff,
        Jesús M. González-Barahona, Gregory R. Madey, and John Noll,
        editors, *Open Source Software: New Horizons*, volume 319, pages
        130–142, Heidelberg, May 2010. Springer.

[McG06] Gary McGraw. *Software Security: Building Security In.* Pearson
        Education, Inc., 2006.

[MTD+09] Ralph Morelli, Allen Tucker, Norman Danner, Trishan
        de Lanerolle, Heidi Ellis, Ozgur Izmirli, Danny Krizanc, and
        Gary Parker. Revitalizing computing education through free
        and open source software for humanity. *Communications of the
        ACM*, 52(8):67–75, August 2009.

[NBM08] Douglas S. Noonan, Paul M. A. Baker, and Nathan W. Moon.
        Open source software potential index (ospi): Development con-
        siderations. *Online*, 2008.

[OSI]   OSI. http://www.opensource.org/licenses.

[Per]   Bruce Perens. http://slashdot.org/articles/99/02/18/
        0927202.shtml.

[Per99] Bruce Perens. Open sources: Voices from the open source revo-
        lution. *The Open Source Initiative*, pages 171–188, 1999.

[Ray00] Eric Steven Raymond. *The Cathedral and the Bazaar*. O'Reilly,
        2000.

[Ray01] Eric Steven Raymond. *The Cathedral and the Bazaar*. O'Reilly,
        2001.

[Sal08] Peter H. Salus. *The Daemon, the Gnu, and the Penguin: How
        free and open source software is changing the world*. Reed Media
        Services, 2008.

[Staa] Richard Stallman. http://www.gnu.org/gnu/manifesto.html.

[Stab] Richard Stallman.   http://www.gnu.org/philosophy/use-free-
        software.html.

[Sta99] Richard Stallman. *The GNU Operating System and the Free
        Software Movement*. O'Reilly, 1999.

[Sta09] Richard Stallman. Why 'open source' misses the point of free
        software. *Communications of the Association for Computing
        Machinery*, 52(6):31–33, June 2009.

[Tid05] Jenifer Tidwell. *Designing Interfaces: Patterns for Effective In-
        teraction Design*. O'Reilly, 2005.

[Tor91] Linus Torvalds. What would you like to see most in minix?
        USENET, August 1991.

[Tor99] Linus Torvalds. *The Linux Edge*. O'Reilly, 1999.

[uml]   http://en.wikipedia.org/wiki/unified_modeling_language.

[Whe]   David A. Wheeler.   http://www.dwheeler.com/essays/floss-
        license-slide.html.

[wp-a] http://en.wikipedia.org/whttp://en.wikipedia.org/wiki/
        browser_wars.

[wp-b] http://en.wikipedia.org/wiki/2004_indian_ocean_earthquake.

[wp-c] http://en.wikipedia.org/wiki/free_software.

[wp-d] http://en.wikipedia.org/wiki/gnu_general_public_license.

[wp-e] http://en.wikipedia.org/wiki/history_of_linux.

[wp-f] http://en.wikipedia.org/wiki/linux_kernel.

354   *References*

[wp-g]   http://en.wikipedia.org/wiki/ sahana_foss_disaster_management_system.

[wp-h]   http://en.wikipedia.org/wiki/us_vs._microsoft.

[You99] Robert Young. Giving it away: How red hat software stumbled across a new economic model and helped improve an industry. *Open Sources: Voices from the Open Source Revolution*, pages 113–126, 1999.

Index

A

Abstraction, 9–10
Accessors (getters), 162, 165, 170
Adding new features, 134–139,
    151–162, 341–350
    adding new domain class,
        164–166, *See also* Domain
        class development
    class design principles and
        practice, 162
    client request, 152–154,
        341–343
    database impact, 138–139,
        193–202
    defining project for
        implementing, 350
    documentation issues, 139,
        158
    impact on code base, 135–139
    impact on design and code
        base, 343–349
    impact on domain classes,
        154–158
    modifying domain classes,
        155–158
    new use cases, 135–136
    refactoring new code base,
        169–171, 197–201
    security impacts, 139
    team discussions, 139
    UI impact, 230–239
    unit testing, 166–169,
        196–197, 201
Admin access, 76
Agile development, xviii, 9, 27–29,
    42, 117, 144, 267, 291,
    295

Agricultural applications, 24
AIM, 66
Alpha release, 288
Alpha testing, 130
Amazon database, 71
Amsterdam, 19
Analysis, *See* Code analysis
Android Development Tools
    (ADT), 84
Apache licensing, 284
Apache Portable Runtime (APR)
    project, 288
Apache Software Foundation, 41,
    274, 276
Apache Web server, 71
Apprentice, 269
Architectural pattern, 30, 87–89,
    See also Software
    architecture
ArgoUML, 303
Assessment methodologies,
    271–273
Authentication (secure login),
    97–100
Availability requirements, 305, 327

B

Backup and recovery, 82, 181–182,
    306, 327
Bad smells, 108–111
Bazaar, 74
"Becoming a user first," 58–60
Benevolent dictator model, 42,
    265–266, 270, 274
Beta release, 288
Beta testing, 130
"Big picture" nouns, 145, 154

BioBricks Foundation, 24
Bottom-up development, 8–9, 28,
      37
Branch, 73
BSD, 284
Buffer overflows, 96
Bug fixing, *See* Debugging
Bug marshalls, 280
Bug reports, 59–60, 129
Bug tracking, 64, 67, 77–81, 130,
      254, 275, 286
Bugzilla, 77
Bulletproofing, 158–162, 308
Bundled and unbundled software,
      2–3
Business models
      proprietary vs. FOSS, 6–7
      Red Hat, 14

C
C++, 32, 70
CAMBIA project, 24
The Cathedral and the Bazaar
      (Raymond), 41, 265, 287
Certification, xxiv
Chat rooms, *See* IRC chat
      channels
Check out, 73
Class design and implementation,
      See Adding new features;
      Domain class
      development
Class diagram, 300
Classes
      bad smells, 109–110
      database table naming, 179
      design principles and practice,
            162–166
      effects of adding new features,
            138
      identifying instance variables,
            145–146
      naming, 33, 108
      refactoring, 112

Client-oriented projects, xviii, 27,
      38–40, 267, *See also*
      RMH Homebase
      approach for using this book,
            xix
      comparing
            community-oriented
            model, 42–44
      members, roles, and tasks,
            44–47, *See also* Software
            development team
      project start-up and
            governance, 267–270
      scheduling, 48–50
Client-server architecture, 30, 71,
      88, 307
      concurrency issues, 100–104
      RMH Homebase system
            architecture, 89
      version control approach, 74
Client-side code, 88
Codd, E. F., 180
Code analysis, 107
      debugging, *See* Debugging
      refactoring, *See* Refactoring
      software metrics, 110–111
Code base, 11, 63
      debugging, *See* Debugging
      functional enhancements, *See*
            Adding new features
      help and, 258–259, 261–263
      identifying bad smells,
            108–110
      refactoring, *See* Refactoring
      sandbox version, 107, 143
Code injection, 96, 97, 216–217
Code management tools, 63, 67
      bug tracking, 64, 67, 77–81
      documentation support, 36,
            68
      IDE, 43, 67, 68–70
      software stack, 67, 70–72
      version control, 31, 63, 67, 68,
            72–77, *See also* Version
            control

Code modification, adding new
    features, *See* Adding new
    features
Code modification, refactoring, *See*
    Refactoring
Code reading, *See* Reading code
Code refactoring, *See* Refactoring
Code release and distribution,
    284–289, 307, 328
  alpha and beta status, 288
  hosting sites, 285–286
  numbering schemes, 288
  release branches, 288–289
  release management, 55–56,
    289
  release manager, 280, 289
  release strategies, 287–289
Code repository, 45, 73, 74
  managing, 76–77
Code synchronization, *See*
    Synchronization
Code synchronization repository,
    42–43, 76, 267
Code testing, *See* Testing
Code writing, *See* Writing code
Coding standards, 33–34
Cohesion, 92
  maximum cohesion principle,
    89, 92
  metrics for evaluating, 93–94,
    111
Collaboration norms and
    etiquette, 56–58, 64
Collaboration tools, xviii, 43,
    63–67, 306, 328
  asynchronous communication,
    64–65
  communication channels, 54
  hosting sites, 285–286
  shared documents, 66–67
  synchronous communication,
    65–66
  videoconferencing, 47, 65–66
Commentary documentation,
    34–36, *See also*

Documentation
  bad smells, 109
Commit privileges, 73, 77
Committers, 278–280
Communication channels, 54, 267
Communication methods and
    tools, *See* Collaboration
    tools
Communication norms and
    etiquette, 56–58, 64
Community building, 273–283, *See
    also* Collaboration tools;
    Project governance
  forums, 276–277
  FOSS project foundations,
    275–276
  hosting sites, 285–286
  incubation, 274–277
  recruitment, 275
Community member roles,
    278–280
Community membership levels,
    269
Community-oriented projects,
    xviii, 27, 39–40
  approach for using this book,
    xix
  comparing client-oriented
    model, 42–44
  FOSS development model,
    41–42
  organization, 277–281
  project evolution, 40–42
Community-oriented projects,
    joining and newcomer
    contributions, 50
  "becoming a user first," 58–60
  communication channels, 54
  good citizenship norms, 56–58
  initiating involvement, 53
  motives for, 50–51
  project selection, 52–53
  reading/improving
    documentation, 53–54
  working with code, 55–56

Community strength, 271, 272
Compilers, 68
Component-based programming,
        9–10, 308
Component diagram, 300
Computing Curricula 2008, xxiv
Concurrency management,
        100–104, 192–193, *See
        also* Synchronization;
        Version control
Concurrent Versions System
        (CVS), 73–74
Conflict management, version
        control, 74–76
Conflict resolution, 270, 282
Consensus building, 270, 281–282
Content management systems, 10
Contributor roles, 278
Copyleft license, 12
Copyright and reuse notice, 17,
        83–84, 209, 307, 329–330,
        See also Licensing
Core developer privileges, 77
Coupling, 93
        metrics for evaluating, 93–95,
        111
        minimum coupling principle,
        89, 93
        multi-level bug example,
        133–134
Crashing, 129
Creative design, 56
Cross-site scripting, 96, 97,
        217–218
CRUD, 182–183, 191, 195, 234
Custom software, 4–5
Cyber communication etiquette,
        56–58, 64

D
Database, 174
Database design, 173, 330–332
        actions with tables, 182–188
        backup and recovery, 181–182

connecting program to
        database, 176–178
CRUD, 182–183, 191
database creation and
        initialization, 175–176
normalization, 180–181
principles and practice,
        174–182
security issues, *See* Database
        security
table creation, 183–185
table insertion, deletion, and
        updating, 187–188
tables, 178–182
table searching, 185–187
UI design and, 222–224
Database management systems
        (DBMSs), 174, *See also*
        Database modules;
        MySQL
        backup tools, 182
Database modules, 30, 330–332
        design principles and practice,
        174–182, *See also*
        Database design
        effects of adding new features,
        138–139, 193–202
        layering principle, 90–92
        locking, 73, 103–104, 192–193
        multi-tier pattern, 88
        preventing concurrency
        problems, 102–104
        unit testing example, 123
Database security, 88, 188–193
        concurrency control, 192–193
        database-level permissions,
        189
        table locking, 192–193
        user-level permissions,
        189–192
Data clumps, 109, 112
Date-time calculations, 163–164,
        308
Deadlocks, 102–103, 190, 191
Debian community, 274

Debugging, 28, 107, 129–130
    bug tracking, 64, 67, 77–81,
        130, 254, 275, 286
    Linus' Law, 77
    multi-level bug example,
        133–134
    project incubation and, 275
    project newcomer
        contributions, 55
    submitting bug reports, 59–60
    tools, 68, 69–70, 130
    UI design and, 224–229
    user interface example,
        131–133
Democratic meritocracy
    transition, 273–283, *See*
    also Community building
Design document, 144–147,
    308–309, 311
Design patterns, 29–31
Developer team roles, 42, 45,
    279–280, *See also*
    Software development
    team
Developing nations and FOSS, 18
Development timelines, 306, 328
Disaster management domain
    constraints, 282–283
Disaster management software,
    See Sahana
Disaster preparedness system
    (NYC), 21
Documentation, 34–36, 51, 55,
    243, *See also* Technical
    writing; User support
    adding new functionality, 139
    commenting while reading
        code, 149
    good interface design
        principles, 206
    knowing the audience,
        244–246
    language translation, 56
    localization, 245

    principles of good writing,
        246–249
    project newcomer
        contributions, 53–54, 55
    quality assessment, 272
    reading a design document,
        144–147
    refactoring and, 35
    support tools, 36, 68
    tags, 35–36
    understanding current system,
        143–144
Document sharing, 66–67
Domain analysis, 144, 292–295
Domain class development,
    143–151, 303
    adding new domain class,
        164–166
    bulletproofing new functions,
        158–162
    class design principles and
        practice, 162–166
    design document, 144–147,
        308
    documenting new features,
        158
    effects of adding new features,
        151–162, *See also* Adding
        new features
    examining domain classes,
        150–151
    modifying existing classes,
        155–158
    reading code, 147–150
    refactoring new code base,
        169–171
    understanding current system,
        143–151
    unit testing new code,
        166–169
    using existing functionality,
        163–164
Domain classes, *RMH Homebase*
    application, 150, 330–332
Domain constraints, 282–284

Domain modules, 30
　developing, *See* Domain class
　　development
　unit testing examples,
　　121–123
Drawing and visualization tools,
　303–304
Drupal, 10, 254–255, 307
Duplicate code, 109, 111–112

E
EasyEclipse user forum, 277
Eclipse, 68–69, 77, 84, 170
　incubators, 274
　pluggable architectures, 307
　test suite development, 117
Economic impacts, 18–19
Efferent coupling, 93–94
Efficiency requirements, 305, 327
E-mail etiquette, 56–58
Emoticons, 57
Encryption of password, 214–216
Epoch timestamp, 163
Error correction, 82, *See also*
　　Debugging
Etiquette guidelines, 56–58, 64
European Union (EU), 18
Expert, 269
Expert user, 279
Extreme programming, 9, 267

F
Feature envy, 109
File sharing, 66
Firefox, 14–15, 41, 52, 130, 252,
　　255–257, 266, 307, *See*
　　also Mozilla
Formal methods, 119
Forums, 54, 65, 244, 253–257,
　　276–277
　communication etiquette,
　　56–58
FOSS certification, xxiv
Free and open source software
　　(FOSS), xvii, 1, 4–5,

　　11–12
　advantages, xvii–xviii, 22–23
　development model, 41–42,
　　See also Software
　　development
　four freedoms, 23
　"free" vs. open source, 13–14
　joining a project, *See*
　　Community-oriented
　　projects, joining and
　　newcomer contributions
　licensing, 14, 16–18, *See also*
　　Licensing
　origins and growth, 12–16,
　　265–266
　project evolution, 40–42,
　　265–266
　project foundations, 275–276
　security compared to
　　proprietary, 217–218
　worldwide impact, 18–19, 24
Free-riders, 278, 279
Free software, 12–13
　licensing, 12, 16
　open source vs., 13–14
Free Software Foundation, 12
French Gendarmerie, 19
"Frequently Asked Questions"
　　(FAQs), 251–253
Functionality assessment, 271
Functionality enhancement, *See*
　　Adding new features
Function and class libraries, 10

G
Genetics applications, 24
Getters (accessors), 162, 165, 170
GIMP, 16
Git, 74
Global impacts, 18–19, 24
GNU, 12
GNU Affero GPLv3, 17
GNU General Public License
　　(GPL), 13, 16–17, 39, 41,
　　284, 307

GNU Image Manipulation
        Program (GIMP), 16
Google Code, 285
Google Groups, 65
Governance, *See* Project
        governance
Government organizations, 19
Graphical user interface (GUI),
        See also User interface
        modules
    design and development, *See*
        User interface design and
        development
    layering principle, 90–92
    multi-tier pattern, 88
Greenfield systems, 11

H
Help, on-line, *See* On-line help
Hosting sites, 285
HTML code, 71
    embedded PHP and user
        interface, 208–213
    on-line help, 261–263
Humanitarian FOSS (HFOSS),
        19–20, *See also Sahana*
    domain constraints, 282–283

I
iCalendar, 308
id (unique identifier), 148–149
Image manipulation software, 16
Incubation, 274–277
Indentation standards, 34
Indexes, 251, 252
Information hiding principle, 162,
        165
Infrastructure support, 56
InnoDB, 103–104
Input validation errors, 96
Instance variables, identifying,
        145–146
Integrated development
        environment (IDE), xxii,

43, 67, 68–70, 77, 112,
        See also Eclipse
Integration testing, 121
Intellectual property, proprietary
        software model, 6
Internet Explorer, 3
Internet Relay Chat (IRC)
    channels, 54, 64, 65
    communication norms, 56–58
Interoperability constraints, 84,
        306, 328
Interpreters, 68
IRC chat channels, *See* Internet
        Relay Chat (IRC)
        channels
IT technician role, 45

J
Java, 32
Joining a community-oriented
        project, *See*
        Community-oriented
        projects, joining and
        newcomer contributions

L
Lack of cohesion of methods
        (LCOM) metric, 93–94,
        111
LAMP, 70–72, 84, 283
    database creation and
        initialization, 175–176
Language translation, 56
LaTeX, 23
Latin American countries, 18
Launchpad.net, 52
Layering principles, 89–92
    refactoring code violations,
        113, 114–116, 234–235
Lazy class, 110
Lazy consensus process, 282
Lead developer, 31, 44, 47, 77,
        269, 270, 275, 279, *See*
        also Project leader

Leadership, 42, 45, 265, *See also*
    Project governance;
    Project leader
Legacy systems, 10–11
Lesser General Public License
    (LGPL), 17, 284
Libraries, 10
Licensing, 16–18, 83–84, 111, 284
    compatibility, 17
    copyleft and free software, 12
    copyright notice, 17, 83–84,
        209, 307, 329–330
    GPL (GNU General Public
        License), 13, 16–17, 39,
        41, 284, 307
    Lesser GPL, 17, 284
    Microsoft terms, 4
    project success measure, 271
Line length standards, 33
Linus' Law, 77
Linux, 13, 40–41, 52, 266
Live server, 43
Localization of documentation, 245
Lock-in, 2–3, 6, 18, 19, 23
Locking, 76, 103–104, 192–193

M
Mailing lists, 54, 63–65
    etiquette, 56–58, 64
Maintainability requirements, 306,
    327
Major number, 288
Mass-marketed software, 4
Maturity models, 271
Maximum cohesion principle, 89,
    92, *See also* Cohesion
Meetings, 65–66, 267, 270
Memory safety violations, 96
Mercurial, 74
Merge, 73
Meritocracy, 42, 51, 269, 278
    democratic meritocracy
        transition, 273–283
Method extraction, 112
Methods

    bad smells, 109
    identifying, 146–147
    naming, 33, 108
Micro number, 288
Microsoft Visual Studio, 68
Microsoft Windows Vista, 5
Microsoft Word and "Office"
    bundling, 2–4
Milestones, 48, 66
Minimum coupling principle, 89,
    93, *See also* Coupling
Minor number, 288
Mission statement, 58
Model-view-controller (MVC)
    pattern, 30, 88
    refactoring, 113
    RMH Homebase system
        architecture, 89
    user interface design, 207–210
Monopolistic behavior, 2–3
Mozilla, 14–15, 17–18, 41, 77, 130,
    266, *See also* Firefox
Multi-tier pattern, 30, 88
    layers, 90
    RMH Homebase system
        architecture, 89
    unit test design strategy,
        128–129
Mutators (setters), 162, 166, 170
MyISAM, 103–104
MySQL, 31, 71, 174, *See also*
    Database modules
    actions with tables, 182–188
    backup tools, 182
    database design using,
        173–182, 330–332, *See*
        also Database design
    IDE, 68
    LAMP stack, *See* LAMP
    locking, 103
    security issues, *See* Database
        security
    SQL injection attacks, 96, 97,
        216–217
    table locking, 192–193

tables, 178–182
using relations, 183–184
working with programming
languages, 176–177

N
Naming tables, 179
Naming variables, methods, or
classes, 33, 108
Need principle, 162, 163
NetBeans, 68, 280–281
Netscape, 4, 14–15, 266
Network protective licenses, 17
New project conception, 291, 303
design alternatives, 308
design document, 308–309
domain classes, 303, *See also*
Domain class
development
performance, platform, and
process requirements,
305–307, 327–328
system architecture, 307, *See
also* Software architecture
user interface, 304, *See also*
User interface design and
development
New project conception,
requirements gathering,
292, 311–328
domain analysis, 292–295,
312–316
use cases, 297–303, 311,
317–326
user stories, 295–297
New York City, disaster
preparedness system, 21
New Zealand Open Source Society
(NZOSS), 64
Non-disclosure agreement (NDA),
38
Non-profit organizations, 19–20,
280–281
Normalization, 180–181
Novice, 269

O
Object integrity principle, 162, 165
Observer, 45
On-line forums, *See* Forums
On-line help, 31, 37, 82, 245,
249–250, 258–263
code base and, 258–259,
261–263
screen shots and thumbnails,
250, 261
step-by-step guidance, 250,
259–260
user access and navigation,
250, 259
OpenBRR, 271
Open discussion forums, *See*
Forums
OpenOffice, 4, 16, 23, 52
Open Source Initiative (OSI), 13
Open source project starting
points, 265–266
Open source software, 5, 12, *See
also* Free and open source
software
factors driving open source
movement, 5–7
free software vs., 13–14
Open Source Software Potential
Index project (OSSPI),
18
Open source software repositories,
11, *See also* Code
repository
Organization of FOSS projects,
277–281

P
Package build tools, 68
Parallel inheritance hierarchies,
109
Password encryption, 214–216
Password recovery, 216, 240
Patches, 77, 79
Pattern matching, 186
Peer-to-peer pattern, 30

Perens, Bruce, 13
Performance, platform, and
    process requirements,
    305–307, 327–328
Performance assessment, 272
Performance constraints, 82
Permissive software in the public
    domain, 16–17
Persistence, 174
PHP, 31–32, *See also RMH
    Homebase*
    coding standards, 33–34
    date-time functionality,
        163–164
    Eclipse plug-in architecture,
        68
    LAMP stack, 70, 283, *See also*
        LAMP
    on-line help, 258
    scripts, 71
    tags, 35–36
    unit test tools, 119
    user interface design, 208–213
    working with MySQL, 177
Pipe-and-filter pattern, 30
Platform constraints, 84
Pluggable architectures, 307
Plug-in architecture, 68
Politics, 23, 274
Primary key, 181, 183
Primitive obsession, 110
Privilege-associated
    vulnerabilities, 96
Programming, *See* Writing code
Program reading, *See* Reading
    code
Project goals and mission
    statement, 58
Project governance, 265
    benevolent dictator, 42,
        265–266, 270, 274
    commit privileges, 73, 77
    communication channels, 54,
        267

comparing community- and
    client-oriented models, 42
consensus and conflict
    resolution, 270, 281–282
democratic meritocracy
    transition, 273–283, *See
    also* Community building
domain constraints, 282–284
free-standing vs. umbrella
    organization, 275–276
hosting sites, 285–286
incubation, 274–277
member roles, 278–280
membership levels, 269
meritocracy, 269
organization, 277–281
origins and evolution, 265–266
oversight, 280–281
progress assessment, 270
proprietary vs. FOSS, 41, 265
quality assessment, 271–273
releasing code, 284–289, *See
    also* Code release and
    distribution
starting a client-oriented
    project, 267–270
task assignment, 269–270
team meetings, 65–66, 267,
    270
Project hosting sites, 285–286
Project leader, 47, 274, 278–279,
    See also Lead developer
Project milestones, 48
Project sponsors, 21, 269, 273,
    275, 280–281, 285
Project start-up, 267–270
    communication channels, 267
Project wiki, 309
Proprietary software, 1, 5
    business model, 6
    customer frustration with, 6
    FOSS competition financial
        impacts, 18
    security compared to FOSS,
        217–218

Proprietary software development
 developer characteristics, 7
 non-disclosure agreement, 38
 project failure rate, 5–6
 transition to FOSS project,
  40, 266
Public domain software, 16–17
Public Library of Science, 24

Q
QSOS, 271
Quality assessment, 271–273
Quality assurance teams, 77

R
Race conditions, 96, 100, 102–103
Raymond, Eric, 41–42, 265, 287
Reading code, 29, 31–32, 147–150
 avoiding refactoring, 149–150
 commenting, 149
 project newcomer
  contributions, 55
 refactoring, 29
 starting from top, 147–148
 unique keys or identifiers,
  148–149
Really simple syndication (RSS)
 feeds, 65
Recruitment, 275
Red Hat, 14, 284
Redundant function, 169
Refactoring, 29, 107, 111–114
 added code and, 169–171,
  197–201, 233–239
 adding documentation, 35
 avoiding while reading code,
  149
 duplicate code, 111–112
 examples, 114–116
 method extraction, 112
 types, 112–113
Reference manuals, 244, 251–253
References, 351–354
Refused bequest, 110
Relational databases, 174

Relational operators, 183–184
Release branches, 288–289
Release management, 55–56, 289,
  See also Code release and
  distribution
Release managers, 280, 289
Release plan, 267
Release strategies, 287–289
Reliability requirements, 305, 327
Repository, *See* Code repository
Requirements analysis, 144, 154,
  291–292, 317–326, *See*
  also New project
  conception; Use cases
 agile approach, 144
 domain analysis, 292–295,
  312–316
 performance, platform, and
  process requirements,
  305–307, 327–328
 user stories, 295–297
Requirements document and task
  assignment, 270
Risk assessment, 273
RMH Homebase, 11, 20, 311
 adding new functionality,
  135–139, 151–162,
  195–202, 230–239,
  341–350, *See also* Adding
  new features
 client-server pattern, 88
 database access privileges,
  189–192
 database tables, 178–180
 debugging examples, 131–134,
  224–229
 design document, 144–147
 domain analysis, 312–316
 domain classes, 150, 330–332
 downloading information, 311
 Eclipse IDE, 68–69
 example code, 32
 general design goals, 329
 layering principle, 91
 on-line help, 258–263

open source license notice, 83
overall design characteristics,
    328–339
password encryption, 214–216
password recovery, 216, 240
project implementation
    schedule, 336
project scheduling examples,
    48–50
refactoring examples, 114–116
requirements, 311–328
sandbox version, 107, 143,
    173, 268
secure login, 97–100
system architecture, 89,
    329–330
team dynamics, 45–47
unique identifier (id), 148–149
unit tests, 117–119, 121–128,
    167–168
use cases, 37, 144, 311,
    317–326
user interface design, 333–339,
    See also User interface
    design and development
user roles, 298–299, 313
workshops, 257
RMH Homeroom, 291–308
Ronald McDonald House, 20, 292,
    312, *See also RMH
    Homebase*
RSS feeds, 65
Run-time system constraints, *See*
    Software development
    run-time constraints

S
Sahana, 20–22, 39
bug report example, 59–60
contributor communication
    channels, 54, 64
disaster management domain
    constraints, 282–283
FAQs, 252–253
forums, 254

lazy consensus process, 282
Volunteer Management
    system, 313
wiki, 66–67
Sahana Foundation, 275–276,
    280–281
Sandbox version, 107, 143, 173,
    268, *See also* Staging
    server
Sarcasm, 57
Scalability assessment, 272
Scheduling, 48
development timelines, 306,
    328
milestones, 48, 66
RMH Homebase project
    implementation, 336
shared documents, 66–67
team meetings or
    videoconferences, 47
to-do lists, 48, 66
Scientific publication, 24
Screen shots, 250, 261
Scripts, 71
Secure login (authentication),
    97–100
Security, 95–100
architectural vulnerabilities,
    96–97
database, 88, 188–193, *See
    also* Database security
initial design considerations,
    305, 327
new functionality effects, 139
password encryption, 214–216
quality assessment, 272
user interface design, 213–218
user-level, 97–100
user-level permissions,
    213–214
Self-organization, 278
Sequence diagram, 300
Server, 43
Server-side code, 88
Sessions, 100–102, 210, 212

Setters (accessors), 162, 166, 170
Shared documents, 66–67
Shuhari, 269
Simplified English, 245
Skype, 66, 267, 328
Software, 1–2
    types, 2–5
Software architecture, 29, 87
    architectural patterns, 30,
        87–89
    concurrency, 100–102
    initial design considerations,
        307
    layering principle, 89–92
    maximum cohesion principle,
        89, 92
    metrics for evaluating
        cohesion and coupling,
        93–95
    minimum coupling principle,
        89, 93
    model-view-controller pattern,
        30, 88, 113, 207–210
    pluggable architectures, 307
    quality assessment, 272
    RMH Homebase, 89, 329–330
    security vulnerabilities, 96–97,
        See also Security
Software developers, 7
Software development, 8, 27–29,
        See also Agile
        development
    code reading, *See* Reading
        code
    coding, *See* Writing code
    coding vs. components, 9–10
    course organization and
        sample syllabi, xix–xxii
    FOSS development model,
        41–42
    individual vs. team
        programming, 9
    legacy vs. greenfield systems,
        10–11

    top-down vs. bottom-up, 8–9,
        28
    using patterns, 29–31
Software development run-time
    constraints, 82
    licensing, 83–84, *See also*
        Licensing
    performance, 82
    platform, 84
    Web hosting, 83
Software development team, 44
    communication/collaboration
        tools, *See* Collaboration
        tools
    consensus and conflict
        resolution, 270, 281–282
    governance, *See* Project
        governance
    individual vs. team
        programming, 9
    initial design considerations,
        306, 328
    joining a project, *See*
        Community-oriented
        projects, joining and
        newcomer contributions
    leadership, 45, 47
    meetings, 267
    member roles, 278–280
    members, roles, and tasks,
        44–47
    membership levels, 269
    RMH Homebase example,
        45–47
    team dynamics, 47–48
Software documentation, *See*
    Documentation
Software framework, 30
Software metrics, 93–95, 110–111
Software project failure rates, 5–6
Software security, *See* Security
Software stack, 67, 70–72, 267
Software testing, *See* Testing
Source code editors and
    translators, 68

Sourceforge, 11, 20, 21, 40, 52,
    285–286, 311
Speculative generality, 110
Spiral development, 8–9
Sponsors, 21, 269, 273, 275,
    280–281, 285
SQL, 174, *See also* MySQL
SQL injection, 96, 97, 216–217
Staging server, 43, 267–268, 306,
    328, *See also* Sandbox
    version
Stallman, Richard, 12–14, 16, 19
Strongly protective licenses, 17
Structured Query Language
    (SQL), 174, *See also*
    MySQL
Subversion (SVN), 73–74, 84
"Supporting" nouns, 145, 154
Supporting resources, xxiii
Synchronization, 74–76, 102, *See
    also* Version control
    client-server pattern, 88
    code synchronization
        repository, 42–43, 76, 267
    race conditions and deadlocks,
        102–103
Synthesis, *See* Writing code

T
Table locking, 103–104, 192–193
Tables, database, 178–182
    actions with, 182–188
    creation, 183–185
    insertion, deletion, and
        updating, 187–188
    normalization, 180–181
    primary keys, 181, 183
    searching, 185–187
Tags, 35–36
Task assignment, 269–270
Team communication etiquette,
    56–58, 64
Team communication tools, *See*
    Collaboration tools
Team leader, 45, 47, 80, 270, 287

Team meetings, 65–66, 267, 270
Team programming environment,
    See Software development
    team
Technical writing, 243–249
    elements of presentation, 244
    knowing the audience,
        244–246
    principles of good writing,
        246–249
    Simplified English, 245
Temporary fields, 110
Test-driven development (TDD),
    9, 117, 120, 167
Testers, 280
Testing, 107, 117–118
    added code or functionality,
        166–169, 196–197, 201,
        233–234, 239
    alpha and beta, 130
    database module example, 123
    domain class examples,
        121–123
    fallibility, 119
    project newcomer
        contributions, 55
    sequencing strategy, 128–129
    system establishment, 267
    tools, 67, 68, 117, 119
    unit test design, 120–121
    unit test modules, 30
    use case example, 125–128
    user interface module
        example, 123–125
Test suite, 30, 117
    designing, 120–121
Thumbnail images, 250, 261
Timelines, 306, 328
To-do lists, 48, 66
Top-down development, 8–9, 28,
    37
Torvalds, Linus, 13, 41, 42, 266
Training, 257, *See also* Tutorials
Transaction processing pattern, 88
Translation of languages, 56

Trunk, 73
Tutorials, 31, 37, 244, 249, 257

U
Umbrella organizations, 275–276
Unified Modeling Language
(UML), 300–301
Unique key or identifier, 148–149
United Kingdom, 19
Unit testing, *See* Testing
Unit test modules, 30, *See also*
Testing
Usability assessment, 271
Use case diagram, 300–301
Use cases, 297–303, 311
adding new functionality,
135–136
design document, 144–147,
308
help tutorials and, 37
RMH Homebase, 37, 144, 311,
317–326
testing example, 125–128
UML, 300–301
writing, 301–303
Useless functions, 113, 169,
197–198
User documentation, 51, 55, 135,
243–244, *See also*
Documentation;
Technical writing; User
support
User forums, *See* Forums
User guides, 54
User interface design and
development, 205, 304,
333–339
adding new features, 230–239
database modules and,
222–224
debugging, 224–229
design principles and practice,
205–207
documentation, 206
ensuring security, 213–218

model-view-controller pattern,
207–210
quality assessment, 271
screen drafts, 304
sessions, 212
unit testing and refactoring,
233–239
working with code, 218–229
User interface failures, 96
User interface modules, 30, 201
debugging example, 131–133
design, *See* User interface
design and development
effects of adding new features,
136
layering principle, 90–92
multi-tier pattern, 88
open discussion forums, 54,
56–58, 65, 244, 253–257
performance constraints, 82
unit test design, 121
unit testing example, 123–125
unit testing new code,
233–234, 239
User involvement in development,
28, 42, 45
"becoming a user first," 58–60
bug finding, 129
community building, 275
membership levels, 269
submitting bug reports, 59–60
User-level security, 97–100
User roles, 144, 278, 298–299, 313
User stories, 295–297
User support, 243, *See also*
Documentation
knowing the audience,
244–246
live user training, 257
on-line help, 31, 37, 82, 245,
249–250, 258–263
quality assessment, 272
reference manuals, 244,
251–253
technical writing, 243–249

tutorial training, 31, 37, 244, 249, 257

V
Vendor lock-in, 2–3, 6, 18, 19, 23
Verbs, 146, 154
Version control, 31, 63, 67, 68, 72–77, 267, 306, 328
    conflict management, 74–76
    release branches, 288–289
    release numbering schemes, 288
Videoconferences, 47, 65–66
Virtual meetings, 65
Visualization tools, 303–304

W
Waterfall model, 8
Weakly protective licenses, 17
Web hosting constraints, 83
White screen of death (WSOD), 129
Wiki, 309
Wikipedia, 72, 76
Wiki tools, 66–67
WINS stack, 70
Working copy, 73
Workload balancing, 269
Write access privileges, 73, 76–77
"Writer," 4
Writers, 280, *See also* Technical writing
Writing code, 32–34
    commentary documentation, 34–36, *See also* Documentation
    standards, 33–34
Writing use cases, 301–303

X
XCode, 68
xfig drawing tool, 304